Curriculum theory and design
in physical education

Curriculum theory and design in physical education

ANTHONY A. ANNARINO

Professor of Physical Education, Purdue University,
West Lafayette, Indiana

CHARLES C. COWELL

Professor Emeritus, Purdue University,
West Lafayette, Indiana

HELEN W. HAZELTON

Professor Emeritus, Purdue University,
West Lafayette, Indiana

SECOND EDITION

Illustrated

The C. V. Mosby Company

ST. LOUIS • TORONTO • LONDON   1980

Printed in the United States of America

The C. V. Mosby Company
11830 Westline Industrial Drive, St. Louis, Missouri 63141

Library of Congress Cataloging in Publication Data

Annarino, Anthony A
  Curriculum theory and design in physical education.

  Edition for 1955 by C. C. Cowell and H. W. Hazelton,
published under title: Curriculum designs
in physical education.
  Bibliography: p.
  Includes index.
  1. Physical education and training—Curricula.
2. Curriculum planning. I. Hazelton, Helen W.,
joint author. II. Cowell, Charles Clarence,
1896-   Curriculum designs in physical education.
III. Title.
GV363.C63   1980   613.7'0712   80-282
ISBN 0-8016-0297-1

TS/VH/VH 9 8 7 6 5 4 3 2 1   01/D/007

To

physical education teachers who "turn kids on"

Preface

The primary function of a curriculum is to translate educational philosophies and theories into a series of progressive, meaningful, and guided experiences for children and youths to attain long-range goals. This curriculum, by which people are educated, is a cooperative undertaking in which all educational specialists will make a contribution to the unified, sequential planning process. In this process the physical education specialist should be an integral and forceful member of an educational team responsible for its design.

A curriculum design as a "scheme or plan of something to be done" not only involves an understanding of the basic mechanics of curriculum design, but it must also be based on the theoretical and philosophical principles underlying curriculum development. This concept is reflected by the inclusion of "theory" in the title for this revision of Professors Cowell and Hazelton's classic curriculum text.

Therefore, based on the principle that curriculum planning is a scientific process resulting in a creative product, the content of this revision retains a basic socioeducative philosophy fundamental to curriculum development but is progressively designed so that the curriculum planner moves through a logical developmental process that culminates in an effective curriculum plan appropriate for any school setting.

Substantive changes in this revision include the identification and analysis of contemporary curriculum theories and traditional and innovative approaches to curriculum design for the purpose of minimizing the gap that exists between theory and practice. This is accomplished by a logical presentation of topical content consisting of five major parts divided into sequentially related units. The text is designed so that the curriculum planner or student moves through a systematic learning process—from an understanding of curriculum theory and foundations to application of design that should culminate in an effective K-through-12 physical education curriculum appropriate for a school or community educational setting.

This goal is achieved by mastering the identifiable competencies stated for each unit, through the use of the reactors for class and group interactions, by exploring alternative solutions for the unit situational problems, by completing the unit learning activities on an individual or group basis, and by using the selected resources that provide current information relevant to curriculum theory and design.

The nature and function of the curriculum is viewed in Part One. Specifically covered are dynamics that effect and affect it, such as educational theories, the school and society, the learner, the learning process, philosophical principles and inferences, objective taxonomies, and organizational procedures.

Growth and developmental characteristics, motives, purposes, interests, and needs of the learner, preschool through secondary, are identified in Part Two as implications for a learner-centered curriculum approach.

The introductory units in Part Three critically examine current issues and trends and their implications for curriculum organization and planning. Various types of contemporary school organizational, operational, and supervisory practices are described. Societal trends and legislative actions such as Title IX, accountability, mainstreaming, and competency-based education are analyzed as to their effect on present and future curriculum planning. The major portion of Part Three moves from curriculum foundations to implementation by comparing examples of conventional and innovative scheduling patterns, curriculum guide designs, activity programs, instructional materials, and instructional strategies.

Another unit in Part Three specifically focuses on handicapped children and youths relative to their specific needs for individualized education programs, assessment and evaluation, and instructional modifications. Examples of assessment techniques and sample programs are provided.

The last unit in Part Three discusses the pros and cons of required or voluntary college and university basic instructional programs. Administrative policies and principles are provided for attendance, scheduling, grading, and credits. Changing curricular offerings and sample programs are described as they relate to contemporary educational values and student interests.

The chief criterion for the acceptance of any activity in the curriculum of any educational institution is, "Does the activity contribute to the educational purpose of the school?" Intramural, recreational, interscholastic, and intercollegiate athletic programs can meet this criterion and can be extensions of a basic instructional program in physical education by educational management establishing sound policies based on platform statements, standards, and principles given in Part Four.

Curriculum planning and assessment are two closely related aspects of sound educational practice. Curriculum assessment is an ongoing process that requires the use of the best available measurement techniques for providing evidence as to the effectiveness of the curriculum for attaining educational objectives. Part Five concerns itself with this problem by justifying a need for assessment, describing the best available instruments for evaluating various components of the curriculum, and, more importantly, indicating what to do with the results.

The curriculum planner must have a comprehensive knowledge of all the current educational theories and practices related to curriculum theory and design in physical education. This can be acquired through the extensive and current resources provided in the appendices.

As previously indicated, substantial changes were made in revising this classic curriculum text of Professors Cowell and Hazelton to include current theories, trends, and practices, but it is permeated with their basic physical education philosophy, in hope that it will influence a new generation of physical educators as it did former generations.

The major changes in this text resulted from a sharing of ideas, thoughts, and programs with students, colleagues, and friends. A debt of gratitude is owed to the innovative teachers and supervisors who generously contributed their creative program ideas and to Thomas J. Loughrey, University of Missouri–St. Louis, who so thoughtfully reviewed the manuscript, offering comments and helpful advice.

A special thanks to Mrs. Millie Newton and Mrs. Virginia Cunningham for laboriously translating scribbling into readable copy and to a very special person, Betts Annarino, for being an understanding and patient wife.

Anthony A. Annarino

Contents

PART TWO

CURRICULUM CONTENT

PART THREE

CURRICULUM ORGANIZATION

PART FOUR

THE EXTENDED CURRICULUM

PART FIVE

THE CURRICULUM: SYNTHESIS AND ASSESSMENT

Appendix B

Selected reading articles, 410

Curriculum theory and design
in physical education

PART ONE

CURRICULUM DYNAMICS

UNITS

1 Curriculum theory and design: an overview
2 The school and society: effectors and affectors
3 The learner: a directive force
4 Learning: a fundamental process
5 Philosophy: principles and inferences
6 Objectives: focus and direction
7 Curriculum guide: planning and designing

Let the main objective of this, our didactic, be as follows: To seek and find a method of instruction, By which teachers may teach less, and learners learn more.

JOHN AMOS COMENIUS

The curriculum . . . is the total situation or group of situations available to the teacher and school administrator through which to make behavior changes in the endless stream of children and youth that passes through the doors of a school.

FRANCIS J. BROWN

1 Curriculum theory and design: an overview

COMPETENCIES

After completing this unit, you should be able to:

Acquire an understanding of the value and need for a well-planned curriculum.

Explain past and contemporary curriculum theories.

Formulate a functional theoretical framework for curriculum planning and designing.

Identify the elements contained in a curriculum pattern through a problem-solving process.

Analyze a physical education experience and those relationships that exist between the experience and learner outcomes.

Identify the important characteristics of a good physical education as guidelines for curriculum planning.

Isolate the unique contributions in a physical education program to the learner's purposes.

Define the following:

Activities
Correlated curriculum
Course of study
Curriculum
Curriculum guide plan
Enriched curriculum
Experiences
Horizontal curriculum
Integrated curriculum
Vertical curriculum
Theory
Curriculum theoretical structure

Discipline of human movement
Movement form
Human movement phenomena
Movement analysis
Motor learning task analysis
Developmental state
Purpose-process curriculum
Student-centered curriculum
Subject-matter curriculum
Design

3

PERSPECTIVE

PRINCIPLE: The physical education curriculum consists of selected and planned learning experiences that provide opportunities for students to achieve objectives.

The curriculum, defined and carried out as a series of meaningful and guided experiences directed toward the attainment of specific objectives, is the basic instrument of the educative process. It is the medium by which theoretical and philosophical concepts are translated into an effective design or plan that will affect the instructional process.

This defined perspective implies that there is a need to identify a curriculum theory and a philosophical base that will provide intelligent power, direction, and insight into curriculum problems. Statements in forms of principles, laws, rules, and definitions that describe, explain, and predict the nature of the discipline must be identified in order to formulate a conceptual curriculum theory. This theory is used as a framework for making effective decisions and judgments in curriculum planning, designing, and rules of practice.

This theoretical approach is essential to move us to critically think about the problems of curriculum development, to make us sensitive to various possibilities in solving the problems, and to see the relationship between the parts—the elements— and the total curriculum. These elements are determined by investigating the nature of the individual, the nature of society, the nature of the discipline's content, the nature of the instructional process, and the nature of the learning process.

Specifically, the elements that are contained in a curriculum pattern are the ones found when we seek answers to the following questions and proceed to act on the information:

1. What are the needs, problems, and interests of these boys and girls at the various developmental levels at which we find them?
2. What are the problems that modern American youth face in a contemporary society?
3. What are presuppositions and principles that guide us in life and education: our philosophy, our basic beliefs?
4. How does one learn? Why does one learn?
5. What are the justifiable objectives and developmental goals of our discipline?
6. What kinds of experiences are not only best suited for achieving our objectives, but also contribute to growth of further experiences?
7. How are these experiences structured and sequenced in a program?
8. Which design model and instructional strategy is most appropriate for creating an effective teaching-learning environment?
9. How can results be appraised in terms of the established objectives?

Answers to these questions should yield data-based information that can be used as a scientific and philosophical rationale for formulating a tentative physical education curriculum theory.

This information-seeking process involves an investigation of the following three areas for more specific questions:

1. Human movement phenomena
   a. Why do humans move?
   b. How do humans move?
   c. What happens when humans move?
2. Physical education body of knowledge
   a. What are the relationships between theory and practice?
   b. What are the best practices?
3. Philosophy
   a. What values are important to the teacher?

b. What is right?
c. What is true?
d. What is adequate?

It is understandable why the establishment of a physical education curriculum theory is a difficult task. As new data appear and philosophical viewpoints differ in the profession, theories are revised, modified, or rejected. The development of any educational theory is a continuous, laborious process but is essential if the curriculum is to have focus and direction.

A review of past and present theories, perspectives, and conceptual frameworks for physical education curriculum planning reflects the problem of specifying one approach that best describes a rationale for the development of a physical education program.

Linda Bain (1978), in attempting to systematically review the status of the curriculum theory of physical education, identified the following six theoretical perspectives that best described the philosophical base from which the curriculum operates: (1) movement form, (2) movement analysis, (3) discipline of human movement, (4) developmental state, (5) motor learning task analysis, and (6) student motives and purposes. Ann Jewett and Marie Mullan (1977) developed a purpose-process curriculum framework based on the assumption that the primary concern of physical education is the individual human being moving in interaction with the environment. Camille Brown and Rosalind Cassidy (1963) were the earliest educators to describe physical education as the school program for studying human movement. Their description included a theory of human movement and a theory of program development and change, both interrelated in such a way as to describe a theory in physical education.

This brief analysis of past and present curriculum theories indicates that they have evolved from two basic approaches, either a subject matter–oriented or student-centered approach. The rationale proposed in this text for curriculum planning and designing will be an eclectic scientific and philosophical base that includes both a subject matter–oriented and a student-centered orientation with a functional approach.

A FUNCTIONAL APPROACH TO PHYSICAL EDUCATION CURRICULUM PLANNING AND DESIGNING

The problem of curriculum development and design is not whether the subject matter of physical education or the learner should be considered, but the realization that both must be considered in relation to each other. Physical education should not choose between or compartmentalize learner-centered and subject-centered education. It must consider the interrelationships involved. Every learning situation includes a learner, a purpose, a content, and a process. Each plays an important part in the learning experiences of the student.

A functional approach to a curriculum theory considers that the physical education curriculum consists of all the situations that are consciously selected and organized for the purpose of developing the personalities of its pupils by new insights, sense of values, skills, or abilities. The theory's function is to stimulate experience that will result in desirable growth and development of appropriate psychomotor, cognitive, and affective outcomes.

No one will deny that content or subject matter is an important element in curriculum design. We recall that to the physical educator subject matter means *activities* and *experiences* but these activities and experiences are meaningless without purpose.

The older idea was that subjects possessed certain inherent values. For culture, the classics were prescribed. For disciplinary value, mathematics was perhaps prescribed. If one were exposed to the right "subjects," he would become an educated person. This is no more true of an education than is the concept of society as a conglomerate of art, business, and politics. Society, however, is a system into which group life is united by human relationships. Society is a structure and a pattern representing interrelationships of people. Similarly, education of the right sort implies unity of experience and the understanding of relationships.

The physical education curriculum, rather than stressing "subjects," stresses unified experiences for children and youth. Can one name an experience of a more integrating nature than a baseball game? The game of baseball is more than a summation of separate skills, attitudes, judgments, and meanings. Each of these affects the others through its relationships to the game as a whole; it belongs to a system of related causes that make the game of baseball.

At one period we tried to teach character education based on a series of desirable traits. On Monday we taught morals, on Tuesday manners, on Wednesday respect for property, and so on. Newer knowledge of how people learn greatly weakens the case for separate "courses" for teaching character or teaching by traits. Real educational values stem from the "wholeness" of the individual and the pattern of learning experience to which the individual is exposed. The values we seek grow out of the total experience of the game. The more closely the game experiences are related to the school as a whole, the home, and the community, the more effective will learning become and the longer will desirable behavior changes endure.

Physical education cannot accept solely the traditional concept of a curriculum as an arrangement of "subjects," each of which has some peculiar value in itself. Conversely, the values and purposes that result as outgrowths of the students' experiences in physical education stem largely from this subjective need.

Physical education cannot solely accept the traditional concept of a curriculum as an arrangement of "subjects" distributed by a scatter-gun technique. There is a need to define intent and purpose by the teacher. The learner takes physical education with purposes. The "feeling" comes with mastery and achievement of a skill, esteem from a peer group, excitement and new experience, status in a group, or simply belonging to a group. The planner of the new curriculum therefore must think first of the learner's purposes instead of "just content." The planner asks, What is our unique contribution to the fulfillment of these purposes?

To create, extend, or modify purposes in children and youth and then to help them to satisfy these worthwhile purposes are the chief educational contributions of physical education. Purposes come first. The quality and extent of the experiences, with their resultant skills and abilities that satisfy the purposes, require some discrimination on the part of the curriculum planners in designing a program.

Another consideration in planning and designing is ensuring that the curriculum makes a maximum contribution to the movement performance by children and youth based on their developmental state. This can be achieved by accepting their developmental stages as aids in the discovery and statement of physical education purposes in the school (i.e., the formulation of a framework for determining the most appropriate sequencing and grade placement of physical education experiences.)

Correlated with these developmental stages is the progression of learning movement skills. The first learnings in life are motor learnings, and the child perceives the world and the objects in it in terms of perceptual data based on movement. The child learns up and down, left and right, inside and outside from these data and moves along a simple to complex or closed to open skill progression interrelated with cognitive, social, and emotional development through childhood and adolescence.

The whole human developmental process should be viewed as a succession of interrelated and integrated events with new potentials, purposes, needs, and interests emerging in the natural process of growth and development. As these capacities develop or change, they need to be reintegrated at increasingly more complex levels in the gymnasium, in the pool, or on the playing fields. An understanding of the process of growth and development is basic to curriculum planning and designing.

In defining a design as a "mental scheme or plan of something to be done," many factors are involved in its development for a physical education curriculum. Observing a physical education curriculum in action, one may or may not sense the relationship between what the students are doing in the gymnasium and pool or on the playing fields and some structure, pattern, or design of the curriculum as a whole. Even afer a prolonged observation, one may still find it difficult to sense a pattern of relationship between what one sees in the activities and the stated general purposes of the school that adorn the principal's office. It may be difficult to understand how any of the observable activities "hang together" to make a well-conceived and continuous program of physical education for children and youth.

The observer may see no relationship between what is being done in sixth grade and what is being done in the seventh grade or between the activities in physical education and the educational aims of which the principal speaks with pride. The physical education teacher can regurgitate learned "objectives" of the program and have them listed on the bulletin board for students and visitors to see, but a critical analysis of the content or the process of instruction indicates very little relationship to the stated objectives.

Curriculum planning and designing involve a clarification of our general social and educational philosophy (see Unit 5), as well as the principles of physical education compatible with this philosophy. It is necessary to understand the nature of our society and the demands of physical education resulting from contemporary social problems as well as to pay more attention to the nature and needs of human beings and to the potential problems of living in a complex technological society. There must be an understanding of the nature of the learning process and how to select and organize learning experiences in accordance with the learner's abilities, needs, and interests. There must be a relationship between all these factors and the objectives to be achieved. Finally, there is need for a program of testing and evaluating to assist learning and instruction and to reveal the degree of progress in attainment of the objectives of the physical education curriculum. These relationships between objectives, principles, subject matter (content), instruction, and evaluation are illustrated in Figs. 1 to 4.

CHARACTERISTICS OF A GOOD PHYSICAL EDUCATION PROGRAM

There are definite areas within which the physical education teacher should have reasonable proficiency if a good program is to result. We shall consider here the general characteristics of a good program.

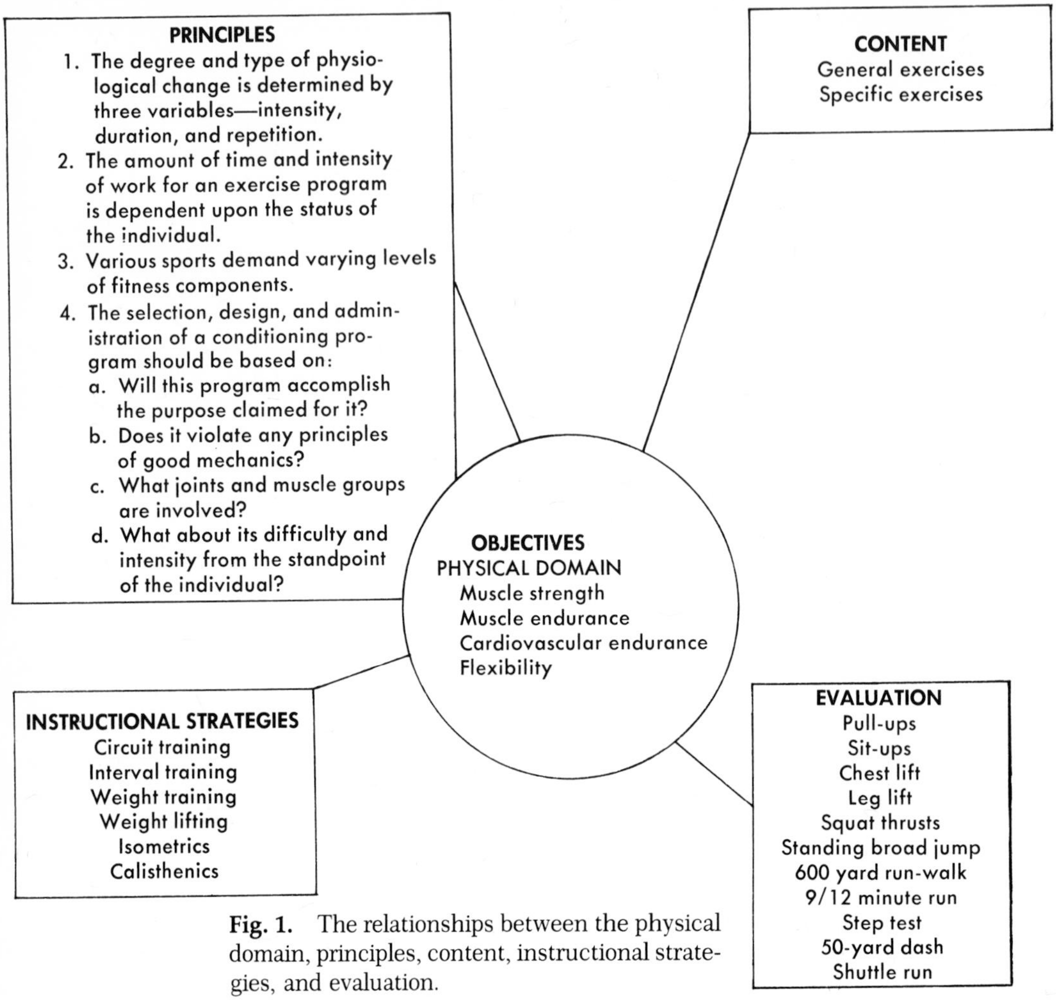

PRINCIPLES
1. The degree and type of physiological change is determined by
   three variables—intensity,
   duration, and repetition.
2. The amount of time and intensity
   of work for an exercise program
   is dependent upon the status of
   the individual.
3. Various sports demand varying levels
   of fitness components.
4. The selection, design, and administration of a conditioning program should be based on:
   a. Will this program accomplish
      the purpose claimed for it?
   b. Does it violate any principles
      of good mechanics?
   c. What joints and muscle groups
      are involved?
   d. What about its difficulty and
      intensity from the standpoint
      of the individual?

CONTENT
General exercises
Specific exercises

OBJECTIVES
PHYSICAL DOMAIN
Muscle strength
Muscle endurance
Cardiovascular endurance
Flexibility

INSTRUCTIONAL STRATEGIES
Circuit training
Interval training
Weight training
Weight lifting
Isometrics
Calisthenics

EVALUATION
Pull-ups
Sit-ups
Chest lift
Leg lift
Squat thrusts
Standing broad jump
600 yard run-walk
9/12 minute run
Step test
50-yard dash
Shuttle run

Fig. 1.   The relationships between the physical
domain, principles, content, instructional strategies, and evaluation.

The essential characteristics of a good physical education program are very similar to those of any good program of education, since home economics education, science education, language arts education, and such subjects, draw their basic principles from the same sources as physical education. We have seen that these principles come from an analysis of the nature and needs of society, the nature of the individual, the nature of the learning process and basic principles of curriculum development, organization and administration. Physical education is an integral part of the educational process and draws its principles from the same sources. The following eight fundamental characteristics might well be major concerns of a physical education curriculum.

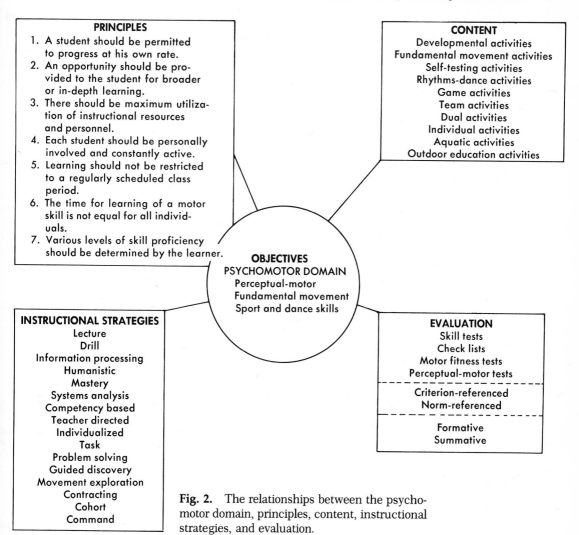

PRINCIPLES
1. A student should be permitted to progress at his own rate.
2. An opportunity should be provided to the student for broader or in-depth learning.
3. There should be maximum utilization of instructional resources and personnel.
4. Each student should be personally involved and constantly active.
5. Learning should not be restricted to a regularly scheduled class period.
6. The time for learning of a motor skill is not equal for all individuals.
7. Various levels of skill proficiency should be determined by the learner.

CONTENT
Developmental activities
Fundamental movement activities
Self-testing activities
Rhythms-dance activities
Game activities
Team activities
Dual activities
Individual activities
Aquatic activities
Outdoor education activities

OBJECTIVES
PSYCHOMOTOR DOMAIN
Perceptual-motor
Fundamental movement
Sport and dance skills

INSTRUCTIONAL STRATEGIES
Lecture
Drill
Information processing
Humanistic
Mastery
Systems analysis
Competency based
Teacher directed
Individualized
Task
Problem solving
Guided discovery
Movement exploration
Contracting
Cohort
Command

EVALUATION
Skill tests
Check lists
Motor fitness tests
Perceptual-motor tests
- - - - - - - - - - -
Criterion-referenced
Norm-referenced
- - - - - - - - - - -
Formative
Summative

Fig. 2. The relationships between the psychomotor domain, principles, content, instructional strategies, and evaluation.

A good physical education program is one that is conceived as an integral part of the total educational effort of a school.

The physical education program recognizes and contributes to the achievement of the common educational purposes of the school, such as citizenship, character, health, and similar purposes, as well as to the achievement of its own unique purposes.

The physical education teacher is found in faculty meetings, on curriculum, evaluation, or other all-school committees. Thus the teacher has a broad view of a comprehensive program of education, and the children and youth under his or her influence sense some emphasis on common values and unity of experience as they move from the gymnasium to the shop, science laboratory, and classroom.

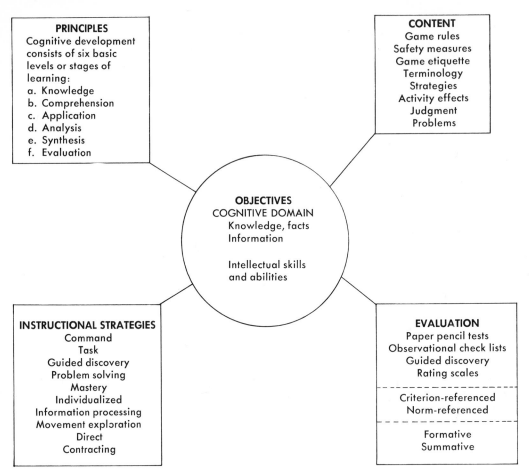

Fig. 3. The relationships between the cognitive domain, principles, content, instructional strategies, and evaluation.

A good physical education program, therefore, is not a "special" or isolated area but is planned with relationship to other areas of learning.

A good physical education program is one that is well-balanced in that it provides experiences that will stimulate growth and development in the physical, psychomotor, cognitive, and affective domains.

Play has been called "nature's way of education." It is a fundamental means of education and antedates the use of textbooks, classrooms, and teachers for this purpose.

If we trace the development of "physical exercises" as a "subject" in the curriculum to "physical training" and finally to *physical education*, we realize that the concept of the teacher's responsibilities changed from "giving exercise" and "relief drills," sandwiched between "lessons," to the concept of a development supervisor, a guardian, and a developer of human personality.

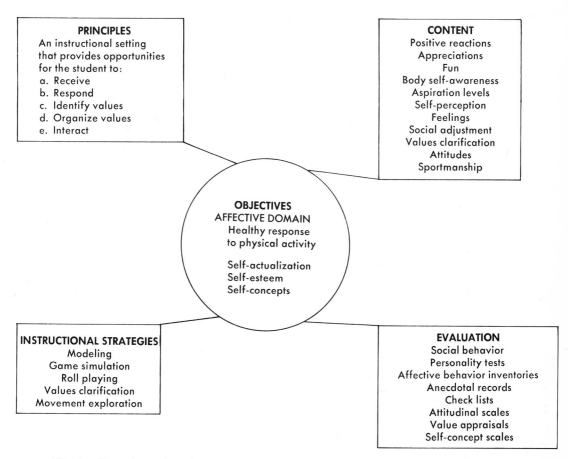

Fig. 4.   The relationships between the affective domain, principles, content, instructional strategies, and evaluation.

The unity and integrity of experiences would not be possible if the teacher of physical education assumed that physical development was his or her sole responsibility. The various aspects of development—emotional, social, intellectual, and physical—are interdependent and interrelated.

As children and youth engage in physical education activities, they develop fitness and movement skills, but at the same time they gather certain information, understandings, meanings, and concepts. They develop habits, ideals, interests, tastes, appreciations, and attitudes.

Needless to say these behavior components do not just "happen." The teacher must be constantly cognizant of integrated development.

A good physical education program is based on the interests, needs, purposes, and capacities of the people it serves.

Not only must a school program be planned with full understanding of the nature of the society it serves, but a full understanding of the individual is also important.

Interest is evidence of a purpose being satisfied. We sustain educational effort by building interests, helping students establish and realize their purposes, and meeting their basic needs for activity, success and mastery, recognition, belonging, status, esteem, and similar persistent motives.

Since children differ greatly in capacities, we must be sure that the children with lesser abilities do not feel inferior and cease trying. Gifted boys and girls, when not challenged, often develop poor habits and attitudes of superiority.

A good physical education program provides experiences that are related to basic areas of living and compatible with the maturity level of the pupils.

In terms of the various maturity levels, we ask, At each age level, through what experiences will individuals or groups of learners secure the needed competencies and understanding?

Simply to list the major areas in which growing competency is needed is quite inadequate. Curriculum planners, for example, must attempt to break down citizenship (as one major area) into more specific elements if they are to be of concrete help to teachers and students. This is difficult. Many factors are involved, but we must try!

Students must know what is right and effective in American society. They must become willing to behave in a manner that is right and effective—attitudes and ideals of goodwill, tolerance, and public welfare must be engendered. Appropriate skills in getting along with other people, in thinking clearly, and in expressing oneself become necessary. Habits of industry and honesty must be developed. Surely, this constitutes a major task for the physical education teacher—even by example!

A good physical education program is an integral part of the community it serves.

A community or neighborhood is a primary or "face-to-face" group, the members of which have needs, manners, traditions, or interests in common. The school, most frequently through its parent-teacher association, unites the community in action in a spirit of fellowship by improving the personal relationships between individuals in the group.

The school and its physical education program have certain responsibilities to plan the curriculum in relation to the needs of the community. The school must retain the characteristic of flexibility; it must meet different needs and developments in the community. On the one hand, it must initiate certain functions and services as these are needed, and on the other, it must drop activities no longer meeting a need.

The physical education area must provide wholesome and attractive experiences in the form of extraclass activities for young and old alike.

The physical education area can provide effective service within the community for all citizens. It can encourage a harmonious and cooperative relationship among the various town and city agencies operating the leisure-time programs of the community.

A good physical education program is one that through adequate facilities, time allotment, equipment, and leadership, encourages and provides a wide range of desirable pupil activities.

One type of facility, equipment, and supplies may foster a dull, devitalized, individual, and stilted formal program. Another type may meet the instructional needs of pupils and result in educational values of a higher order.

It is self-evident that if children are to learn to swim, swimming facilities are imperative; that in learning to play tennis, tennis courts are important: and that to learn to square dance, provisions must be made for music and space. Games such as soccer, field hockey, softball, and volleyball demand a certain minimum square footage as well as balls and other equipment. There is also the question of bean bags, deck tennis rings, horseshoes, paddle tennis paddles, shuffleboard disks and cues, volleyballs, basketballs, footballs, baseballs, bats, bases, and a host of additional supplies.

Ball games of all kinds are so universal in America that skill in catching, throwing, batting, or kicking balls is a must, not only for skills proficiency, but also for good "gang" contacts that are so necessary to personality and social development of children and youth. Needless to say, one ball for a class of 30 children who are trying to learn skills is a rather futile experience for teacher and pupils alike.

The content of instruction in the physical education program depend on the factors previously mentioned. Games, sports, athletics, "lead-up" games—even games of low organization—take space. Aquatics require a place to swim; adapted activities, to be really effective, take special facilities and equipment. Rhythmical activities, self-testing activities, camping and outdoor activities, social and recreational activities certainly require more than a "bandbox" gymnasium and a gravel playground.

A good physical education program is one that cooperates closely with the guidance program of the school.

It is assumed that every school has fairly well-defined guidance policies and practices. It is hoped that the guidance process is considered an integral part of the curriculum. We cannot separate one kind of learning from another. A child in the gymnasium is forming an emotional attitude toward the activity, his teacher, his school, and his classmates just as surely as he is learning to do a forward roll or dribble a basketball.

Guidance should not be separated from instruction. It cannot be thought of as a detached and separate educational function. Yet, although the fullest cooperation of all teachers is the ultimate solution to the guidance problem, the task of coordinating effort and of collecting and systematizing accurate information is the function of the guidance specialist.

The teacher of physical education in a good program contributes to this area because:

1. He or she has contact with the same pupils, sometimes for a consecutive period of several years and gets to know them well.
2. He or she deals with human beings through action and performance. In this way he or she sees the "whole" child in action and notes strengths and weaknesses, absence or presence of mobility and dynamic drive, degree of emotionality or emotional tone, social acceptance, and a host of other ways in which the child is unique.
3. The informality of the learning situation results in more informal student-teacher relationships, of value for effective guidance.

Clinical psychologists and counselors

agree that failure on the part of the child to enter into social play activities is a symptom of valuable clinical significance, that a child's social contacts with other personalities are to a large extent made by way of common motor activities, and that we get a more adequate view of personality in action on the playground than in the narrow confines of a clinical laboratory or classroom alone.

Data from the playground, gymnasium, and athletic field can contribute to the cumulative guidance records of children and youth if we are to understand the individual as a total personality and wish to label our physical education programs "good."

A good physical education program is one that fosters and encourages the professional growth and welfare of the teachers involved.

A workable philosophy of education based on sound principles plus continuous growth on the part of the teaching staff is the foundation of a good physical education program. Participation in school planning, membership and interest in curriculum study groups, membership and participation in one's professional organizations, and frequent reading are related to a good program. Despite facilities, equipment supplies, and time allotment, a good teacher is the most important factor in the situation. We cannot improve physical education programs without improving physical education teachers.

The old theory of curriculum development suggested that one sifted ideas from "experts" via textbook writers and national curriculum groups and these finally got down to the teachers. The present theory is that curriculum revision is increasingly in the charge of those responsible for school programs—supervisors, administrators, but most important, teachers. Things start to happen in individual schools and spread, rather than happening "systemwise" at the command of a superintendent higher up. Every teacher should feel some responsibility for curriculum development by participating in its overall planning. They can make valuable contributions to this process, since curriculum development is essentially the result of team effort. By its very nature, it must draw on many kinds of competencies.

REACTORS

1. Persistent problems of living at the various developmental levels become guides to the curriculum development of boys and girls and therefore are underlying elements in curriculum design.
2. A curriculum design is needed in order to think about the problems of curriculum development, to make us sensitive to various possibilities in solving the problems, and to see the relationships between the parts—the elements—and the total pattern or design.
3. Content or subject matter is the most important element in curriculum design.
4. Physical education cannot accept the traditional concept of a curriculum solely as an arrangement of "subjects," each of which has some peculiar value in itself.
5. Even after analyzing the needs and problems of society, understanding the learner's needs and characteristics, we are forced to deal with experiences and strategies—"things to do with."
6. Things start to happen in individual schools and spread, rather than happening "systemwise" at the command of administration.
7. If we think of the curriculum as the "life and program of the school," the curriculum of any school has many facets.
8. The definition of curriculum implies that there is a need to indentify a curriculum theory and a philosophical base that will

provide insight into curriculum problems.

9. Physical education should not choose between a learner-centered or a subject matter—oriented approach to curriculum planning and designing.
10. The inexperienced physical education teacher's chief difficulty is usually the result of the absence of associative ideas and illustrations to expand and make more meaningful curriculum content.

SITUATIONAL PROBLEMS

1. In too many schools, physical education (including athletics) is treated as a "dangling appurtenance to the academic structure" instead of an integral part of it. While children are carefully classified and scheduled for classes in English or mathematics, students are often assigned to physical education whenever they have a free period and often in groups including two or three different grade levels. Furthermore, physical education teachers (often due to their own lack of interest) are left off certain important school committees, such as those dealing with philosophy, curriculum, or guidance. Examine the characteristics of a good physical education program listed in this unit.
   a. Can you rank these characteristics in some definite order of priority as to importance? Try to do so.
   b. List the characteristics of a good school as a whole. Are there any essential differences between this list and the one suggested as containing the criteria of a good physical education program? Would you expect them to differ greatly? Why?
2. If we think of the curriculum as the "life and program of the school," the curriculum of any particular school has many facets. Let us spend a week in a secondary school and note some of the activities going on. A few of these are as follows:
   Classroom activities, usually organized around "subjects"
   Home economics, dramatic, and other club programs
   The school council, the athletic associations, and similar student organizations
   Intramural and interscholastic athletics

Assembly programs
School paper, yearbook, and other student publications
School dances and other social affairs
Trips to industries, and so forth, sponsored by the school
Counseling services
Health services of the school
Examine each of these activities, answering How do they fit into the curriculum design? How do they contribute to a well-balanced curriculum? Do any of these activites violate basic principles of learning and development? The basic assumptions underlying the nature of our democratic society? The function of the school in our society?

LEARNING ACTIVITIES

1. Curriculum characteristics.
   a. Examine the characteristics of a good physical education program listed in this unit.
   b. Supplement this list.
   c. Rank the characteristics in some definite order of priority.
2. Curriculum elements.
   a. Determine and list the elements that comprise a curriculum theory and design.
   b. Identify and draw relationships between these curriculum elements and the characteristics of a good physical education program.
3. Develop a chart for the six theoretical perspectives for a physical education theory proposed by Linda Bain.
   a. Identify the major concepts for each perspective.
   b. Indicate whether the perspective is a student-centered or subject matter–oriented approach.
4. Activities and experiences.
   a. Select and analyze a physical education activity or experience as to its integrated effect on the learner.
   b. Indicate how the following activites can contribute to a well-advanced physical education curriculum:
   Assembly programs
   Intramurals
   Interscholastics

Counseling services
Health instruction
Field trips

UNIT EVALUATIVE CRITERIA

Can you:

1. List the good characteristics of a good school as a "whole"? Contrast and compare these characteristics and those of a good physical education program.

2. Determine on what basis and justification administrators and teachers make decisions for incorporating a variety of activities into the "life and program of the school"?

3. Give a rationale for a well-developed curriculum theory being an aid for curriculum planners to solve curriculum problems?

4. Formulate a physical education curriculum eclectic theory with a functional approach?

RESOURCES

AAHPER. *Curriculum improvement in secondary school physical education.* Washington, D.C.: The Alliance, 1973.

AAHPER. *Echoes of influence for elementary school physical educator.* Washington, D.C.: The Alliance, 1977.

AAHPER. *Knowledge and understanding in physical education.* Washington D.C.: The Alliance, 1969.

AAHPER. *This is physical education.* Washington, D.C.: The Alliance, 1965.

AAHPER. *Tones of theory.* Washington, D.C.: The Alliance, 1972.

American Educational Research Association. *Curriculum.* Review of Educational Research 39:2, pp. 283-375, June 1969. (Also June 1960, 1963, and 1966 issues).

Association for Supervision and Curriculum Development. *Curriculum decisions—social realities.* Washington, D.C.: The Association, 1964.

Association for Supervision and Curriculum Development. *Influences in curriculum change.* Washington, D.C.: The Association, 1968.

Association for Supervision and Curriculum Development. *Perspectives on curriculum development, 1975-1976.* Washington, D.C.: The Association, 1976.

Bain, L. Status of curriculum theory in physical education. *JOPER*, March 1978, pp. 25-26.

Beauchamp, G. A. *Curriculum theory.* Wilmette, Ill.: Kagg Press, 1975.

Berman, L. *New priorities in the curriculum.* Columbus, Ohio: Charles E. Merrill Publishing Co., 1968.

Berman, L. M., & Roderick, J. A. *Feeling, valueing, and the art of growing: insights into the affective.* Washington, D.C.: Association for Supervision and Curriculum Development, 1977.

Brown, C., & Cassidy, R. *Theory in physical education.* Philadelphia: Lea & Febiger, 1963.

Carr, W. G. *Values and the curriculum: a report of the fourth international curriculum conference.* Washington, D.C.: National Education Association for the Study of Instruction, 1970.

Doll, R. C. *Curriculum improvement, decision-making and processes* (2nd ed.). Boston: Allyn & Bacon, Inc., 1970.

Eisner, E. W., & Vallance, E. Five conceptions of curriculum: their roots and implication for curriculum planning. In E. W. Eisner & E. Vallance (Eds.), *Conflicting conceptions of curriculum.* Berkeley, Calif.: McCutchan Publishing Corp., 1974.

Goodlad, J. I. *The changing school curriculum.* New York: Fund for Advancement of Education, 1966.

Heitmann, H. M. (Ed.). *Organizational patterns for instruction in physical education.* Washington, D.C.: American Alliance for Health, Physical Education, and Recreation, 1971.

Huebner, D. (Ed.). *A reassessment of the curriculum.* New York: Teachers' College, Columbia University, 1964.

Jewett, A. E., & Mullan, M. R. *Curriculum design: purposes and processes in physical education teaching—learning.* Washington, D.C.: AAHPER, 1977.

Mackenzie, M. N. *Toward a new curriculum in physical education.* New York: McGraw-Hill Book Co., 1969.

Nixon, J. E., & Jewett, A. E. *An introduction to physical education* (8th ed.). Philadelphia: W. B. Saunders Co., 1974.

Smith, B. O. (Ed.). *Perspectives of curriculum evaluation.* Monograph Series on Curriculum Evaluation. Chicago: American Educational Research Association and Rand McNally & Co., 1967.

Tanner, D., & Tanner, L. *The curriculum development.* New York: Macmillan Publishing Co., Inc., 1975.

Trump, J. L., & Baynham, D. *Focus on change: guide to better schools.* Chicago: Rand McNally & Co., 1961.

The creative person transcends the limits of history and time by realizing new facets of himself and by relating to the demands of existence in new ways.

CLARK E. MOUSTAKES

2 The school and society: effectors and affectors

COMPETENCIES

After completing this unit, you should be able to:

Identify the forces in society, evolving from early times to the present, that affected educational trends.

Trace and correlate the role and purpose of physical education with changing educational trends.

Interpret the relationships between the socioeconomic forces that play on the school, the goals society seeks to achieve through the school, and the elements that constitute the design of a curriculum.

Define the following:
Culture
Customs
Mores
Society
Trend

PERSPECTIVE

PRINCIPLE: Education takes place in a society that is always changing.

Dewey has said that "history is the past of the present." We understand the present more completely if we examine it both in retrospect (historically) and in prospect—in its relationship to the possible future.

Education takes place in a society that is always changing. Obviously, the basic element in the design of a curriculum must therefore be consideration of the forces operating within the societal structure. Contemporary physical education, with today's technology, sedentary occupations, and a 40-hour or less work week, has different educational and social functions to perform than in the early 1880s when men and even children often worked at physical labor from dawn to dark and play was looked on as a most questionable activity—or even as an invention of the devil.

In recent years the philosophies and theories of education have changed, and curriculum adjustments have resulted. Physical education teachers and administrators, with increased knowledge of child development and better understanding of the pressures of modern society on youth, now realize that well-planned physical education in the schools can contribute to making life happier, more wholesome, and more effective.

If we think of education as "fitting for life," the aims of primitive education and the aims of modern education are identical. With the more stable, less changeable environment of the primitive child, education was concerned with his/her adjustment to the immediate environment, largely through the development of body habits—motor skills. Physical skills learned in prim-

itive childhood were closely interwoven with the economic, social, and recreational life of the tribe. The home was the sole agency of formal education, involving conscious instruction in whatever crude arts the adult members of the family practiced. The problems that primitive children faced were vivid, specific, and life related, with the further advantage of constant practice. To the primitive child the technical processes of his/her elders—warfare, hunting, agriculture, and home industries—were vastly more understandable than are our own systems of industries to the more civilized child. There was no limit to the kind of knowledge of various crafts possessed by primitive humans, and the children acquired it as they grew. The basis of primitive childhood education was "less telling by parents and more doing by children."

The absence of curriculum problems in primitive education is well illustrated in a statement by Margaret Mead, an outstanding anthropologist:

I once lectured to a group of women—all of them college graduates—alert enough to be taking a course on primitive education. I described in detail the lagoon village of the Manu tribe, the way in which the parents taught the children to master their environment, to swim, to climb, to handle fire, to paddle a canoe, to judge distances, and calculate the strength of materials. I described the tiny canoes which were given the three-year-olds, the miniature fish spears with which they learned to spear minnows, the way in which small boys learned to calk their canoes with gum and how small girls learned to thread shell money into aprons. Interwoven with a discussion of more fundamental issues, such as the relationship between children and parents, and the relationship between younger children and older children, I gave a fairly complete account of the type of adaptive craft behavior which was characteristic of the Manus and the way this was learned by each generation of children. At the end of the lecture, one woman stood up and asked the first question 'Didn't they have any vocational training?'*

This questioner, obviously, had never developed the concept of a curriculum design based on such elements as the nature of the individual to be educated, the needs of society, the purposes of education, the kind of teaching procedures and school organization needed, and the appraisal of results.

Complexities in curriculum construction increase as the complexities of civilization increase. They go hand in hand. The gymnasiums, athletic fields, and swimming pools of today are merely educational substitutes for the forest, field, and stream of earlier years.

THE OLD WORLD TRADITION

Our dominant heritage came from northern Europe. Since a curriculum of public education is a product of socioeconomic forces, it finds its purposes and fundamental philosophy in the social and cultural setting in which it exists. Society very early began to realize that men and women could be improved through education, and the curriculum soon became the means of translating these beliefs—the social and educational philosophy—into teaching procedures.

The European tradition was our early guide, for the American settlers were transplanted Europeans. Until our forebears thought through the nature and meaning of democracy as the kind of social organization they wanted for their new country, the economically and socially favored groups tended also to be favored educationally.

In Europe, the concepts of divine destiny and the divine right of kings went with the educational cultivation of a social and intellectual elite. Classes and castes made social mobility virtually impossible and the idea of equality and opportunity for all a myth. The ruling classes not only set the goals of education but also controlled the curriculum designed to achieve them.

The Latin grammar school, the secondary school of the early American colonial period, bore all the earmarks of the European secondary school. It was a product of the Renaissance, dedicated to the mastery of Greek and Latin classics.

Many of our early Southern colonists represented the ruling classes of England and were motivated largely by economic motives in coming to America. With their aristocratic background, it was quite natural that they were not mainly interested in education for the masses. Even in the north, the apprentice style of education represented the practical emphasis on education for the masses while the tutorial system and the Latin grammar schools were for the more favored classes. This occurred despite the fact that these were children of early immigrants who came to this continent motivated by ideals of political and religious freedom.

A curriculum of Latin, Greek, and rhetoric aimed at preparing lawyers, ministers, and medical doctors, with drill the method and rigid classroom discipline the atmosphere, met the particular needs of a particular group in the early colonial period. The names of William Penn, Roger Williams, and Edward Hopkins, who had been

*From Mead, M. Our educational emphasis in primitive perspective, *The American Journal of Sociology*, May 1943, pp. 633-639. By permission of *The American Journal of Sociology* and the University of Chicago Press.

educated in similar schools abroad, lent prestige and popularity to these techniques and resulted in the establishment of the Boston Latin School in 1635. From this school came such signers of the Declaration of Independence as John Hancock, Samuel Adams, Benjamin Franklin, and others. Other former students include such famous names in American history as Cotton Mather, Ralph Waldo Emerson, Henry Ward Beecher, Edward Everett Hale, and Charles Eliot.

In 1743, against much opposition from certain wealthy, and influential people, Benjamin Franklin began to think of the need for a different kind of secondary school—one that would prepare youth for business and "the several offices of civil life" the colonies were developing. Business required competencies in bookkeeping, navigation, surveying, and business administration. The professional man needed history, public speaking, government, and political science. The need for French was more important than the need for Latin. In 1751 Franklin opened a modified version of his academy in Philadelphia.

By the mid-nineteenth century, neither the needs of the students nor the needs of society were met by the nonfunctional curriculum of the old Latin grammar school, and it ceased to exist in that form. By its very nature it was the school of the aristocracy. It failed to keep pace with the developing ideals and needs of the times.

As the concept of democracy developed—the concept that the safety of the new nation lay in the hands of the people—the idea of the nature of education changed. The public school became the setting where "all the children of all the people" would be educated. The function of the curriculum was to translate social and education philosophy into teaching procedures and ways of living, actual behavior.

The school curriculum, however, has been accused of "educational lag," of permitting a serious gap between educational practice and the almost miraculous developments in science and technology. If the school and its curriculum in physical education is to march out of step, always a few steps behind the society it is to serve, it will be unable to accept the challenge of the needs of people in a highly technological age.

Obviously, from what has been said—and aside from sheer common sense—it can be seen that the bases on which any curriculum is built change with new socioeconomic trends and forces. The school, therefore, faces a change in its pattern of responsibilities from time to time. The curriculum that changes with the social structure must be a living, dynamic thing. Since the American school is grounded in the democratic ideal, it must advance the ideals of the society that maintains it by public taxation. As our society grows in complexity, a greater burden is thrown on the school. By changing the curriculum we really mean changing the experiences of students. The curriculum is the means by which appropriate educative experiences are assured. It is not something of intrinsic value, but rather a means to an end. As new socioeconomic forces play on the school, the goals society seeks to achieve through the school become important elements in curriculum design.

In examining the history of education, we see various emphases at different periods. Plato was trying to make the citizen "the guardian of the state to be philosophical, high spirited, swift-footed and strong." The religion of the Puritan stressed educational objectives in terms of faith and stern duty. The growth of science emphasized reflective thinking, a disciplined and well-ordered mind. The present threats to our democratic way of life demand emphasis on an understanding of the nature, principles, and ideals of democracy and the development of zeal to defend these. Citizenship, therefore, becomes an important ultimate objective of education.

In 1860, Herbert Spencer,* one of England's great educational scholars, conceived of education as "complete living" and suggested that education is something more than telling, that it is an activity phenomenon and should include:

1. Those activities that directly minister to self-preservation (health-safety).
2. Those activities that, by securing the necessities of life, indirectly minister to self-preservation (vocation).
3. Those activities that have for their end the rearing and discipline of offspring (family).
4. Those activities that are involved in the maintenance of proper social and political relations (citizenship).
5. Those miscellaneous activities that make up the leisure part of life, devoted to the gratification of the tastes and feelings (leisure time).

The efforts to adjust the character and curriculum of the school to meet the needs of children, youth, and adults in a democratic setting have been determined, remain continuous, and are very much in process today.

BASIC TRENDS IN THE MODERN WORLD

It is difficult to realize that the American child in the fifth grade will spend his adult life in a culture quite different from the one he/she experienced as a fifth-grader. The environment and experiences of future generations will be even more different. We cannot think of the needs of children or give answers to their questions solely on the basis of our own experience as children. The goals of education in the most rapidly changing culture in the history of the world present fearsome challenges to the individual and the educator alike. As Mead reminds us of the task in hand:

We have given our children an incomparable heritage of independence, willingness to go out into new places among people, willingness to stand on their own feet and answer for their own deeds. Now because the task ahead is more exacting than any task Americans have yet faced, we must use the knowledge which the new sciences of human behavior have given us, to create the conditions of the strength that will be needed, to give protection against loneliness, new sources within the self, new capacities for moving into that future which is the only earthly future to which a democracy can commit itself, a future in which only the general direction of the next step is clear, in which men have the faith to say, although the night is dark, and they are far from home, 'I do not ask to see
> The distant scene
> One step enough for me.'*

We speak of "education for change." Permanency is merely an illusion. We are swamped with economic and technological changes. Yet we cherish the ideals of a life of reason, hope, and conditions wherein the welfare of the individual is prominent and the true goals for functioning in a society might be realized for all.

The early leaders of America saw in the public schools the progressive realization of the nation of their visions. In the old-fashioned community of the time where people were conscious of their dependence on one another, kin sympathy was strong. The attitudes and ideas of what was right and wrong, desirable and undesirable present-

---

*Modified from Spencer, H. *Education: intellectual, moral and physical.* New York: Hurst & Co., 1860, p. 17.

*From Mead, M. The impact of culture on personality development in the United States today. *Understanding the child*, January 1951, p. 18.

ed few serious problems. Educational purposes were stated solely in terms of the individual's mastery of subject matter and the acceptance of dualism—which thought of learning as occurring "in the mind," and while this took place, the emotional, esthetic, and social aspects of the learner were unaffected.

However, as emerging social problems became more complex and values at times more undefinable, the resultant policies and actions of very large and diversified social groups were the causes for change. Education became virtually interested in the whole person. The emphasis was on learning as a whole—the unity of man—and the rejection of dualism. It was strongly realized that the school was a vital part of the total cultural pattern of society and had increasing responsibilities for giving attention to the social process—the personal-social interactions—involved in education for living. Such goals as keeping children and youth healthy, assisting them in becoming socially useful by finding their places in the economic scheme, and developing in them the full responsibilities of citizenship, moral and spiritual values, and intellectual curiosity and power gave direction to education.

Physical education, paralleling the direction of education, realized that Johnny did not leave his mind in the classroom when he entered the gymnasium. He brought with him his hopes, fears, intellectual abilities, curiosities, weak muscles, clumsiness, enlarged tonsils, physique, values, appreciations, and life-style. Physical education adopted the notion of the unity of the total organism. It became concerned with not only the physical aspect of the learner but also his/her total being. The acceptance of this theory that the teacher of physical education—above all others—should be concerned with the learner in toto and view him/her as a sociopsychobiological creature and not merely as a dancer, pitcher, or fullback places a unique responsibility on such teachers. They, like all teachers, must constantly strive to identify those forces or trends in a contemporary or future world that are determinants of behavior in the same individuals that they as teachers seek to change by the educational process. Unless the teacher has an awareness and understanding of the complexities of an ever-changing society, then his/her own education as well as the education of students is apt to be futile.

EDUCATIONAL PURPOSES OF TODAY AND THE FUTURE

Determining the relationships between an evolving nature of society and educational trends can provide us with insight and direction for curriculum planning. Even though we have many scientific facts on which to construct a curriculum of physical education, we must always face the philosophical question, To what end? We must constantly seek answers to questions like, What is right and just? What is adequate? What do these facts mean in terms of purpose and value? Theory and philosophy should not be competitive but should complement one another. The first supplies fact judgment and means, the second, value judgment and ends. Theory does not tell us what we ought to do, it merely tells us what we must do if we are to achieve our purposes.

Since education is concerned with purposefully directed learning for producing desired changes in behavior, it is important that we think in terms of the *direction of change*.

To this end, Bruce E. Joyce,* in addressing physical educators at a Secondary

---

*From Joyce, B. E. *Curriculum and humanistic education: moralism and pluralism.* Paper presented at Secondary School Physical Education Curriculum Conference, 1971.

School Physical Education Curriculum Conference, stated the following as goals of curriculum planning:

1. To create environments which enable individuals to actualize themselves on their own terms—emotionally, intellectually, and socially.
2. To create environments which help people reach each other and live with an expanding common consciousness—one which not only embraces the traditional liberal values of mutual respect and protection of the rights of others, but also reaches out to explore the development of expanded human experiences through new dimensions of relationships with others.

Physical education adds the physical dimension and faces an added challenge of meeting these goals in the gymnasium and pool or on the athletic field and playground.

Each goal cited here presents a challenge to physical education teachers and all other teachers because it is difficult to isolate components of personality and deal with them separately. We deal with the total individual in total situations wherein we hope to have the student develop the abilities, understanding, attitudes, or appreciations mentioned earlier.

To decrease the difficulty as well as to indicate the importance of our task, we must segment each goal into objectives that represent types of human behavior and development that contribute to the attainment of these goals.

Objectives and experiences must be devised in the swimming lesson, the basketball period, the organization of the athletic association, all of which contribute in various ways to the ultimate outcome—a graduate, a citizen, devoted to the principles of democracy and zealous in upholding them.

Without this type of analysis, the selection of curriculum experiences would be impossible for curriculum planning. No principal or teacher would deny the fact that in order to make a football team, boys must take part in playing football by teams and achieve a host of immediate objectives, such as catching, blocking, punting, passing—all done in relation to what other teammates are doing—as these fit into the plan of the team.

William Van Til, in addressing the National Association of Secondary School Principals, posed the question, "What should be taught and learned in secondary schools?" He listed 16 concerns that secondary education should consider. They were as follows:

(1) war, peace, and international relations; (2) overpopulation, pollution and energy; (3) economic options and problems; (4) governmental processes; (5) consumer problems; (6) intercultural relations; (7) world views; (8) recreation and leisure; (9) the arts and aesthetics; (10) self-understanding and personal development; (11) family, peer group and school; (12) health; (13) community living; (14) vocations, (15) communication; and (16) alternative futures.*

Even though some of these concerns can be considered as unique and specific to physical education, all of them must be considered as directly or indirectly affecting the goals and objectives of curriculums.

Physical education, as an integral part of the total educational process, cannot minimize its responsibilities for contributing to the personal growth and usefulness of every boy and girl. It can be a vital force in preparing every student to assume full responsibilities of citizenship. It can help satisfy individual needs for happiness by stimulating curiosity, an awareness of the inner joy and satisfaction of intellectual and physical achievement, and an appreciation

*From Van Til, W. Address to the National Association of Secondary School Principals, Washington, D.C., February 1976.

of the values on which this nation was founded and that must continue to nourish it today.

We must face and resolve present and future issues. The National Society for the Study of Education Yearbook* (1976), which deals with "Issues in Secondary Education," identifies eight issues that confront education for preparing today's students to live in the twenty-first century. They are as follows:

(1) The Individual—how can secondary education best foster the fullest development of the individual's potentialities and experiences as a fully functioning, self-actualizing person?

(2) Values—how can secondary education best help youth to develop and apply humane values so that the democratic dream might be achieved and experienced by Americans and other citizens of the world?

(3) Social Realities—how can secondary education best equip youth with the vision, knowledge, and competencies needed to cope with the social realities . . . in the present and emerging future?

(4) Drawing on Man's Experiences—how can secondary education best utilize the . . . experiences of mankind . . . in the education of contemporary youth?

(5) Environment and Setting—how can secondary education best draw upon present and prospective school facilities and buildings and the life and institutions of communities and thus maximally use the total environment and setting for learning experiences of youth?

(6) Organization—how can secondary education best create, test and use enriching and effective ways of organization for the better education of youth?

(7) Teaching Strategies—how can secondary education best mobilize and use instruc-

tional resources and processes for learning experiences for youth?

(8) Administering, Supervising and Improving—how can secondary education draw upon all affected groups . . . in administering supervising and improving the education enterprise?

As to the future, Alvin Toffler, who coined the term, "future shock," critically decries today's curriculum, with its segmented, air-tight compartments, saying that it does not give credence to contemporary and future human needs. To help avert future shock:

The curriculum of tomorrow must include not only an extremely wide range of data-oriented courses, but a strong emphasis on future-relevant behaviors skills. It must combine a variety of factual content in what might be termed "life know-how." It must find ways to do both at the same time, transmitting one in circumstances or environments that produce the other.*

However, even with an awareness of the problems in the "past" and envisioning the problems of the "future," we must also be concerned with the "now." it might be well to identify and synthesize rather specifically the trends in the attempt to bring the basic elements of the curriculum in line with the needs of the individual and the needs of society, here and now. Some of these are as follows:

1. While interested in the future, we try to make the most of present living. We are interested in each child here and now. Taking turns and sharing, being a "good sport," faithfulness in adversity, working for the "good of the team," and having a sense of humor became objectives from the nursery school through the remainder of formal education.

*From *National Society for the Study of Education Yearbook*. Washington, D.C.: National Educational Association, 1976.

*From Toffler, A. *Future shock*. New York: Bantam Books, 1971, p. 418.

2. Facts and skills are not only important because of their inherent value but because they contribute to the total development of boys and girls. We are interested not only in what John does to the football or what Mary does with the dance, but also in what the football does to John and what the dance does to Mary. We say that modern education is child centered rather than subject centered.

3. Because we live in a rapidly changing world, our aims, materials, and strategies are less static and more flexible. Modern physical education is more than "muscles and sweat."

4. At one time the curriculum and the textbook were synonymous. Today, we think of the curriculum in terms of all the guided experiences young people have under the control of school authorities.

5. The school is no longer isolated from the community, but the school utilizes the resources of the community. Education is not limited to the four walls of the classroom.

6. Learning is not dictated, prescribed, and controlled by text and teacher. Learning involves the total personality of the learner. It is generally influenced and motivated by the learner's values and purposes. Boys and girls want strength, grace, skill, and health for something. They want to be accepted, be with their friends, overcome self-consciousness, be less clumsy and awkward, and have a clearer skin. Learning is active. It comes through experiences involving planning, self-discovery, self-direction, self-evaluation, exploration, and thinking.

7. We learn to be sociable, not solely by studying about life, but also through active participation in group and community living. It is difficult to learn to swim by correspondence. It is in childhood and youth that the common motor experiences of children and youth at play socialize the individual. The most important factor in the development of personality is contact with other personalities. Play situations represent the "great common denominator," the social "melting pot."

8. The word "extracurricular" is falling into misuse. No clear distinction now exists between curricular and extracurricular activities. All experiences affected by the school are considered part of the curriculum. Intramural games, dramatics, orchestra, and interscholastic athletics are an integral part of the curriculum.

9. Traditional instructional, curricular, and organizational patterns need to be critically examined in light of newer educational theories, innovative instructional models and strategies, and application of technology.

10. Evaluation is not based solely on final results, but should be an immediate specific and continous process for detecting the direction and degree of behavioral changes.

11. Finally, the physical education teacher is not a "rammer" of facts and skills into the brains and muscles of pupils. The teacher is a "development supervisor," a guardian and developer of individual human personalities who uses the unique contributions of physical education as a means toward these ends.

In summary, it would be presumptuous to assume that by teaching a youngster to hit a tennis ball or perform a polka step all the problems of society will be solved. However, the total educational curriculum can be the medium for individual self-discovery and self-realization. It should be the steering gear for society. Physical education, as one spoke in that gear, can make its unique contributions to these ends by providing a series of rich and meaningful experiences under trained and dynamic leadership. There must be general agreement as to the particular direction and, more specifically, the means for accomplishing these tasks. These are the purposes of this book.

REACTORS

1. If education takes place in a society . . . without continous awareness of the problems of society:
   a. We shall have a rather unrealistic perspective of our objectives.
   b. We shall run the risk of educating people for a world that no longer exists.
2. The aims of primitive education and the aims of modern education are identical.
3. As a civilization becomes more complex, education and physical education tend to be somewhat divorced from life.
4. A curriculum should change society and reflect society.
5. Educational leadership in the organization of children's activities requires knowledge and skill that make the organized activities as natural as unorganized, but more certain of educational results.

SITUATIONAL PROBLEMS

1. In a radio discussion concerning the meaning of culture, Archibald MacLeish* said:

   Culture is one of the things you don't define. It is too close to life itself to be defined. You describe it. You begin by clearing your head of the notion which Webster's dictionary gives you that culture has something to do with taste and aesthetics. Maybe it did in the nineteenth century in the ladies' Browning societies. Actually what you mean by the culture of a people is the way of life of that people: its civilization—its contribution to common civilization—the things its people value and the things they don't value—the way they make music—the way they express themselves—their habits of life—their works of art—their novels—their history—the things they have learned in their effort to penetrate the common mystery and experience of mankind by the instruments of poetry and science—briefly, what they are, what they do, what they are like.

   Ask some 70-year-old men and women:
   a. How they made a living
   b. What games they played in youth
   c. The nature of their school experiences

   *From MacLeish, A. San Francisco Conference of the United Nations, 1945.

   d. The heroes they admired in adolescence
   e. Their modes of transporation and communication
   f. Their general use of leisure time in youth

   Contrast their experiences with yours of today. How would you account for the differences? What are the curriculum implications of the culture modern man has created for himself? Does education have some responsibility for consciously changing the culture patterns?

   Examine the concepts of physical education during:
   a. The age of Pericles
   b. The days of Julius Caesar
   c. The American colonial period
   d. The present day

   What essential differences existed among individuals of these four different cultures?

2. During the 1700s manpower was the principal source of energy. Today only about 2% of our industrial power has its source in muscular power. Where formerly a majority of the people of the country were engaged in agriculture in order to feed the total population, now perhaps no more than 15% is required. Even when all labor is done by machines, men and women need healthy minds and muscles. If sturdy systems are not developed during the normal labor of the day, what is the requirement placed on education for the development of substitutes for maintenance of physical and mental health? Can the task be accomplished by two 20-minute periods of physical education each week?
3. In the lists below and on p. 27, match the corresponding numbers in the "satisfaction goal" column to the "fundamental tendency" out of which each grows.

   Fundamental tendency
   1. To be physically active
   2. Spontaneous play, hobbies
   3. Complex and varied drives operating in mating
   4. Self-preservation
   5. Manipulation and experimentation

6. Fear of the unknown, untried, strange
7. Preference for gregarious behavior
8. Recognition
9. Group status
10. Achievement and mastery

Satisfaction goal

1. Finding explanations for unknown causes
2. Spontaneous play, hobbies
3. Many forms of dancing
4. Wearing a "school letter"
5. Learning to swim
6. Abstaining from starches and sweets
7. Learning a trade
8. Hunting, fishing, agriculture
9. "Making" a team
10. Joining a club

LEARNING ACTIVITIES

1. Identify and differentiate between the concepts of physical education during:
   a. The age of Pericles
   b. The days of Julius Caesar
   c. The American colonial period
   d. The present day
2. Examine and compare the early historical purposes of physical education with contemporary purposes.

3. Give examples of how the activities of a physical education program can be the means for satisfying some of the motives of our culture.
4. Interpret the statement, "We can alter the results only by determining and manipulating the factors which cause them," and apply your interpretation to a physical education situation.
5. Predict what changes could occur in physical education due to future cultural changes.

UNIT EVALUATIVE CRITERIA

Can you:

1. Identify the forces in society that affect curriculum development in physical education?
2. Determine the curriculum implications of the culture modern man has created for himself?
3. State and justify the purposes of education and indicate which purposes are unique to physical education?
4. Envision what physical education will be in the future?

RESOURCES

Benedict, R. *Patterns of culture.* Boston: Houghton Mifflin Co., 1934.

Bookwalter, K. W., & Vanderzwaag, H. J. *Foundations and principles of physical education.* Philadelphia: W. B. Saunders Co., 1969.

Brown, F. J. *Educational sociology* (2nd ed.). New York: Prentice-Hall, Inc., 1954, chap. 4.

Cowell, C. C. *Scientific foundations of physical education.* New York: Harper & Brothers, 1953, chap. 2.

Cowell, C. C., & France, W. *Philosophy and principles of physical education.* Englewood Cliffs, N.J.: Prentice-Hall, Inc., 1963.

Gorer, G. *The American people.* New York: W. W. Norton & Co., Inc., 1948.

Kelley, E. C., & Rasey, M. *Education and the nature of man.* New York: Harper & Brothers, 1952.

Mead, M. *And keep your powder dry.* New York: William Morrow & Co., Inc., 1942.

Nash, J. B. *Physical education: Interpretations and objectives.* New York: A. S. Barnes & Co., Inc., 1948, chap. 2.

Nixon, J. E., & Jewett, A. E. *An introduction to physical education.* Philadelphia: W. B. Saunders Co., 1969.

Obertueffer, D. *Physical education, a textbook of principles for professional students.* New York: Harper & Brothers, 1951.

Obertueffer, D., & Ulrich, C. *Physical education.* New York: Harper & Row, Publishers, Inc., 1970.

Smith, B. O., Stanley, W. O., & Shores, J. H. *Fundamentals of curriculum development.* Yonkers, N.Y.: World Book Co., 1950, chap. 1.

Toffler, A. *Future shock.* New York: Random House, Inc., 1970.

Van Dalen, D. B., Mitchell, E. D., & Bennett, B. L. *World History of physical education.* Englewood Cliffs, N.J.: Prentice-Hall, Inc., 1971.

Weston, A. *The making of American physical education.* New York: Appleton-Century-Crofts, 1962.

Williams, J. F. *The principles of physical education.* Philadelphia: W. B. Saunders Co., 1949.

Ziegler, E. Z. *Problems in the history and philosophy of physical education and sport.* Englewood Cliffs, N.J.: Prentice-Hall, Inc., 1968.

Individuality and identity emerge from the deep levels of the self, from the resources and talents that exist in each of us to be formed and shaped into a particular being in the world.

ABRAHAM H. MASLOW

3 The learner: a directive force

COMPETENCIES

After completing this unit, you should be able to:

Identify and interpret those human growth and developmental forces and their significance for curriculum planning.

Translate, by means of the curriculum, the conditions, experiences, and materials that will encourage the unfolding and development of what nature has hidden in the learner.

Determine what constitutes the best education for the learner at particular stages of development.

Formulate principles from the growth and developmental implications to serve as guidelines for program planning.

Define the following:

Ability	Maturation
Characteristics	Nature
Development	Needs
Drives	Nurture
Environment	Principle
Growth	Readiness
Heredity	Tension
Interests	Values

PERSPECTIVE

PRINCIPLE: The directive forces of basic personality needs and the growth and developmental characteristics of the learner, at whatever grade level, are important elements to be considered in curriculum development.

Children and youth can be educated only to the extent that we understand how and why they learn or, more specific for physical education, how and why they play. We cannot be effective in dealing with children and youth without an understanding of the progressive stages of strength and endurance development; an awareness of when and why social interactions begin to develop; the ability to perceive play through the eyes of a highly imaginative child or a skill-motivated youth; the ability to recognize the shifting of play goals from a simple joy in activity itself to interest in acquiring skill; and a discernment of changes from individualism to a desire to organize and be a member of a team.

The individual is a complex, ever-changing organism in terms of physiological, psychological, and sociological growth and development. An insight into these areas provides for us a direction for curriculum planning. We speak of nature and nurture, heredity and environment. Education is always a bipolar process—the one pole man, the other pole his environment. Experience becomes the interaction between these two as the human organism makes adjustment to a situation.

Instead of instinct, we now speak of "unlearned cores of behavior," unlearned tendencies to respond, basic drives and tensions, persistent types of self-assertion. Biologically founded education considers the nature and needs of the learner. It adopts the concept of the gardener rather than that of the builder and thinks of develop-

ment as the expression of heredity in a favorable environment. It is concerned with the provision of conditions and experiences that permit children and youth to most completely realize their potentialities.

The potato sprout grows toward light. Similarly, the young child plays because he/she attempts, unconsciously, to resolve a dynamic biochemical disequilibrium—an imbalance, a tension. We call this phenomenon the "activity drive." The child stops when he/she incurs an "oxygen debt," rests until the oxygen supply is built up and the debt paid, and dashes off again to play.

Nature, as exemplified by the activity drive, initiates action without direction. Random activity or infantile play represents, like the behavior of the potato sprout, *unconscious* purpose at work. The child by nature is active. Education or nurture, biologically viewed, is concerned with the mysterious process of development in which nature expresses itself under the influence of appropriate nurture. Here we come face to face with *conscious* purpose as a directional force as a result of our provision of external influences that take on meaning and purpose for the individual. We start with basic activity drive—an unlearned core of behavior that provides no conscious direction. Conscious or intentional education gives guidance and direction to the natural learning processes.

An organism has needs. A stone has no needs. In order to live, grow, and develop, and organism must be continually satisfying needs. Life involves the satisfaction of all sorts of physical, mental, emotional, and social needs.

We shall see that certain elements of the curriculum which must be considered in curriculum design are the directive forces of basic personality needs and the developmental characteristics of the learner at whatever grade level we might be working.

To be effective, education has to know what the needs of life are, under what conditions and at what age level children undertake to meet them, by what processes they meet them, what subject matter or experiences are best suited to meet them, and what sort of person is best fitted to assist children to satisfy their needs.

Children may have the most adequate nutrition, sunlight, good air, and grassy playgrounds with adequate equipment and supplies, yet optimum growth and development may still not be attained due to educational mismanagement—for example, an attempt to teach first graders the zone defense in basketball. This extreme example is used to emphasize that *readiness* may determine the acceptance or rejection of a learning experience. Obviously, first-grade children are not *ready* physically, socially, or psychologically to accept such instruction. It is beyond their developmental level, out of their experience; therefore it meets no actual need in their lives.

DEVELOPMENTAL CHARACTERISTICS OF THE LEARNER AS FACTORS

Convention and tradition, rather than scientific understanding, have formed the basis of most school curricula. Curriculum patterns used at the start of the century are no longer valid today. Changing society and newer knowledge of principles of child growth and development and of the nature and conditions of learning make the difference. With the focus of attention in American education on the full development of the individual rather than merely on subject matter, provision in the curriculum must be made for a wide range of psychosocial needs. Emotional and social maturity, self-confidence, and self-realization become developmental ends to which the curriculum becomes the means.

Not only must the school be grounded in the American ideal of democracy in order to perform its great social functions, but it must also consider the developmental characteristics of individual students. It must ask not only, What does society require? but it must ask of pupils, Are they mature, immature, girls, boys, strong, weak? For example, boys and girls who have achieved sexual maturity present different educational problems from prepubescent boys and girls. The school must ask, What are the fundamental forces *within* the growing organism that seek expression and satisfaction? Here we refer to the dynamic usage of the term *need*. Instrumentally or functionally, this term refers to the means and conditions that are necessary for the satisfaction of those fundamental forces active in youth that seek expression and satisfaction, and for which the curriculum becomes the means of satisfaction. We turn now to examine these important elements of the curriculum more closely.

We think of physical education as being concerned with physical activities—as a leadership of the basic drives and tensions, the primary motivations, the organic needs, the fundamental urges, the tissue needs, the first-order drives of growing boys and girls. Our subject matter consists of a program aimed to satisfy the biological instigations for activity, excitement, and new experience as well as the socially acquired drives for recognition, approval, and group status. The development of methods and techniques to these ends in physical education are important curriculum problems.

At each school level we must ask, What constitutes the best development and education for children or youth at this particular stage in their experience? The answer is sought in facts and principles discovered through research into genetic growth and development. The kindergarten child, for example, is immature physically and socially and outstandingly active, but fatigues easily and has a very short interest span, is egocentric and a rugged individualist—does not like to share toys and usually plays in small groups of three or four if engaged in group play—and likes to imitate, dramatize, and create.

The teenage adolescent—to skip several vaguely defined developmental stages—represents a changed picture. Story plays, mimetic exercises, and mere climbing, balancing, pushing, and pulling are not adequate for this need stage. The teenager makes different demands on the surrounding culture, being in a period of rapid growth, and having acquired a number of motor skills. Personal appearance and the opposite sex receive attention. Cooperation, team play, and organization become prominent in his/her thinking and feeling. Desire for group approval is strong, yet there is a strong surge toward autonomy and self-realization. It has been said that, "You can always tell an adolescent but you can't tell him much." From a curriculum standpoint, however, we recognize that learning to think and act for oneself is an essential part of growing up.

Conclusion: Developmental characteristics of the learner represent an important element in the design of a curriculum. They must be taken into account.

ABILITIES, INTERESTS, NEEDS, AND READINESS AS IMPORTANT DIRECTIONAL FORCES

Ability is defined as natural talent or acquired proficiency. Since the physical educator is primarily concerned with motor ability, this definition should be applied within that context. This definition takes on a greater significance when watching children in the intial stages of learning a new skill. Why do some children perform the skill immediately while others have difficulty? It is obvious that certain components of motor ability or even degrees of proficiency required for learning a skill are inherited traits, while others are developed by experience. The physiological and psychological components comprising motor ability and their acquisition must be of major concern to the curriculum planner.

There is a difference between following the whims or fancies of children and using their interests in the development of a curriculum. Interest is evidence of purpose that results in sustained effort and maximum meaning.

How are the needs of the organism, from the amoeba to man, met? That which meets a need may be called a *value*. If one has an uncomfortable feeling called hunger, a sandwich becomes a value. If one is lonesome, companionship becomes a value.

At all stages of the development of the individual certain basic needs must be met if he/she is to live wholesomely and learn effectively. Evidences of needs and ways of satisfying them vary at different levels of growth. A problem in curriculum development is the planning of a program with direct reference to the kind of needs most characteristic at each age level.

As development supervisors, physical educators are concerned with the physical aspects of growth and development and the fulfillment of such basic physical needs as good food, fresh air, physical activity balanced by rest and relaxation, and the correction of physical defects. At the same time, however, they are likewise concerned with the satisfaction of basic emotional and social needs of children and youth, factors that are equally important. For example, good food may be supplied, yet anxiety, fear, or excitement may prevent its being eaten or properly assimilated. Playgrounds and gymnasiums may be available, yet tension and excessive competition with its resulting worry and lack of security may actually result in arresting development. The psychomatic concept of medicine recognizes the profound importance of biological integration—of the interrelationship of mind and body. In the child's every act on the playground, intellectual, emotional, and volitional activity are involved. The girl playing volleyball and the boy playing basketball will approach the game intellectually and with imagination to the extent that they feel the game is worthwhile and they have strength of purpose with respect to it. Their feeling or appreciation will depend on their understanding of the game and their will to master the game. As a result of clearer understanding, more appreciation and endeavor result. The total individual responds to each situation with his/her *whole* being.

For purposes of simplification, we think of needs, drives, tensions, and motives as being vaguely synonymous. We may think of needs from the dynamic point of view in relation to "disturbing situations." The latter are "provokers of needs." They cause tensions that orient us in the direction of goals of satisfaction. From the standpoint of implemental usage of the term we think of *goal resources*—means, conditions, experiences that will enable the student to satisfy his/her needs. We help students to learn, to achieve internal equilibrium or satisfaction, and to resolve tension by helping them achieve goal satisfactions. Table 1 indicates some functions of the physical education curriculum with reference to need satisfaction. A curriculum that provides goal re-

sources for satisfaction of the needs indicated would always be meaningful and dynamic; it would be a curriculum in which children and youth would engage in vital experiences and in which the persistent problems of living would be faced, and physical, social, and emotional needs would, to a greater extent, be met.

Since we note genetic growth and development taking place in children by observing changes in behavior, there is some indication that some children may be more ready and able to profit by instruction than others. The nursery school child pounds clay and manipulates it most often without producing forms recognized by the adult. He/she climbs, pushes, and pulls but finds games of even low organization of little interest because he/she has attained neither the level of coordination nor the comprehension to want to participate in them.

This variable, termed *readiness,* refers primarily to those levels of physical and mental maturation that may influence the child to enter into physical education activities with meaning, interest, and a reasonable chance to successfully achieve. The inability to isolate this variable as to its interaction with and effect on the physiological, psychological, and emotional factors creates somewhat of a problem. However, readiness, with all its complexities and controversial implications, must be given consideration by the curriculum planner. It represents the time when the learner is able to profit by instruction. After the child reaches a certain stage of development, he/she can do easily and quickly what could not be done even with much training at an earlier stage. The climbing, balancing, pushing, pulling, random manipulation of the kindergartner; the scribbling and dabbing at the easel; the primitive sense of rhythm; the simple pattern of play with blocks—all these activities are

Table 1. Functions of the physical education curriculum with reference to need satisfaction

Disturbing situations (causes of tensions)	Goal resources (implemental usage of "needs")	Goal satisfactions (resolution of tensions)
Experiencing threats to bodily comfort (pain, hunger, sex demands, need for sleep)	Our function as teachers is to help to provide the goal resources in the form of conditions, materials, experiences, and opportunities that will make desirable goal satisfactions possible for the student. How goal resources may be provided and how learning experiences may be organized is the burden of the curriculum.	Improved health, physical well-being, rest, marriage
Being bored, finding life dull and monotonous; lacking activity; wanting physical "play"; having unsatisfied curiosity		New adventure, exploration, experience, zestful activity, creativeness, self-expression
Feeling weak and like a failure, feeling inferior; feeling thwarted and disappointed		Success, mastery, and achievement; sense of leadership and power
Being unwanted, being unloved; being rejected by one's peers; knowing loneliness; being "left out"		Friends, being loved and given intimacy and tenderness by those whose love and approval one seeks; sense of belonging to a larger social unit; participating in group ventures
Being ignored or looked down on; being regarded with scorn, contempt, disapproval; being emotionally insecure		Rewards of being looked up to, recognized and approved, admired and appreciated; having status in one's group
Experiencing lack of orientation in life; being uncertain of ideals and goals worth following; being uncertain about one's purposes and abilities in life; having an unclear picture of the conscious "self"; having a muddled attitude toward the major issues of life		Clearer concept and picture of oneself; clear ideals of life accomplishment and of self; clarification of masculine and feminine roles; acceptance of one's bodily characteristics; philosophy of life that gives consistent direction to behavior and life; religious belief; unity of purpose
Being worried, anxious, fearful that one will be deprived of goal satisfaction or that needs will not be met; experiencing threats to one's security		Peace of mind, security, release from tension; some well-defined purposes and a stable philosophy of life or religious belief

building psychological and educational readiness for more and more complicated growth to come. People are ready to profit by experience when they understand what they are learning and see some purpose in it.

For curriculum development, a thorough understanding of the common growth sequences is highly important. Without this understanding, physical education teachers cannot anticipate when children will most likely be ready for the various types of experiences available in the curriculum. Some understanding of the complete growth cycle is important. When do children prefer tag to toys, basketball to dodge ball, high and broad jumping to galloping and skipping, coeducational activity to activity limited to their own sex?

It is true that what society values and expects of children is always a factor in determining behavior, yet the subtle factors of physical and mental maturation influence, initially, the interest and willingness to learn.

INDIVIDUAL DIFFERENCES— INEVITABLE AND DESIRABLE

Obviously, all children of the same chronological age are not in the same stage of maturation. We see in seventh-graders, for example, a wide variation in skills. An inflexible and stereotyped curriculum will see many children bored and unchallenged, whereas others will be *straining* unduly to keep up. This presents the important problem of individual differences in relation to the curriculum.

Although we plan activities aimed at the level of the "average" pupil, the average never represents any one individual. Patterns of development are individual. Generalizations concerning maturation are of great importance to the curriculum maker, but the application of the principles involved must be made on an individual basis.

Flexible and innovative physical education programs allow for individual variation in levels of maturation and skill at any one time and permit individuals to change activities as abilities change. Individualized instructional programs account for maturity and bodily structure as well as for skill. They are designed to consider individual differences so that maximum satisfaction and maximum learning may be obtained by the participants.

Personality types should be accepted and respected. We should understand that each individual is unique. The sensitive, bookish boy should not be maligned because he does not come out for football in order to make a "regular fellow" out of him. Physical education teachers are rather prone to impose on their students a somewhat preconceived type of personality—usually the overactive, extrovert type.

Nature has expended great ingenuity in making our children as diverse as they are. Certainly, the function of education is not to root out all these diversities and reduce the student group to a uniform mass. The world needs a variety of powers and character. Each boy and girl holds within him or her unique potentialities and should have full opportunity to develop them for all they are worth. America's strength comes from a unique source—strength through diversity. Democracy implies freedom for each individual to develop the unique potentialities that are within him/her. For this, education is required—a particular kind of education.

Large physical education classes containing children of a wide age range represent curricula based on mere convenience. All children are not essentially alike, although certain central tendencies exist in any group. That no single impersonal method of treatment is possible for all cases is axiomatic.

As guardians and developers of personality, teachers of physical education, by means of the curriculum, have the task of providing the conditions, experiences, and materials that will encourage the unfolding and vigorous development of what nature has hidden in the child. A critical analysis of teaching strategies, organizational patterns, procedures, and types of experiences is needed to determine the best means to these ends.

REACTORS

1. Development is the expression of heredity in an environment.
2. It is essential to distinguish conscious purposes from uncommon purposes; also, contrast between directional forces from within the organism and directional forces outside the organism.
3. A static curriculum does not reflect new information related to the learner's growth and development.
4. The learner is an ever-changing organism in terms of physiological, psychological, and sociological growth and development.
5. The teacher of physical education can educate children adequately only to the extent to which he/she understands them.
6. A physical education curriculum must provide for variances in individual rates and levels of maturation.
7. The application of principles derived from the learner's growth and developmental stages must be made on an individual basis.

SITUATIONAL PROBLEMS

1. A certain professor of biology spends a great part of his time gaining intimate knowledge of various living organisms ranging from amoebas, sweet peas, and fruit flies to chimpanzees. He cultivates them and studies them. He has to find out certain things about these various organisms if he is to cultivate them successfully.
   a. Their nature
   b. The traits and capabilities that nature put into them at the beginning
   c. How they resemble each other and how they differ
   d. The main laws of development and how these laws apply to various organisms
   e. How their development is affected by things in the world outside—what conditions are necessary for their full development (i.e., their needs)

   Only when the biologist knows these things can he cultivate his organisms successfully and obtain the finest specimens. He may know all about rabbits but he will know little about children unless he studies them, for no organism differs so much from other organisms as does the human being. In children, for example, there are an immense number of capabilities and tendencies not found in other organisms. The biologist is successful with organisms insofar as he knows their nature and is able to assist them most effectively in meeting their needs.

   This biologist has children in the elementary school. He describes the "activity" program in the primary grades, votes against appropriation of funds for a school playground, and describes the physical education program as an unnecessary "fad and frill."

   Develop an outline of a statement supporting an educational program for children incorporating the biological point of view that the father applies to the cultivation of his laboratory organisms but not to the cultivation of his own children.
2. Development is the expression of heredity in a favorable environment. The seed may be of very great importance, but the soil on which it is cast and from which it draws its nourishment has an important influence on its growth. With a given seed the farmer concentrates his attention on the chemistry of

the soil and its cultivation, realizing that no effort will produce more than the potentialities of the seed allowance. But without every effort to meet the needs of the growing plants for food, air, sunlight, water, protection from pathogenic bacteria, and other conditions suitable for their growth at every stage of life, the farmer's plants will not achieve optimum development.

Describe a favorable environment in the physical education situation for elementary school children. If we would help children achieve their optimum deveopment, what must we know of their nature and what conditions must be supplied under which their needs can best be met? What sort of physical, emotional, mental, and social needs demand satisfaction if the children are to adjust adequately to their environment?

3. The principal of an elementary school looks on you—a physical education supervisor—as a specialist in child development. He wants you to speak to his primary grade teachers concerning maturation or "readiness" with reference to types of toys, playground apparatus, games, and so forth, which should be made available at these grades.

Outline your talk.

LEARNING ACTIVITIES

1. Characteristics, needs, and interests
   a. Review the current literature and compile the characteristics, interests, and needs of the learner from grades K through 12.
   b. Categorize these factors under physiological, psychological, and sociological areas.

c. Classify the factors specific for each school grade division.
   d. Indicate whether for boys, girls, or both.
2. Implications for curriculum development
   a. Interpret and state the implications of growth and developmental stages for curriculum development, based on the data from project 1.
   b. Follow the same procedures as specified in project 1, b to d.
3. Development of principles
   a. Develop a set of principles based on the implications stated in project 2.
   b. Identify the principles specific for each school grade division.
   c. Identify a set of general principles applicable to all school grade divisions and sex.
   d. Follow the same procedures as specified in project 1, b to d.

UNIT EVALUATIVE CRITERIA

Can you:
1. Differentiate, by definition and example, between abilities, needs, interests, and readiness?
2. Identify the growth and developmental characteristics, interests, and needs of the learner specifically for a school grade division?
3. Assess the children's characteristics, needs, and interests and explain their relationships to curriculum development?
4. Interpret the relationships between maturation and learning in physical education?
5. State principles of physical education that can be verified by documented evidence?

RESOURCES

Annarino, A. A. *Fundamental movement and sport skill development*. Columbus, Ohio: Charles E. Merrill Publishing Co., 1973, pt. I.

Breckenridge, M. E., & Murphy, M. N. *Growth and development of the young child*. Philadelphia: W. B. Saunders Co., 1963.

Breckenridge, M. E., & Vincent, L. E. *Child development*. Philadelphia: W. B. Saunders Co., 1965.

Cowell, C. C. *Scientific foundations of physical education*. New York: Harper & Brothers, 1953, chap. 3.

Espenschade, A. S. Motor development. In W. R. Johnson (Ed.), *Science and medicine of exercise and sports*. New York: Harper & Row, Publishers, Inc., 1960.

Espenschade, A. S., & Eckert, H. M. *Motor development*. Columbus, Ohio: Charles E. Merrill Publishing Co., 1967, chap. 6, 7, 8, and 9.

Gesell, A. & Amstruda, C. S. *Developmental diagnosis*. New York: Harper & Brothers, 1947.

Hartley, R. E., Frank, L. K., & Goldenson, R. M. *Understanding children's play*. New York: Columbia University Press, 1952.

Havighurst, R. J. *Human development and education*. New York: Longmans, Green, 1953, chap. 1.

Jerisild, A. T. *Child development and the curriculum*. New York: Bureau of Publications, Teachers College, Columbia University, 1946, chap. 1.

Olson, W. C. *Child development*. Boston: D. C. Heath & Co., 1949, chap. 1.

Smart, M. S., & Smart, R. C. *Children development and relationships*. New York: Macmillan Publishing Co., Inc., 1967, pt. II, III, IV.

Strang, R. *An introduction to child study*. New York: Macmillan Publishing Co., Inc. 1959.

Williams, J. F. *The principles of physical education* (5th ed.). Philadelphia: W. B. Saunders Co., 1959, chap. 3.

Don't believe what your eyes are telling you. All they show is limitation. Look with your understanding. Find out what you already know, and you'll see the way to fly.

RICHARD BACH

4 Learning: a fundamental process

COMPETENCIES

After completing this unit, you should be able to:

Interpret the similarities and differences that exist in traditional and current learning theories and their implications for motor learning.

Identify the variables and factors that affect the learning process and to what degree.

Analyze a physical education experience as to the specific types of tangible and intangible learnings that may result.

Synthesize and translate learning principles into effective teaching strategies.

Define the following:
Education
Experience
Learning
Motivation
Principle
Process
Theory

PERSPECTIVE

PRINCIPLE: Learning is a fundamental process of life.

Two factors are fundamental in the educative process. On the one hand there is the immature, undeveloped being, and on the other hand there are definitive aims, meanings, and values. To bring this being into proper relation with these purposes, there must be a control of the interaction of the individual with his/her environment. This interaction is designated as experience. By means of the curriculum we provide experiences that contribute to the individual's physiological, psychological, and sociological development. The learner is the beginning and the end. Although the learner's growth and development are the ideal, the experiences inherent in the curriculum become the involved instruments, or means.

Education is the process of change in the behavior of the human organism. We educate people by changing them as individuals. Obviously, education implies development in the individual by the process of learning, as distinguished from mere physical growth. Life is a process of continuous interaction between organism and environment. Education as a *process* connotes activity, doing, progressive operation. Education as a *product* is the residuum of any experience—the result left by learning experience or activity.

The results of learning are often spoken of as knowledge and information, habits and skills, attitudes and ideals, modes of thought, and standards of value. Would anyone deny that physical education activities involve sensory experience demanding the perception of distance, weight, and patterns, such as offensive and defensive formations? Is not memory—prompt mental response—necessary and employed in signals, rules, plays, and formations? Our chief stock in trade is skill—prompt physical response—as children learn to throw, catch, dance, swim, and integrate these skills into complex patterns in games and other activities.

Does physical education involve problem solving that makes children think in terms of causes and effects, in finding reasons, in applying principles, and in coming to conclusions? Do any appreciations, enjoyments, tastes, attitudes, or ideals become the outcomes of play experience? We as teachers may ask ourselves, What types of learning are involved in a game of softball when boys or girls learn to bat? Distinguish a curve ball from a straight ball? Remember the signals? Comprehend why a "hit and run" play is desirable? Plan on where to make a play with two men on base and the ball hit to them? Hold their tongues when they are called "out" in a close decision? Like the game of baseball and develop a strong feeling of loyalty to the team?

The game of baseball involves all these learning activities and many more. Learning is always multiple. Boys and girls are unified organisms and learn from all aspects of the game situation. The curriculum maker has a serious obligation to determine just how to derive valid educational objectives from these types of learning and how to translate them into teaching strategies.

TYPES OF LEARNING

If one expects to be successful in and to enjoy activities, there are numerous learnings involved. In tennis, for example, one must learn the proper grip on the racket for the various strokes and what strokes to use under various circumstances. In soccer one must learn to trap, dribble, pass the ball, and recall the techniques and functions of the various players who make up the team. No player can define adequately his/her own place on the team without some concept of the function and responsibility of every other player on the team. A first baseman, for example, cannot play his/her role adequately without knowing the roles of the second baseman, the center fielder, and the other six players on the team. These types of learning, such as knowledge of rules, strategy, skills, agility, strength, reaction time, endurance, and speed, are subject to measurement and appraisal with considerable reliability. Since skills and knowledge are the outcomes of the curriculum that are most easily evaluated, we tend to stress these to the exclusion of other outcomes important to a balanced curriculum. These are the tangibles, and we, as teachers, tend to direct our energies chiefly to them.

Our tests and and measurement courses in physical education spend endless amounts of time and research in measuring learnings such as skill, physical fitness, and rate of achievement. These are of primary importance, of course. By comparison, however, we tend to slight and leave unplanned in the curriculum those less tangible facts, principles, skills, and processes not usually considered an integral part of the learning at hand.

Do we teach for an understanding of the physiological training process involved with boys on a basketball squad or girls on a field hockey squad? What understanding of the elementary principles of physiology of activity is left with students? Do students know how to lay out a tennis court? The history and etiquette of the game? How to choose and care properly for various types of athletic equipment?

These learnings are an important part of the students' learning at any level. They require an alert, well-educated, and many-sided teacher. They are an integral part of the curriculum but must not be left to chance. They must be planned for and taught.

More or less intangible learnings are represented, chiefly, by attitudes, values, and appreciations. They are the valuable by-products of experiences on the playground, in the gymnasium, or in the pool. Students come away from the gymnasium interested or bored, liking or disliking, with a high sense of moral values or a callousness to sports ideals, with a feeling of fear or self-confidence, with an attitude and facility for cooperation or one of the "lone wolf."

These attitudes, of course, are *learned* just as shooting a basket is learned. But they are learned solely by having experience in situations that call forth these attitudes and surround them with true social meaning. They are not learned as a *separate* part of the curriculum but are developed out of *total* experience in the type of group situations so common to the gymnasium and the playing field. Unfortunately, our techniques for teaching these important things and our methods of evaluation are utterly inadequate. The psychologist finds it difficult to apply precise statistical procedure to the evaluation of these most precious outcomes.

Despite the lack of quantitative measures for sportsmanship, initiative, honesty, resourcefulness, trustworthiness, cooperativeness, and like traits, no curriculum worker would deny them, exclude them, or fail to recognize the importance of teaching them. A good parent's evaluation of a school's physical education program should not be based solely on the son or daughter's abilities to "make the team," but also by those cooperative tendencies that are developed after making it. In a similar manner, the school should be judged not only by the student's grade in American history but also by the degree of social consciousness the student develops by means of experiences in history.

PRINCIPLES OF LEARNING

We have earlier considered the relationship of the curriculum to the nature of the society in which we live. We have also referred to the importance of considering the nature of the individual to be educated —the learner. Integrally related to the nature of the learner are the numerous characteristics of the learning process that must be examined in terms of important principles for the guidance of learning.

Principles represent statements based on the best information, currently available, that lead to effective action. Principles are guiding rules for action toward our objectives and are based on tested thinking, research, or best held opinion. Principles are basic beliefs or judgments derived from facts that guide us to action.

In attempting to apply this definition and abstract learning principles from the current literature pertaining to learning, one is confronted with conflicting theoretical and experimental evidence. The problem is further compounded by the lack of relationship that exists between learning theories and current educational practices. Therefore the listing and interpretation of all available learning principles are beyond the scope of this book. The reader is referred to the most current educational psychology and motor learning texts for more detailed information.

However, neither adequate assumptions about curriculum construction nor sensible curriculum planning can be made without some understanding of how learning becomes most effective.

This understanding is based on the following four general principles that indicate how any learning undertaking should be approached, regardless of the types of learnings sought:

1. *Learning is always related to something.* The learner must have a goal. There must be a motive, a purpose, a challenge. Learning serves needs; motivation within the learner stimulates action.
2. *Learning is an active, not a passive, process—an adjustment that goes on within the learner to meet needs, solve problems, and achieve purposes.* The learner strives to move in the direction of goals related to the motivation. The boy or girl who wants to "make the team" will train, will develop skill, and may make individual selfish wishes subservient to the team wishes. These behaviors reflect motives related to the recognition, the social status, the new adventure and excitement, the "fun," and the sense of achievement and mastery that team membership can satisfy.
3. *Although learning depends on activity, it is the intense effort that hastens learning.* Value concepts resulting from insight and purpose inherent in physical education activities are dynamic and lead to goal action. The learner must desire to possess the specific skill mentioned as a teacher objective. What the teacher has in mind as an objective—say, learning to play tennis—must for the student become a value, something desirable or sought after. Once it has become a value, the teacher's objective has been translated into the learner's purpose.
4. *Every learning situation involves volitional, intellectual, and emotional relationships. It involves purpose, weight, and feeling.* The physical education teacher who stresses isolated and unintelligible skills and unrelated facts, who constantly criticizes and blames rather than encourages and praises is blocking the learning process.

If the learning situation permits the

learner to manipulate ideas as well as arms and legs by participating in planning the experiences, executing the plan, and evaluating the outcomes of experiences, then the learner's thinking, as well as acting or feeling, is involved. Without this threefold effect, poor learning—or no learning at all—results.

In summary, the process of learning is a function of a number of variables or factors. In learning a motor skill, one must have a purpose or goal, a clear mental picture of the movement as a whole, a desire to learn, effective instruction, concentrated attention, purposeful practice, absence of physical and mental fatigue, proper distribution of practice periods, confidence in the ability

to improve, knowledge of progress, success, and praise. The teacher controls the learning process only by controlling and manipulating these variables and factors. Any event, including learning, is the product of existing conditions. The teacher's task is to determine what these conditions are and to change them if necessary.

The development of an educational practice based on an understanding of the learner and the nature and conditions of learning must consider the basic desire of children and youth to learn. It should appeal to preexisting desires for play and a joy of mastery and achievement, realizing that lasting change must come from within the individual.

REACTORS

1. All learning is related to something.
2. There is a distinction between scientific and educational theory.
3. We educate people by changing them as individuals.
4. Motivation is central in the curriculum because it is in response to basic needs that humans adapt and learn.
5. Practicing without a definite purpose is like walking without a destination in view—you never arrive.
6. The influence of emotions is one of the important factors in determining behavior.
7. When we cannot know exactly what we are seeking, it is impossible to measure our approach to the thing sought.
8. Physical education has often been long on activity and short on understanding.
9. Competition is an effective motivating force.
10. Although all interests are learned, the learner's level of maturity has a marked bearing on the relative ease of developing them?

SITUATIONAL PROBLEMS

1. You are a member of a junior high school curriculum committee and have been assigned to a subcommittee on "Classes of

Objectives and Types of Learning." Representatives of each educational area of the school (science, mathematics, home economics, physical education, and so forth) have been asked what activities they use to achieve the following objectives after each type of learning.

Type of learning	Objective
a. Sensory experience	Perception (of size, length, speed, sound, dimension, texture)
b. Memory	Prompt mental response (principles, rules, facts, associations, names, football plays)
c. Motor skills	Prompt physical response (writing, throwing, vaulting, swimming, typing, pronouncing)
d. Problem solving	Concepts (causes, effects, relationships, conclusions, applications)
e. Emotional experience	Personal attributes (tastes, appreciations, attitudes, ideals)

As a member of the committee and spokesman for physical education, make your case.

2. One of the important principles of teaching is that "learning should be unitary, not fragmentary." Another principle is that "all learning is related to something." A game is more than a summation of isolated skills. Continual practice on isolated skills in baseball and seldom playing the game of baseball would never result in a good baseball team because of the gap between the isolated skills and the practical applications in game situations.

Unitary learning in the baseball situation means the practical applications of skill, concept, knowledge, understanding, or insight to the complex task of advancing your own runners around the bases and preventing your opponents from doing so. To do this, deeper comprehension and all the higher mental processes are brought into operation if the team is to be successful. Learning to play the game of baseball becomes purposeful in terms of cause and effect, relationships, functions, understandings, and insights, as well as skills.

The school curriculum committee of which you are a member is concerned with the fact that so much of the "isolated" or fragmentary instruction in citizenship in the classroom appears to be ineffective. You are asked, from the standpoint of unity of learning experience, where you believe the instruction is at fault. In total sport situations, such as developing hockey, soccer, or football teams, you have been more successful in developing effective behavior correlated in the words "citizenship" and "sportsmanship."

List all the various behavior components or personal attributes that are learned in a game situation.

LEARNING ACTIVITIES

1. Learning in physical education
   a. Define:
      (1) Skill
      (2) Motor skill
   b. Define and differentiate by example between:
      (1) Motor performance
      (2) Motor ability
      (3) Skill learning
   c. Define and differentiate by example between:
      (1) Closed skill
      (2) Open skill
2. Theories of learning
   a. Identify and state the basic principles for the following:
      (1) Association
      (2) Cognition
      (3) Information processing
   b. Analyze the previously stated principles as to similarities and differences.
3. Skill acquisition
   a. Select two models for skill acquisition:
      (1) State and label the stages of learning a skill for each model
      (2) Interpret the stages of each model for application to teaching
4. Factors and variables affecting learning
   a. Identify the most important factors and variables governing what is learned in a physical education situation.
   b. List and justify principles of learning related to the factors and variables.
5. Learning criteria
   a. Determine the chief criterion of learning for the following examples:
      (1) When a student has learned to play tennis
      (2) When a student is a "good sport"
      (3) When a student is socially developed
      (4) When a student has learned to appreciate a performance in a gymnastic meet

UNIT EVALUATIVE CRITERIA

Can you:
1. Identify and determine the relative importance of all the factors and variables that affect learning?
2. Compare the basic concepts for the traditional and current learning theories?
3. Explain and state implications of a working model for skill acquisition?

RESOURCES

Biehler, R. F. *Psychology applied to teaching*. Boston: Houghton Mifflin Co., 1971, chap. 1 and 3.

Cratty, B. *Movement behavior and motor learning*. Philadelphia: Lea & Febiger, 1954, chap. 1 and 2.

DeCecco, J. P. *The psychology of learning and instruction*. Englewood Cliffs, N.J.: Prentice-Hall, Inc., 1968, chap. 1.

Drowatzky, J. N. *Motor learning: principles and practices*. Minneapolis: Burgess Publishing Co., 1975, chap. 3 and 11.

Fitts, P., & Posner, M. *Human performance*. Belmont, Calif.: Brooks/Cole Publishing Co., 1967.

Gage, N. L. Theories of teaching. In E. R. Hilgard (Ed.), *Theories of learning and instruction: sixty-third yearbook of the National Society for the Study of Education*. Chicago: University of Chicago Press, 1964.

Gagne, R. *Conditions for learning* (2nd ed.). New York: Holt, Rinehart & Winston, 1970.

Gentile, A. M. *A working model of skill acquisition with application for teaching*. Quest, Jan. 1972, **17**:3-23.

Hilgard, E., & Bower, G. *Theories of learning*. New York: Appleton-Century-Crofts, 1966.

Krathwohl, D., Bloom, G., & Basia, B. *Taxonomy of educational objectives. Handbook II: Affective domain*. New York: David McKay Co., Inc., 1964.

Oxendine, J. B. *Psychology of motor learning*. New York: Appleton-Century-Crofts, 1968, pt. I.

Robb, M. *Dynamics of motor skill acquisition*. Englewood Cliffs, N.J.: Prentice-Hall, Inc., 1972.

Singer, R. *Motor learning and human performance*. New York: Macmillan Publishing Co. Inc., 1968, chap. 8.

Singer, R., & Dick, W. *Teaching physical education—a systems approach*. Boston: Houghton Mifflin Co., 1974, chap. 2.

Science merely gives us the tools. It is the rest of education which teaches us how to use those tools.

JAMES BRYANT CONANT

5 Philosophy: principles and inferences

COMPETENCIES

After completing this unit, you should be able to:

Identify the basic tenets for each of the traditional schools of philosophy.

Apply the basic tenets of each of the traditional schools of philosophy to physical education.

Critically analyze and select those ultimate inferences and principles for the purpose of developing a physical education philosophy.

Translate a physical education philosophy into objectives, instructional strategies, and curriculum content.

Define the following:
Eclectic
Idealism
Naturalism
Philosophy
Pragmatism
Realism
Science

PERSPECTIVE

PRINCIPLE: Sound practice in physical education can emerge only when there is a wide acceptance of fruitful principles and generalizations on which a system of thinking can be founded.

Philosophy represents the ultimate inferences and principles that determine our thinking and action. The value system that we evolve and personally cherish becomes the means by which we interpret events and control our actions. The most important thing about any person is his/her philosophy. Whether or not an individual has ever heard the word "philosophy," one's philosophy sets the scale and shapes the pattern of one's thinking and living. It is a series of value assumptions that become a source of direction and a guiding light in decision making when alternatives present a dilemma.

The answer to every educational question is ultimately influenced by our philosophy of life. Every system of education must have an aim. Each teacher has a pattern of meaning and values that controls choice of educational objectives, way of organizing learning experiences, and beliefs as to what is good, better, or best.

Whereas philosophy formulates ends, education offers suggestions as to how these ends may be achieved. The function of the curriculum is to translate educational philosophy into learning experiences and teaching procedures. The most powerful elements in determining what goes on in a physical education program are the values—those conditions of life and learning that the teacher cherishes and deems important.

Our business is education. As teachers we are neither in the entertainment business nor engaged in enhancing our personal prestige and reputation at the expense of the students. We are "development supervisors," guardians and developers of human personality. We should constantly test the soundness of our philosophy by reexamining the validty of our beliefs, opinions, concepts, ideas, impressions, and values in terms of the scientific bases for what we do as physical education teachers and coaches. The quality of physical education is determined by the kind and quality of educational experiences offered, and we as teachers can aid in determining these. Educational philosophy is concerned with self-criticism, the criticism of one's own experience when it asks: What is true? What is right? What is adequate? What are the purposes and values of these activities? Whenever we examine critically our educational theories, hypotheses, and generalizations in the light of data already available, we are educational philosophers.

Since philosophy is the only source of direction from which practice springs, this unit aims to help its readers think through their respective philosophies and internalize them with the hope that more intelligent and effective educational practice results.

NEED FOR A PHILOSOPHY OF PHYSICAL EDUCATION

Philosophy speaks in terms of aims, science in terms of results. Philosophy helps us to decide what we want to happen to people on the playing fields, in the gymnasium, or in the pool, science shows us how to make it happen. The "what" and "why" precede the "how." A theory of values is most important. Without a consideration of values, we have no answer to the question, What is educationally desirable? The answer to this question is basic to every educational policy, including physical education policies, athletic policies, safety, and health education policies. The impatient teacher, however, seeks some cut-and-dried conception of "how to do it," despite the fact that administering and teaching a program of physical education is a continuous problem-solving enterprise requiring a system of reflective educational thinking and based on some valid understanding of what physical education is. When assumptions are made, the careful student inquires into the grounds which may reasonably be said to support them.

Many physical education curriculums lack direction, unity, and balance. The central purposes of programs are not clear. Guiding principles, if present, are not consistent. A society, a school, a department of physical education will "hang together" to the extent that there is common agreement (policy) as to what things are important (i.e., valuable). Part of our job as teachers is to give some leadership in determining what should be taught in order to give some selective control and direction to the growth and development of children and youth. The questions arise, What should the content of physical education be? and What criteria of choice are most important?

To idealize in terms of standards is not difficult. Only as each school and physical education department conceives of itself as a force in molding human welfare and personality and develops an underlying philosophy cherishing certain values will changes in educational method, time allotment, space, equipment, and the like come about. More important than standards are the values affected by them. When one seeks certain values, standards begin to appear, for standards are established rules or models that grow from taking a look at the values desired. Each school sets its own standards in terms of the values it seeks.

PHYSICAL EDUCATION AND THE TRADITIONAL SCHOOLS OF PHILOSOPHY

For thousands of years, teaching among humans was a part-time indirect activity without teaching "specialists." In time, the human race developed its productivity to a point where there was leisure time for cultural activities. Teachers appeared on the scene and gradually began to systematize their work through various arrangements, and schools came into existence. Although we use the word *school* to identify a building, it is the system of teaching that is the school, philosophically speaking. In this sense we refer to a group of people held together by the same teachings, beliefs, opinions, and methods or followers or disciples of a teacher, leader, or creed in such terms as "gentlemen of the old school," or the French impressionistic school of painters, or the naturalistic school of novelists.

American education today is undergoing strains and stresses. The rise of new issues and of old issues in new forms creates considerable turbulence in social trends and forces, often resulting in sweeping changes. Considerable soul-searching and philosophizing is going on as a result.

It is our purpose in this brief survey of the tenets of three of the traditional schools of philosophy to determine some of the changing goals and purposes of education from the past that grew out of idealism, naturalism, and pragmatism as they have implications for physical education. It is from these variations of thought that our educational philosophy of today has come.

Although it can be said that perhaps nowhere can educational philosophy be found which wholly exemplifies idealism, naturalism, or pragmatism, a brief and rather superficial examination will be made of all three. The reader is asked to consider the practical implications of these beliefs in physical education theory and practice.

PHYSICAL EDUCATION AS IDEALISM

Idealism, popularly, means faith in the moral quality of the universe or an attitude of mind that is prone to represent things in the light of abstract perfection. Idealism, philosophically, implies that man can know the world only through the senses—by perception. It is known only through the ideas of the knower. Thought and purpose take a more central place. It has been said that idealism may better be called the philosophy of idea-ism. The essential idea in classical idealism is that the universe has spiritual purpose.

To further identify and clarify the principles of idealism applied to education, we offer the following:

1. Philosophical viewpoints and educational objectives
   a. Mind and spirit are real forces in the universe.
   b. Values are part and parcel of reality.
   c. The individual realizes selfhood only in society. Brotherhood is the social objective of education.
   d. The older generation should give the new the benefit of past experience. Tradition is important if it has stood the test of time. Cultural heritage is important.
   e. Book learning and the development of an intellectual elite are important in stressing culture, knowledge, and development.

   f. Education is worthwhile for its own sake, as it brings the student to seek truth, beauty, and goodness.
   g. The ideal character of persons and society is the ultimate objective of education.
   h. All good education is character education.
2. Curriculum content
   a. The curriculum experiences should show the three "racial aspects of achievement": intellect, creation, and will.
   b. Experiences, activities, life situations, and studies should be selected that contribute to the development of the ideal human character and an ideal society.
   c. The best ideas in all the conventional branches of liberal and vocational education should be presented so that they become ideals.
   d. Individual growth and character come through freedom of the will and through self-activity, and the ultimate responsibility should rest with the will of the student.
   e. We should learn from the past by scrutinizing carefully our cultural heritage of the finest in literature, music, art, and ethics so that children will be exposed to what is "noble, generous, and faith-provoking."
3. Organization of learning experiences: method
   a. The student's judgment should be cultivated by thought-provoking questions and by setting up situations that demand decision and choice on his/her part.
   b. The student's potential should be developed by environmental surroundings and influences that create problems to be resolved by the student's own decisions and active efforts.
   c. Intellectual culture, art, morality, and religion should provide the only satisfactory philosophical bases of education.
   d. Students should learn that "ideas are not true because they work. They work, if they work at all, because they are true."
   e. Interest permeates all school activity. Child-centered procedures consider indi-

vidual differences in children's natures and maturity levels.

f. Idealism is eclectic in methodology of education but not in philosophy.

4. Pupil and teacher

a. The teacher prepares the young for many critical experiences before they actually occur. He/she conceives objectives.

b. The pupil is considered a "self," a spiritual being.

c. The body is considered "the home of the mind."

d. The individuality and uniqueness of pupils are considered a supreme value.

e. The teacher sees the pupil in the "process of becoming" and aids him/her in actualizing the potential present at birth.

f. The teacher is a worthy model to be imitated, creates the learning environment and atmosphere, and structures the learning situation.

g. As he/she sets up learning opportunities for the student, the teacher encourages and seeks active response from the learner.

5. Evaluative criteria

a. The student is well rounded, balanced, and well grounded in the sciences, arts, and humanities.

b. The standards of judgment are those ideals established according to the best achievements and traditions of the past.

c. Superior selfhood with regard for truth, beauty, and goodness, growing out of intellectual, esthetic, and moral experiences that result in seeking the truth, transcends ugliness and conquers evil.

As physical educators, let us look at some of the facts, issues, and problems in American education that might be of concern to us as idealists:

1. By what criteria of truth shall we judge physical education programs? Is there just one standard or are there several?

2. By what standard can we validate our aims and values in physical education?

3. Do we develop greater force of moral charac-

ter by having teachers set certain standards of learning and conduct for pupils, or do learning activities derive their value solely from being liked by the students?

4. Just what does democratic regard for the individual mean?

5. If more external control is restored in physical education, how, at the same time, shall we build initiative, self-reliance, and moral autonomy in children and youth?

6. Idealism asks, Why has the mind a body? whereas, naturalism asks, Why has the body a mind? What is our reply as idealists?

7. Is there a religious dimension to physical education that we have neglected in our search for a value underlying all things?

8. What obligation do teachers of physical education have to persuade students to "take life seriously and to search strenuously for something worthy of their complete and absolute allegiance"?

9. What good is a healthy body if the soul that animates it is diseased or corrupt and thus confuses good with evil? Is character building the cliché that many physical educators make of it, or is it an educational responsibility? If we are idealists, we search for psychological values in physical education. Are we in the entertainment business, the business of exploiting youth for our own personal gain, or the profession of education?

Because learning involves change, including a change in values, a philosophy of physical education is deeply committed to potentialities in the direction of change.

PHYSICAL EDUCATION AS NATURALISM

Naturalism is characteristic of modern rather than ancient thought, but today its concepts more closely approximate idealism. Naturalism, however, considers man as a biological organism and as a product of organic evolution. It rejects the supernatural or mystic concept of life and regards nature as the criterion of values. Behavior has as its end the establishment of equilibrium, or satisfaction (i.e., success in adjustment). Since adjustment is the process by which organisms meet their needs, the physical educator as a naturalist must know what the needs of life are. What conditions do children normally lean toward to satisfy these needs, by what processes are these needs met, and what experiences on the playing fields, in the gymnasium, or in the pool are best suited to meet these needs?

From the biological point of view, we must think of the child as a living whole, or organism. To aid children in reaching their optimum development, we must know their nature and supply the conditions under which their needs can best be met. Education is a dynamic process going on in response to inner needs and by means of self-activities. The human child is confronted with a complex, humanly constructed, ever-changing environment. He/she has an action system that is imperfect at the start but is in the process of maturing. This necessitates much trial and error before adjustments are satisfactory. Hence planned education by teachers with progression in mind facilitates learning and makes it more rapid and effective.

The physical educator accepts the fact that the child comes into the world with "unlearned cores of behavior," tendencies to respond, which were once referred to as instincts. All normal children tend to be physically active, to be curious, to explore, to seek excitement and new experience, to become increasingly gregarious and eventually social, and to play. These forms of behavior are universal, and all educative efforts must start from such instinctive tendencies.

Physical educators, as naturalists, have long recognized that the origins of physical education are to be found in unlearned cores of behavior. We use native human tendencies to be active, to combat threat of bodily harm, and to avoid boredom, inactivity, and monotony by new adventure, exploration, zestful activity, and self-expression. We help conquer feelings of failure, weakness, and inferiority by providing opportunities to strive for success, mastery, and achievement. Humans, being gregarious animals, resent being unwanted, unloved, or rejected by their peers. Physical education contributes to a sense of belonging to a larger social unit by allowing for sharing and participating in team games and other group ventures.

Some principles of naturalism applied to education follow:

1. Philosophical viewpoints and educational objectives
   a. The goal is to educate according to nature by preserving the natural virtues of the individual and creating a society based on individual rights.
   b. "Teachers do not teach subjects, they teach pupils." Attention is directed to the person being taught.
   c. There is no use in making a person mentally fit and neglecting physical fitness. Education is for the body as well as the mind.
   d. There should be a healthy balance between mental and physical activities.
   e. Education should be pleasurable and should therefore be in accord with the present development of the student's physical and mental equipment that makes him/her "ready" for learning.
   f. Spontaneous self-activity in the acquisition of knowledge is an important part of education.
2. Curriculum content
   a. Curriculum is a careful and systematic organization of content according to the laws of growth and development (e.g., infancy, childhood, early adolescence, adolescence, adulthood).
   b. Activities are selected according to the

developing maturity level and interests of the pupils.

c. Plentiful opportunity for informal exercise of senses, muscles, and speech is given at each developmental level. Physical education activities of various types supply important developmental needs.

d. Herbert Spencer's* (1860) education for "complete living" presents naturalistic objectives that suggest curriculum content as follows:

(1) Those activities that directly minister to self-preservation (health-safety).

(2) Those activities that, by securing the necessities of life, indirectly minister to self-preservation (vocation).

(3) Those activities that have for their end the rearing and discipline of offspring (education for family life).

(4) Those activities that are involved in the maintenance of proper social and political relations (citizenship).

(5) Those miscellaneous activities that make up the lesser part of life, devoted to the gratification of tastes and feelings (leisure time).

3. Organization of learning experiences: method

a. Education, to fulfill its function, should be attuned to the natural and periodic rhythms of development in children and youth.

b. The child learns with the entire body as he/she builds perceptions and establishes relationships. In a sense, the child educates himself/herself in great measure.

c. A child's predilections for and liking for an activity are good indices for the kind of activity that will contribute to his/her education at a given stage of development.

d. The child is a body, a little animal. One of the first requirements is that he/she be a healthy, vigorous animal, capable of withstanding the wear and tear of living; hence activity rather than passivity is a keynote to method.

e. The method of instruction is primarily

---

*Modified from Spencer, H. *Education: intellectual, moral and physical.* New York: Hurst & Co., p. 17.

inductive, reasoning from particular facts or individual cases to a general conclusion; discovering generalizations, for example, "The longer the tube, the lower the note" or "A falling barometer indicates rain."

4. Pupil and teacher

a. The teacher is a guardian and developer of human personality rather than a taskmaster. He/she exemplifies the concepts of the gardener rather than those of the builder.

b. The teacher is the guide and hunter leading the pupil to adventure and new experience but lets the pupil "bag the game."

c. Nature expended great energy to make people different. Each pupil has unique potentialities and therefore separate and distinct learning needs and requires different types of learning activities.

5. Evaluative criteria

a. Naturalism favors extroversion or interest in the outer or objective world. The extrovert is a person of action, who expresses feelings through skeletal activity, by doing something. Dominated by external and social values, he/she is able to achieve empathy with others.

b. Education recognizes the "organismic needs" concept and accepts the theory that there are fundamental forces within the individual that seek expression and satisfaction (e.g., the need for activity, affection, recognition, group status, and achievement). These are "natural states" of humans and education must aid in satisfying these basic needs.

c. Education is not simply mental; it is also physical and moral. The teacher, knowing the pupil, determines the goal but the pupil furnishes the impulse toward his/her own development. The ultimate criterion is not, What has the child learned? but What has the child become?

Physical educators acting as naturalists recognize that:

1. The biological conception of education em-

phasizes the organism as a center of reactions.

2. When the child confronts the world into which he/she is born, he/she is already equipped with certain capacities, innate powers, and natural tendencies that determine fundamental needs. The primary responses to the environment shall be in the attempt to meet these needs.

3. Individual development as progress toward maturity represents the unfolding of native abilities within the limits of inherent capacity and is an important concept for progression in education.

4. Learning comes through self-activity. Activity is the sole source of the development of capabilities planted in the organism by heredity.

5. Playing is a form of self-activity that is worthwhile for its own sake, but at the same time, playing should be under conditions and with suggested materials that shall result in adequate physical exercise, social interaction, and the standards and practices of moral conduct.

6. Learning lies in the recognition of a need and the carrying out of constructive acts to meet it. A child's adjustment to the environment is something that he/she must effect for himself/herself through individual activities.

7. Education at the nursery school and primary levels is most important because it comes first and lays the foundation for what follows.

8. As the most characteristic spontaneous activity of the child, play becomes the basis of the educational process in the early grades.

9. Play, resulting most directly from the native interests of the child, furnishes the best natural stock on which to graft desirable habits of action, feeling, and thought.

10. It is through play that the child first represents the world to himself/herself, permitting the teacher to introduce him/her to the world of social relations, build a sense of independence and mutual helpfulness, and provide initiative and motivation.

11. Humans are psychobiological units, and

psychosomatic medicine verifies that physical activity is necessary to their growth, health, and happiness—mental as well as physical. The body is the instrument through which the mind expresses itself.

12. The biological conception of education puts into the foreground the ideal of the whole self. Mind and body cannot be educated in isolation from each other.

We end this discussion by saying that physical education has a cognitive aspect and is bound up with bodily conditions and motor activities. In every school task, intellectual, emotional, and volitional processes play a part, each being necessarily involved; hence methods of instruction that ignore any of them lack vitality and the normal reality of life. Consider the self-expression in playing a game of baseball. Many learnings merge into a single pattern of playing the game as a whole. The game of baseball, a total situation and a stimulus pattern, calls for response to a number of different stimuli, but these stimuli are interrelated, one to the other. The child learns to bat (skill), to distinguish a curve ball from a straight ball (visual perception), to remember signals (memorization), to comprehend why a "hit and run " play is in order (understanding), to plan on where to make a play with two men on base if the ball comes to him/her (thinking), to hold his/her tongue when the umpire calls him/her "out at the plate" (modification of emotional reaction), and to like the game of baseball and develop great loyalty to the team (attitudes and ideals). We see here that in the activity of the organism all parts, organs, specialized structures, and physical and mental tendencies are interdependent and interrelated.

PHYSICAL EDUCATION AS PRAGMATISM

Pragmatism, from its etymological origin, refers to a theory or method of dealing with real things in the sense of being practical or efficient. As a philosophy, it began as a revolt against the intellectualistic speculation that characterized idealism and most modern speculative philosophy. Pragmatism contends that the truth or validity of a principle or belief depends on its effect on practice. The central problem of pragmatism is, What is truth and how it is to be distinguished from error?

Pragmatism is often referred to as experimentalism or implementalism and sometimes as Deweyism. Life is largely a matter of finding out what is workable, and this finding out is an experimental procedure. Truth can be proved only by results. We are always experimenting—seeking better results. It follows that our conception of truth must coincide with what we find. This is pragmatism's central point of view, and it is evident that it is strongly involved in the phenomenon of change and progress—giving up what is good for what is better. One applies the pragmatic test—experiments— to describe how truths are developed, how errors are corrected, and how, in general, old truths are adjusted to new situations. The experimentalist opposes the idea of absolute values, a static society, or a static education. His/her basic interest is continued improvement of practice, making testing of thought a better guide to action. Pragmatism, therefore, is the experimental method of science.

Applied to education, pragmatism stresses the importance of first-hand experiences; reasoning with data in the solution of problems; teaching children how to think rather than teaching them what to think; education involving the whole organism—it should be "for both hands and minds of children"; and, because "life only educates," the school not being divorced from life. Therefore functional, meaningful, purposeful learning should be stressed.

Some generalizations concerning educa-

tion operating under the philosophy of pragmatism would appear as follows:

1. Philosophical viewpoints and educational objectives
   a. Learning is an activity phenomenon. Learning, like thinking, always begins in the midst of movement and activity.
   b. Experience is vital to learning. In coping with ever-changing experience, the student carries away the residue of one experience to solve problems faced in subsequent experience.
   c. Dewey's definition of education as "the continuous reconstruction of experience as adds to the meaning of experience and increases ability in its subsequent direction" leads to the popular statement that the "general objective of education is more education."
   d. Dewey, as the leading exponent of pragmatism, was the first to team philosophy with education by defining philosophy as the "general theory of education."
   e. Life is primarily social, at the same time that it is individual. Social efficiency, or effectiveness in maintaining social relations, is an important general objective of education.
   f. Problems and projects challenge the powers of insight and stimulate interest and thinking; therefore isolation of the elements of any problem faced is basic to its solution.
   g. The most important test of truth is, Does it work? Thinking, as associated with the scientific method, is highly valued and encouraged.
2. Curriculum content
   a. Information becomes knowledge when it is put to use; therefore the testing of hypotheses or "hunches" by experimentation in any area of curriculum content is important.
   b. Students are encouraged to accept "natural laws" and scientific generalizations as ways of telling them what has happened or what they may expect to happen.
   c. The most fundamental criterion for the selection of curriculum content is its per-

tinence to present life; therefore school practices should give pupils a sense of reality by projects and problems demanding use of workshops, laboratories, and libraries, thus inspiring educational experimentation.

3. Organization of learning experiences: method
   a. Creative and constructive projects are employed so as to broaden the cycle of learning. "Core" projects that cut across subject matter lines and escape the frozen rigidity of departments, courses, time, and schedules are encouraged. The emphasis is on meaning and the integration of learnings from many fields around some central theme or purpose. This is exemplified in the better "unit" plans.
   b. Learning experiences are devised that avoid making passive receivers of pupils waiting to be impressed; the purposefulness and meaningfulness of projects catch the imagination and encourage students to reach and engage in valued experience.
4. Pupil and teacher
   a. Pupils are primarily organisms. The pragmatist does not regret that when the student comes to school he must bring his body with him.
   b. The doctrine of individual differences respects individuality of pupils, yet desirable social relationships of all kinds are encouraged.
   c. The teacher avoids the cloistered and formally academic by keeping close to experience and having students draw real meanings from it in a social setting.
5. Evaluative criteria
   a. Pupils are expected to be not only contemplative but also active (i.e., doers as well as thinkers).
   b. Pupils are expected to be optimistic, somewhat impetuous, and democratic, seeing and protesting what is wrong in society about them and looking toward a brighter future, despite the present and past.
   c. Pupils have a sense of reality about the

school and its operations; they want to have a part in them and are willing to engage in experimentation that might improve them.
   d. Democracy is enhanced by having each student progress to maximum capability but with some special ability so as to make a contribution for the common social good of all.

If a physical educator accepts some of the tenets of the philosophy of pragmatism, these are some of the things he/she would do and believe:

1. Being "child-centered," he/she would be concerned with the needs and purposes of students and adjust the curriculum accordingly.
2. He/she would consider student purposes before abilities, realizing that students want abilities in order to achieve purposes that to them are important.
3. The educator would stress natural activities (games and sports) in the program rather than formal gymnastics and the like, thereby bringing the activities closer to life.
4. He/she would teach skills, but always reintegrate them into the broader patterns in which they are used. Students would see the application of the skills to the game as a whole. Bunting in baseball is practiced after team failure due to poor bunting ability. Pivoting and stopping are practiced after repeated fouls for "traveling" in basketball.
5. Rather than calling plays from the bench, he/she would have the players develop understanding, insight, game intelligence, and ability to adapt "on their own" to changing game situations.
6. The teacher would stress learning by doing, but along with the doing, real understandings would be developed. The "what" and the "why" accompany the "how."
7. He/she would give the pupils an opportunity to express their opinions and ideas and to make suggestions of "how to improve things."
8. He/she would see that practice in sports and

physical education in classes would be pleasurable experiences.

9. The educator would know that progression in instruction is based on past experience, and, at the same time, it continuously leads on to future experience. It is thereby implementing Dewey's idea of education as involving "continuous reconstruction of experience."
10. He/she would organize classes as "miniature societies" and would stress democratic ideals, in the belief that the characteristics of the individual are derived partly from society and that the individual helps determine the nature of the social group of which he/she is a part.
11. He/she would organize instruction in units that represent a series of worthwhile experiences bound together around some project theme of central interest, for example, a unit in track sports, field events, diving, or lawn games.

To those of us in physical education the "activity movement" is not new. The activity and experiences of pupils have always been important considerations. The question of meaningfulness has scarcely been a real problem to us, for play is an activity that supplies its own drive. We are essentially people of action and, we hope, of thought as well. We are pragmatists to a degree.

A PHYSICAL EDUCATION PHILOSOPHY

What is the meaning of physical education? The answer to this question is the function of a philosophy of physical education. The answers must give unity to the truths from the various schools of thought. This philosophy is perforce *eclectic*, which simply means selective. It will be a composite system of thought made up of views borrowed from various other systems that seem to afford a sound practical theory. We create this system by selecting from all sources those elements that are sound in logic and have proved most useful in educational programs. The eclectic is the only method left open for a philosophy of physical education. The function of physical educators as philosophers resolves itself into that of critical selection if a complete philosophy of physical education is to be approached. Our thinking today has rightfully been influenced by all the thinking that has gone before us. The soundness of our philosophy will be determined by the validity of the principles we select and incorporate into our composite system. We must find unity in diversity, for we seek social and psychological as well as biological values.

REACTORS

1. Philosophy represents the ultimate inferences and principles that determine our thinking and action.
2. Philosophy differs from science.
3. Our physical education and social philosophy should be compatible.
4. In recent years, the philosophy of education has changed, and curriculum adjustments have resulted.
5. The function of the curriculum is to translate educational philosophy into learning experiences and teaching strategies.
6. It is from the variations of thought of different schools of philosophy that our educational philosophy is developed.
7. The eclectic is the only method left open for a philosophy of physical education.

SITUATIONAL PROBLEMS

Illustrate by application the operation of each of the following principles:
1. Science determines means, whereas philosophy determines ends.
2. Science gives us knowledge, but only philosophy can give us wisdom.

3. What changes we try to bring about in our students as individuals and in society will depend on our value assumptions—our philosophy.
4. Attitudes and ideals evolve progressively with the experiences that create them.
5. Educational philosophy and social philosophy should be fully compatible.
6. Educational philosophy cannot be divorced from the society it serves.
7. The principle of balance between individual freedom and group welfare is basic in a democracy.
8. The human problems of living together are constantly in a state of flux, and therefore superior education is needed to solve them.
9. Personality is molded by the type of social organization to which the individual belongs.
10. The success of a group depends on integrating the efforts of the individuals.
11. It is in early play groups that social understanding and sensitivity are first cultivated.
12. Cultural values to which we often pay only passing notice exert a powerful force on behavior patterns.
13. Cultures are changed by changing the value systems—the philosophies—of individuals in large numbers.
14. The most important factor in the development of personality is the presence of other personalities.
15. Patterns of acceptable behavior vary from culture to culture and produce personality differences.
16. Philosophical principles are based on insight, understanding, and experience.
17. Principles based on scientifically estab-lished facts do not change, whereas principles based on concepts of philosophy are subject to change.
18. A coach's philosophy is evident in speech, attitude, and example.
19. Values are learned through experience.

LEARNING ACTIVITIES

1. Formulate a philosophy of physical education.
2. Select and state principles and ultimate inferences as bases for the development of a philosophy.
3. Analyze, identify, and compare each sentence and/or paragraph of your philosophy with the traditional schools of philosophy.
4. Formulate an aim of physical education.
   a. State the relationship(s) and uniqueness of your aim to an aim of general education.
5. Formulate a definition of physical education.
   a. Analyze your philosophy, aim, and definition as to relationships and compatibility.

UNIT EVALUATIVE CRITERIA

Can you:
1. Determine the changing goals and purposes of education from the past that grew out of idealism, naturalism, and pragmatism as these philosophers have implications for physical education?
2. Answer the question, What is the meaning of physical education?
3. Formulate, interpret and justify your philosophy of physical education?
4. Identify the values that represent your choice of objectives, teaching style, and beliefs as to what is good, better, or best?

RESOURCES

Barrow, H. M. *Man and his movement: principles of his physical education.* Philadelphia: Lea & Febiger, 1971.

Bookwalter, K., & Zanderzwag, H. J. *Foundations and principles of physical education.* Philadelphia: W. B. Saunders Co., 1969.

Brown, C., & Cassidy, R. *Theory in physical education.* Philadelphia: Lea & Febiger, 1963.

Bucher, C. A. *Foundations of physical education* (8th ed.). St. Louis: The C. V. Mosby Co., 1979.

Burns, H. W., & Brauner, C. J. *Problems in education and philosophy.* Englewood Cliffs, N.J.: Prentice-Hall, Inc., 1965.

Cowell, C. C., & France, W. L. *Philosophy and principles of physical education.* Englewood Cliffs, N.J.: Prentice-Hall, Inc., 1963.

Davis, E. C. *Philosophies fashion.* Dubuque, Iowa: William C. Brown Co., Publishers, 1961.

Davis, E. C., & Miller, D. M. *The philosophic process in physical education.* Philadelphia: Lea & Febiger, 1967.

McCloy, C. H. *Philosophical bases for physical education.* New York: F. S. Crofts & Co., 1940.

Spencer, H. *Education: intellectual, moral and physical.* New York: Hurst & Co., 1860.

Steinhaus, A. *Toward understanding of health and physical education.* Dubuque, Iowa: William C. Brown Co., Publishers, 1963.

Thompson, J. C. *Physical education for the 1970's.* Englewood Cliffs, N.J.: Prentice-Hall, Inc., 1971.

Webster, R. W. *Philosophy of physical education.* Dubuque, Iowa: William C. Brown Co., Publishers, 1965.

Zeigler, E. F. *Problems in the history and philosophy of physical education and sport.* Englewood Cliffs, N.J.: Prentice-Hall, Inc., 1968.

In every living person change is continuous. In the presence of another, change is accelerated. If, in a group, one person has vision and tries intelligently to guide this change toward realizing this vision—he is a teacher.

ARTHUR H. STEINHAUS

6 Objectives: focus and direction

COMPETENCIES

After completing this unit, you should be able to:

Identify, analyze, and compare physical education objectives from the early 1900s to the present as to changing educational theories and philosophies.

Formulate, state, define, and interpret general objectives for a physical education curriculum that can be justified by a valid educational theory and philosophy.

Design performance objectives, based on the best available evidence, to be achieved by the learner at each grade level for attainment of the stated general objectives.

Define the following:

Aim	Organic
Goal	Neuromuscular
Objective	Interpretive
Ultimate	Social
Ideal	Emotional
General	Physical fitness
Terminal	Motor fitness
Behavioral	Perceptual ability
Performance	Psychomotor
Instructional	Cognitive
Curricular	Affective

PERSPECTIVE

PRINCIPLE: The primary function of a curriculum is to provide experiences for changing a student's behavior. The type, degree, and direction of changes are determined by objectives.

The purposes of general education and specifically physical education are ever-challenging issues. Traditionally accepted objectives are being critically examined due to the changing demands of society and to a divergence of educational theories and philosophies. The result of this examination has caused professional disagreement as to focus, direction, labels, definitions, and interpretations of objectives. The problem is further compounded by a periodic shifting of emphasis as to the relative importance of the objectives. Controversy is healthy and stimulating for any profession but only to the extent that directional goals are not lost in the confusion that may exist when teachers ask, In what direction shall we change the values of our pupils? For it is then that they are face to face with determining objectives. For them it is time to review the basics and fundamentals of the discipline in retrospect—where we have been; in introspect—where we are now; and in prospect—where we are going?

Some attention has already been given to the nature of society, the nature of the learner, the nature of learning, and an examination of educational theory and philosophy. It is from the nature and relationships of these phenomena that educational purposes must be derived.

Consideration of objectives implies preferences, choices, and values that guide us in the selection and organization of curriculum experiences. Whenever we consider the direction in which we want to change the values of our pupils, we are dealing with objectives, for values represent goals of achievement. Values come from the direction and character of our goals in life. As teachers we want pupils to be strong, skilled, able to resist fatigue, agile, socially aware and sensitive and emotionally responsive to ideas, difficulties, order, ideals, and beauty. Before we can educate others we must know what is to be taught.

In formulating objectives, the teacher has some determining purpose in mind, for education is purposive; it has an end in view. Objectives are ends or goals that serve as agents for directing and organizing learning experiences. Education achieves high order when the high purposes of the teacher and the purposes of the pupil are similar—when teacher *objectives* become pupil *purposes*.

ULTIMATE OR IDEAL OBJECTIVES

If learning is the progressive change in the direction of some goal we set (e.g., fewer errors on a typewriter, a higher batting average in baseball, or more fluency in speaking French), then *education is the consciously controlled or purposefully directed process designed to produce the desired changes in behavior*. When we speak of effective citizenship, good sportsmanship, self-realization, sound character, or similar, more remote or long-range outcomes or objectives, they must be considered as ideal or ultimate objectives of any educational process. We can agree that to become a good citizen, or even a healthy one, or an individual of sound character requires the development of all sorts of desirable understandings, interests, habits, ideals, concepts, principles, and attitudes. We can further agree that we cannot teach good citizenship by simply giving a course in the subject. Every teacher and every discipline have a unique contribution to make to the ultimate objectives that permeate all areas of the school.

The master artist-teacher does not memorize all the components contributing to the making of an educated citizen, but recalls these ideals, concepts, interests, attitudes, and understandings to mind intuitively in planning and teaching in an effort to humanize physical education.

OBJECTIVES: AN OVERVIEW

Historically, physical education objectives have undergone changes. These changes and differences in labeling, defining, interpreting, and weighting values have been the result of educational trends and variances in major theoretical positions These positions have been categorized as (1) education of the physical, (2) education through the physical, (3) movement education, and (4) play education. Since each portion has its strengths and weaknesses, does it not seem reasonable that by synthesizing the strengths and discarding the weaknesses of the various theories, the result would be a physical education theory that could unify the profession as to focus, direction, and purpose?

It is usually agreed that the ultimate objectives of education are those intended to improve all students regardless of their vocational inclination (we want all students to be healthy, to be functioning and contributing members of society). It is likewise quite generally agreed that guidance in all aspects of living is the function of all teach-

ers. We should be concerned with the total personality of the student and interested in his/her nonspecialized activities, such as those involving self-realization, human relationships. (belonging, gaining status in the group, developing a sense of mastery and achievement), and civic responsibility. *We teach students first and physical education second.*

Recent statements of the aims of education place great emphasis on developing curricula that take into account social realities, human values, the needs of individual learners, and bodies of knowledge derived from disciplinary and interdisciplinary studies. It is the responsibility of the school to direct these social processes. Physical education, as a social process, is concerned with progressive change in behavior originating from the stimulus of big muscle play activities in groups, whether this education be called movement experiences or skill experiences. All human activity is based on movement, and since physical education's unique contribution is physical activity, it is the education of and through movement. The function of physical education is to combine the basic principles of movement and the common elements of activity as subject matter for learning and instruction.

The learner is a progressively developing, integrated organism. His/her progressive growth and developmental stages are accompanied by functional development in basic movement and more complex skills. The progression from fundamental movement skills to sport skills is the teaching and learning construct. Activities for the development of fundamental movement skills are presented prior to those requiring a higher degree of refined and specialized skill learnings. Specifically, the teaching of the fundamental movement skills of running, jumping, changing direction, and ball handling provide a foundation for the more complex sport skills of the pivot in basketball, the spike in volleyball, the long jump in track and field, the dribble in soccer, the scoop and throw in baseball, and the ace in tennis. Other physical abilities such as balance, weight transfer, agility, and speed can be developed as foundations for the acquisition of new skills.

The development of perceptual qualities becomes an integral outcome of all these activities. Through propulsive and receptive activities the child learns to focus his/her attention on a select number of specific stimuli from a mass of sensory intake. Target throwing with a ball develops the child's ability to coordinate vision with gross skills. Group game activities provide opportunities for a student to develop body image awareness and to distinguish laterality.

Prerequisites for skill learning are varying degrees of strength, muscle and cardiovascular endurance, and flexibility. These are not only immediate needs but are also needed for future demands of living.

If one expects to be successful in and enjoy these activities, there are other learnings to be acquired: a knowledge of rules and strategy, an understanding of the elementary principles of the physiology of activity, how to layout a backyard badminton court, etiquette and safety rules of a game, and how to purchase and properly care for various types of sports equipment. These are tangible learnings that must be considered in the development of objectives.

Less tangible learnings consisting of values, attitudes, appreciations, socialization, sportsmanship, honesty, cooperativeness, and emotional well-being present different objective problems. The inability to precisely measure and evaluate the behavioral changes that occur in these traits makes it difficult to select our techniques of teaching for these important learnings. However, they cannot be excluded from curriculum planning. Teachers must be cognizant of their relative importance in the total experience of the learner. They are valuable byproducts of a satisfying movement or skill experience. If an individual acquires a degree of skill that affords pleasure in participation, he/she will participate; will be socially active with the group in that activity; and will use the activity as an outlet for emotional well-being.

It may be difficult to apply statistical procedures to evaluate these outcomes, but we must always be aware that by structuring the learning environment and teaching by modeling, we can produce positive effects in these less tangible objectives. Activities taught solely for the purpose of activity do not fulfill the objectives. Teachers must have the ability to interpret objectives operationally, understand the nature of activity thoroughly, know which teaching strategies produce which effects, and be able to relate the relative contribution of activities to stated objectives.

Objectives should be weighted as to their relative value. This weighting is determined by the growth and developmental stages of the learner, teaching behavior and styles, teacher competencies, and teacher values. Other criteria can be the uniqueness of the objective to the goals of general education, the feasibility of measurement, and the degree of objective and accurate evaluation.

OBJECTIVES: MEANING AND SIGNIFICANCE

The classification and interpretation of physical education have been stated in a variety of ways. The more traditional objectives are indicated on p. 64 in a rather informal manner.

Table 2. Developmental objectives of physical education*

Organic	Neuromuscular	Perceptual
Proper functioning of the body systems so that the individual may meet adequately the demands placed upon him/her by the environment; a foundation for skill development	Harmonious functioning of the nervous and muscular systems to produce desired movements	Ability to receive and distinguish among available cues in a given situation in order to perform more skillfully
Muscle strength	Locomotor skills	Spatial relationships
Maximum amount of force exerted by a muscle or muscle group	Walking, skipping, sliding, leaping, pushing, running, galloping, hopping, rolling, pulling, jumping	Ability to recognize objects as being in front, behind, below, to the right or left of one's self
Muscle endurance	Nonlocomotor skills	Visual-motor coordination
Ability of a muscle or muscle group to sustain effort for a prolonged period of time	Swaying, twisting, shaking, stretching, bending, hanging, stooping	Ability to coordinate vision with gross motor skills involving hands, body, and/or feet
Cardiovascular endurance	Game-type fundamental skills	Figure-ground relationships
Capacity of an individual to persist in strenuous activity for periods of some duration; this depends on the combined efficiency of the blood vessels, heart, and lungs	Striking, catching, kicking, stopping, throwing, batting, starting, changing direction, bouncing, rolling, trapping, volleying	Ability to select stimuli from a mass of sensory intake or to select a limited number of stimuli on which to focus attention
Flexibility	Motor factors	Body balance (static, dynamic)
Range of motion in joints needed to produce efficient movement and to minimize injury	Accuracy, rhythm, kinesthetic awareness, power, balanced reaction time, agility	Ability to maintain static or dynamic equilibrium
	Sport and dance skills	Dominancy
	Soccer, softball, volleyball, wrestling, track and field, football, baseball, basketball, archery, speedball, hockey, fencing, golf, bowling, tennis, dance	Consistency in the use of the left or right hand or foot in throwing and striking
	Recreation skills	Laterality
	Shuffleboard, croquet, deck tennis, hiking, table tennis, swimming, horseshoes, boating	Ability to distinguish the difference between left and right sides of the body and between left and right within one's own body
		Body image
		Awareness of the parts of the body or the whole body and the relationships to space

*Reprinted from Annarino, A. A. *Fundamental movement and sport skill development*. Columbus, Ohio: Charles

Cognitive	Social	Emotional
Ability to explore, to discover, to understand, to acquire knowledge, and to make value judgments	Adjustment to both self and others by integration of the individual to society and the environment	Healthy response to physical activity through a fulfillment of basic needs
Knowledge of game rules, safety measures, and etiquette	Ability to make judgments in a group situation	Development of positive reactions in spectatorship and participation through either success or failure
Use of strategies and techniques involved in organized activities	Learning to communicate with others	Release of tension through suitable physical activities
Knowledge of how the body functions and its relationship to physical activity	Ability to exchange and evaluate ideas within a group	Outlet for self-expression and creativity
Appreciation for personal performance; the use of judgment related to distance, time, space, form, speed, and direction in the use of activity implements, balls, and self	Development of the social phases of personality, attitudes, and values in order to become functioning members of society	Appreciation of the esthetic experiences derived from correlated activities
Understanding of growth and developmental factors affected by movement	Development of a sense of belonging and acceptance by society	
Ability to solve developmental problems through movement	Development of positive personality traits	
	Learnings for the constructive use of leisure time	
	Development of attitude that reflects good moral character	

T. Merrill Co., 1973, pp. 4-5.

1. *Organic power, the ability to maintain adaptive effort*—an attempt to strengthen muscles, develop resistance to fatigue, and increase cardiovascular efficiency.
2. *Neuromuscular development*—an attempt to develop skills, grace, a sense of rhythm, and an improved reaction time.
3. *Personal-social attitudes and adjustment*—an attempt to place pupils in situations that encourage self-confidence, sociability, initiative, self-direction, and a feeling of belonging.
4. *Interpretive and intellectual development*—an attempt to encourage pupils to approach whatever they do with active imagination and some originality, so that they contribute something that is their own.
5. *Emotional responsiveness*—an attempt to have pupils express joy at participation in "fun" games and sports, accept challenges that mean overcoming difficulties, get a thrill out of cooperative success or teamwork, and develop an increased appreciation of esthetic experiences in the dance, a game, or water ballet.

With some modifications, the traditional terminologies may still be acceptable. However, because of changing educational theories and philosophies, there is a need to critically analyze the traditional objectives as to definitions, interpretations, and specificity. The developmental objectives shown in Table 2 are the results of an analysis and indicate a transition from the traditional to a more developmental set of objectives. However, one of the problems in attempting to place all behaviors into separate categories or compartments is the overlap or interrelatedness of not only the categories but of the behaviors.

Since education is concerned with changes in behavior, another classification scheme or taxonomy has been proposed. This scheme translates educational objectives into behavioral characteristics and categorizes them into three domains: psychomotor, cognitive, and affective (Bloom, 1956; Krathwohl, 1964). By analyzing outcomes, placing them in these domains in a hierarchical form, and adding a fourth domain—the physical, the curriculum designer has a sound basis for planning a progressive and meaningful curriculum.

To bring order out of the chaos and confusion that exist, the operational taxonomy for physical education objectives illustrated on pp. 65 to 69 is proposed.

PERFORMANCE OBJECTIVES

In curriculum planning, ultimate and general objectives are easy to state because they are somewhat abstract and remote. They look good on paper but lack specificity by indicating to the student and teacher exactly what is to be accomplished in this lesson *today* or in this unit *this week*. There is a need to specify what is to be learned, to what degree, and under what condition in order to create realism for each lesson or unit. The learner must have a clear definitive picture of what he/she is trying to accomplish and to what degree of achievement. Without clearly defined objectives, it is difficult to determine and select the appropriate instructional content and strategy and to evaluate the worth of the program.

One method for writing instructional objectives in behavioral terms is proposed by Mager (1962). He identifies three basic components that should be included in an instructional or performance objective. They are (1) an identified terminal behavior that is observable and measurable, (2) the situation or conditions under which the behavior will be performed, and (3) the criterion or criteria that indicate the standard of performance necessary for fulfilling the objective.

The following examples are given to compare traditionally stated objectives of

OPERATIONAL TAXONOMY FOR PHYSICAL EDUCATION OBJECTIVES

A:0 Physical domain (organic development)
Proper functioning of the body systems so that the individual may adequately meet the demands placed on him/her by the environment

A:1 *Strength*
Maximum amount of force exerted by a muscle or muscle group

A:1.1 Static (isometric)
Maximum force exerted without any change in muscle length

A:1.2 Dynamic (isotonic)
Release of maximum force in the shortest period of time

A:2 *Endurance*
Capacity to persist in strenuous activity for periods of some duration

A:2.1 Muscle
Ability of a muscle or muscle group to sustain effort for a prolonged period of time

A:2.1a Static
Ability of a muscle or muscle group to sustain effort in a fixed position

A:2.1b Dynamic
Ability of a muscle or muscle group to repeat effort in a movement

A:2.2 Cardiovascular
Ability to persist in strenuous activity dependent on the combined efficiency of the blood vessels, heart, and lungs

A:3 *Flexibility*
Range of motion in joints

A:3.1 Extent
Ability to extend joint motion as far as possible in various directions

A:3.2 Dynamic
Ability to repeat flexing and extending movements

B:0 Psychomotor domain (neuromuscular development)
Harmonious integration of the nervous and muscular systems to produce desired movements

B:1 *Perceptual-motor abilities*
Those abilities needed for recognition, interpretation, and response to stimuli for performing some type of task

B:1.1 Balance
Ability to maintain body position or equilibrium

B:1.1a Static
Maintaining a specific stationary body position

B:1.1b Dynamic
Maintaining equilibrium while performing a movement

Continued.

**OPERATIONAL TAXONOMY FOR PHYSICAL EDUCATION
OBJECTIVES—cont'd**

B:1.2 Kinesthesis
Awareness of the position and movement of one's body or parts in space
  B:1.2a Body image
    Self-concept of one's body and its relationship between one's self, others, space, and the world around
  B:1.2b Body awareness
    Recognition and control of the body and its parts
  B:1.2c Laterality
    Distinction of the difference between left and right sides of the body and between left and right within one's own body
  B:1.2d Directionality
    Distinction between and among left, right, up, down, front, back, and distances in space
  B:1.2e Dominance
    Consistency in the use of a preferred side in performing a task
B:1.3 Visual discrimination
Ability to receive, recognize, and differentiate between and among objects in space through visual cues
  B:1.3a Visual acuity
    To differentiate and understand various sights
  B:1.3b Visual tracking
    To follow objects with coordinated eye movements
  B:1.3c Visual memory
    To recall and reproduce movement from past visual experiences
  B:1.3d Figure-ground relationships
    To distinguish and select an object from its surrounding background
  B:1.3e Perceptual constancy
    To recognize familiar objects presented in a different size or manner
B:1.4 Auditory discrimination
Ability to receive, recognize, and differentiate between and among sounds
  B:1.4a Auditory acuity
    To receive and distinguish varying pitch and intensity of sounds
  B:1.4b Auditory tracking
    To locate sounds and follow their movements
  B:1.4c Auditory memory
    To recognize sounds from past experiences
B:1.5 Visual-motor coordination
Ability to integrate visual cues and specific body parts to produce a desired movement

OPERATIONAL TAXONOMY FOR PHYSICAL EDUCATION
OBJECTIVES—cont'd

B:1.5a Eye-hand coordination
Relationship of the eyes with the hands to gain control, accuracy, and steadiness

B:1.5b Eye-foot coordination
Integration of the eyes and foot to judge accurately the speed and direction of an object for kicking movement

B:1.5c Eye-hand-foot coordination
A combination of the above

B:1.6 Tactile sensitivity
Ability to receive and use cutaneous cues for enhancing motor performance

B:2 *Fundamental movement skills*
Manipulative skills involving the body or an object

B:2.1 Body manipulative skills
Those movements restricted to moving one's self by locomotion from space to space; nonlocomotor movements of moving one's self or body part within a space

B:2.1a Basic locomotor skills moving the body from one place to another

B:2.1aa Walking
B:2.1ab Running
B:2.1ac Leaping
B:2.1ad Jumping
B:2.1ae Hopping

B:2.1b Basic nonlocomotor skills moving a part or body part within a place

B:2.1ba Bending
B:2.1bb Stretching
B:2.1bc Twisting
B:2.1bd Turning
B:2.1be Hanging
B:2.1bf Posture

B:2.1c Locomotor combinations
Combining two or more locomotor skills

B:2.1ca Skipping
B:2.1cb Galloping
B:2.1cc Sliding
B:2.1cd Starting
B:2.1ce Stopping
B:2.1cf Changing directions

Continued.

OPERATIONAL TAXONOMY FOR PHYSICAL EDUCATION
OBJECTIVES—cont'd

B:2.1cg Falling
B:2.1ch Landing
B:2.1ci Rolling
B:2.1d Nonlocomotor combinations
Combining two or more nonlocomotor skills
B:2.1da Swaying
B:2.1db Swinging
B:2.1dc Lifting
B:2.2 Objective manipulative skills
Use of the various body manipulative movements in propulsive and receptive skills
B:2.2a Propulsive skills
Giving impetus to an external object
B:2.2aa Throwing
B:2.2aaa Underarm
B:2.2aab Sidearm
B:2.2aac Overarm
B:2.2ab Pushing
B:2.2ac Pulling
B:2.2ad Striking
B:2.2ae Lifting
B.2.2b Receptive skills
Receiving of external objects
B:2.2ba Catching
B:2.2bb Trapping
B:2.3 Sport skills
More complex skills that apply specifically to performance in a sport, game, or dance
B:2.3a Individual skills
B:2.3b Dual skills
B:2.3c Team skills

C:0 Cognitive domain (intellectual development)
C:1 *Knowledge*
C:1.1 Game rules
C:1.2 Safety measures
C:1.3 Game etiquette
C:1.4 Terminology
C:1.5 Body functions
C:2 *Intellectual skills and abilities*
C:2.1 Use of strategies

OPERATIONAL TAXONOMY FOR PHYSICAL EDUCATION OBJECTIVES—cont'd

C:2.2 Use of judgment related to distance, time, form, space, speed, and direction in the use of activity implements, balls, and self
C:2.3 Solution of developmental problems through movement
C:2.4 Understanding the relationship of physical activity to body function and structure
C:2.5 Knowledge of the immediate effects of activity
C:2.6 Knowledge of long-range effects of activity

D:0 Affective domain (social-personal-emotional development)
  D:1 *A healthy response to physical activity*
  D:1.1 Development of positive reactions through either success or failure in activity
  D:1.2 Appreciation of the esthetic experiences derived from correlated activities
  D:1.3 Recognition of the potential of activity as an outlet for tension release, and use of leisure time
  D:1.4 Ability to have "fun" in activity
  D:1.5 Spectator's appreciation of outstanding physical performance
  D:2 *Self-actualization*
  D:2.1 Awareness of what the body is capable of doing at a specific time
  D:2.2 Knowledge of what one is and the ability to accept this knowledge of one's capacity and potential
  D:2.3 Willingness to set a level of aspiration that is within reach and motivation to seek this level
  D:3 *Self-esteem*
  Self-perception refers to all of an individual's basic beliefs about himself/herself based on past experience; self-esteem refers to the individual's personal evaluation of these beliefs
  D:3.1 Individual's development of perceptions of his/her general physical ability or of physical performance in a specific activity

physical education to performance (behavior) objectives:

PHYSICAL DOMAIN

Traditional objective: The student should develop endurance or stamina.
Performance objective: The student in gymnasium attire and on a 440-yard track will demonstrate his/her present cardiovascular endurance level by completing the 12-minute run/walk test and covering a distance of 1.5 (boys) or 1.25 (girls) miles.

PSYCHOMOTOR DOMAIN

Traditional objective: The student should be able to putt.
Performance objective: The student will demonstrate the proper techniques of the putt by putting a golf ball into a cup 6 inches in diameter from a distance:
1. 3 feet, three of five times
2. 8 feet, three of five times

COGNITIVE DOMAIN

Traditional objective: The student should learn the rules of volleyball.

Performance objective: The student will demonstrate knowledge of the game of volleyball by answering questions on a written test, achieving a score of 70% or better.

AFFECTIVE DOMAIN

Traditional objective: The student should learn to appreciate the game of soccer.

Performance objective: The student will demonstrate a positive appreciation by completing two or more of the following:

1. Volunteering to officiate
2. Participating in a soccer varsity or intramural program
3. Viewing or scoring a soccer game outside of class
4. Assisting a classmate in learning and evaluating skill
5. Displaying leadership in a class soccer activity

The explicit components (change, standard, condition) give to the learner direction and meaning for practice, immediate feedback and reinforcement, and a measurement of achievement.

One can foresee the major task that confronts the curriculum planner in translating the ultimate and general objectives to performance objectives. Data based on research and field testing experiences are needed to provide estimates of minimal and maximal standards of performance for all grade levels. Effort in these directions are being made by various states, communities, and individuals. It is hoped that in time we will have a comprehensive set of performance objectives that will be reflected in the content and methodology of a curriculum that has meaning and significance.

REACTORS

1. Characteristics, needs, and interests of the learner are the bases for selecting objectives.
2. If an objective cannot be objectively measured, it should not be stated as an objective.
3. Only the physical objective of physical education can be justified.
4. Historically, physical education objectives have undergone few changes.
5. There is no relationship between methodology and objectives.
6. There may be differences between teacher objectives and student purposes.
7. Only in terms of the goals that an individual accepts, the values he/she seeks to serve, and the understanding he/she achieves does practice become a functional aspect of learning.
8. General objectives of physical education not only establish goals of learning but also determine the criteria for evaluating the success or failure of the learning and teaching effort.

SITUATIONAL PROBLEMS

1. The curriculum, as the life and program of the school, consists of acitvities and experiences. The school uses these to achieve its educational purposes or objectives. If we think of the curriculum in physical education as the means of education, what specific ways does it contribute to the following ends?
   a. Health
   b. Command of fundamental processes
   c. Worthy home membership
   d. Vocational efficiency
   e. Citizenship
   f. Worthy use of leisure
   g. Ethical character
   These are all ultimate objectives. Why? Can you translate them into immediate objectives?
2. You have accepted the development goals (objectives) of physical education.
   a. Physical development
   b. Psychomotor development
   c. Cognitive development
   d. Affective development

Activities	Markedly	Somewhat	Only slightly	Not at all
1. Kindergartners playing in the sandbox				
2. Fifth-grade students learning a Swedish folk dance for use in a United Nations performance				
3. Adults playing chess				
4. College students playing team basketball				
5. High school students putting on a public modern dance recital				
6. High school students riding horses				

Design a chart (above) indicating the degree (markedly, somewhat, only slightly, not at all) to which each activity listed can contribute to each of the four objectives.

LEARNING ACTIVITIES

1. Curriculum guide general objectives
   a. Select, state, and define objectives of physical education for a curriculum guide plan.
   b. Operationally define objectives for each school grade division.
   c. Determine and indicate a weighting percentage value allotted to each objective for the school grade divisions.
   d. Justify your selection, definition, and weighting values of the objectives by an educational theory and philosophy.
2. Curriculum guide performance objectives
   a. Select a physical education activity and design three performance objectives for each of the four domains specifically for a school grade division.
   b. Select a different activity and design three performance objectives for each of the

four domains for each school grade division.
   c. Design performance objectives for the total learning experiences and activities selected for the curriculum guide plan. Classify the performance objectives by domain headings and school grade division. (NOTE: Activity 2c will be completed after Unit 19.)

UNIT EVALUATIVE CRITERIA

Can you:
1. Defensibly justify by documentation the educational theory and philosophy that determined your selection, definition, interpretation, and weighting values of the curriculum guide's objectives?
2. Identify the criteria components of behavioral change, standard, and condition for each of your performance objectives?
3. Validate the standard component of your performance objectives by data-based information?

RESOURCES

AAHPER. *Knowledge and understanding in physical education*. Washington, D.C.: The Alliance, 1969, pt. II.

Annarino, A. A. *Fundamental movement and sport skill development*. Columbus, Ohio: Charles E. Merrill Publishing Co., 1973, pt. I.

Bookwalter, K., & Zanderzwag, H.J. *Foundations and principles of physical education*. Philadelphia: W. B. Saunders Co., 1969, chap. 3.

Bloom, B. (Ed.). *Taxonomy of educational objectives. Handbook I: The cognitive domain*. New York: David McKay Co. Inc.., 1956.

Brown, C., & Cassidy, R. *Theory in physical education*. Philadelphia: Lea & Febiger, 1963, chap. 5.

Jewett, A. E., Jones, L. S., Luneke, S. M., & Robinson, S. M. Educational change through a taxonomy for writing physical education objectives. *Quest*, 1971, *15*, 32-38.

Krathwohl, D. R., et al. *Taxonomy of educational objectives. Handbook II: The affective domain.* New York: David McKay Co., Inc., 1964.

Mager, R. *Preparing instructional objectives.* Palo Alto: Fearon Publishers, 1962.

Nash, J. B. *Physical education: interpretations and objectives.* New York: A. S. Barnes & Co., Inc., 1948.

Nixon, J. E., & Jewett, A. E. *Physical education curriculum.* New York: Ronald Press Co., 1964, chap. 2.

Nixon, J. E., & Jewett A. E. *An introduction to physical education.* Philadelphia: W. B. Saunders Co., 1969, chap. 6.

Oberteuffer, D., & Ulrich, C. *Physical education.* New York: Harper & Row, Publishers, Inc., 1970, pt. I.

Popham, W. J., & Baker, E. L. *Establishing instructional goals.* Englewood Cliffs, N.J.: Prentice-Hall, Inc., 1970a.

Popham, W. J., & Baker, E. L. *Systematic instruction.* Englewood Cliffs, N.J.: Prentice-Hall, Inc., 1970b.

Curriculum development is essentially the result of cooperative effort and by its very nature draws upon many kinds of competencies.

VIRGIL E. HERICH

7 Curriculum guide: planning and designing

COMPETENCIES

After completing this unit, you should be able to:

Organize and chair a departmental physical education curriculum committee.

Interpret how an effective curriculum guide translates philosophy and objectives into specific planning and development procedures.

Function effectively as a physical education curriculum committee member.

Identify the basic elements in a curriculum and specify design procedures.

Explain not only the "how" of curriculum development but also the "why."

Develop and utilize administrative policies necessary to implement an effective comprehensive program.

Define the following:

Administration
Course of study
Curriculum guide
Organization
Policy

PERSPECTIVE

PRINCIPLE: The term *curriculum guide* refers in reality to a guide for teachers and students of physical education that indicates how educational philosophy and theory are translated into action.

In the days when the curriculum was viewed as a body of specific subject matter indicating what should be learned by the students, the terms *course of study* and *curriculum* were treated as synonyms. Since the material was listed in logical order of presentation in the course of study, this became the actual curriculum.

The state department of education was often the original source of these curriculum outlines. The superintendent and principal, as curriculum specialists, made a few additions and passed them on to the individual teachers. The supervisor or principal was responsible for checking to see that the course of study was being followed religiously.

As changes in curriculum interpretation and practices occurred, there was a shift from overcentralization and stereotyped courses of study toward including in the curriculum all the educative experiences children and youth have under the auspices of the school. Since the curriculum is what pupils do and not what administrators set down on paper in a course of study, teachers became more involved and, as a result, now have greater freedom in determining the quality of life that results from learning experiences and how these experiences are organized. In other words, the old "course of study" instead of being followed rigidly under close supervision now becomes a "curriculum guide."

CURRICULUM FRAMEWORK

The term *curriculum guide* is preferred to *course of study,* as it is in reality a guide for teachers and students and indicates how educational philosophy and theory are translated into action. The teacher actively participates in the creation and represents the efforts and thinking of many people working in a coordinated manner.

The curriculum now involves something more than mere sequence of "subject matter" separated into grades or areas. The curriculum is concerned with the learner's growth and development, "out of class" activities, guidance services, school social life, work experience, and any other type of activity related to the school program and the learning experiences of students.

In contrast to the prepared plans handed down from above, curriculum development encourages teachers, students, and parents to be participants and thinkers rather than mere reactors to the ideas of others. The curriculum in physical education and the related policies are not a "one-man show." Policies are basic agreements made after examining all the most valid evidence—pro and con—available. A policy represents some recognizable attitude, purpose, or set of values that has been more or less crystallized after examining all available data.

Once policy is established, a program is the way to implement or give effect to the policy. Naturally, the soundness of the program will depend on the validity of the policy or the extent to which it is based on scientific facts and principles, the nature of the society, the nature of the individual, and the nature of the learning process. In this process we search for principles of growth and development and seek ways in which we might make provisions, at each level of development, for physical, social, emotional, and intellectual needs of children and youth.

If we started by asking ourselves how we can improve the educational program in physical education, we could hardly avoid opinions from our colleagues in sociology, medicine, psychology, philosophy, and the general field of education. It is true that our group would be formed largely of people concerned directly with physical education, but what education needs above all else is teamwork in the solution of curriculum problems. We talk to ourselves too much. We need multidisciplined thinking in which teachers, scientists, or parents of different vocations try to understand each other's problems with a view to helping one another solve them.

Growth in ability to cooperate is fostered only by sharing in cooperative action. Curriculum development involves such action. A philosophy of education must be developed and accepted, and an experimental attitude must be developed by the teaching staff, administrators, and supervisors in the determination of objectives. Learning experiences, teaching percentages, and methods of evaluating growth must be determined within the general framework of some curriculum pattern.

Each individual school involved in a curriculum improvement program must initiate the program so that teachers can participate effectively at their professional level. The program should be tailored for local needs. These teachers, as an effective group in a school concerned with curriculum development and improvement, should concern themselves with some broad frame of reference. "Putting parts into a framework" has been described as an important aspect of the learning process. The framework is primary and essential. In

curriculum planning, this is also true. In this respect, the curriculum guide or framework assumes major importance.

Today, the major responsibility for curriculum planning is in the physical education teachers functioning as cooperative members of school or departmental curriculum committees. The experience of teachers working cooperatively for the purpose of planning the physical education curriculum should result not only in an improved curriculum for the students but also in increased competency and professional growth for the individual teacher.

However, to serve as a functional and effective committee member, the teacher must have the ability to organize and determine the structure and function of a curriculum committee, a knowledge of the basic elements included in a curriculum, and a thorough understanding of design procedures.

CURRICULUM COMMITTEES: STRUCTURE AND FUNCTION

The entire personnel of today's schools must think and plan together and eventually implement by action the school's educational program. Every school system, regardless of size, should have some administrative group to coordinate the study, planning, execution, and evaluation of curriculum policies and practices.

The total curriculum program of a school system may be the responsibility of a general school curriculum committee with representation of all areas, including physical education. This will assure physical education's contributions to the educational purposes that should permeate all areas of the school system. Thus physical education will not be isolated but will always be seen in relation to the total educational program.

Representation of each department on a

general school curriculum committee will indicate that an effective total curriculum is not a "one-person" or "one-department" job. When important ultimate or ideal objectives are recommended by such a committee, we can see that we cannot plan solely in terms of subjects.

Curriculum planning involves the scientific method or the method of reflective thinking, as all good planning must.

1. Goals are determined. The "problem" is defined.
2. The total school situation is studied for all facts and clues bearing on the problem.
3. The best hypotheses are advanced as the possible solutions to the problem.
4. The most likely and promising hypothesis is selected.
5. Procedures are carefully planned to test the hypothesis, isolating experimental factors wherever possible by using controls.
6. Trying out or testing the hypothesis is done by carrying out the experiment with care.
7. Conclusions are drawn.
8. Inferences are made based on the conclusions.
9. The curriculum is revised or specific policies and procedures are changed as a result of continuous evaluation.

Reflective or critical thinking is not the monopoly of any field of study. It is not limited to the physics or chemistry laboratory or to the mathematics classroom. It may apply anywhere and to any problem. In this case we apply it to the physical education curriculum. Suppose that education for democracy is an important school objective. How would the curriculum committee in physical education proceed with the development of a functional curriculum for certain behavior outcomes? How should we proceed to determine the type and degree of changes in the behavior of boys and girls with respect to this important objective?

In any curriculum-building program, the teachers who are to execute the program

cannot do so intelligently without having participated in its development. Even though the school personnel and the community together may plan the general curriculum framework, the detailed development of the curriculum falls on the shoulders of individual teachers. Certainly, if the teacher is unaware of the educational goals of the curriculum, he/she can hardly be expected to help pupils to attain these goals.

System-wide committees that cut across several levels of the school system and are responsible to some central curriculum coordinating council are necessary as the need arises. Some of these are as follows:

1. Central health committee
2. Physical education committee
3. Audiovisual aids committee
4. Guidance and counseling committee
5. Mathematics committee

These committees, having representation from the various grade levels, get down to the "grass roots," keep the curriculum down to earth by improving instructional practices, and actually help the individual teachers translate educational philosophy into teaching strategies.

Some of the functions of these committees are as follows:

1. Preparing instructional materials in terms of grade progression
2. Showing how content may be selected and organized for the purpose of achieving "all-school" objectives
3. Maintaining close relationships with individual local school staff

Through these committees, general policies and plans for curriculum improvement sift upward from the classroom teachers to a central committee whose task it is to coordinate basic agreements, philosophy, objectives, and procedures and to see that the composite thinking of all teachers is consolidated into the statement of the points of view acceptable to the majority.

PHYSICAL EDUCATION CURRICULUM COMMITTEES

Physical education deals with both *system* and *grade,* and these affect all children of all grades in all schools. The organization of a physical education committee for curriculum development and/or improvement is illustrated in Fig. 5. The following organizational chart indicates the structure of a physical education curriculum committee. The suggested activity subcommittees may be modified, depending on the situation. The suggested membership and function of the groups and individuals involved in committees are as follows:

I. Coordinating committee
  A. Membership: The principals of the schools involved, the responsible school system heads of physical education, and one physical education teacher representative from each of the following school levels:
    1. Primary grades
    2. Intermediate grades
    3. Junior high school or middle school
    4. Senior high school
  B. Function: To coordinate the work of the various subcommittees, to standardize the progression for the various grade levels, to guide the development of the elements in the curriculum based on the approved curriculum design, to harmonize the physical education program with other school areas, and to provide to all subcommittees the results of the following information:
    1. Community survey
      a. Historical background of the community
      b. Community economy and tax structure
      c. Social structure

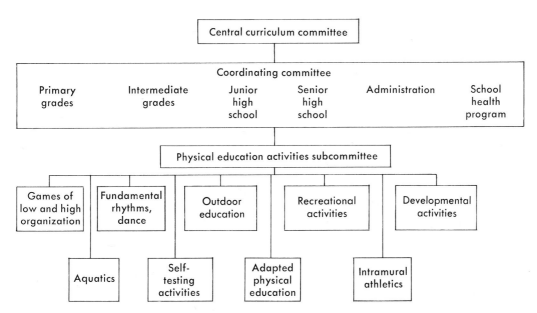

Fig. 5. Suggested organization for curriculum improvement in physical education.

    d. Public and commercial recreational facilities

    e. Population and trends projections

2. School survey

    a. Indoor and outdoor facilities

    b. Equipment and supplies

    c. Enrollment and projections

    d. Number of classes

    e. Size of classes

    f. Number and qualifications of teaching personnel

    g. Organization and administrative structure

    h. Daily and yearly time modules

3. Curriculum guide foundations: The coordinating committee's responsibility includes formulating the foundations for curriculum guide development. These foundations are as follows:

    a. A specific definition of physical education and a clear conception of the curriculum

    b. Data-based information concerning the characteristics, needs, and interests of the community's youth categorized under physiological, psychological, and sociological areas

    c. Translation of the foregoing information into teaching and learning principles

    d. A statement of a physical education philosophy

    e. A stated aim

    f. Listing and defining the general objectives of the school and physical education

4. School policies: The curriculum guide plan can also include instructional, intramural, and athletic administrative policies. These policies can be developed by the coordinating committee or assigned to subcommittees. Specifically, policies should be developed for the following areas:

    a. Attendance and excuses

    b. Budget and requisition

    c. Equipment, supplies, and facilities

        (1) maintenance

        (2) storage

        (3) use

    d. Discipline procedures

    e. Classification, testing, and marking

    f. First aid and accident procedures

    g. Legal liability

    h. Safety and health rules

    i. Medical examinations

    j. Dress

    k. General instructions for teachers at all levels

    l. Scheduling of facilities

        (1) instructional program

        (2) intramurals

        (3) athletics

        (4) special school and community groups

    m. Interscholastic athletics

        (1) medical examinations

        (2) eligibility

        (3) travel

        (4) budget

        (5) awards

    n. Intramurals

        (1) eligibility

        (2) awards

        (3) supervision

II. Subcommittees

  A. Membership: Criteria should be interest, grade division representation, expertise, and degree of involvement in the teaching of physical education.

  B. Function: To select and organize experiences and activities for the school grade levels, to provide scope and sequence for the selected activities and experiences, to determine the most effective instructional strategies and curriculum designs, to develop instructional materials, and to determine valid and reliable methods for evaluation.

Total involvement of the teachers and the school in designing a curriculum guide plan will result in a program in which all teachers can effectively participate at their professional level, in improved professional growth for the teachers involved, and, more importantly, in a meaningful curriculum for the students. Improving physical education depends primarily on improving physical education teachers.

REACTORS

1. Curriculum planning is a continuous process.
2. We cannot improve education without improving teachers.
3. Is the physical education curriculum trying to do too much?
4. Membership on all-school committees would perhaps be the best type of in-service education for teachers.
5. In curriculum planning and development, "Small deeds done are better than great deeds planned."
6. Physical education programs can be improved by improving physical education teachers.

SITUATIONAL PROBLEMS

1. Success in any venture depends, among other things, on careful planning. Sound policies and procedures result from careful consideration of factors and conditions regarded as most essential to success. Group action cannot be intelligent without planning.

   You are chairman of the department of physical education in a senior high school of 1,000 boys and girls. Your new principal has come to town with a strong reputation as a curriculum specialist. After several weeks of looking over the physical education program he calls you into his office and in a friendly tone says, "Mr. X, I have tried to find some organizational pattern in our physical education program. I see little relationship between courses from year to year or between units from month to month. Even the daily lessons seem unrelated to some tangible curriculum pattern or design. As chairman of the department, I am asking you to organize your staff into working committees and within two months present an out-line of a curriculum guide for physical education for boys and girls of the freshman and sophomore classes."

   Comply with his request.
2. The trends and characteristics of good education may be categorized under five main headings, as follows:
   a. Teaching tools of learning for a purpose. Facts, principles, and skills are not learned as ends in themselves but rather as a means of achieving some purposeful end.
   b. Practicing living in a democracy. Learning citizensip and the democratic way of life is more effective through practicing social living in the school and community.
   c. Relating the school program to real-life problems. The school plans its program around problems of living to which democratic values are applied.
   d. Recognizing child growth as a total process. The school program is guided by an understanding of human behavior and child growth as a total process.
   e. Recognizing the fact that no two pupils are alike. The school program recognizes the needs of individual pupils.
   State specifically how a good curriculum guide in physical education translates these trends and characteristics into specific planning and development procedures.
3. Select some ultimate objective, such as "sportsmanship," that cuts across a number of instructional fields, and outline the manner of preparing a curriculum guide or bulletin for this topic.
4. You, as supervisor of physical education in a city of 30,000, have been charged by your superintendent to produce an "athletic policy" for the school system. A policy is a basic agreement made after considering all of the most valid evidence obtainable. How would you proceed to define such a policy? Whose help would you seek? Why is it important that educational policies, athletic policies,

and public relations policies be clearly defined and democratically derived?

LEARNING ACTIVITIES

1. Visit a large, medium, and small city school corporation.
   a. Secure a list of facilities and administrators for grades K through 12.
   b. Outline an organizational chart for developing a grade K through 12 physical education curriculum for one of the corporations.
   c. Indicate the functions of the various committees.
   d. Indicate the structure of the various committees.

2. Examine various curriculum guide plans for different size school corporations. Identify the similarities and differences related to organization and content.

UNIT EVALUATIVE CRITERIA

Can you:
1. Organize a curriculum development committee and interpret procedures and responsibilities?
2. Identify the basic elements of a curriculum guide plan?
3. Translate the philosophical and relationship objectives for a curriculum guide plan?
4. Explain the differences between a curriculum guide plan and a course of study?

RESOURCES

Association for Supervision and Curriculum Development. *Curricular concerns in a revolutionary era.* Washington, D.C.: The Association, 1971.

Baley, J. E., & Field, D. A. *Physical education and the physical educator.* Boston: Allyn & Bacon, Inc., 1970.

Barrow, H. M. *Man and his movement: principles of his physical education.* Philadelphia: Lea & Febiger, 1971.

Bookwalter, K., & Vanderzwag, H. J. *Foundations and principles of physical education.* Philadelphia: W. B. Saunders Co., 1969.

Brown, C., & Cassidy, R. *Theory in physical education.* Philadelphia: Lea & Febiger, 1963.

Bucher, C. A. (Ed.). *Dimensions in physical education* (2nd ed.). St. Louis: The C. V. Mosby Co., 1974.

Bucher, C. A. *Foundations of physical education* (8th ed.). St. Louis: The C. V. Mosby Co., 1979.

Burns, H. W., & Brauner, C. *Problems in education and philosophy.* Englewood Cliffs, N.J.: Prentice-Hall, Inc., 1965.

Cowell, C. C., & France, W. L. *Philosophy and principles of physical education.* Englewood Cliffs, N.J.: Prentice-Hall, Inc., 1963.

Cratty, B. J. *Social dimensions of physical activity.* Englewood Cliffs, N.J.: Prentice-Hall, Inc., 1967.

Cratty, B. J. *Psychology and motor activity.* Englewood Cliffs, N.J.: Prentice-Hall, Inc., 1970.

Davis, E. C., & Miller, D. M. *The philosophic process in physical education.* Philadelphia: Lea & Febiger, 1967.

Daughtrey, G. *Methods in physical education and health for secondary schools.* Philadelphia: W. B. Saunders Co., 1967.

Felshin, J. More than movement: an introduction to physical education. Philadelphia: Lea & Febiger, 1972.

Harrow, A. J. *A taxonomy of the psychomotor domain.* New York: David McKay Co., Inc., 1972.

Heidenreich, R. R. *Improvements in curriculum.* Virginia: College Readings, Inc., 1972.

Heitmann, H. M. *Organizational patterns for instruction in physical education.* Washington, D.C.: American Alliance for Health, Physical Education, and Recreation, 1971.

Insley, G. S. *Practical guidelines for the teaching of physical education.* Reading, Mass.: Addison-Wesley Publishing Co., Inc., 1973.

Ismail, A., & Gruber, J. *Motor aptitude and intellectual performance.* Columbus, Ohio: Charles E. Merrill Publishing Co., 1967.

LaPorte, W. R. *The physical education curriculum.* Los Angeles: University of Southern California Press, 1968.

Larson, L. A. *Curriculum foundations and standards for physical education.* Englewood Cliffs, N.J.: Prentice-Hall, Inc., 1970.

Mackenzie, M. M. *Toward a new curriculum in physical education.* New York: McGraw-Hill Book Co., 1969.

Metheny, E. *Connotations of movement in sport and dance.* Dubuque, Iowa: William C. Brown Co., Publishers, 1965.

Metheny, E. *Movement and meaning.* New York: McGraw-Hill Book Co., 1968.

Nixon, J. E., & Jewett, A. E. *Physical education curriculum*. New York: Ronald Press Co., 1964.

Nixon, J. E., & Ulrich, C. *Tones of theory*. Washington, D.C., American Alliance for Health, Physical Education, and Recreation, 1972.

Oxendine, J. B. *Psychology of motor learning*. New York: Appleton-Century-Crofts, 1968.

Siedentop, D. *Physical education—introductory analysis*. Dubuque, Iowa: William C. Brown Co., Publishers, 1972.

Singer, R. N. *Psychomotor domain: movement behaviors*. Philadelphia: Lea & Febiger, 1972a.

Singer, R. N. *Readings in motor learning*. Philadelphia: Lea & Febiger, 1972b.

Slusher, H. S., & Lockhart, A. S. *Anthology of contemporary readings*. Dubuque, Iowa: William C. Brown Co., Publishers, 1966.

Thompson, J. C. *Physical education for the 1970's*. Englewood Cliffs, N.J.: Prentice-Hall, Inc., 1971.

Webster, R. W. *Philosophy of physical education*. Dubuque, Iowa: William C. Brown Co., Publishers, 1965.

Willgoose, C. E. *The curriculum in physical education*. Englewood Cliffs, N.J.: Prentice-Hall, Inc., 1979.

Ziegler, F. *Problems in the history and philosophy of physical education and sport*. Englewood Cliffs, N.J.: Prentice-Hall, Inc., 1968.

PART TWO

CURRICULUM CONTENT

UNITS

Physical education in curriculum construction should study and appraise all the pertinent facts with respect to the characteristics of the individuals to be educated.

JESSE FEIRING WILLIAMS

Unfortunately, the maintenance of the game rather than the identity of players becomes most important.

R. D. LAINZ

8 Selection of activities and experiences

COMPETENCIES

After completing this unit, you should be able to:

Select meaningful physical education experiences that have a direct relationship to objectives of the school.

Identify young people's expectations and translate them into relative criteria for the selection of curricular experiences.

Recognize that student expectations are individual and establish a curriculum of experiences in terms of these individual expectations.

Conclude that physical education activities are not merely ends in themselves but possible means by which children and youth solve problems of daily living.

Define the following:
Criteria
Experiences
Interactions
Needs
Purposes
Expectations

PERSPECTIVE

PRINCIPLE: Learning is the result of interactions by the individual and the environment. These interactions are experiences that are primarily activated by purpose and interest.

The content of the physical education curriculum should have a direct relationship to the objectives of the school. There are numerous criteria that might be applied in the selection of curriculum activities. The teacher's concept of the role of the school in modern society, and in turn the role of physical education in the school, suggests many.

1. Since schools are publicly supported for the benefit of society, are the activities conducive to social ideals in a changing democratic society?
2. Do the activities have a direct relationship to the overall objectives of the school?
3. Do the activities contribute to the solution of problems that boys and girls meet in everyday life? Are the activities useful or merely traditional?
4. Do the activities capitalize on previously acquired knowledge, skill, and interests of pupils? Do they simplify and promote learning in further learning situations?
5. Do the activities abound in possibilities for affective developments such as interests, values, attitudes, ideals, tastes, and appreciations?
6. Do the activities have play value so that children engage in them in their "out-of-school" hours?
7. Do the activities make unreasonable administrative demands in terms of space, equipment, leadership, time allotment, or amount of noise?

In selecting learning experiences in physical education, the value of the content of these experiences may be appraised in terms of the basic criteria suggested by the questions just stated. These questions focus attention primarily on criteria that apply to all areas of education, including physical education.

RELATION OF CRITERIA TO OBJECTIVES

When we state objectives, we define the goals we desire to achieve. Objectives imply preferences, values, and directions in which we wish to change young people. For the selection of experiences best suited to attain these goals, criteria are needed to govern this selection. Criteria represent value judgments or "yardsticks" in the selection of activities designed to achieve objectives.

The selection of appropriate learning experiences in physical education is one of the most crucial problems of physical education curriculum construction. We need to develop and improve fitness qualities—strength, endurance, and flexibility; these are important objectives. In selecting conditioning activities to achieve these objectives we apply criteria and ask, To what extent does this activity (for example, circuit training) contribute to the maximal development of these qualities?

Cognitive development can only be achieved if the learner is involved in the cognitive process.

If proficiency in the performance of motor skills is an objective, we must understand the specific demands and requirements of a variety of activities. Additional criteria must be applied for manipulating environmental and practical settings in order to provide more positive experiences for enhancing performance.

If the affective area is to be effected, experiences must be structured that provide social interaction under controlled emotional pressure that demands moral decisions and the development of self-concepts.

NEED AND SOURCES OF CRITERIA

Rapid social changes, greatly increased leisure time, the increase of mental and physical illnesses, crime, and delinquency, our newer knowledge of growth and development—all these suggest the need for a revision of criteria in selecting physical education activities and possibly additional revision of school curricula. Another important source of criteria is the findings of the research studies concerning the dynamics of human behavior that reveal the needs and problems of youth. Concern over physique, "going steady," being unpopular, lack of social and game skills, self-consciousness, inadequate recreation facilities, and similar conditions creates considerable tension within adolescents and has implications for the curriculum.

In a complex industrial culture each person faces certain persistent problems of living—achieving—achieving recognition, approval, appreciation and status; finding new experiences, excitement, and adventure; satisfying the desire for affection, for being wanted, and for a sense of belonging; and developing some sense of power, achievement, mastery, or accomplishment.

In selecting activities for the physical education curriculum and in deciding how these experiences should be organized, preference should be given to those experiences that apply in the daily lives of the pupils and meet present and future needs. In the process of selecting learning experi-

ences, there are numerous factors that may serve as selective criteria, such as pupil age, pupil sex, place, type of community, climate, leadership, available space, facilities, and equipment. These are tangible criteria, but we must also ask, What do the students want?

STUDENT EXPECTATIONS

Although we stress skills and abilities, we forget that students want skills and abilities *for* something. Motivation is central in the curriculum because we learn those things that are necessary to satisfy our needs. Therefore it is important that we try to find out what purposes or long-range motives people attempt to satisfy when they come to us with a hockey stick, tennis racquet, gold club, basketball, or swimming cap in hand. Purposes tell us something of the goal expectations sought by children and youth. Our task as teachers is to help students secure goal resources by which they may achieve their expectations. Table 3 lists the activity expectations of students.

A curriculum based on student purposes and expectations would always be meaningful and dynamic; it would be a curriculum in which children would engage in vital experiences for meeting their own daily problems of living, where permanence of learning would be at a maximum. Purposes and expectations of students must be criteria in selecting experiences. Our task as educators is to create within students worthwhile purposes and expectations, to modify and extend purposes already held by students, and, in some cases, to help them to change undesirable purposes. Our next duty is to help them find the goal resources (skills, abilities, and knowledges) to achieve their goal satisfactions—to help them go where they want to go and do what they want to do.

Although we establish a curriculum of activities in terms of the central tendency of

Table 3. Physical education program content*

Activity	Team	Indi-vidual	Life-time	K	1	2	3	4	5	6	7	8	9	10	11	12
Angling/casting		X	X												X	X
Aquatics		X	X			X	X	X	X	X	X	X	X	X	X	X
Archery		X	X								X	X	X	X	X	X
Badminton		X	X								X	X	X	X	X	X
Basketball	X							X	X	X	X	X	X	X	X	X
Bicycling		X	X					X	X	X	X	X	X	X	X	X
Bowling		X	X								X	X	X	X	X	X
Dance/rhythms		X	X	X	X	X	X	X	X	X	X	X	X	X	X	X
Fencing		X	X											X	X	X
Field hockey	X													X	X	X	X
Games/relays	X			X	X	X	X	X	X	X	X					
Golf		X	X									X	X	X	X	X
Gymnastics		X					X	X	X	X	X	X	X	X	X	X
Handball		X	X										X	X	X	X
Movement explora-tion		X		X	X	X	X									
Orienteering		X	X												X	X
Physical fitness/conditioning		X	X	X	X	X	X	X	X	X	X	X	X	X	X	X
Racquetball		X	X					X	X	X	X	X	X	X	X	X
Recreational /group games	X		X	X	X	X	X	X	X	X	X	X	X	X	X	X
Riflery		X	X												X	X
Self-defense		X	X								X	X	X	X	X	X
Soccer/speedball	X							X	X	X	X	X	X	X		
Softball /mushball	X		X					X	X	X	X	X	X	X		
Table tennis		X	X					X	X	X	X	X	X	X		
Tennis		X	X					X	X	X	X	X	X	X		
Touch football	X		X					X	X	X	X	X	X	X		
Track/field		X			X	X	X	X	X	X	X	X	X	X		
Tumbling/self-test-ing		X		X	X	X	X	X	X	X	X	X	X			
Volleyball	X		X				X	X	X	X	X	X	X	X		
Weight training/weightlifting		X	X											X	X	X	X
Wrestling		X										X	X	X	X		

*From *Motion and direction*. Indiana State Department of Public Instruction, 1977, pp. 43-44.

fairly common needs and purposes of children and youth—realizing that these differ at different maturity levels—we nevertheless realize that purposes are individual. John may want to learn to play football to overcome a feeling of inferiority and inadequacy. Mary may be interested in modern dance to overcome awkwardness and develop a more socially acceptable figure. Terri may want to learn to play tennis to satisfy the desire for a sense of achievement or mastery, whereas Tony is interested in social acceptance and recognition.

Physical education activities mean many things to many people. We see that the activities are not merely ends in themselves but possible means by which children and youth solve some of the persistent problems of living.

The following units in Part Two will graphically illustrate the relationships that exist between student age characteristics, developmental objectives, and activities.

REACTORS

1. Teaching moral values as a separate part of a school curriculum is a questionable response to an unquestioned need. Lessons in character cannot be "clamped on" like a gadget to some corner of the educational program.
2. Physical education activities should be purposeful, natural, and useful rather than for the entertainment of others or to uphold traditions.
3. Norms and achievement standards for physical education activities should be the result of valid research results.
4. Pupils should understand to the limits of their ability the scientific ends we are trying to accomplish by means of physical education activities.
5. By "changing the curriculum" do we mean changing the experiences of boys and girls?

SITUATIONAL PROBLEMS

1. The high school principal stands before her faculty members who are about to embark on the cooperative venture of reevaluating their school curriculum. She points her finger in the direction of the physical education teachers (for no apparent reason) and says, "Somewhere along the line in our curriculum study we, as a group, must take hold of the basic psychological factors involved in meeting the 'needs' of youth. What do people need for optimum happiness and adjustment? The recent survey by our students entitled, 'What I Expect the High School to Do for Me' highlighted the following expectations of these students:
   a. To help find what interests me most
   b. To help me get along with other people
   c. To prepare me for college
   d. To help me develop physically and keep well
   e. To help me in my social adjustments
   f. To understand the studies I am taking
   g. To give me an all-around education
   h. To help me be a good citizen
   i. To teach me to study more effectively
   j. To develop my personality
   k. To make good friends
   l. To build character
   m. To give me a better understanding of world problems
   n. To teach me to take on responsibility and carry through with it
   "I challenge each of you to formulate selective criteria based on these expectations representing value judgments that will aid you in the selection of learning materials and experiences most appropriate for the meeting of their needs and expectations."

   In addition, a teacher of physical education in this school assumes that an activity is valid and significant only if it satisfies at least one of the criteria given. Indicate after each how some learning experience in physical education may be organized to satisfy the criterion in question.

LEARNING ACTIVITIES

1. List three criteria that would aid in the selection of physical education experiences for each of the following main headings:
   a. Criteria related to the overall objectives and purposes of the school as a whole
   b. Criteria related to the learning process
   c. Criteria related to the needs of youth
2. Devise a comprehensive list of physical education activities through library research. Do not impose limiting criteria, such as equipment, facilities, personnel, environment, or location.
   a. Select major activity headings (e.g., team activities) and group the activities under the appropriate headings.
   b. Categorize the activities as appropriate for the basic program, intramural programs, and athletic programs.
   c. Classify activities as most appropriate for the school grade level.
   d. Design the following chart:
      (1) A horizontal column indicating the general objectives of physical education
      (2) A vertical column indicating the major activity headings from 2a
      (3) Using a 10-point scale (10 = high and 1 = low), use your best judgment in rating the potential contribution of the activity to each of the objectives
      (4) Total and compute an average for each horizontal and vertical column
3. Survey an elementary, middle, junior high school, and high school as to:
   a. Facilities (indoor and outdoor)
   b. Personnel
   c. Equipment
   d. Supplies
   e. Community resources
4. Based on the survey, select appropriate activities for that situation and for each school division.

UNIT EVALUATIVE CRITERIA

Can you:

1. Interpret the relationships between objectives to be achieved and curricular experiences that students should be provided to achieve the objectives?
2. Select activities appropriate to the criteria of facilities, environments, equipment, supplies, and personnel in school organizational schedules?
3. Identify the sources of criteria for the selection of physical education experiences at a given grade level?
4. Explain the procedures and state a rationale for their use in selecting experiences for a physical education curriculum?

RESOURCES

AAHPER. DGWS sports guides. Washington, D.C.: The Alliance.

AAHPER. How we do it game book. Washington, D.C.: The Alliance, 1959.

Annarino, A. A. Teaching soccer in physical education. Cincinnati: Tri-State Co., 1956.

Annarino, A. A. Teaching tumbling in physical education. Cincinnati: Tri-State Co., 1956.

Annarino, A. A. Teaching volleyball in physical education. Cincinnati: Tri-State Co., 1962.

Annarino, A. A. Developmental conditioning for physical education and athletics. St. Louis: The C. V. Mosby Co., 1976.

Annarino, A. A., & Purvis, D.: Calisthenic programs for physical education. Cincinnati: Tri-State Co., 1961.

Baley, J. A. Gymnastics in the schools. Boston: Allyn & Bacon, Inc., 1965.

Broer, M. Individual sports for women. Philadelphia: W. B. Saunders Co., 1971.

DeWitt, R. T. Teaching individual and team sports. Englewood Cliffs, N.J.: Prentice-Hall, Inc., 1972.

Dintiman, G. B. A comprehensive manual of physical education activities for men. New York: Appleton-Century-Crofts, 1970.

Dratz, J. P., & Coker, H. L. Men's physical education handbook. Dubuque, Iowa: William C. Brown, Co., Publishers, 1961.

Fait, H., Shaw, J. H., & Fox, G. I. A manual of physical education activities. Philadelphia: W. B. Saunders Co., 1956.

Hess, L. A. Merrill sports series. Columbus, Ohio: Charles E. Merrill Publishing Co.

Lees, J. T., & Schellenberger, B. Field hockey. New York: Ronald Press, 1971.

Moody, D. L., and Hepner, B. J. Modern foil fencing: fun and fundamentals. Calif.: B & D Publications, 1972.

Paterson, A., & West, E. L. Team sports for girls. New York: Ronald Press, 1971.

Physical education activities series, 31 vols. Dubuque, Iowa: William C. Brown Co., Publishers.

Saunders physical activities series. Philadelphia: W. B. Saunders Co.

Seaton, D. C., Clayton, I. A., Leibee, H. C., & Messer-smith, L. Physical education handbook. Englewood Cliffs, N.J.: Prentice-Hall, Inc., 1975.

Sports education series. Boston: Allyn & Bacon, Inc.

Stanley, D. K., & Waglow, J. F. Physical education activities handbook for men and women. Boston: Allyn & Bacon, Inc., 1966.

Umbach, A. W., and Johnson, W. R. Successful wrestling: its bases and problems. Dubuque, Iowa: William C. Brown, Co., Publishers, 1972.

Wadsworth sports skills series, 26 vols. Belmont, Calif.; Wadsworth Publishing Co., Inc.

Play is the child's life, he lives on it and reveals himself through it.
AMY R. HOLWAY

9 Nursery school and kindergarten

CONTENTS   **Perspective**
Activity program
Organization and planning

COMPETENCIES

After completing this unit, you should be able to:

Understand and appreciate the meaning and value of play.

Recognize distinct periods in the growth and development of a child from ages 3 to 6.

List and define fundamental locomotor, nonlocomotor, receptive, propulsive, and other perceptual motor abilities.

Organize and plan a physical education daily and yearly program for a nursery school and kindergarten.

Define the following:

Movement exploration
Perceptual-motor abilities
Perceptual-motor development
Sensory-motor development
Unlearned cores of behavior
Play leadership
Direct supervision
Recess
Creative tendency
Play therapy
Manipulation
  Unspecified
  Specific
  Meaningful
Pre-school
Nursery school

PERSPECTIVE

PRINCIPLE: At play, the child does not merely manipulate things; ideas, as well, are manipulated.

Children enact in their own spheres all the activities they observe in the larger world about them and by so doing are educating themselves with customs, actions, people, and things. The motive behind the physical expression of these mental images is the activity drive, the desire for and love of activity—"function pleasure" in movement. The results in terms of education are growth in power to observe, to imagine, to accumulate and organize knowledge of environment, and to express these in body movement that forms a basis for psychomotor development.

As civilization advances and we become more and more city-dwelling people accustomed to the passive pastimes of watching others in activity on television or in the movies and there is neither space nor provision for children's play, we grow farther removed from the environment in which self-education beyond the earliest years of childhood is possible. We ignore at our own risk the biological development of the human species. It is more important than ever that we understand and appreciate the meaning and value of play. If we do this to the point of providing ample time, space, facilities, and leadership for the play of children, we are providing a most valuable means of real education in which the young child participates spontaneously and with abounding joy.

Genetically, we recognize distinct periods in the growth of a child: infancy, prepuberty, puberty, adolescence, postadolescence. In curriculum planning and devel-opment we account for these periods and the various developmental or age characteristics of children at each level. We recognize that each stage of development brings certain irresistible impulses—tendencies to actions of certain kinds. Each period seems to indicate that certain activities are so prominent that we must conclude that they result from certain directional forces from within the child as well as certain directional forces from the environment outside the child. There is a time when children are intense in their desire to learn to crawl, walk, skate, dance, swim, play ball, and so forth. They will expend enormous amounts of energy and endure much fatigue to become expert in these activities. This, then, is the age when they should learn these things or be afterward deficient in them and in the particular related social and emotional development that invariably accompanies these motor skills.

At the age of 5 or 6 years, children's impulses express themselves in free, active, spontaneous play. Their individual concepts are very simple and crude. They are strongly individualistic and have little interest in group games. They are essentially nonsocial. Interest is centered in the activity itself and not in a remote end, as in adult play. The motive is joyful use of their own bodily powers for the pure fun of doing. They are not respecters of traditions. Each is a law unto himself/herself. The native interest at this age is in such racially old activities as running, climbing, jumping, pulling, pushing, throwing, and digging, through which large fundamental groups of muscles are developed.

Given a favorable opportunity, these unlearned cores of behavior (often referred to as "instincts" in our older literature) will find expression in self-made games and play. However, now that space is restricted and there are large groups of children, or where other circumstances make impossible this freedom of movement and liberty of action, the physical education curriculum can provide the child with wholesome substitutes in the form of a variety of movement experiences. In place of fences and trees to climb, we can supply jungle gyms, horizontal ladders, climbing ropes, and swings. The development of perceptual-motor abilities becomes an integral outcome of play activities. Through throwing and catching activities, the child develops the ability to perceive objects in space and can learn to focus his/her attention on a selected number of specific stimuli from a mass of sensory intake. Kicking activities give an observable indication of a child's dominancy movement in low-structured game activities requiring a sense of laterality. Individualistic tag games provide a body image awareness as a physical being occupying a space. Target throwing with a bean bag or ball establishes the child's ability to coordinate vision with gross movement skills. Children can externalize concrete mental images when they imitate by playing horse, bear, fireman, train, or auto, and engage in other mimetic activities. Most important at this nursery school–kindergarten age, when children are imaginative and inventive to a marvelous degree, is the true individual expression that results from these movement experiences.

Activity experiences for this age group can be somewhat structured, but the curriculum planner or teacher should not disregard the "play" concept and its importance as a factor in education.

As stated earlier, at play, the child does not merely manipulate things; ideas, as well, are manipulated. In play, some factor urges the organism to express itself. Usually some inner desire of the child is seeking an outlet—some outlet denied by the adult environment. Physical education should structure an environment abundant in situations and materials that will lead to activity—purposive planning and resultant manipulation of the body and objects. Toys (trucks, balls), materials (clay, dishes), equipment (swings, ropes, balance beams, jungle gyms) are simply stimuli that arouse the play response and enable the child to explore, construct, and control a world of his/her own.

One must be aware of the difference between play supervision and play leadership versus domination of children's play. Although children at this age crave activity and life intensely, the young child's imagination outruns his/her skill and judgment. His/her resources are limited, attention fleeting, and enthusiasm breaks down. Even though the child rebels at domination, he/she is constantly seeking for aid in achieving desires, and when leadership (not domination) is given and accepted, he/she will submit to endless direction. Thereby, activities become more satisfying and educationally different.

At this age children enjoy games with much repetition but of short duration, in which the climax is quickly reached, that make very slight demand on the attention, and that require very little endurance. Long before children are ready for sports as such, they begin to build vitality and develop their bodies through play. At first they develop the large muscles by learning to walk, jump, swing, roll, climb, push, pull, and dig. They experiment again and again and learn to manipulate their bodies by the trial-and-error method. They learn to make their legs and feet take them where they want to go and their arms and hands do what they want them to do. Later when these basic skills are mastered, they concentrate on gaining more specific coordination of the smaller muscles. They learn that objects have different color, texture, weight, and sound. They learn to use fingers more skillfully in fashioning objects out of clay, in cutting figures from paper, in stringing spools, and in drawing lines that can later be recognized as pictures or printing.

Thus the physical education program begins in the home or the nursery school with the preschool child. When, in the first grade, we see a 6-year-old girl who jumps rope skillfully and rapidly in time with a singing chant, we realize that she has achieved this coordination of body muscles and the eye and ear through her earlier years of play.

ACTIVITY PROGRAM

The term *activity program* is most applicable to the nursery school–kindergarten curriculum. It should provide a series of well-selected activities suitable to preschool children and offer opportunities for children to explore movement through experimentation and problem solving.

The program must be integrated and correlated with the rest of the class program. It must, among other things, take into consideration the following:

1. Ages of children
2. Number and preparation of teaching personnel
3. Place of parents or aides in the program
4. Weather
5. Arrangement of rooms, facilities, equipment, and the indoor and outdoor spaces involved
6. Hours
7. Grouping of children
8. Other class activities
9. Play and work periods
10. Objectives and outcomes

The program for nursery school–kindergarten children should consist of six major activity areas, namely, movement exploration, rhythmical activities, developmental activities, games, self-testing, and perceptual-motor skills.

Movement exploration is a general classification. It may be used as an instructional technique or activity. As a technique, the teacher may present a problem or situation that permits creative expression through movement. As an activity, it uses mimetics, story plays, and small equipment and apparatus to develop fundamental movement skills.

Rhythmical activities consist of creative movement, singing games, and fundamental rhythmical movements.

Developmental activities should contribute to strength, endurance, agility, balance, flexibility, and good posture. Many standard exercises can be modified for this age group with the emphasis on mimetics (hopping bunny, galloping horses, etc.).

Games can be modified as to rules, strategy, and skills. Low-organization games should be used that involve body and object manipulative skills or, more specifically, locomotor and nonlocomotor movement skills, propulsive and receptive movement skills, and other perceptual motor abilities.

Self-testing includes the use of apparatus and small equipment, such as balance beams, incline board, climbing ladders, jungle gym, and ropes. It will also include individual stunts, partner stunts, individual tumbling stunts, partner tumbling stunts, and simple pyramids.

Perceptual-motor skills encompass all voluntary motor acts. There is some limited evidence to indicate that specific improvement in these abilities may transfer to academic learning disabilities. Selected activities in this area should aid in the development of laterality, body awareness, spatial relationships, visual perception, and auditory acuity. These perceptual qualities are inherent in the other activity areas.

ORGANIZATION AND PLANNING

In organization and planning, the maximum use of the outdoor playground area for a guided program or for free play (recess) should be considered. The playground is an institutional center for child life and a substitute for the environment that existed and educated children in all facets of life years ago. The playground, under the supervision of experts in child development, supplies a variety of activities and experiences that satisfy the developmental needs of children. It can be a laboratory for the development of social behavior as well as physical skills. Its experiences can be the foundation for a value system. In this phase of education, the physical education or classroom teacher can be a positive influence for its effectiveness.

The following activity classification and time allotment table indicates recommended major activity areas and percentages for the nursery school–kindergarten program.

ACTIVITY CLASSIFICATION AND TIME ALLOTMENT

Activities	Nursery school (%)	Kinder-garten (%)
Movement exploration	10-20	20-30
Rhythmical activities	20-30	20-30
Developmental activities	5-10	10-15
Games (low organization)	10-20	20-30
Self-testing	20-30	10-30

REACTORS

1. Children do not have to be taught to play.
2. Children express through play how they feel about what has happened to them, although they may not reproduce what actually happened.
3. Young children identify themselves with the world about them, which inspires stories of animals who keep house, think thoughts, and have conversations just as they do.
4. Play differs from work. Artistic work differs from work on the assembly line.
5. Today's playground is a laboratory of social behavior.
6. The child does not merely manipulate things; ideas, as well, are manipulated.
7. Each developmental stage seems to indicate that certain activities are so prominent that they result from directional forces from within the child as well as directional forces from the environment.
8. Unlearned cores of behavior (instincts) will find expression in self-made games and play.
9. "Every little boy has inside of him an aching void which demands interesting and exciting play. If you don't fill it with something that is interesting and exciting and good for him, he is going to fill it with something that is interesting and exciting and isn't good for him." (T. Roosevelt)

LEARNING ACTIVITIES

1. Observe the characteristics of the young child.
   a. Differentiate between the nursery school–kindergarten child as to physical and social characteristics.
   b. Note developmental characteristics.
2. Observe at least three preschool children at some form of activity:
   a. Record specifically and briefly what you observe concerning each child's behavior.
   b. File the data for each child on a separate 5×7 file card with the child's age and sex at the top.
   c. During class, all class members pool their cards; separate and categorize the cards by age and sex.

d. Give each category to a class member.

e. Summarize and report the findings.

3. List all the desirable and possible activities for nursery school–kindergarten programs under the following headings:

Circle games	Mimetics
Ball activities	Simple apparatus use
Rhythmical activities	Stunts
Story plays	Low-organization games
Simple dances	Self-testing
Exercises	

a. Devise a chart with horizontal heads for 3-, 4-, 5-, and 6-year-olds and a vertical column listing the activities just given.

b. Indicate by a check the appropriate activity for the age group.

4. List desirable materials and equipment for nursery school–kindergarten children.

5. Illustrate by example each of the three methods of handling play materials:

a. Unspecified manipulation (usually before 2 years).

b. Specific manipulation (consider the nature of the material).

c. Meaningful manipulation (adapted to the problem).

UNIT EVALUATIVE CRITERIA

Can you:

1. Define play and identify specific outcomes for the nursery school–kindergarten child?

2. Identify stages of growth and development for these age groups and formulate implications for physical education activities and experiences?

3. Design a daily, weekly, and yearly physical education program for nursery school–kindergarten?

4. Observe children at play and identify positive and negative social behavioral traits?

5. Determine the effect of a physical education program on perceptual-motor learning and cognitive development?

6. Synthesize the research related to perceptual-motor training and its contribution to improving academic learning disabilities?

RESOURCES

AAHPER. *The significance of the young child's motor development.* Washington, D.C.: The Alliance, 1971.

AAHPER. *Echoes of influence for elementary physical education.* Washington, D.C.: The Alliance, 1977.

Aitken, M. H. *Play environment for children: play space, improvised equipment, and facilities.* Bellingham, Wash.: Educational Designs and Consultants, 1972.

Annarino, A. A. *Fundamental movement and sport skill development.* Columbus, Ohio: Charles E. Merrill Publishing Co., 1973.

Arnheim, D. E., & Pestolesi, R. A. *Elementary physical education: a developmental approach* (2nd ed.). St. Louis: The C. V. Mosby Co., 1978.

Blocks, S. D. *Me and I'm great: physical education for children three through eight.* Minneapolis: Burgess Publishing Co., 1977.

Corbin, C. B. *Inexpensive equipment for games, play, and physical activity.* Dubuque, Iowa: William C. Brown Co., Publishers, 1972.

Corbin, C. B. *Motor development.* Dubuque, Iowa: William C. Brown Co., Publishers, 1973.

Dauer, V. *Essential movement experiences for pre-school and primary children.* Minneapolis: Burgess Publishing Co., 1972.

Espenschade, A. S., & Eckert, H. *Motor development.* Columbus, Ohio: Charles E. Merrill Publishing Co., 1967.

Fait, H. F. *Physical education for the elementary school child.* Philadelphia: W. B. Saunders Co., 1976.

Flinchum, B. *Motor development in early childhood: a guide for movement education with ages 2-6.* St. Louis: The C. V. Mosby Co., 1975.

Gallahue, D. *Motor development and movement experiences for young children.* New York: John Wiley & Sons, Inc., 1976.

Gallahue, D. L., Werner, P., & Luedke, G. *A conceptual approach to moving and learning.* New York: John Wiley & Sons, Inc., 1975.

Gerhardt, L. *Moving and knowing: the young child orients himself in space.* Englewood Cliffs, N.J.: Prentice-Hall, Inc., 1973.

Latchaw, M., & Egstrom, C. *Human movement.* Englewood Cliffs, N.J.: Prentice-Hall, Inc., 1969.

Logsdon, B., et al. *Physical education for children: a focus on the teaching process.* Philadelphia: Lea & Febiger, 1977.

The world goes forward on the feet of little children but the adults in the world build the road those feet are to travel.

RUTH ANDRUS

10 Grades 1 and 2

CONTENTS   Perspective

Activity charts

COMPETENCIES

After completing this unit, you should be able to:

Identify, interpret, and validate principles underlying a physical education program for children in grades 1 and 2.

Select activities and experiences for grades 1 and 2 based on physiological, psychological, and sociological factors.

Design performance objectives from developmental objectives to be achieved by first and second graders.

Organize activities into a meaningful curriculum pattern for grades 1 and 2.

Define the following:
Development
Chronological age
Maturity
Readiness

PERSPECTIVE

PRINCIPLE: The life of young children is a mingling of fact and fancy with everything so new that they have not learned to distinguish reality from fancy as adults do.

Our philosophy consists of the ultimate presuppositions and principles that guide our thinking and action. Here are listed a few of the principles that serve as "light to the eyes and a lamp to the feet" when dealing in physical education with children in grades 1 and 2.

1. Development means the process of becoming; the expression of heredity in a favorable environment—progress toward maturity.
2. Chronological age is a crude index to maturity. Children develop at different rates. Education should be geared to the course of human development. The first six years are the most important and vital that the child will ever experience because they are the first.
3. Maturity is related to growth and developmental characteristics.
4. "Readiness" refers to maturation and represents the time at which the child is able to profit by instruction. The goals of education should be in line with goals of development.
5. After children reach a certain stage of development, they can do easily and quickly what they could not do even with much training at an earlier stage.
6. The long period of human infancy and childhood decreed by nature is the important period that determines the man or woman yet to be. It takes time to grow up!
7. The experiences children have, at any stage of their growth, are just as important to them at their level of maturity as our adult experiences are to us.
8. We use the child development approach in planning the physical education curriculum when we apply the facts and principles learned from the actual study of children themselves.
9. We must keep the idea of interrelatedness of development in mind. Motor development is related to social development, since, in the elementary grades, a child's social contacts with age-mates are to a large extent made through play activities.
10. Children lacking physical strength and skill have few social contacts. Having less strength and skill, strong emotional reactions, such as fear and anxiety, result when they are confronted with situations demanding strength and skill. Feeling "different," they tend to avoid play situations and so begins the circle of events inimical to his best total development.
11. The growing child is our center of interest when we consider curriculum development. The implications are that physical education teachers will ascertain, if possible, the potential capacities of their pupils and bring these children into contact with such experiences in their natural and social environments as will stimulate optimum physical, psychomotor, affective, and cognitive development.

AGE CHARACTERISTICS (Grades 1 and 2)

To understand the play of children requires knowing many things about them: their stage of development, other ability to coordinate, and the extent to which their respective interest spans allow concentration on any one form of play material. We must know when they first enjoy playing alongside other children and in groups. We must understand the imagination with which they conceive and elaborate their play and games that they invest with so much meaning to themselves and that are so often not understood by adults. The play life of young children is a mingling of fact and fancy with everything so new that they have not yet learned to distinguish reality from fancy, as adults do. The teacher of physical education can educate children adequately only to the extent to which he/she understands them.

Physiological characteristics
1. Reaction time slow; coordination poor; need a large variety of large muscle activities; enjoy fighting, hunting, chasing, and climbing.
2. Active, energetic, and responsive to rhythmical sounds.
3. Bones soft and easily deformed.
4. Hearts easily strained.
5. Sense judgment and perception developing.
6. Eye-hand coordination developing; still inept in use of small muscles.
7. General health precarious; susceptibility to disease high and resistance low.

8. Loss of deciduous teeth.
9. Constantly active, sitting or standing; love chasing, being chased, exploring, and climbing.

Psychological characteristics
1. Short attention span.
2. Curious, want to find out things; inquiring natures.
3. Development of ability to control organs of speech.
4. Repetition of activities enjoyed.
5. Reasoning ability limited.
6. Interested in almost everything.
7. Creative desire present; highly imaginative.

Sociological characteristics
1. Dramatic, imaginative, and imitative; curiosity strong.
2. Enjoy fighting, hunting, chasing, and climbing.
3. Right is that which wins approval or provides satisfaction; annoyed by conformity.

Grades 1 and 2
CURRICULUM DESIGN—RECREATIONAL ACTIVITIES

Noon hours, after-school hours, and Saturdays provide periods of informal group relationships so attitudes, and for building desirable personality attributes. Starting with second graders, games, short treasure hunts, "dress-up" costume parties, and similar activities provide not only pleasurable activity

Development objectives		
Cognitive	**Affective**	**Psychomotor**
Know several individual and several group activities for after-school play	Learn the spirit of "give and take" in group play	Develop ability to use skills learned in school in after-school activities
Understand the value of new friends	Develop respect for school equipment and others' property	Have the personal resources and skills to be busy and happily active when alone
Know how and what to suggest for group recreational activity	Learn to give and follow directions	Have adequate endurance to keep up with peers
	Appreciate the need for group planning	
	Learn to value group activities and "feel at home" in a group	

4. More enjoyment through nature, pets, and stories.
5. Participate as much as possible in playing games; play best in groups of three or four.
6. Do not accept criticism well.
7. Do not lose graciously.
8. Like to be the center of the stage; enjoy being "it."
9. Individualistic, independent, self-assertive, daring, and adventurous.
10. Casual comradeship, chums changing from time to time.

ACTIVITY CHARTS

The charts on pp. 100 to 113 illustrate the relationships between developmental characteristics, objectives, and activities. Each activity area or curriculum content provides opportunities for achievement, growth, and development. The developmental objectives and evaluative criteria can be used as bases for designing performance objectives specific for each activity and grade level.

The activities presented in the following charts do not constitute ready-made units for the designated activity area. They are suggested activities and are not all-inclusive but should provide assistance in formulating and developing more fully each aspect of the curriculum. Serious consideration, at this level, must be given as to whether the activities are to be taught by a physical education specialist or by a classroom teacher. Further consideration must be given to integrating and correlating physical education activities with classroom activities.

Text continued on p. 114.

necessary for putting to use what is learned in the physical education periods, for creating social hikes, parties, story-telling trips to places of interest, nature study, apparatus stunts, swimming, but also opportunity for planning and carrying out certain responsibilities.

Suggested units	Suggested activities	Evaluation criteria
Free-time fun	Singing games (ten little indians) Dress-up party Dramatic activities Story plays Handicrafts Story telling Trips to places of interest	Who participates? Who avoids participation? What children seem to be poorly adjusted socially? What evidence is shown of improved social awareness by broader inclusion of others as friends?
Making new friends	Treasure hunt Roller skating party Picnics Halloween costume party Toasting marshmallows Beach party Fun in the snow (fox and geese) Sledding, skating, sliding	Are children growing in ability to take some responsibility in planning and carrying plans to completion? Are they contributing ideas and suggestions during the evaluation period after some special event?

Grades 1 and 2
CURRICULUM DESIGN—AQUATICS

Aquatics, in the broad sense, refers to any sport practiced on or in the water. For first- and second-
wheels, sailing boats, skipping stones, playing water tag or "Find the Coin," riding on rafts, or going
drive"—doing something and having something happen as a result—and to the increased freedom of
that a sand pile, a roomful of toys, or the playground apparatus is enjoyed.

Developmental objectives		
Cognitive	**Affective**	**Physical and psychomotor**
Understand the need for sanitation—why take a soap bath, before swimming in pool	Learn to cooperate with the teacher and to do their best	Learn correct methods of elementary strokes
Know the safety value of learning to swim	Understand proper behavior (etiquette) in the water	Develop proper breathing
Develop wholesome respect for water—water can be a friend	Appreciate that activity in water can be fun	Be able to apply a sense of rhythm to swimming movements
Understand the importance of following regulations and instructions	Appreciate safety precautions around water for themselves and others	Make progress in developing endurance
Know the bare fundamentals of swimming	Develop confidence in the water	Develop the use of buoyancy as applied to floating
Understand how to breathe properly while in the water		
Know when and when not to go into the water		
Understand the principles necessary to be successful swimmers		

grade children it may mean playing with water, pouring, wading, splashing, building dams and water swimming. Love of paddling, wading, and swimming is due in a large measure to the "activity the body when fewer or more comfortable clothes are worn. Water is enjoyed for the same reasons

Suggested units	Suggested activities	Evaluation criteria
Feeling at home in the water *or* Making water your friend	Blowing bubbles while exhaling with face under water Walking across shallow end of pool Counting fingers with hands and eyes under water Picking up an object off the pool bottom Jumping into the water while holding noses Submarine float on "tummies" Turtle dive from edge of pool Motor boat breathing Mud turtle float Jelly fish float Sitting in the water Lying in the water	Are they tense or relaxed? Are they timid or fearless? Can they float? Have they learned to exhale under water and inhale out of it? Do they know how to enter and leave the pool? Can they jump or dive into the water? How far can they swim? Has a check list been made of the suggested activities listed, to see how many each child can do? Do they know and obey the safety rules? Do they know and follow the sanitary rules?
Stunts that help us learn to swim	Overarm stroke while standing waist deep, and exhaling with faces under water Mississippi steam boat Dutch windmill Dog paddle Treading water Push off, glide, and "steamboat" Glide, "steamboat," and overarm Water tag Side glide Lily pad float Push off and glide Back glide	

Grades 1 and 2
CURRICULUM DESIGN—GAMES (low organization)

Games for this age level should allow much freedom and vigorous activity. Movement activities developed, there should not be too much emphasis placed on the refining of these skills.

Developmental objectives		
Cognitive	**Affective**	**Physical and psychomotor**
Learn to catch, throw, run, and dodge through their own activity.	Learn to "take turns"	Learn eye-hand and eye-foot coordination
Be able to learn rules and their purposes through group participation	Develop courtesy regarding mistakes of others.	Understand emphasis in muscular activity is on speed and agility
Understand that for "group" success "teamwork" is necessary	Do their best; appreciate standards of achievement	Develop skill in the execution of fundamental movements
Learn how to make simple equipment with which to play (bean bags, etc.)	Learn to play in group	Develop perceptual motor abilities
Know there is a correct way to perform most activities and this correct way can be learned	Learn sportsmanship; games have rules and everyone should abide by them	
Develop some idea of physical growth and development; muscles grow bigger and stronger with use	Learn they cannot always be "it" or the leader; followers are important, too	
Invent ways of playing games more successfully	Satisfy a feeling of belonging and being wanted	
Choose activities with accident prevention in mind	Lean self-control under emotional stress of the game	
Learn to understand instructions and rules of simple games	Learn to be "fair" in choosing players	
	Develop social sensitivity	
	Learn to win without boasting or lose without an alibi	

involving running, throwing, and jumping should be used. Although muscles and skills are being

Suggested units	Suggested activities	Evaluation criteria
Perceptual-motor activities	Throwing, catching bean bags and balls of various sizes: bean bag circle throw, hound and rabbit, teacher and class	Do they have a degree of skill in throwing and catching (measured by check lists, progress charts, rating scales)?
Fundamental movement skills	Accuracy: ring toss, target throw Walking the fence: balance beam Stopping, dodging, kicking, and jumping: crossing the brook, hopscotch, statues	Do they have a degree of skill in throwing for accuracy and distance? Can the children climb to the top of a jungle gym? How many "rungs" can children traverse on the horizontal ladders?
Team games	Red rover Dodge ball Kick ball Kick the can Capture the flag Line soccer	Do the activities contribute to the development of muscular strength? Endurance? Agility? Improved reaction time? Coordination? Do the activities provide opportunities for the development of socially useful traits, such as cooperation, sympathy, tolerance?
"It" games; chasing and fleeing	Tag games: squat, channel, tree, cross, bird catcher, fox and chickens, hide and seek, three deep, midnight, black Tom, club snatch, cops and robbers	What meaning and significance do the activities have for the children? Do they engage in activities learned at school after school hours?
Relays	Inch worm Eraser In and out Jump stick Over and under ball pass Hopping	Do children know the rules and follow them? Do the children always want to be "it" or never want to be "it"? Are the children accepted by the group?

Grades 1 and 2
CURRICULUM DESIGN—RHYTHMICAL ACTIVITIES

Rhythmics are actions set to music. Children respond to rhythm in most of their bodily movements. employ imaginary elements, games with accompaniment, singing games, and various types of danc- individual capacity through the medium of music. The ability to use one's body as an instrument to emotional growth—especially at an age when some form of motor activity is the basic response to

Developmental objectives		
Cognitive	**Affective**	**Physical and psychomotor**
Learn to put ideas derived from stories, poetry, and music into movement form	Appreciate music and dancing	Acquire a fundamental sense of rhythm
Develop individual rhythmical patterns in running, walking, skipping, hopping, galloping, and sliding to music	Appreciate the fact that one can have fun dancing in a group and that it helps one make friends	Acquire ability to direct body movements according to directions furnished by the teacher
Learn the right from the left foot	Learn to experience and appreciate the rhythmical patterns of other people (Indians, Chinese, etc.)	Learn to perform fundamental movements as a partner
Identify the accompaniments for walk, hop, skip, run, jump	Enjoy dramatizing and "acting out" a story or play, telling a story in rhythmical movements	Learn to respond by changes in direction and dynamics (loud, soft, heavy, light) and by level (high, low)
Identify a simple musical phrase		Learn to beat time for walking, running, hopping, skipping
Realize that all dancing is based on rhythm		Create simple rhythmic patterns
Understand that through rhythms and dancing we can express feelings and tell stories		

Fundamental rhythms such as skipping, marching, hopping, and dramatic and mimetic rhythms that
ing all provide freedom and the opportunity to develop voluntary expressive movements suited to
express subtleties of feeling, thought, and movement is highly desirable for adequate social and
most stimuli.

Suggested units	Suggested activities	Evaluation criteria

Mimetic play	Five in a boat
	Hobby horse
	Rabbit in the hollow
		Do the children show evidence of joy?
		Can they keep time?
		Is there evidence of creativeness and
		  active imagination?
		How well can they translate feeling
		  and thought into movement?

Fundamental move- ments	Marching Skipping Running Hopping Galloping Jumping Stepping Clapping	
Dramatic rhythms: a day at the circus, toys	Animals: horses, elephants, bears Toys: bounding balls, tops, trains, toy soldiers Rag dolls	
Singing games	A-hunting we will go London bridge Muffin man	
Folk dances	Chimes of Dunkirk The crested hen Little Miss Muffet	

Grades 1 and 2
CURRICULUM DESIGN—SELF-TESTING ACTIVITIES

Self-testing activities involving fundamental skills, such as walking the balance beam slowly, bounc-children with a wide variety of activities that build skill and confidence. Stunts such as bear walk, points of carry-over outside the class period, leading to self-competition for improvement.

Developmental objectives		
Cognitive	Affective	Physical and psychomotor
Understand what they can or cannot do	Understand the meaning of kindness, sympathy, and friendliness and value these traits	Have ability to make use of simple stunts
Develop a concept of safety	Appreciate the need of sharing and "taking turns"	Use apparatus to represent trees, logs, streams
Develop respect for other person's ability	Are irritated by quarreling and arguing when the group is trying to learn skills	Have ability to make a short "approach run" for a jump
Learn that practice leads to improvement	Feel elated at their own initiative and ability to exert self-control	Develop strength, agility, endurance power
Self-satisfaction comes with achievement	Appreciate the need and value of group discipline, orderliness, and safety precautions in relation to fun and rapid learning	
Develop the concept of stunt skills to the point of carry-over to after-school play	Develop self-confidence	

ing balls, jumping rope in a variety of ways, or throwing and catching a bean bag or ball, provide
rabbit hop, flipping the pancake, and traveling across the horizontal ladder develop interest to the

Suggested units	Suggested activities	Evaluation criteria
Fun on the jungle gym	Climbing to the top of the "castle" Climbing (hands only) Hang tag "Skin the cat" Chinning	How many stunts in each category can they do? Who are the "actives" and who are the "fringe members"? Do they try these stunts on the school playground when not under instruction? How have they improved in strength, endurance, agility, power? How do they rank in terms of an achievement test using their own group for norms?
Tumbling stunts	Log roll Single squat Jump Jump and turn Backward jump Backward jump landing on one foot Wheelbarrow Human rocker	
Simple stunts: let's play circus	Bear walk Camel walk Lame duck Chicken walk Duck walk Mule kick Crab walk Frog leap Full squat Dead man Push up Front somersault Back to back rise Heel click Frog handstand	
Combative stunts	Tug of war Rooster fight King of the hill	
Track and field achievement tests: Have I improved?	Throw ball for distance and accuracy Jumping the brook: broad jump High jump Hop-skip-jump	

Grades 1 and 2
CURRICULUM DESIGN—OUTDOOR EDUCATION

Young children love to play with soil, sand, and clay. They like to roll in the grass, pile stones, dig in the soil and test in many ways their powers over materials and natural forces in the great outdoors. nature study, outdoor cooking, and other camping experiences may be enjoyed by large numbers of

Development objectives		
Cognitive	Affective	Physical and psychomotor
Learn what not to touch, what not to taste, how to find their way home, how to protect trees and plants, how to catch and clean a fish	Develop a keen "taste" and appreciation for reading based on rich outdoor experiences	Learn that walking, cutting wood, pitching tents, building fires and other camping activities will build sound bodies
Know where the sun rises and sets, read a sun dial, tell the direction of the wind, read a compass, distinguish poison ivy	Develop a love of nature that will persist in years to come	Develop skills in first aid
Learn to recognize different kinds of bugs, trees, and leaves and to enjoy the simple life outdoors	Appreciate the need for teamwork in putting up tents, building campfires, cooking meals	Learn to identify various animals, flowers, birds, trees
Learn the principles of safety and first aid	Learn not to be afraid of bugs and insects	Develop ability to tramp over rough terrain and find their way
Develop some understanding of nature and desire to conserve its beauty		Learn skills of observation and perception of things in the world of nature
Know that play in fresh air and sunshine whets the appetite and is fun		Develop ability in building fires and cooking simple foods
		Develop skills in using simple camping equipment

the moist sand with hands and feet, or shape and mold clay to their fancy. They like to till and plant Many cities set aside rugged and isolated sections of their parks as day or weekend camps where younger schoolchildren.

Suggested units	Suggested activities	Evaluation criteria
Living like Indians	Hiking to the lake Choosing a camp site Putting up the tent Gathering the wood Building the campfire Keeping the fire from spreading Paddling a canoe or rowing a boat Playing Indian games Planning the meal Cooking the meal Cleaning up Telling campfire stories: becoming a member of the tribe	What observations have the pupils made? Have they benefited socially? Did pupils participate in the planning, execution, and evaluation of the activity? Which boys and girls seem unduly tired and unable to keep up with the group? Do they understand the fundamentals of conservation? Of safety? Have they learned to recognize simple facts of nature—types and kinds of trees, cardinal points of the compass, direction of sun rising?
A class picnic	Selecting the site Planning the meal Planning the games and activities Planning the campfire program	Do children show an interest in nature? Are they afraid of the woods?
Snow games	Making a snow man Making a snow hut Making a snow fort	Has a checklist of basic skills such as making and controlling a fire, grilling a hamburger, knowing the points of the compass, and baiting a hook for fish been made? Has a checklist achievement scale for the group been compiled?

Grades 1 and 2
CURRICULUM DESIGN—DEVELOPMENTAL ACTIVITIES

The school is not a clinic providing medical services but a place for education. Good body mechanics muscle tone, organic efficiency, and absence of undue fatigue contribute to good body mechanics.

Developmental objectives		
Cognitive	**Affective**	**Physical and psychomotor**
Understand the difference between tenseness and relaxation	Develop a feeling of security through absence of physical anomalies	Learn skill in executing good body mechanics in lying, sitting, walking standing
Learn the "feel" of correct standing by training through kinesthetic sensing; know what good posture is and how to achieve it	Learn the handicapped child is aided in the prevention of loneliness, moroseness, self-consciousness, and sensitivity by building up a self-regarding attitude through opportunities rich in wholesome compensations and substitutions	Develop skill in relaxation (*This is learned!*)
Know that certain exercises help overcome weakness in specific parts of the body		Develop adequate muscle tone and strength to maintain proper body alignment
Understand that muscular strength is necessary in order to sit well, stand well, grow tall		Develop levels of strength, speed, agility, and endurance for activity participation
Understand that one must have speed, agility, strength, and endurance to play games	Appreciate good posture and grace in self and others	
	Begin to develop an awareness of what the body is capable of doing	

may be learned. Children, through kinesthetic reaction, must "feel" correct body alignment. Good

Suggested units	Suggested activities	Evaluation criteria
Building a good body (At this age children can be taught the "feel" of good posture and learn to assume good positions. A beginning can be made in "posture consciousness" even at this early stage.)	Parent- or teacher-controlled: Good nutrition, the ability to relax, freedom from fatigue Well-fitting clothes and shoes Proper seating that supports the lower back and permits the feet to be flat on the floor Sleeping on a firm flat bed without a pillow Games: Outdoor, involving running, skipping, jumping, climbing, and playing on horizontal ladder, jungle gym, etc Skip and stoop, statues, Indian walking race	Is there decreased evidence of fatigue posture? Do children know how to assume good standing, sitting, and walking posture? What percentage of the children show improved posture? Improved nutrition? Improved muscle tone? Are children's seats properly adjusted? Is there some evidence of posture consciousness? Have checklist criteria been met?
Let's grow straight posture cues: head up; chin in, neck back; abdomen flat; back straight; shoulders relaxed (not stiff or forced back); knees straight; feet parallel (weight on outer borders)	Games (adapted to posture element): Ten steps on still pond Pussy wants a corner (wall) I say stoop Hang tag Slapjack (with posture board on head) Numbers change (with posture board on head) Playing statue (emphasizing statue with correct posture) Relays: shuttle walk relay (with bean bag or posture board on head), over and under relay, crab walk relay Stunts on mats: bridging, elbow press, rocker (holding feet)	
Physical fitness: endurance, strength, agility, speed, flexibility	Fleeing and tagging games Stunts Combatives Mimetic exercises Circuit training	

ACTIVITY CLASSIFICATION AND TIME ALLOTMENT

Activities	Grade 1 (%)	Grade 2 (%)
Aquatics	0-5	0-10
Games (low organization)	10-20	20-30
Rhythmical	20-30	20-30
Self-testing	15-20	20-30
Developmental	5-10	5-10
Outdoor education	5	5-10
Recreational	5	5-10

REACTORS

1. Urbanization forces large numbers of children to live in apartments and homes with limited yard space.
2. Competence in motor activities is related to the social-emotional development in children.
3. First and second graders are involved in the activity of a simple game, cheer every time a teammate scores, and then become unconcerned about the score when the game is over.
4. Never do for a child, what the child can do for himself/herself.
5. Principles serve as "light to the eyes and a lamp to the feet" when dealing in physical education with children in grades 1 and 2.

LEARNING ACTIVITIES

1. Design a chart that identifies, contrasts, and compares physiological, psychological, and sociological characteristics between children in grades 1 and 2.
2. Formulate principles from the preceding data.
3. Select major activity areas.
   a. List the appropriate subactivities for each area
   b. Indicate time allotments by percentages
4. List the appropriate play equipment and supplies for children of these grades.

UNIT EVALUATIVE CRITERIA

Can you:
1. State, interpret, and validate principles to be used in developing a physical education program for grades 1 and 2?
2. Draw relationships between developmental characteristics, objectives, and activities?
3. Select activities and organize and design an effective program for grades 1 and 2?
4. Develop instructional units and strategies appropriate for these grade levels?

RESOURCES

AAHPER. *Echoes of influence for elementary physical education*. Washington, D.C.: The Alliance, 1977.

Aitken, M. H. *Play environment for children: play space, improvised equipment, and facilities*. Bellingham, Wash.: Educational Designs and Consultants, 1972.

Anderson, M. H., Elliott, M. E., & LaBerge, J. *Play with a purpose*. New York: Harper & Row, Publishers, Inc., 1972.

Annarino, A. A. *Fundamental movement and sport skill development*. Columbus, Ohio: Charles E. Merrill Publishing Co., 1973.

Arnheim, D. E., & Pestolesi, R. A. *Elementary physical education: a developmental approach* (2nd ed.). St. Louis: The C. V. Mosby Co., 1978.

Boorman, J. *Creative dance in the first three grades.* New York: David McKay Co., Inc., 1969.

Corbin, C. B. *Becoming physically educated in the elementary school.* Philadelphia: Lea & Febiger, 1969.

Corbin, C. B. *Inexpensive equipment for games, play, and physical activity.* Dubuque, Iowa: William C. Brown Co., Publishers, 1972.

Corbin, C. B. *Motor development.* Dubuque, Iowa: William C. Brown Co., Publishers, 1973.

Dauer, V. *Essential movement experiences for preschool and primary children.* Minneapolis: Burgess Publishing Co., 1972.

Fait, H. F. *Physical education for the elementary school child.* Philadelphia: W. B. Saunders Co., 1976.

Gallahue, D. L. *Motor development and movement experiences for young children.* New York: John Wiley & Sons, Inc., 1976.

Gallahue, D. L., Werner, P., & Luedke, G. *A conceptual approach to moving and learning.* New York: John Wiley & Sons, Inc., 1975.

Logsdon, B., et al. *Physical education for children: a focus on the teaching process.* Philadelphia: Lea & Febiger, 1977.

Metzger, P. A. *Elementary school physical education readings.* Dubuque, Iowa: William C. Brown Co., Publishers, 1972.

Vannier, M., Foster, M., & Gallahue, D. *Teaching physical education in elementary schools.* Philadelphia: W. B. Saunders Co., 1973.

We look for and find projections of freedom and spontaneity in the children's graphic expressions, in their art, song and dance, their capacity for abandonment.

KATURAH WHITEHURST

11 Grades 3 and 4

CONTENTS   **Perspective**
            Activity charts

COMPETENCIES

After completing this unit, you should be able to:

Analyze the age characteristics for third and fourth graders and formulate implications for curriculum planning.

Design performance objectives from developmental objectives to be achieved by third and fourth graders.

Select activities and experiences for third and fourth graders based on their physiological, psychological, and sociological characteristics.

Organize activities into a meaningful curriculum pattern for third and fourth graders.

PERSPECTIVE

PRINCIPLE: At this age the interest in play is shifting a bit from simple joy in movement itself to some interest in the end to be attained.

At 8 or 9 years of age, children are still quite strongly individualistic, but the motive for physical activity is no longer purely a love of movement. The interest in play is shifting a bit from simple joy in movement itself to some interest in the end to be attained. "Social and sports consciousness" is beginning to appear. The desire to become recognized members of the group leads these children to notice their companions somewhat by their attainments. The result is greater effort to acquire skill. Free, spontaneous play, however, still holds the largest share of interest. Some of the basic beliefs pertinent to curriculum development in physical education at this level are as follows:

1. Guidance for the rapidly maturing young is always important. This means plentiful outdoor play for physical growth and a variety of group movement activities to encourage the child's expanding interests.
2. Early childhood, when children are less sensitive and self-conscious, sets the stage for a golden period for learning of movement skills.
3. At this age, interest in the use of the body as a medium of expressing movement is strong. "Tag" takes precedence over toys, manipulation of bats and balls over other tools or toys.
4. Sensory pleasure or "fun" is sheer joy that comes from running, jumping, using the muscles, and testing one's budding capacities. In hopscotch, roller skating, bicycling, swimming, and all forms of physical activity, the elementary years provide the period of practice in the perfection of physical education lessons already learned and in the extension of new skills.

5. Movement skills at these age levels—even as before and after—are of great importance because in our culture much social contact with other children centers around them.
6. These are years of rapid muscle growth—hence the great interest in physical activity, and the boasting of strenth, and the selection of leaders based on strength standards and skill.

AGE CHARACTERISTICS (Grades 3 and 4)

Physiological characteristics
1. Improved coordination in fundamental movement skills
2. Endurance increasing
3. Growth steady
4. Eye-hand coordination good
5. Poor posture possibly present
6. Physiologically, girls almost a full year ahead of boys
7. Permanent teeth appearing
8. Sex differences not of great consequence
9. Individual differences distinct and clear
10. Accident-proneness due to mobility

Psychological characteristics
1. Attention span increasing; developing a sense of achievement
2. Reasoning ability increasing because pupils have had more experiences
3. Imaginative; love rhythmical sounds and movements
4. Like to imitate their "ideals"
5. Interest in organized games increasing but pupils do not readily grasp complicated game rules
6. Adult approval strongly desired
7. Repetition of activities enjoyed
8. Competitive activities especially liked

Sociological characteristics
1. Easily excited; easily hurt by criticism
2. At times, like to brag

Text continued on p. 128.

ACTIVITY CHARTS

Grades 3 and 4
CURRICULUM DESIGN—AQUATICS

Where facilities and adequate assistance are available, swimming should be an integral part of the agencies like the YMCA, YWCA, or sport clubs do have them, every effort should be made for a individualized or at least carried on in small groups with similar instructional needs. At these ages

Developmental objectives		
Cognitive	Affective	Physical and psychomotor
Learn that the water will hold them up if they relax	Develop pool etiquette	Progress in ability to tread water, to float, and to master fundamental strokes
Learn that it is harder to get to the bottom than to come to the top	Develop good health habits in and around the pool	Coordinate breathing with proper movements
Learn that swimming underwater can be fun, too	Learn that safety for selves and others in and around the pool is important	Develop endurance
Learn that one who "fights" the water makes little progress	Learn that breathing with confidence in water relieves fear	Are able to dive into the water
Learn why proper breathing is necessary in the water	Learn that being able to swim develops a feeling of security	Develop proper form
Learn that safety practices are important		Know proper entries into the water
Understand that progress will come faster if they take one thing at a time		Develop the ability to swim in a straight line and to change directions
Have knowledge of water sports and how they serve and contribute to enjoyment		
Have knowledge of the basic swimming strokes		
Learn to respect and not to fear the water		
Learn that form improves with practice		
Learn that mobility in water is similar to that on land		

physical education program at all grade levels. Where schools do not have facilities and community cooperative program of instruction. Because of the wide range of ability, instruction will be largely definite and systematized instruction in the mastery of the basic strokes should be started.

Suggested units	Suggested activities	Evaluation criteria
Different methods of propulsion in water—learning fundamentals of new strokes	Kickboard Elementary crawl Dog paddle Steam boat Paddleboat Side stroke and glide Practice various swimming strokes	Has fear of water been overcome? What strokes have been learned? How far can children swim? Do they know safety rules? Do they swim in their leisure time? Are they relaxed in the water? Are they selfish or considerate of others?
Testing confidence	Dead man's float Follow the leader Jump into water Swimming underwater Recovering various objects from under the water	How far can they kick-glide? Can they open their eyes underwater? Are proper fundamentals being learned?
Water relays	Water relays	
Fun in the pool	Water rodeo Water tag	
Swim in safety	Practice correct breathing while swimming Safety skills	

Grades 3 and 4
CURRICULUM DESIGN—GAMES AND SPORTS (including games of low organization)

At this grade level we normally find most children physically and socially "ready" for some of the more
ities in line with the further development of the growing child. Captain ball, kick ball, dodge ball, and
develop skill, coupled with a growth in social attitudes and sensitivity, increases the opportunity and
Children neither learn to catch and throw correctly without instruction nor do they learn to make
these developmental objectives, and this grade level is a focal point in this process.

Developmental objectives		
Cognitive	**Affective**	**Physical and psychomotor**
Know that ability in most sports events depends on the learning of fundamental skills	Learn to accept defeat as gracefully as victory; the "give-and-take" of social life among peers is important	Develop endurance through more intensive activity
Learn that rules of most events are arbitrary but for maximum group enjoyment they should be observed	Learn to take turns and to work with a group; learn what it means to "play fair"	Learn that activity helps the individual to gradually improve movement skills
Learn how to play and be safe at the same time	Develop fundamental skills and know acceptable physiques can help in being accepted in group activities	Learn that as bones and muscles develop, activities can be performed more readily and with greater skill, as neural maturation and practice make specific coordination easier
Learn that knowledge of the game gives more enjoyment to playing	Become willing to accept the fact that some people are more skilled in some activities than others	Know that increased skill usually means increased enjoyment
Understand that the game, first of all, should be played for the enjoyment of it		Learn to obey the body's demands for rest and relaxation

highly organized individual and group games. These games represent a natural progression of activ-
soccer represent games somewhat modified to conform to abilities of this age group. Keen desire to
practice for "playing fair," being a "good sport," and developing moral judgments and values.
moral decisions "instinctively." Good teachers use teaching situations to have children achieve

Suggested units	Suggested activities	Evaluation criteria
Let's race: my place in a relay	Tag games Run couple run Line relay Fetch and carry Base running Kick the bag Run home	Is competition evidenced, yet fellowship unstrained? Do all the children join in with the spirit of the group? Is there evidence of improved reaction time, agility, speed, strength, endurance, flexibility?
Playing together: becoming a team player, let's choose sides, group play	Line soccer Newcomb Dodge ball Batball Three deep Fist fangs The beater goes round Three days Hopscotch Jacks Old gray wolf Hide and seek Pig Blind man's bluff One old cat Rounders Blackman Cowboys and Indians	Do the children know when to run, correct distance to "lead" off base, etc? Do they enjoy the game? Do the show signs of improving their sportsmanship? Can they throw overhand, underhand, sidearm? Do they have good timing for throwing and catching? Do they play games learned at school during leisure time? Do they know the rules of the game? Do they share equipment? Do they experience average success in the games? Are they improving in game skills?
Seasonal "lead-up" games with balls: soccer type, basketball type, softball type, flag football type, volleyball type	Dodge ball Kick ball Baseball Target throw Circle baseball Throwing Catching Batting balls Indoor ball Newcomb Line soccer Keep away Schlag ball	
Individual activities: track and field	Dashes Jumping Relays	

Grades 3 and 4
CURRICULUM DESIGN—RHYTHMICAL ACTIVITIES

Rhythmical activities are splendid socializing activities as well as providers of vigorous, strong, and more, the experiences should lead children out of self-consciousness and timidity into confidence and accompaniments of loud or soft clapping or chanting are possible. Each form of rhythmical activity singing games to folk dances to square dances is a normal progression.

Development activities		
Cognitive	**Affective**	**Physical and psychomotor**
Understand simple dance steps	Consider it fun to be able to dance	Have skill in performing simple dance steps
Know how to make their bodies move to the beat	Include dancing in party activities	Improve in body coordination
Find satisfaction in expression through rhythm	Consider ability to dance a social asset	Learn smoothness in movement and poise
Know that today we enjoy many forms of dance	Appreciate simple tunes, moving and dancing, and rhythm	Develop a sense of rhythm
Give own interpretation to dances	Know that the social graces are learned	Develop the feeling of balance and timing in rapid and intricate movements
Are aware that some people have a better sense of rhythm than others		Develop strength and endurance, especially in the abdominal and leg muscles
Know that rhythm helps one to relax		Improve in eye-hand and eye-foot coordination, poise, and balance
Know that rhythm helps balance and coordination		

free movements that permit children to express practically every emotion we may isolate. Further-
poise. Percussion instruments like rattles and drums may be made by the children themselves, or
should reveal a progressive development through the year and lead to more difficult forms. From

Suggested units	Suggested activities	Evaluation criteria
Let's dance	Dramatic rhythms: imitating animals, occupations Creative rhythms appropriate to seasons, holidays, etc.	Do children enjoy dancing? Is there individual interpretation? Is skill in dancing acquired? Do the children have a feeling of rhythmic patterns?
How we move	Walking, running, skipping, spinning, sliding, turning, and jumping with music	Can they turn and spin without losing rhythm? Can they dance with others?
Singing and folk games	Skip to My Lou Yankee Doodle Jolly is the Miller	Are they improving rhythmical coordination? To what degree have they mastered each dance?
The American way	Indian War Dance Going to the Circus Cowboys Thanksgiving	Are they developing poise?
Across the sea	Folk dances from other countries	

Grades 3 and 4
CURRICULUM DESIGN—SELF-TESTING ACTIVITIES

Self-testing activities should promote strength, endurance, and agility for the student while serving as ting, balancing, kicking, bouncing balls, jumping, and leaping, children move on to stunts and tum-a wide variety of materials and instill skill and confidence in their use. Progression should consider the

Development activities		
Cognitive	Affective	Physical and psychomotor
Learn that others improve by attempting to do things	Learn to establish standards for themselves	Learn that practice makes the muscles stronger; function makes structure
Learn by watching others and imitating them	Learn that self-competence can be fun	Learn that daily practice helps one to maintain and improve skills
Understand need for correct form	Develop self-confidence and are motivated to self-improvement	Understand that satisfactory performance in stunt achievement tests should be a goal
Feel satisfaction in improving at certain skills	Learn to evaluate and judge own ability	Learn that grace, poise, and muscular coordination are goals
Understand that practice develops self-improvement	Learn that increased skill receives group approval	
	Develop courage	

evaluation devices for the teacher. From the fundamental skills of catching, dodging, throwing, bat-
bling that allow for a great range of interest and ability. These activities should acquaint children with
level of agility, balance, flexibility, and strength developed by stunts previously mastered.

Suggested units	Suggested activities	Evaluation criteria
Stunts without equipment	Duck walk Leapfrog Crab walk Knee dips	Is strength of arms, legs, and backs increasing? Can they walk a straight line for balance test?
Stunts on mats Stunts on bar	Ankle throw Forward roll Headstand Cartwheel Backward roll Pyramid building Handspring Somersault	How well do they perform each stunt? Have exercises been mastered? Has courage and self-assurance been developed? Are stunts enjoyed? Is there an increase in endurance? Do they possess agility and grace? How do they rate on stunt skill tests? How far can they walk on a balance beam?
Let's play circus Climbing fences	Elephant walk Rolling, squatting, elbow balance, and foot clap Cock fight	
I can walk a plank	Walking narrow board, rail, or balance beam	
Test yourself	Stunts with soccer balls and volleyballs, Indian clubs and duck pins Through stick Jump and reach Modified push-ups Jumping, running, hopping, and climbing Gripping bar	
Ropes	Jumping Climbing	
Apparatus	Hoops Beams Wands Parachutes	

Grades 3 and 4
CURRICULUM DESIGN—DEVELOPMENTAL ACTIVITIES

This is an educational aspect of the physical education curriculum and not a clinical one. It deals with variations in structure that profoundly affect the symmetry of body development are not treated in this under the direction of a physical therapist. This unit should emphasize development.

Development objectives		
Cognitive	**Affective**	**Physical and psychomotor**
Understand correct posture	Are confident that defects can	Learn to relax when tired
Know the benefits of good eating	be corrected or compensated	Develop good nutritional habits
and sleeping habits	for	Are able to use good body
Know how to overcome deficiencies	Develop self-pride in the body	mechanics
Know how to relax	Accept themselves and work for	Overcome deficiencies as much
Know that strong muscles are less	correction	as possible
likely to be injured	Are happy with feelings of well-	Practice good health habits
Learn that proper exercise can help	being and possession of	Engage in as many skills as
to develop muscles in the correct	healthy bodies	possible
way		Work on basic exercises for
Know why healthful living is		their bodies
important		Develop in strength, endurance,
Know how to use exercise		and flexibility

Grades 3 and 4
CURRICULUM DESIGN—OUTDOOR EDUCATION

Understanding the importance of ecology, developing new and sympathetic interests in nature, and learned. This is the age to begin to work with children as a group with common, strong interests in

Developmental objectives		
Cognitive	**Affective**	**Physical and psychomotor**
Know nature as related to	Enjoy living with a group	Bring craftsmanship skills into
recognition of common animals	Develop an appreciation of	play
and plants	nature	Learn correct skills used in
Know general camping rules and	Adjust to being away from home	camping
routines (pitching a pup tent,	Respect outdoor danger, but lose	Learn use of camping tools
making a simple bed)	unfounded fears	Build up endurance by hiking
Understand the values of outdoor	Develop comradeship and	Learn precautions for the
activities, recreation, and play	companionship	protection of the feet
Understand the heritage of outdoor	Accept "safety first" as their goal	Are able to hike over obstacles of
living	Develop respect for other	nature
Learn to adapt themselves to	people's property	
distance and time in terms of		
their own abilities (on hikes)		
Know the position of the main stars		
(pointers for direction)		
Learn the position of the sun with		
respect to time and direction		

individuals and groups in the establishment of conditioning and proper body mechanics. Pathological program. These should be referred to the orthopedic physician who usually prescribes treatment

Suggested units	Suggested activities	Evaluation criteria
Let's look at ourselves	Self-appraisal after developing adequate concepts of correct body movements	Have the children developed body control?
Let's get strong	Discussion periods on general activities	Do they know and practice good health habits?
What is good for us	Practice on good body mechanics and conditioning	Do they know what good health is? Are they able to identify improper position habits used in sitting, walking, running, etc.?
Let's rest	Period of rest and learning how to relax	Do they take pride in the care and development of their bodies?
Improving our bodies	Stretching Correct walking Running	Is there improvement in fitness factors?

feeling a sense of pride and responsibility for the wildlife and natural resources of our land are outdoor activities.

Suggested units	Suggested activities	Evaluation criteria
Hiking	Short, half-day hikes	Can the children name common plants and animals?
Cooking out	Roasting food	Can they build fires safely?
Roughing it	Overnight outings	Do they appreciate nature? Do they enjoy the outdoors?
Let's make camp	Pitching a tent Star identification	Has self-confidence been increased? What common camping activities can be performed with skill?
Visiting the farm	Identifying plants and animals (collection of specimens)	Do they have the desire and ability to help others?
Snow games	Fox and geese Making angels	

Grades 3 and 4
CURRICULUM DESIGN—RECREATIONAL ACTIVITIES

Recreational activities, creative crafts, sports, music, hobbies, and camping under the leadership of ciations, and good associations. Noon-hour and after-school recreation provide numerous opportuni- the development of recreational skills.

Developmental objectives		
Cognitive	**Affective**	**Physical and psychomotor**
Accept "followership" as being as important as leadership	Learn to take setbacks without undue emotional upset	Use skills in everyday situations
Recognize their own frustrations	Find being sociable self-rewarding	Feel at home in game situations
Understand the importance of group planning	Accept rules and regulations of games	Develop sufficient skills to become desirable members of some group
Know the names and skills for activities the group enjoys	Appreciate decorum and esprit de corps	Evaluate skills in comparison with others
Learn to start or continue to play familiar games with the teacher absent	Learn to sacrifice self for the benefit of the group	Improve in recreational skills
	Improve in mental attitude	Desire to learn new and more advanced social skills
	Learn some rules of etiquette for self-conduct and dealing with others	
	Widen range of friendships; play with others besides classmates	

3. Like to tease and punch others; do not have much empathy for each other
4. "Showing off" not uncommon; display dramatic forms and actions
5. Friendly and interested in other people, but also seem to enjoy special friends
6. Strong curiosity
7. Want to belong to a group; often have special "friends"
8. Often careless in appearance; noisy and argumentative
9. Becoming more independent, but still want adult protection
10. Like group activities better than individual activities
11. Like to think that they are needed
12. Often show contradictory social traits by fighting with their best friends yet are most sympathetic when someone is hurt or in trouble
13. Assume and follow leadership in small, self-organized play groups
14. Tend to compare themselves with others and show concern over lack of skill, failure, and loss of prestige
15. Begin to recognize the needs and desires of their peers and identify with group purposes and responsibilities
16. Able to work out minor social problems at play with enough satisfaction to keep the group intact
17. Unless so taught, discrimination against children of a different race or social position absent
18. Sexual modesty more apparent

good educators may result in good habits with respect to use of leisure time, good attitudes, appre-
ties for informal group relationships that are most effective in creating desirable social attitudes and

Suggested units	Suggested activities	Evaluation criteria
Worthy use of leisure time Playing with friends Out of school play	Hikes Parties Dances Tree Tag Volleyball (modified) Croquet Picnics Free-play Marshmallow roasts Charades "Dress-up" parties	Are the children learning to wait their turns in games? Can they be followers as well as leaders? Are new friends made easily? Are they developing desirable personality attributes? Do they know and participate in several games? How are individuals rated by the group (sociometric test)? Do they show good sportsmanship?

A classification and percentage time allotment plan is presented for grades 3 and 4 from the preceding charts.

ACTIVITY CLASSIFICATION AND TIME ALLOTMENT

Activities	Grade 3 (%)	Grade 4 (%)
Aquatics	0-5	0-5
Games and sports	10-20	20-30
Rhythmical	20-30	10-20
Self-testing	10-20	20-30
Developmental	5-10	5-10
Outdoor education	5-10	5-10
Recreational	5-10	5-10

REACTORS

1. Elementary school physical education is the basis of child development and progression.
2. Children start at an earlier age to be "sports conscious" due to the emphasis on "big-time" athletes in our culture.
3. Third and fourth graders' interest in play shifts from just the joy of movement itself to some interest in the end to be attained.
4. In our culture, a great deal of social contact with other children focuses on movement skills.

LEARNING ACTIVITIES

1. Design a chart that identifies, contrasts, and compares physiological, psychological, and sociological characteristics between children in grades 3 and 4.
2. Formulate a set of principles from the preceding data.
3. Select major activity areas.
   a. List the appropriate subactivities for each area.
   b. Indicate time allotments by percentages.
4. Observe third- and fourth-grade children at play. What are they doing or playing?

UNIT EVALUATIVE CRITERIA

Can you:

1. State, interpret, and validate principles to be used in developing a physical education program for grades 3 and 4?
2. Draw relationships between developmental characteristics, objectives, and activities?
3. Select activities and organize and design an effective program for grades 3 and 4?
4. Develop instructional materials and strategies appropriate for these grade levels?

RESOURCES

AAHPER. *Echoes of influence for elementary physical education.* Washington, D.C.: The Alliance, 1977.

AAHPER. *The significance of the young child's motor development.* Washington, D.C.: The Alliance, 1971.

Annarino, A. A. *Fundamental movement and sport skill development.* Columbus, Ohio: Charles E. Merrill Publishing Co., 1973.

Arnheim, D. E., & Pestolesi, R. A. *Elementary physical education: a developmental approach* (2nd ed.). St. Louis: The C. V. Mosby Co., 1978.

Bookwalter, K., & Vanderzwag, H. J. *Foundations and principles of physical education.* Philadelphia: W. B. Saunders Co., 1969.

Bucher, C. *Physical education and health in the elementary school.* New York: Macmillan Publishing Co., Inc., 1971.

Corbin, C. B. *Inexpensive equipment for games, play, and physical activity.* Dubuque, Iowa: William C. Brown Co., Publishers, 1972.

Cratty, B. J. *Social dimensions of physical activity.* Englewood Cliffs, N.J.: Prentice-Hall, Inc., 1967.

Dauer, V., & Pangrazi, R. P. *Dynamic physical education for elementary school children.* Minneapolis: Burgess Publishing Co., 1975.

Fait, H. F. *Physical education for the elementary school child.* Philadelphia: W. B. Saunders Co., 1966.

Felshin, J. *More than movement: an introduction to physical education.* Philadelphia: Lea & Febiger, 1972.

Kirchner, G. *Physical education for elementary school children.* Dubuque, Iowa: William C. Brown Co., Publishers, 1976.

Schurr, E. *Movement experiences for children.* New York: Appleton-Century-Crofts, 1975.

Vannier, M., Foster, M., & Gallahue, D. *Teaching physical education in elementary schools.* Philadelphia: W. B. Saunders Co., 1973.

When an adult loses sight of a child as a human being, when he fails to recognize the child's presence as a person, there is no reality between them, there is no relationship.

CLARK MOUSTAKES

12 Grades 5 and 6

CONTENTS	**Perspective**
	Middle school concept
	Activity charts

COMPETENCIES

After completing this unit, you should be able to:

Specify the cause and effect of physiological and sociological variances for children in grades 5 and 6.

Interpret those variances that exist for school organizational and curriculum patterns.

Design performance objectives to be achieved in all activities for each grade level.

Select and sequentially organize appropriate activities for grades 5 and 6.

Define the following:

Middle school

Sport

Lead-up game

PERSPECTIVE

PRINCIPLE: Earlier maturing of children, expansion of recreational resources, and cultural impact are causing changes in school organizational and curriculum patterns.

This age group presents a marked change in the trend of interest in games and activity. These children are less individualistic; the motive for the activity is more subjective. The desire to organize appears, "sides" and teams are chosen. The end to be attained—unlike that in infantile play—takes on equal importance with the joy in the activity for its own sake. Games with "rules" are desired, and the game must involve keeping score. Real team spirit is still weak, for each tends to think of himself/herself as the team.

Children of this age desire to test their strength, skill, speed, and endurance with their peers in climbing, jumping, wrestling, racing, swimming, etc. The ambition to attain physical fitness, to excel their peers, supplies the motive for practice in these activities.

This is also the most suitable age for the acquisition of basic sport skills for the girls as well as the boys. Cultural stereotyping of the girl's roles is changing to widespread development of women's athletic programs and expanding work roles of women. These changes will affect the interest and needs of girls. Therefore activities selected for boys and girls for these grade levels should not differ except in such parameters as biological maturation, physiological growth, skill performance, and sociological adjustments.

These additional facts and principles should guide the planning and development of the curriculum:

1. In these grades individual differences become more numerous. Some children are experiencing the problems of adolescence, whereas others remain unchanged for the time being. In this stage of growing up, friendships fluctuate due to new interests. Boys and girls begin to show more marked differences in interests; however, group activities should be provided for both sexes.

2. By the sixth grade, most girls will have reached the menarche, whereas only half the boys have become pubescent. This creates some problems in instruction and in selection of activities. Even though this is still the skill development stage, many are becoming more "sport conscious."

3. The variations in developmental growth within these grade levels call for curriculum content and teaching-learning environments that reflect diversified needs and interests.

4. Earlier maturing by today's children, access to community recreational facilities, and the growth of public and private sport clubs provide justification for the curriculum planner to introduce games with increased organization and individual and dual activities that were formerly taught in high school programs. These are games, with modifications, such as soccer, basketball, volleyball, and football. Individual and dual activities such as golf, tennis, badminton, and archery are also included.

MIDDLE SCHOOL CONCEPT

The aforementioned facts and principles, in addition to other educational needs, are having an effect on school reorganization, for example, the introduction of the middle school concept. This organizational pattern is for children between the elementary and high school years. A typical middle school includes grades 6, 7, and 8 or a grouping of grades 5 to 8.

This reorganizational pattern will cause physical education curriculum planners to view children with a broader range of motor abilities. Sequential and progressive planning must ensure a transitional process from basic skill development to more complex learnings for each student. Consideration must also be given to changing interests and needs due to cultural and environmental changes. Administrative techniques and instructional strategies must be critically analyzed to meet these changes.

AGE CHARACTERISTICS (Grades 5 and 6)

Physiological characteristics
1. Accessory muscles more developed
2. Increasingly conscious of their bodies
3. Active games liked by boys and girls
4. Not a period of great growth in height and weight
5. Muscular strength not keeping pace with growth
6. Reaction time improving
7. Awakening interest in competitive sports
8. Sex differences appearing
9. Coordinations good
10. Bodies sturdy and healthy in appearance
11. Legs in a period of rapid growth in comparison with upper bodies
12. Noticeable difference in the strength of the boys and girls

Psychological characteristics
1. Increased interest in games of higher organization
2. Hero worship strong
3. Attention span increasing
4. High sense of pride in regard to their skills
5. Strongly concerned about their peer groups
6. Some easily discouraged, possibly giving up when unsuccessful
7. Have great confidence in adults
8. Strive to gain teacher approval
9. Have usually grasped the meaning of time and want to get things done on time

Sociological characteristics
1. Process of physical maturing accompanied by inconsistent emotional feelings
2. Desire to belong and peer differences causing confusion at this level
3. Easily excitable
4. Interest in boys shown by girls
5. Affection from adults liked
6. Emotional outbursts not uncommon
7. Respond strongly to praise and commendation
8. Critical of adults and actions
9. Boys generally not fond of girls, but girls have crushes on older boys
10. Developing a sense of pride
11. Will do almost anything to gain recognition
12. Do best work if encouraged by adults
13. Gain great satisfaction through ability to achieve; hate to lose or make mistakes
14. Desire recognition from the group
15. Teamwork greatly increased; leadership qualitites show
16. Like parties and enjoy taking part in planning and conducting them
17. Like to feel they are wanted
18. Loyal to team or gangs
19. Group interest; strongest attachments to same sex

Text continued on p. 146.

ACTIVITY CHARTS

Grades 5 and 6
CURRICULUM DESIGN—AQUATICS

Water games and stunts related to swimming, if systematically planned, can eliminate fear, build
These may all include the various important fundamentals of swimming. The fourth-grade tendency
pupil will be mastering the skills of various strokes.

Developmental objectives		
Cognitive	Affective	Physical and psychomotor
Know the different swimming strokes	Know and practice good pool etiquette	Increase skills in diving and swimming all strokes
Understand why proper breathing is necessary	Gain self-confidence	Increase endurance
Understand why a shower should be taken before and after a swim	Do not encourage nonswimmers to take dares	Increase coordination between arms and legs
Know simple ways to save a life (use of boat, stick, etc.)	Accept some responsibility for the safety of others	Are able to float and tread water
Understand that swimming requires a great ideal of energy and one can tire quickly	Learn to feel at home in the water	Improve breathing
Understand why we respect other people's rights in the water		
Understand reasons for swimming in protected areas and other safety rules		

confidence, and develop breathing and buoyancy skills as well as coordination and proper stroking.
to merely "play" in the water after learning to swim in a perfunctory fashion should be gone; now each

Suggested units	Suggested activities	Evaluation criteria
Testing confidence and buoyancy	Beginner's object finding Follow the leader Keep away Buoyancy flat Glide for distance Breathing while in water Floating Treading water	Have the children made progress in elementary swimming skills, such as ability to retrieve object in 3 feet of water, blow bubbles 12 times breathing in through the mouth and out through the nose, push off and hold glide for 5 seconds, flutter kick and glide 15 feet, and dive in and swim 25 feet?
Different methods of propulsion in the water	Human paddle Breast stroke Crawl stroke Side stroke Back stroke	Do they show evidence of increasing endurance in water? Do they demonstrate ability to progress in the various swimming strokes, such as elementary crawl, back, side, and breast strokes?

Grades 5 and 6
CURRICULUM DESIGN—GAMES AND SPORTS (including low organization and lead-up

From the fifth grade on, interest in team games is paramount. Games should be "fun," provide vig-
planned program adapts games to the maturity level of the players. At this level, "lead-up" games are
such as soccer, basketball, volleyball, football, and hockey. They give instruction and practice in
practically all the skills of the sport being taught. Contests based on these characteristic elements of
learning.

Developmental objectives		
Cognitive	**Affective**	**Physical or psychomotor**
Understand standards of good sportsmanship and cooperation	Know the duties of officials and appreciate the difficulty of their job	Develop basic game and movement skills
Understand the etiquette of various sports	Learn to adjust to other students who differ from themselves	Increase endurance as the muscles develop and coordination improves
Know and understand the rules of games	Accept followership as being as important as leadership	Improve in speed and accuracy
Make strategic judgments in game situations	Appreciate that team participation develops sociability	Develop resistance to fatigue through more intensive activity
Have some clear concepts of elementary physiology of activity	Endure hardships with teammates	Know how to relax and use rest periods
Understand the importance of game fundamentals	Feel "at home" in a group	

games)
orous activity as well as mental challenges, and be based on rules and friendly competition. A well-
important and popular. These are games involving elements and situations related to team sports
fundamental athletic skills and rules of the game, yet are part of a total game situation. They involve
each major sport make for keen interest and a resultant increase in attention, energy output, and

Suggested units	Suggested activities	Evaluation criteria
Seasonal lead-up games	Soccer tag Soccer keep away Line soccer Soccer dodge ball One old cat Schlag ball Pin baseball Newcomb Netball Spot set-up Mass volleyball Captain ball Twenty-one Three-two-one Seven spot basketball Shuttle pass	Do the children show evidence of enjoyment? Do they demonstrate a degree of good sportsmanship? Do they demonstrate conformity to the rules established by the group? Do they show a degree of skill on achievement tests? Do they play these games outside of school? Do they demonstrate fitness development with skill development?
Team sports (with modifications)	Basketball Softball Volleyball Flag football Soccer Speedball Field hockey	
Individual sports	Tennis Golf Badminton Track and field Wrestling (boys) Archery Bowling	

Grades 5 and 6
CURRICULUM DESIGN—RHYTHMICAL ACTIVITIES

Children of these ages are no longer satisfied with imitating high-stepping horses or fairies on tiptoe. the sixth grade they will perform square dances to the "calling" of one of their own group and begin

Developmental objectives		
Cognitive	Affective	Physical and psychomotor
Express rhythmical feelings in various ways Understand the differences in the basic rhythms and tempos Understand that poise and balance are achieved through dance activity Know that graceful body movements, coordination, and timing learned in rhythmical activities aid in other movement activities Understand the fundamental dance steps	Know personal feelings are expressed and "released" Desire confidence by overcoming awkwardness Seek more wholesome boy-girl relationships by dance skills Learn to cooperate with other members of a group or a partner in making delicate and graceful body movements Learn to appreciate other people's skills and abilities	Develop poise and balance Are able to perform fundamental steps Develop skill, grace, and ability in body movements Develop leg, hand, eye, and ear coordination

They now want activities involving partners and more complex dance steps. By the time they reach the fundamentals of social dance steps.

Suggested units	Suggested activities	Evaluation criteria
Dances of many lands	Fist Polka (Finnish) Crested Hen (Danish) Troika (Russian) Turn Around Me (Czech) Come Let Us Be Joyful (German) Klappdans (Swedish) Polly-Wolly-Doodle (American)	Do they demonstrate a degree of joy in the activity? Do they show a degree of improvement in dancing skill? Do they show a degree of skill in ability to interpret and express changes in accent and tempo of music?
American square dance	Captain Jinks Square Dance The Bear Went Over the Mountain Oh, Suzanna Buffalo Bill Goes Around the Outside	Do they show a degree of eagerness to participate? Do they demonstrate ability to make their own dance patterns?
Fundamental dance movements	Slide, gallop Polka Waltz Two-step Schottishe	Do they demonstrate ability to follow the patterns of others?
Contemporary dance		

Grades 5 and 6
CURRICULUM DESIGN—SELF-TESTING ACTIVITIES

Activities that are challenging and satisfy the motive for achievement and mastery yet develop and
to test their skills, but they also have a chance to show their classmates what they can do. Thus, an
children when the social drives and need to be proficient in skills become stronger.

Developmental objectives		
Cognitive	**Affective**	**Physical and psychomotor**
Determine weaknesses and limits and evaluate achievement	Develop an appreciation of their own ability and the ability of others	Are motivated toward better body appearance and strength
Know that practice develops fitness and skill	Develop confidence for participation in a group and learning new activities	Develop muscular coordination
Know different apparatus exercises and their value	Develop an interest in achieving an objective	Performs well in beginning gymnastics
Understand that self-testing activities are primarily for self-competition	Appreciate that different people learn different activities at different rates	Improve reaction time and self-protecting reflexes
Learn that one improves only by attempting to do things	Develop pride, ask, "Can you do this?"	Improve in ability, courage, and self-assurance
	Realize individual capabilities and establishment of individual standards	
	Appreciate that increased ability leads to greater group approval	

test balance, skill, strength, and flexibility are included here. Not only do children have an opportunity opportunity for the satisfaction of normal motives of recognition, group status, and the like is given

Suggested units	Suggested activities	Evaluation criteria
Can you do this?	Sit up, touching elbow to opposite knee Crane twist Jump over stick Rocking horse Cock fight Forward roll Forward barrel roll Headstand Skin the cat Nest hang	Do the participants improve in coordination and skill? Is there evidence of increased endurance? Are all the pupils participating? Is there evidence of spontaneous joy? Do children "spot" (assist) one another in the interest of safety?
Follow the leader	Simple obstacle course	
Rope	Individual jumping Partner jumping Long rope jumping Variations Climbing	
Tumbling and stunts	Rolls Springs Stands Pyramids Partner Fall exercise	
Apparatus	Beams Vaulting Horizontal ladder Side horse Stegel Low horizontal bar	

Grades 5 and 6
CURRICULUM DESIGN—DEVELOPMENTAL ACTIVITIES

In these grades physical processes are slowing up before the preadolescent growth spurt. Children in distances. The strong desire for physical achievement tests the individual to capacity. Good body

Developmental objectives		
Cognitive	**Affective**	**Physical and psychomotor**
Know the importance and practice of good conditioning Know correct body positions: sitting, standing, and lying Know factors that contribute to diet, fatigue, rest, etc. Know that physical exercises may help to maintain correct body alignment Understand the need for exercises Know some good exercises Know muscles grow stronger when used; weaker when not used Are aware of individual differences with respect to anatomical builds	Sense that everyone admires a well-developed body Develop individual pride in own development Realize that some people grow faster than others during this time Accept themselves and have good self-concepts Feel that personal satisfaction comes with improvement Develop healthy attitudes for maintaining physical conditioning	Improve strength in arms, shoulders, backs, and legs Correct defects and strengthen muscles when possible with proper exercise Strengthen correct body posture through daily habits Improve on all physical fitness parameters

these grades are throwing balls farther and lifting heavier objects with greater speed and for greater mechanics should be a concern of the teacher.

Suggested units	Suggested activities	Evaluation criteria
Body mechanics stunts	Duck walk, toes in High-stepping horses Hop toad Rabbit hop Measuring worm Human rocker Turk stand Full squat (head and back erect!) Human wicket Bridging Back to the wall test	Do the children understand the bases for good body mechanics? Can they demonstrate the ability to maintain good body mechanics? Do they show a progressive attitude toward physical improvement? Can they do the 8/12-minute run-walk for endurance? Do they show improvement on various fitness tests?
Strength development	Cargo nets Climbing ropes Weight training	
Endurance development	Circuit training Obstacle courses	
Flexibility development	Stretching exercises Stunts	
Agility and speed	Shuttle runs Dashes Zigzag runs	

Grades 5 and 6
CURRICULUM DESIGN—OUTDOOR EDUCATION

Outdoor education is now clearly recognized as an integral part of the school curriculum. By instinct To rectify one of civilization's mistakes in violating ecological laws we use playgrounds, school camps, good of the race. Let us nurture it!

Developmental objectives		
Cognitive	**Affective**	**Physical and psychomotor**
Read a map and use a compass correctly	Enjoy group activities in the outdoors	Build endurance by hiking
Know the various forms of animals, trees, flowers	Are happy away from home	Develop skill and strength in using an axe
Know the correct way to build a fire and to put it out on "breaking camp"	Learn to be accepted members of a group	Develop craftsmanship skills
Know how to cook over a campfire	Appreciate the beauty of nature	Develop skill in purposely controlling the elements of the environment
Know and can execute general camping skills	Learn to be followers as well as a leader	Develop ability to walk and carry a pack
Know proper foot care while hiking	Accept and carry out orders from those in charge	Develop skills in making a camp and using camping equipment
	Respect the property of others	Develop skill in reading nature: sun dial, stars, etc.
	Develop a sense of usefulness to a group	

and tradition children and youth are fond of the outdoors. The lure of the outdoors is the lure to health. summer camps, and overnight hikes. Nature has planted the love of the outdoors in children for the

Suggested units	Suggested activities	Evaluation criteria
Making camp for overnight	Determining an objective Finding the site How to get there What to take Sharing responsibilities Setting up a pup tent Meals Camp sanitation Fun around the campfire	Is the hiking pack small yet does it contain enough to be comfortable? Are pupils properly dressed and shod? Has the attitude check list to determine the thoughtful "good" campers been applied? Has a check been made on a brief rating scale with regard to packs, clothes, pup tents, and other equipment for each individual before starting and returning?
Outdoor cookery	Gathering twigs and firewood Laying the fire Handling a hot skillet Cooking a meal How to leave a campsite when "breaking camp": no fires, no unburied trash, etc.	Do the children show a degree of ability to select the proper type of cooking fire and fireplace needed? Do they demonstrate ability to share responsibility? Is a degree of "camp spirit" evident? Do they show evidence of joy—camp singing, cheerful help, etc.? Has an individual brief evaluation checklist by students been done, results to be discussed in class?

Grades 5 and 6
CURRICULUM DESIGN—RECREATIONAL ACTIVITIES

Most girls begin to show signs of maturing around 11 and a few in fifth grade will have reached interested in boys, in "dates," and in dancing quite some time before their male classmates are boys are just confused by the attentions aimed at them. The alert physical education teacher will children in various stages of maturity even though they may all be of the same chronological age.

Developmental objectives		
Cognitive	Affective	Physical and psychomotor
Understand that self-consciousness between the two sexes can be overcome through social recreation	Overcome self-consciousness	Develop a knowledge of and skill in social games and activities
	Develop self-control	Develop social skills useful in later life
	Establish and maintain group friendships	
Understand the need of leisure time activity	Develop stronger family relationships	Exhibit leadership in social activities and demonstrate party stunts, games, etc.
Participate creatively in organizing games and parties	Realize the value and enjoyment of companionship	
Understand that enjoyment comes through participation	Are able to relax in a mixed group	
Develop an understanding of the value of activities for later life	Learn to adjust to others' suggestions of play activity	
Understand the importance of party etiquette	Develop the feeling of being accepted by the group	

A classification and percentage time allotment plan is presented for grades 5 and 6 from the preceding charts.

ACTIVITY CLASSIFICATION AND TIME ALLOTMENT

Activity	Grade 5 (%)	Grade 6 (%)
Aquatics	5-10	5-10
Games and sports	20-25	25-35
Rhythmical	15-20	15-20
Self-testing	20-30	20-30
Developmental	5-10	5-10
Outdoor education	5-10	5-10
Recreational	5-10	5-10

REACTORS

1. This is the most suitable age for the acquisition of basic sport skills for the girls as well as the boys.
2. Activities selected for fifth and sixth graders should not differ for boys and girls without exception.
3. Children in these grades are less individual-istic; the motive for the activity is more subjective.
4. The curriculum planner is justified in breaking tradition by introducing individual and dual sports for these grade levels.
5. Since most elementary and high schools differ in organizational patterns, the middle school concept will ease the transitional proc-

menarche, whereas the majority of the boys do not mature until 14. Maturing earlier, the girls are interested at all. As a result the girls often begin to feel that they are "failures," and the less mature provide activities for boys and girls of these grades, knowing that no one type of activity can interest all Noon-hour and after-school programs of the "mixer" type are desirable.

Suggested units	Suggested activities	Evaluation criteria
How to spend your leisure time	School club activities Voluntary community agencies: YMCA, YWCA, Girl Scouts, Boy Scouts Music Dramatics Crafts Intramural athletics	Who are the "good mixers"? The "fringers"? Has an analysis of a time budget been made? What is too much extraclass activity? Has a point system of participation evolved? What should be included? What is a balanced education? What is a well-rounded personality?
Recreational skills	Shuffleboard Table tennis Paddle tennis Horseshoes Deck tennis	

ess for upper elementary and junior high schoolchildren.

LEARNING ACTIVITIES

1. Identify specific physiological, psychological, and sociological differences between fifth and sixth graders and between girls and boys.
   a. Formulate principles incorporating these differences.
   b. Translate these principles into implications for curriculum planning.
2. Select major activity areas.
   a. List the appropriate subactivities for each area.
   b. Indicate time allotments by percentages.
3. Observe a physical education program for this age group.

a. How would you improve it?
b. What would you add?
c. What would you eliminate?

UNIT EVALUATIVE CRITERIA

Can you:
1. Interpret principles based on the characteristics, needs, and interests of the fifth and sixth grader?
2. Draw relationships between developmental characteristics, objectives, and activities for the grade levels?
3. Select activities and organize and design an effective program for fifth and sixth graders?
4. Develop instructional materials and strategies appropriate for these grade levels?

RESOURCES

AAHPER. *Echoes of influence: for elementary school physical education*. Washington, D.C.: The Alliance, 1977.

AAHPER. *Essentials of a quality elementary school physical education program*. Washington, D.C.: The Alliance, 1970.

AAHPER. *Ideas for Golf Instruction*. Washington, D.C.: The Alliance, 1970.

AAHPER. *Knowledges and understandings in physical education*. Washington, D.C.: The Alliance, 1973.

AAHPER. *Physical education '73*. Washington, D.C., The Alliance, 1973.

AAHPER. *Promising practices in elementary school physical education*. Washington, D.C.: The Alliance, 1969.

AAHPER. *Trends in elementary school physical education*. Washington, D.C.: The Alliance, 1972.

Aitken, M. H. *Play environment for children: play space, improvised equipment, and facilities*. Bellingham, Wash.: Educational Designs and Consultants, 1972.

Annarino, A. A. *Fundamental movement and sport skill development*. Columbus, Ohio: Charles E. Merrill Publishing Co., 1973.

Annarino, A. A. *Developmental conditioning for women and men* (2nd ed.). St. Louis: The C. V. Mosby Co., 1976.

Bucher, C. *Physical education and health in the elementary school*. New York: Macmillan Publishing Co., Inc., 1971.

Corbin, C. B. *Inexpensive equipment for games, play, and physical activity*. Dubuque, Iowa: William C. Brown Co., Publishers, 1972.

Dauer, V. P. *Essentail movement experiences for preschool and primary children*. Minneapolis: Burgess Publishing Co., 1972.

Dauer, V. P., & Pangrazi, R. P. *Dynamic physical education for elementary school children*. Minneapolis: Burgess Publishing Co., 1975.

Daughtrey, G., & Woods, J. B. *Physical education programs*. Philadelphia: W. B. Saunders Co., 1976.

Delacato, C. H. *The elementary school of the future*. Springfield, Ill. Charles C Thomas, Publisher, 1965.

Dowell, L. J. *Strategies for teaching physical education*. Englewood Cliffs, N.J.: Prentice-Hall, Inc., 1975.

Espenschade, A. S. *Physical education in the elementary schools* (No. 27 of the series, *What research says to the teacher*). Washington, D.C.: National Education Association, 1963.

Fait, H. F. *Physical education for the elementary school child*. Philadelphia: W. B. Saunders Co., 1976.

Heitman, H. M. *Organizational patterns for instruction in physical education*. Washington, D.C.: American Alliance for Health, Physical Education, and Recreation, 1971.

Humphrey, J. H. *Child learning through elementary school physical education*. Dubuque, Iowa: William C. Brown Co., Publishers, 1974.

Kirchner, G. *Physical education for elementary school children* (3rd ed.). Dubuque, Iowa: William C. Brown Co., Publishers, 1974.

Latchaw, M. *A pocket guide of movement activities for the elementary school*. Englewood Cliffs, N.J.: Prentice-Hall, Inc., 1970.

Metzger, P. A. *Elementary school physical education readings*. Dubuque, Iowa: William C. Brown Co., Publishers, 1972.

Miller, A. G., & Whitcomb, V. *Physical education in the elementary school curriculum*. Engleood Cliffs, N.J.: Prentice-Hall, Inc., 1974.

Nagel, C., & Moore, F. *Skill development through games and rhythmic activities*. Palo Alto, Calif.: National Press, 1966.

Schurr, E. *Movement experiences for children*. New York: Appleton-Century-Crofts, 1975.

Thompson, J. C. *Physical education for the 1970's*. Englewood Cliffs, N.J.: Prentice-Hall, Inc., 1971.

Vannier, M., Foster, M., & Gallahue, D. *Teaching physical education in elementary schools*. Philadelphia: W. B. Saunders Co., 1973.

Wasserman, S. *Table tennis*. New York: Sterling Publishing Co., 1972.

Werner, P. H., & Simmons, R. A. *Do it yourself: creative movement with innovative physical education equipment*. Dubuque, Iowa: Kendall-Hunt Publishing Co., 1973.

The peer group becomes more and more important as the child moves into adolescence. Whereas it tended to supplement the home and the school in the middle childhood, in adolescence the peer group often takes priority over these institutions in its demands for the allegiance of its members.

ROBERT J. HAVIGHURST

13 Grades 7 and 8

CONTENTS   **Perspective**
Activity charts

COMPETENCIES

After completing this unit, you should be able to:

Analyze the differences in characteristics, needs, and interests between these youth and the upper elementary and high school students.

Formulate implications for selection of activities from characteristics of grades 7 and 8.

Select and organize activities in an effective sequence for grades 7 and 8.

Identify advantages and disadvantages of school patterns for grades 7 and 8.

Define the following:
Adolescence
Peer

PERSPECTIVE

PRINCIPLE: Early adolescence is a period of insecurity. At these ages the student is at the "in-between stage" of development—neither a child nor an adult.

One of the outstanding achievements of the junior high school has been its recognition of the needs of boys and girls in the period of early adolescence and its provision for the active life of these youngsters. Student councils, clubs, intramural sports, assemblies, and many extraclass activities found their initial and finest development in the junior high school. These years bridge the gap between the elementary and high schools, and a good physical education program, if well planned, can contribute much to the development of these young people at an important period in their lives.

Early adolescence is a period of insecurity. At these ages, the student is at the "in-between stage" of development—neither a child nor an adult. At this stage, youngsters are concerned about themselves. They are struggling for independence and autonomy—trying to "grow up"—but meeting many frustrations in this process. These frustrations make the transitional process from elementary school to high school a critical period for these youngsters. Other difficulties occur, such as the change from an individualized approach in elementary schools to a departmentalized high school program, the inability of some youngsters to make personal and social adjustments, and problems specific to physical education. Youngsters may not have developed proficiency in the fundamental motor skills and are confronted with more complex sport skills, compounding these frustrations.

The problems at this age level have caused educators to consider an alternative school organizational pattern. One of these alternatives is the middle school plan.

The middle school concept has minimized some of the problems cited but has also created new ones. For physical education, the organizational pattern permits more prescriptive types of programs to compensate for the wide variances in physical growth, social growth, and abilities. However, there has been a tendency to introduce more complex sport skills too early and to develop athletic skills at the expense of a progressive physical education program.

Boys and girls at these ages are at a stage of development when cooperation, team play, and organization are prominent in their thinking and feeling. Physical education activities should be varied and the skills broad enough in nature so that every youngster has an opportunity to refine those fundamental skills needed for the acquisition of more complex sport skills. A well-balanced physical education program vigorous in nature and rich in a variety of activities and experiences can provide wholesome development through the channeling of loyalties, interests, and energies into desirable educational outcomes.

Learning experiences must be provided not only to ease the transition to high school but to prepare these youngsters for life itself. The physical education teacher, and other teachers, must know and understand these youngsters and then walk with them until they are able to walk alone.

AGE CHARACTERISTICS (Grades 7 and 8)

Physiological characteristics

1. Rest needs similar to adults (8 to 8½ hours)
2. Feelings of unlimited resistance and unlimited sources of energy; tire easily but are reluctant to admit it
3. Tend to resist getting sufficient sleep; less energy for studies
4. Period of rapid growth and development; frequent health examinations important
5. Increase in appetite because of rapid growth or "finickiness" with loss of appetite
6. Increased sexual tension
7. Frequent appearance of awkwardness and poor coordination
8. Boys now faster and stronger than girls; girls over a year more mature sexually
9. Readiness for sport skills

Psychological characteristics

1. Deep desire to learn skills
2. Expend much energy in fantasies
3. Consciousness of sex
4. Interest in technical subjects and "gadgets"
5. Abstract reasoning developing more rapidly
6. Increase in attention span
7. Curious and concerned about all happenings and often worried over small matters
8. Imitation of adults prevalent
9. Enjoy practice for improvement

Sociological characteristics

1. Hero and heroine worship prevalent
2. Desire for belonging to a group
3. Recognizing morals and ethics of our culture
4. Desire for excitement and adventure
5. Emotions easily aroused and swayed
6. Strong desire for group status
7. Development of permanent friendships
8. Desire to be like classmates
9. Often shy, self-conscious, and lacking in self-confidence
10. "Show-off" attitude still present
11. Resistant to authority
12. Interests being narrowed
13. "Crushes" on the same or opposite sex
14. Tend to be moody, unstable, and restless

Text continued on p. 166.

ACTIVITY CHARTS

Grades 7 and 8
CURRICULUM DESIGN—AQUATICS

It is to be assumed that students have made regular progress in the swimming programs to which learning process extended over years of time and should not be limited to a "swimming campaign" of a instruction in school, and next to vehicular accidents, drowning is the chief cause of accidental death tional content.

Developmental objectives		
Cognitive	**Affective**	**Physical and psychomotor**
Master some of the fundamental dives	Appreciate water skills	Are able to swim at least 50 yards
Are aware of the different strokes and the usefulness of each	Accept reasons for not "showing off" while in the water	Are skillful in handling water craft such as boats and canoes
Know water safety principles and apply them	Do not try to "bully" others in the water	Are able to do at least two basic dives
Know good swimming etiquette	Respect value and caution of lifeguards	Have ability to float when becoming tired in deep water
Understand responsibilities to others	Have reasonable attitudes toward their own swimming limitations	Have ability to hold breath longer underwater
Know, understand, and obey the safety rules		Develop endurance through longer swims
		Develop good form and speed in the performance of various water activities

they have now been exposed for 6 years. Swimming is a complex skill that involves a progressive
week or so. For many boys and girls the junior high school period is the first opportunity for formal
at this age. If there has been no previous formal instruction, preentry skills should determine instruc-

Suggested units	Suggested activities	Evaluation criteria
Lifesaving	Artificial respiration Forms of rescue	Do they understand the importance of safety around water?
Diving	Back dive Swan dive Jackknife dive Running front dive	To what extent do they use community swimming facilities? Can they execute artificial respiration correctly?
Small craft handling	Canoeing Treading water for 3 minutes Rowing a boat Powerboating Straight sailing Tacking	How many "sinkers," beginners, intermediates, advanced, and junior lifesavers compared to the first of the year?
Skills	Basic swimming Beginner swimming Advanced beginner swimming	

Grades 7 and 8
CURRICULUM DESIGN—GAMES AND SPORTS

As children mature into youth we must make certain that our programs progress with them. Since in young adolescent approaching maturity a wide variety of activities that will prepare him/her to meet youngsters and are excellent means not only for developing physical fitness but also for conveying

Developmental objectives		
Cognitive	Affective	Physical and psychomotor
Know game rules and techniques Understand how body functions and its limitations Apply principles of skill games to new situations Understand the reasons for taking care of equipment Learn the importance of lead-up games for learning fundamentals Develop the ability to make changes in some games to better fit existing situations and improve strategy	Control emotions in game situations Appreciate good winners and gracious losers Accept game rules and official decisions Enjoy competition without undue worry over the outcome Appreciate the importance of teamwork Appreciate the officials' viewpoint Appreciate a high degree of performance	Develop strength, endurance, accuracy, improved reaction time Develop skill in fundamentals and are able to integrate them into game situations Have ability to relax

our rapidly changing world we can only partly anticipate an individual's future needs, we must offer the many situations with confidence. At these ages, team, individual, and dual sports appeal strongly to values that should operate in everyday life.

Suggested units	Suggested activities	Evaluation criteria
Team sports	Flag football Volleyball Basketball Soccer Softball Speedball Field hockey	In how many activities have the youth participated? Do they enjoy the games and sports? Do they accept the decisions of the officials? Have they had an evaluation of all skills, fitness, and improvement by standard achievement tests, both formatively and summatively?
Lead-up games	Volley against the wall Corner kickball Rotation soccer Game of 21 Passing, dribbling, shooting games Tournaments	
Individual and dual sports	Tennis Wrestling Badminton Archery Golf Bowling Track and field	

Grades 7 and 8
CURRICULUM DESIGN—RHYTHMICAL ACTIVITIES

Dancing of any kind should be a skillful, pleasurable performance, not drudgery. New basic or fun-
action result. "Dancing for fun" should be the slogan. The teacher should know the dance thoroughly,
whole. The formal instruction periods should be short or the pupils (the boys especially) will get

Developmental objectives		
Cognitive	Affective	Physical and psychomotor
Understand the fundamental social dance steps	Develop self-control and overcome awkwardness and self-consciousness	Have an increased sensitivity to rhythm in activities
Know that many athletic skills are performed in a rhythmical tempo	Learn to have understanding between boys and girls; the boys are often not interested in dancing at this time while the girls are interested	Develop better posture
Understand the basis for modern, folk, and group dancing		Develop body grace and control
Know dancing etiquette		Are skillful in performing several social, contemporary, square, and folk dances
Are able to express ideas in dance forms	Develop friendliness and fellowship	
	Develop poise and confidence in social activities and groups	

damental steps should be introduced gradually so that a minimum of teaching and a maximum of
teach systematically, and constantly keep each of the steps taught related to the dance pattern as a
discouraged.

Suggested units	Suggested activities	Evaluation criteria
Appreciation of the relationship of music to dance	Rhythmical patterns with names Identifying dance steps to music	Do the students enjoy the activities? Is the program enabling boys and girls to overcome self-consciousness common to junior high school youth?
Folk and square dance	Folk dances Highland Fling Harvest Frolic Take a Little Peek Dive for the Oyster	Do the students understand the values of dance? Are the students able to respond to a rhythmical pattern?
Social and contemporary dancing	Fox-trot Waltz Trends Demonstration of asking for a dance and ways of holding dance partner Ways of changing partners	Is there greater ease in changing partners? Can the students communicate their own experiences and reactions through the medium of dance movements?
Modern dance Jazz Ballet Tap dance		

Grades 7 and 8
CURRICULUM DESIGN—SELF-TESTING ACTIVITIES

Self-testing activities appeal to these youth because through these tests they are given an opportunity development, timing, and coordination. Out of a wide range of possibilities, the teacher should choose remembering that "the correct way to perform is the safe way to perform."

Developmental objectives		
Cognitive	**Affective**	**Physical and psychomotor**
Understand that self-testing exercises are for self-competition rather than for competition with others	Develop an interest in accomplishment	Develop strong arms and legs
Understand that people differ in their level of performance in activities	Develop courage and self-confidence	Develop improved coordination
Know that guided practice improves performance levels	Develop good group relationships through skill and acceptance	Develop agility, endurance, strength, balance, and flexibility
Develop a desire for accomplishment	Learn that satisfaction is received in accomplishment	Improve skill in performing fundamental stunts
Understand the fundamentals of exercise		Improve form in running and throwing
Discover weaknesses and how to correct them		
Understand their own achievements		
Know several different self-testing exercises		
Understand the "warm-up" period in sports		
Know and obey the safety rules in tumbling, stunts, and apparatus		
Identify the component parts and scoring of a routine		

to test skills and to show peers what they can do. These activities offer a valuable means of muscular
those activities that meet the interest and advance the development of the individuals of the group,

Suggested units	Suggested activities	Evaluation criteria
Self-testing stunts	Sit-ups Frog stand for time Push-ups Walk on hands Distance throwing of softball and basketball Number of baskets in 15 seconds Time and distance races	Do the students respect abilities of others? Is there improvement of throwing, form, distance, and time in various individual events? Are the students progressing in their performance of testing activities in terms of their own class? Is there pride in accomplishment? Is creativity exhibited by the development of a gymnastic routine?
Strength tests	Chinning Push-ups Vertical jumps	
Tumbling and stunts	Review basic tumbling skills Springs Somersaults Partners Pyramids Free exercise	
Apparatus	Ropes Even and uneven parallel bars Horizontal bars Balance beam Rings Horse Swedish box	

Grades 7 and 8
CURRICULUM DESIGN—DEVELOPMENTAL ACTIVITIES

The continuous flow through the orthopedic surgeon's office of adult patients with backaches, neu-
youth. From a preventive standpoint, the growing child needs trained assistance to avoid similar
mechanics, good flexibility, strength, and endurance would be solved. We have been afraid of the
levels.

Development objectives		
Cognitive	**Affective**	**Physical and psychomotor**
Demonstrate some understanding of muscle action	Know the conditioning of muscles after injury takes time and patience	Develop and maintain good bodies
Know that a conditioned body is less susceptible to injury and disease	Demonstrate a healthy response to physical activity	Show improvement in fitness factors
Understand and accept their own physical limitations	Show an awareness of what the body is capable of being	
Recognize individual differences in rates of learning various skills		
Know and practice good posture		
Know that it is usually easier to correct defects when young		
Know the relation of good diet to fitness		
Know the immediate and long-range effects of activity		
Understand the relationship of activity to body function and structure		

ritis, and foot and leg symptoms attests the consequences of faulty body alignment uncorrected in difficulties. Had this been forthcoming during the elementary grades the problem of good body words "body mechanics" and "physical fitness." They are still important educational goals at all

Suggested units	Suggested activities	Evaluation criteria
How is your posture?	Posture stunt exercises Exercises that strengthen all body muscles related to good alignment Relaxing activities, water therapy, breaststroke	Do the students take pride in developing their bodies to the fullest extent? Is improvement shown in overcoming deficiencies? Has a fitness test been administered? Have they been tested in the 12-minute run? Are skin-fold measurements taken?

Physical fitness:
  muscle endurance,
  cardiovascular
  endurance, muscle
  strength, flexibility,
  power, speed, agility
	Weight training
	Circuit training
	Interval training
	Calisthenics
	Aerobics
	Jogging	

Grades 7 and 8
CURRICULUM DESIGN—OUTDOOR EDUCATION ACTIVITIES

The deeply rooted, established relations between humans and nature cannot be ignored without loss. squeezed out of life by mechanization. Contact with nature is not only eminently healthy but subjects

Developmental objectives		
Cognitive	Affective	Physical and psychomotor
Know nature, organic and inorganic	Meet demands for getting along with others	Have ability to erect a camp and use various tools
Enjoy outdoor living and activities	Cooperate and share with others	Develop endurance, especially through hiking activities
Are able to care for themselves and others in the outdoors	Develop an outdoor hobby	Perform general camping skills
Know nature's gift to recreation	Understand safety factors involved	Demonstrate handicraft skills
Are able to test for drinking water	Overcome the fear of sleeping out and being away from home at night	Develop power and endurance in their shoulders by canoe paddling, boat rowing, and wood chopping
Demonstrate safety in camping out	Identify themselves with some group with whom they can participate in outdoor activities	Have ability to pack, carry, and erect equipment for overnight sleeping
Are able to read a map and to follow a trail	Accept responsibility of sanitary camping conditions	Demonstrate skills in use of knife and axe
Understand camp sanitation		Demonstrate cooking skills
		Have skill in building and controlling all types of fires

In the rush and racket of modern civilization we must try to replace some of the educational juice
youth to impersonal discipline and engenders humility.

Suggested units	Suggested activities	Evaluation criteria

Nature and you	Selecting camp site
	Camping out with a group
	Knowledge of poison ivy, oak, and
	    sumac
	Identifying animals and their habits
	Identifying trees and placing leaves
	    in a scrapbook
		Do they enjoy outdoor activities?
		Do they cooperate with each other?
		Do they appreciate each other's ability?
		Do they take proper care of
		    equipment?
		Do they understand the dangers of
		    carelessness with firearms?

Orienteering	Proper use of a compass Learning to make a trail Backpacking	Are they good sportsmen with regard to fishing? Can they paddle a canoe? How many common trees can they
Cycling	Bicycle riding in a group	identify? Can they find their way by stars? By
Hunting	Safety lessons concerned with handling firearms Hunting small game	compass?

Outdoor adventure:
    casting, fly type
    fishing
	Fishing derby
	Boating
	A fishing trip to the river, pond, or
	    lake	

Winter sports	Skating Skiing Tobogganing	
Ecology Weather study		

Grades 7 and 8
CURRICULUM DESIGN—RECREATIONAL ACTIVITIES

Youth at this age, especially in mixed groups, are self-conscious and shy. Before long, self-conscious-
Coeducational planning of social activities, committee work, or operating noon-hour "mixers" usually

Developmental objectives		
Cognitive	Affective	Physical and psychomotor
Understand the basic social patterns of the two sexes	Develop leadership qualities	Develop ability in a wide range of leisure time activities
Have a more definite understanding of how to get along with people	Learn to be at ease in a mixed group	Know a number of social games
Understand the rules governing manners in social living	Gain a feeling of acceptance	Develop skill in demonstrating activities
Understand the importance of friends	Release tensions through cultural as well as physical activities	
Understand the worthy use of leisure time	Know how to gain attention without being boisterous	
Understand party conduct	Enjoy companionship of both sexes	
	Develop social etiquette	
	Develop a sense of humor	
	Learn to accept differences in people	
	Are at ease in social situations	

ness is lost in the enthusiasm, and a single circle—holding hands—is accepted as a matter of course.
falls to students under the guidance of physical education teachers.

Suggested units	Suggested activities	Evaluation criteria
In-class	Golf tournament Table tennis Volleyball Badminton Archery Bowling Shuffleboard Dart baseball Social dancing Horseshoes Frisbee	Do all the students have the ability to make new friends? Do they enjoy activities in mixed groups? What pupils are regularly left out of group activities? Do the pupils participate voluntarily? To what extent are students planning, executing, and evaluating their own activities?
Extraclass	School mixers Speedball Softball Group singing Stunt party Bait casting Horseback riding Bowling Parties Picnics Roller skating	

A classification and percentage time allotment plan is presented for grades 7 and 8 from the preceding charts.

ACTIVITY CLASSIFICATION AND TIME ALLOTMENT

Activity	Grade 7 (%)	Grade 8 (%)
Aquatics	5-10	10
Games and sports	20-30	30-40
Rhythmical	10-20	10
Self-testing	10-20	10-20
Developmental	10-15	10-15
Outdoor education	10-15	10-15
Recreational	10-15	10-15

REACTORS

1. Early adolescence is a period of insecurity.
2. The problems of this age group have caused educators to consider alternative school organizational patterns.
3. The middle school concept was initated to minimize the transition from elementary to junior high school.
4. The selection of activities for this age group is critical due to the wide variances in needs, interests, and purposes.

LEARNING ACTIVITIES

1. Identify specific physiological, psychological, and sociological differences between seventh and eighth graders and between girls and boys.
   a. Formulate principles incorporating these differences.
   b. Translate these principles into implications for curriculum planning.
2. Compare and list the advantages and disadvantages of a junior high school organizational plan to that of a middle school.
3. Develop a chart listing the major activity areas and subareas for this grade level.
4. Identify the major differences in characteristics between sixth and seventh graders and eighth and ninth graders.

UNIT EVALUATIVE CRITERIA

Can you:
1. Characterize seventh and eighth graders and indicate similarities and differences between the girls and boys?
2. Translate relationships between characteristics, objectives, and activities into a curriculum plan?
3. Develop instructional materials and strategies for an effective program design?

RESOURCES

AAHPER. *Ideas for golf instruction.* Washington, D.C.: The Alliance, 1970.

AAHPER. *Physical education for high school students.* Washington, D.C.: The Alliance, 1970.

Annarino, A. A. *Developmental conditioning for women and men* (2nd ed.). St. Louis: The C. V. Mosby Co., 1976.

Bucher, C. A. *Administration of health and physical education programs, including athletics* (6th ed.). St. Louis: The C. V. Mosby Co., 1975.

Bucher, C. A. (Ed.). *Dimensions of physical education* (2nd ed.). St. Louis: The C. V. Mosby Co., 1974.

Bucher, C. A., Koenig, C. *Methods and materials for secondary school physical education* (5th ed.). St. Louis: The C. V. Mosby Co., 1978.

Clark, D. E. *Physical education: a program of activities*. St. Louis: The C. V. Mosby Co., 1969.

Daughtrey, G. *Methods in physical education and health for secondary schools*. Philadelphia: W. B. Saunders Co., 1967.

Daughtrey, G. *Effective teaching in physical education for secondary schools*. Philadelphia: W. B. Saunders Co., 1973.

Daughtrey, G., & Woods, J. B. *Physical education programs*. Philadelphia: W. B. Saunders Co., 1971.

Dowell, L. J. *Strategies for teaching physical education*. Englewood Cliffs, N.J.: Prentice-Hall, Inc., 1975.

Essex, M., Bowers, G. R., & Love, M. E. *Ohio guide for girls secondary physical education*. Columbus: Ohio Department of Public Instruction, 1971.

Heitmann, H. M. *Organizational patterns for instruction in physical education*. Washington, D.C.: American Alliance for Health, Physical Education, and Recreation, 1971.

Johnson, P., et al. *Problem-solving approach to health and fitness*. New York: Holt, Rinehart & Winston, 1966.

Kozman, H. C., & Rosalind, C. O. *Methods in physical education*. Dubuque, Iowa: William C. Brown Co., Publishers, 1967.

Miller, A. G., & Massey, D. *Dynamic concept of physical education for secondary schools*. Englewood Cliffs, N.J.: Prentice-Hall, Inc., 1963.

Mosston, M. *Teaching physical education*. Columbus, Ohio: Charles E. Merrill Publishing Co., 1966.

Walker, J., et al. *Modern methods in secondary school physical education*. Boston: Allyn & Bacon, Inc., 1973.

Willgoose, C. E. *The curriculum in physical education*. Englewood Cliffs, N.J.: Prentice-Hall, Inc., 1969.

The adolescent period is a long stretch on the ascending curve of life when childish things we put away, when the limit of growth comes in sight, and when sex impulses rise from whispers to loud voices.

J. ARTHUR THOMPSON

14 Grades 9 and 10

COMPETENCIES

After completing this unit, you should be able to:

Formulate principles for program planning from the characteristics, needs, and interests of ninth and tenth graders.

Use the aforementioned principles for selecting and organizing activities.

Analyze the advantages and disadvantages between various curriculum models for high school programs.

Define the following:
Election program
Selection program
Choice program

PERSPECTIVE

PRINCIPLE: The adolescent often accepts the prescribed values of a peer group, yet searches for models to idealize and copy. Physical education teachers oftentimes serve as these models.

At this period the world often seems "out of phase" with the potentialities of adolescents. They are pounded by dozens of "environmental hammers," consisting of family, neighborhood, peers, church, school, tradition, custom, law, and an "inner self." These forces all contribute to a state of confusion and conflict. They worry about themselves. They wonder whether or not they are "normal." Each is concerned whether his/her growth pattern or skill performance differs from others at the same age.

Society is beginning to expect more mature behavior from these adolescents. It often expects some degree of social and economic independence—yet adults often deny these youth full participation in activities that are socially significant. Therefore through athletic teams, clubs, secret societies, and so forth, they set up a world of their own on which their social life centers.

Adolescents' role in society and their ideas concerning themselves are powerful directional forces in their lives. Physical educators are therefore obligated to devise a curriculum that offers a wide variety of experiences that will (1) give youth a chance to try themselves out, (2) provide opportunities for self-evaluation influenced by success or failure, (3) provide situations that allow them to assume and carry out responsibility, and (4) give them a chance to note the opinions expressed and attitudes betrayed by their peers regarding the results of their efforts. Individualism now merges into group, class, team, or school feelings. The games enjoyed express this expanding of the self and take on the more highly organized competitive features for which teams and clubs are formed, and the individual is lost in his/her desire to further the interest of the team.

The activities of the physical education program are potentially rich in providing recognition and ego satisfaction so that the basic needs of youth may be better met and greater serenity and internal equilibrium will result.

At this age level, the physical education curriculum has, among many others, the following obligations:

1. To provide experience for the development of self-discovery, self-realization, and self-assertion so important in the education of the adolescent
2. To provide activities that reflect the goals of cognitive development through such activities as planning and executing strategy in games, evaluating experiences, and making suggestions
3. To help individuals develop value systems— philosophies—based on the proper recognition of the relationships to fellowmen and the great social problems of our day
4. To build efficient, well-coordinated bodies, free from disease and possessing sufficient speed, strength, agility, endurance, and skill to meet easily the maximum demands of the day
5. To stress lifetime skills that will give tone and color to life long after school days are over
6. To give youth some freedom of choice under friendly guidance in activities so constructed

Text continued on p. 180.

ACTIVITY CHARTS

Grades 9 and 10
CURRICULUM DESIGN—AQUATICS

Unless students have been exposed to progressive lessons in swimming, lifesaving, use of small craft, ability will be found. This fact will tax the ingenuity of the instructor, who must see that each student the time available. Some students may be outright beginners, whereas others are ready for advanced

Developmental objectives		
Cognitive	**Affective**	**Physical and psychomotor**
Understand the use of the various dives and strokes	Appreciate standards of safety for selves and others in the locker room and pool	Are able to administer artificial respiration properly
Understand completely the water safety rules and some type of "buddy" system	Create high standards for cleanliness in and around the pool	Have mastered the ability to relax in the water
Understand the principles of lifesaving	Appreciate the importance of rules of conduct for the beach and pool	Are able to apply methods of rescue in the water
Understand the mechanical and physical principles involved in buoyancy, proper breathing, propulsion	Appreciate water skills and enjoy the water	Are able to demonstrate fundamental strokes (breast, side, back, and crawl)
Understand basic knowledge of using small craft		Are able to tread water and dive satisfactorily
		Are able to apply water balancing techniques (sculling, finning, leveling)
		Are able to apply competitive techniques (racing starts, turns)
		Are able to maneuver small craft

and similar forms of aquatics before the senior high school period, a tremendous range in individual
is accepted at his/her given stage of skill and developed to the maximum degree commensurate with
lifesaving courses.

Suggested units	Suggested activities	Evaluation criteria
Lifesaving	Artificial respiration, approaches, breaks and releases, carries	Can the students pass a Junior Red Cross lifesaving course?
Small craft	Canoeing: entering canoe, paddling, changing seats, righting canoe in water Powerboating Sailing	Can they properly give artificial respiration? Can they perform different types of dives? Is there general progress in skill, speed, and endurance?
Water competition	Speed and distance swimming, starts, turns	Are they able to select proper strokes for various swimming situations? Do they enjoy the water?
Water games	Water polo Water basketball Water relays Relays pushing balloons	Can they perform the various types of strokes?
Synchronized swimming	Basic strokes Somersaults Tandem swimming	
Skills	Basic swimming Beginner swimming Advanced beginner swimming	

Grades 9 and 10
CURRICULUM DESIGN—GAMES AND SPORTS

In many senior high schools, unfortunately, these are the only years of required physical education. carry over into adult leisure time.

Developmental objectives		
Cognitive	**Affective**	**Physical and psychomotor**
Understand proper selection, use, and care of equipment Know the rules and how to officiate at an event Understand and apply democratic principles in selection of players for representative teams Are able to apply to the wholeness of games and athletics and use of skills developed in earlier lead-up games Have improved knowledge of advanced team play Are able to analyze their own abilities for various games	Appreciate clean competition and fair play Try out for varsity sports Develop sportsmanship traits Participate in recreational activities Appreciate advanced skills in games and sports Contribute in some way to the benefit of the group in organized activity	Have well-developed muscular coordination Have skill in more than one sport Show evidence of improved reaction time, endurance, and strength

The program should allow for a wide range of individual skills in a variety of lifetime sports that may

Suggested units	Suggested activities	Evaluation criteria
Team sports	Volleyball in varied forms Flag football Basketball Hockey Baseball Softball Soccer Lacrosse Speedball Team handball	How are training rules kept? Has a rating sheet been used for individual display of skills? Have students made self-appraisals as to skill and attitude? Do they have the right attitude toward competition? Do the students play these sports and games in their leisure time? Do the students show good sportsmanship?
Let's get into condition!	Swat tag Scooters Floor hockey	Do the students limit their play to one sport? To what extent do the students try to be excused from class?
Progressive relays	Running relays Backward relays Wheelbarrow relays Bounce pass relays Over and under relays Jump stick relays Basketball relays	
Individual and dual sports	Golf Wrestling (boys) Handball Archery Badminton Tennis Track and field Racquetball Bowling Skiing	

Grades 9 and 10
CURRICULUM DESIGN—RHYTHMICAL ACTIVITIES (dance)

The dance program in these grades should be a varied program that offers opportunity for further
ment in mixed groups and provide enjoyable social experiences that will add tone and color to their

Developmental objectives		
Cognitive	Affective	Physical and psychomotor
Interpret various social customs and racial characteristics through dance	Enjoy group participation	Promote growth toward accurate rhythm
Express their individual personalities spontaneously	Feel "at home" in activities of a rhythmical nature	Develop skill in dancing with a group (square dance)
Understand various types of dance	Realize that dancing is socially important	Develop good poise, balance, and body control through dance
Understand the value of social contacts through dance	Appreciate the importance of social etiquette at dances	Understand dance activities aid in development of pattern or rhythm in many games
Realize the value of dancing as a lifetime activity	Enjoy participating in or attending dance programs	
Use dance as a creative experience		

Grades 9 and 10
CURRICULUM DESIGN—GYMNASTICS ACTIVITIES

Gymnastics produces complete and well-balanced development of the body.

Developmental objectives		
Cognitive	Affective	Physical and psychomotor
Understand their personal limitations and how to adjust to them	Develop pride in growing ability and achievement	Improve body control and flexibility
Discover personal strengths and weaknesses	Develop courage and self-confidence	Develop strength
Know the importance of skill, strength, speed, and endurance in relation to physical performance	Develop some concepts and attitudes concerning standards of performance	Improve cardiovascular endurance
Show originality and creativeness in activities	Appreciate the attitude of prevention (safety)	Develop poise, grace, balance, and kinesthesis

development through expression in rhythmical movement. It should assist pupils in social adjust-
lives long after their school days are over.

Suggested units	Suggested activities	Evaluation criteria
Adventures in rhythm	Music used as accompaniment for tumbling and athletic fundamentals Cheerleading Free exercise	Do boys and girls mix freely at dances? Can they make a combination of steps fit together to give variety to their dancing?
United Nations festival	Folk dances of countries belonging to United Nations	Do they move smoothly and rhythmically in a square dance?
Tap and clog dances	Tap routines Composition of a tap dance Arkansas Traveler	Can they call a simple square dance? Do they show some degree of interest and skill in dancing? Do the pupils enjoy dancing?
Square dancing	Dive for the Oyster Take a Little Peek	Do the pupils show originality in creating movement rhythmical patterns?
Social dancing	Ballroom dancing Contemporary dancing	
Modern dance Jazz Ballet		

Suggested units	Suggested activities	Evaluation criteria

Stunts and tumbling	Review:
	    Forward roll
	    Backward roll
	    Somersaults
	    Pyramids
	    Cartwheels
	    Headstands
	    Handspring
	Advanced:
	    Combinations
	    Routines
	    Free exercise
		Is muscular development evident?
		Can pupils appraise their own performance and progress?
		Do the pupils enjoy self-competition?
		Has coordination been improved?
		Do pupils assist and spot one another?
		What is the number of stunts performed from selected and graduated checklists for the development of routines?

Apparatus	Balance beams Uneven and even parallel bars Mini-trampoline Vaulting box Rings Horizontal bar Horse Ropes Hoops Balls	

Grades 9 and 10
CURRICULUM DESIGN—DEVELOPMENTAL ACTIVITIES

Every group varies in strength and skill in terms of the "normal distribution" of traits. Weaker and less helped to develop as normally as possible—both physically and psychologically. The constant aim is to physical education program as is possible with a sufficient degree of physical fitness.

Developmental objectives		
Cognitive	**Affective**	**Physical and psychomotor**
Know what good body alignment and development are	Are able to accept their own limitations without withdrawing from the group	Use exercises to the best advantage
Understand principles of elementary kinesiology and physiology	Appreciate the significance of individual differences	Protect themselves against injury
Know safety measures related to accident prevention	Develop personal pride, responsibility, and willingness to maintain good body condition	Improve flexibility, body control, and gracefulness and show increased accomplishments in strength and endurance
Know how to select the most effective conditioning methods		

typical boys and girls have problems that teachers must recognize so that these students may be enable these boys and girls eventually to take part in as many of the joys and benefits of the total

Suggested units	Suggested Activities	Evaluation criteria
You and your body mechanics	Good alignment Good shoes Mechanics of carrying, sitting, lifting, jumping, running How to relax	Do the students demonstrate evidence of strength and endurance (arm and shoulder girdle, foot and leg strength, abdominal strength, upper back strength)?
Keeping in condition	Conditioning exercises Rope jumping Stretching exercises Weight training Aerobics Interval training Obstacle courses Circuit training Jogging	Do they demonstrate evidence of flexibility and good body mechanics (foot mechanics, correct alignment of body segments, sitting position, stooping to pick up light object)? Do they have the ability to relax—absence of muscular tension? Do they show improvement on physical fitness tests?

Grades 9 and 10
CURRICULUM DESIGN—OUTDOOR EDUCATION

The present educational trend emphasizes the importance of camping and backpacking experiences are the training of the powers of observation and accurate inference with regard to the surroundings, ment, altruistic service, and other concomitant outcomes are possible under good leadership.

Developmental objectives		
Cognitive	**Affective**	**Physical and psychomotor**
Know what general camping skills are important	Love the outdoors and value outdoor activities	Develop visual perception
Know the general field of ecology	Appreciate camp safety, property rights, sanitation	Are able to fold and handle a three-man tent
Know how to select a campsite and establish a camp	Appreciate group membership and accept group responsibilities	Are able to pace and measure distance, handle small craft, build a fire without matches, cook a meal, follow a trail
Develop skill in cooking	Desire to help younger or less experienced campers	Can successfully plan for and supervise an overnight hike
Know how to select proper camp equipment (shoes for hiking, clothing, pup tents)		Can plan and conduct a successful evening campfire program
Understand the main principles of ecology		Develop physical qualities needed for hiking, climbing, backpacking

for the all-around education of every individual. Among the most valuable contributions of camp life in addition to the physical benefits. Wholesome fun, social adjustment, self-reliance, joy of achieve-

Suggested units	Suggested activities	Evaluation criteria
Woodcraft	Woodlore and wild life Bird life Trees and how to distinguish them Flowers and edible plants Building fires Building a lean-to and other shelters Getting lost and the way out Weather signs Axemanship	How is their knowledge? Do they observe rules and laws? Do they have demonstrable skills in tracking, woodcraft, fishing, hiking, backpacking? Do they use proper equipment? Keep it in good condition? Is some degree of interest shown? Is some degree of self-dependence and responsibility shown? Do they practice safety measures?
How to fish	Still fishing Casting Trolling Baits and lures	
Hunting safety	Game laws Posted land Crossing fences	
Discovery days	The state park Historical sites Living then and now	
Indian methods	Blazing a trail Subsistence on nature The Indian way	
Hiking	Camping Backpacking Survival skills First aid Outdoor ecology Map and compass reading orientation Equipment	

Grades 9 and 10
CURRICULUM DESIGN—RECREATIONAL ACTIVITIES

Recreational sports of an individual or dual nature fulfill many of the recreation objectives of physical of these lifetime activities. Recreational sports, because of their individual nature and the large num- ment present additional hazards to good education that teachers must surmount by increased inge-

Developmental objectives		
Cognitive	Affective	Physical and psychological
Develop an understanding between boys and girls leading to wholesome boy-girl relationships Demonstrate knowledge of how to use leisure time profitably Demonstrate knowledge of a wide variety of social and recreational activities Develop new acquaintances and keep them Know how to plan a recreational program Learn to render service to a social group	Satisfy a feeling of "belongingness" Develop ability to make new friends and to associate with a group Develop social sensitivity and courtesy Appreciate opportunities for group participation Develop a willingness to accept responsibilities Enjoy all recreational activities Appreciate and enjoy company of others Develop sportsmanship in both play and observation	Develop skills in social conduct Develop sufficient skill in games played by the group to give individual satisfaction Develop poise in social and rhythmical situations Develop a number of social and individual leisure time skills— dancing, shuffleboard, skating Cultivate high quality tastes, appreciations, interests

that they may develop the ability to make wise choices by their own judgment

7. To foster the fun, joy, fellowship, and challenge of the activity for its own sake rather than for something else

Physical education activities contribute in a large measure to the successes, hopes, and ideals that help shape the personality of the adolescent. Since the adolescent often accepts the prescribed values of a group or gang, yet searches for models to idealize and copy, physical education teachers have unique opportunities and responsibilities to foster desirable human relationships within groups and to serve as models for their pupils.

AGE CHARACTERISTICS (Grades 9 and 10)
Physical characteristics
1. Rapid growth and development period, especially for boys who are catching up to girls in size and weight
2. Puberty reached by practically all students at end of this period
3. Rapid increase in muscular development, strength, speed, endurance, and coordination
4. Difficulty, and consequent undue concern, with skin disorders—no doubt due to sex hormones, budding beards (in boys)
5. Definite secondary sex characteristics and changes in physical proportions appearing

Mental characteristics
1. Power of reasoning fairly well developed
2. Interested in using their own thinking as a means of gaining independence; dislike being under the jurisdiction of their parents
3. Eager to perfect skills
4. Aware of attitudes on issues and policies to which they formerly gave little attention
5. Imitation popular
6. Increased initiative
7. Interest shown in the choice of a vocation

education. We have an obligation to see that pupils are graduated with ample training in at least a few bers of pupils in most physical education classes, present a problem. Inadequate facilities and equip- nuity.

Suggested units	Suggested activities	Evaluation criteria
Recreational skills	Cycling Horseshoes Deck tennis Shuffleboard Roller skating Bait and fly fishing Dart games Croquet Table tennis Skateboarding Frisbee	Do the students show evidence of sheer joy and good fun? Do they have ability to plan, execute, and evaluate their own activities? Do they show evidence of etiquette and consideration of others?

Social and emotional characteristics

1. Intense emotions displayed; these emotions often not too well understood or controlled
2. Desire for adventure and excitement
3. Desire to have friends of the opposite sex, to date, and to follow adult patterns in social life
4. Great interest in social relationships; social dancing becomes more interesting for most of them
5. Concerned about their physical attractiveness, dress, and appearance
6. Very strong group loyalty; anxious to conform to group standards in matters of dress, dating, and allowance
7. Permanent friendships beginning to develop; have "crushes"
8. Less responsible because of fear of failure; need encouragement

A classification and percentage time allotment plan is presented for grades 9 and 10 from the charts on pp. 170 to 181.

ACTIVITY CLASSIFICATION AND TIME ALLOTMENT

Activity	Grade 9 (%)	Grade 10 (%)
Aquatics	10-20%	10-20%
Games and sports	20-30%	20-30%
Rhythmical (dance)	10-15%	10-15%
Gymnastics	10-15%	10-15%
Developmental	10-15%	10-15%
Outdoor education	5-10%	5-10%
Recreational	5-10%	5-10%

REACTORS

1. Ninth and tenth graders are pressured by dozens of "environmental hammers."
2. Each adolescent is concerned that his/her growth pattern or skill performance may differ from those of others of the same age.
3. Physical education activities contribute in a large measure to the successes, hopes, and ideals that help shape the personality of the adolescent.
4. Some teachers think the seventh and eighth graders are a joy to work with and that ninth and tenth graders are the most difficult to keep happy and interested.
5. Variances in growth and skill between ninth- and tenth-grade boys and girls have implications for marking and grading.

LEARNING ACTIVITIES

1. Analyze a sample school program for this age group.
   a. Would they contribute to all the objectives?
   b. What would you change?
   c. What would you add?
   d. What would you delete?
2. State implications for physical education program planning from your knowledge of the characteristics, needs, and interests of ninth and tenth graders. Would they differ for boys and girls?
3. Select major activity areas.
   a. List the appropriate subactivities for each area.
   b. Indicate time allotments by percentages.

UNIT EVALUATIVE CRITERIA

Can you:
1. Identify similarities and differences in characteristics, needs, and interests between ninth and tenth graders and students in other grades?
2. Formulate specific principles and draw implications for program planning from the above?
3. Design an effective program with appropriate instructional materials and strategies?

RESOURCES

AAHPER. *Physical education for high school students*. Washington, D.C.: The Alliance, 1970.

Annarino, A. A. *Developmental conditioning for women and men* (2nd ed.). St. Louis: The C. V. Mosby Co., 1976.

Annarino, A. A. *Individualized instructional set: archery, bowling, badminton, golf, tennis*. Englewood Cliffs, N.J.: Prentice-Hall, Inc., 1973.

Bookwalter, K., & Vanderzwag, H. J. *Foundations and principles of physical education*. Philadelphia: W. B. Saunders Co., 1969.

Bucher, C. A. *Foundations of physical education* (7th ed.) St. Louis: The C. V. Mosby Co., 1975.

Bucher, C. A. (Ed.). *Dimensions of physical education* (2nd ed.). St. Louis: The C. V. Mosby Co., 1974.

Bucher, C. A. *Organization and administration of health, physical education, and athletics*. St. Louis: The C. V. Mosby Co., 1975.

Bucher, C. A., & Koenig, C. *Methods and materials for secondary school physical education* (5th ed.). St. Louis: The C. V. Mosby Co., 1978.

Cowell, C. C., & France, W. L. *Philosophy and principles of physical education*. Englewood Cliffs, N.J.: Prentice-Hall, Inc., 1963.

Daughtrey, G. *Methods in physical education and health for secondary schools*. Philadelphia: W. B. Saunders Co., 1967.

Daughtrey, G. *Effective teaching in physical education for secondary schools*. Philadelphia: W. B. Saunders Co., 1973.

Daughtrey, G., & Woods, J. B. *Physical education programs*. Philadelphia: W. B. Saunders Co., 1971.

Dowell, L. J. *Strategies for teaching physical education*. Englewood Cliffs, N.J.: Prentice-Hall, Inc., 1975.

Heitmann, H. M. *Organizational patterns for instruction in physical education*. Washington, D.C.: American Alliance for Health, Physical Education, and Recreation, 1971.

Larson, L. A. *Curriculum foundations and standards for physical education*. Englewood Cliffs, N.J.: Prentice-Hall, Inc., 1970.

Mackenzie, M. M. *Toward a new curriculum in physical education*. New York: McGraw-Hill Book Co., 1969.

Miller, A. G., & Massey, D. *Dynamic concept of physical education for secondary schools.* Englewood Cliffs, N.J.: Prentice-Hall, Inc., 1963.

Mosston, M. *Teaching physical education.* Columbus, Ohio: Charles E. Merrill Publishing Co., 1966.

Nixon, J. F., & Jewett, A. E. *Physical education curriculum.* New York: Ronald Press Co., 1964.

Nixon, J. F., & Ulrich, C. *Tones of theory.* Washington, D.C.: American Alliance for Health, Physical Education, and Recreation, 1972.

Thompson, J. C. *Physical education for the 1970's.* Englewood Cliffs, N.J.: Prentice-Hall, Inc., 1971.

Willgoose, C. E. *The curriculum in physical education.* Englewood Cliffs, N.J.: Prentice-Hall, Inc., 1969.

The entire object of true education is to make people not merely to do the right things, but enjoy them; not merely industrious, but to love industry; not merely learned, but to love knowledge; not merely pure, but to love purity; not merely just, but to hunger and thirst after justice.

JOHN RUSKIN

15 Grades 11 and 12

CONTENTS	**Perspective**
	Activity charts

COMPETENCIES

After completing this unit, you should be able to:

Interpret the needs and interests of eleventh and twelfth graders for the development of a program "fitting them for life."

Design innovative programs that provide choice, selection, election, and development of mastery in skills.

Select activities that are appropriate for these grade levels.

Define the following:

Election

Mastery

Selection

PERSPECTIVE

PRINCIPLE: We should see that youth have the knowledge and experience they need to improve their social, skill, and fitness status to the limit of their capacities.

During this period students go through a rapid and uneven growth both mentally and physically, but they are reaching relative stabilization and maturity. A keen sensitivity to the opposite sex is developing. A decided trend toward eventual independence and autonomy is present. There is an awareness of the basic problems of living, such as health, religion, education, and world and community affairs. Many permanent interests and values are established at this time.

For a great many American children this is the end of formal education. The schools should undertake the responsibility of education for these students and help them to develop healthy attitudes and self-direction. We should see that youth have the knowledge and experience they need to improve their social, skill, and fitness status to the limit of their capacities.

Physical activity interests now grow more specialized. Fewer games, specifically those more highly organized and strongly competitive in character and played with intensity, are the rule. Competition is highly individual for both sexes and at the same time intensely cooperative. Team play reaches its height. Here leadership from physical education teachers may hold high the goal and ideal of personal service and honesty at any cost, teaching the pupil to take success in good grace, to bear defeat stoically, and to value energetic action, fair play, courage, perseverance, individual effort, and cooperation. With this training in their moldable youth and in the best years of their lives, high school youth should learn to act well their part in the adult game of life, with its many emergencies and endless anxieties.

Programs should offer choice, election, and selection of activities taught by more individualized strategies.

AGE CHARACTERISTICS
(Grades 11 and 12)

Physical characteristics
1. Gain greatly in muscular strength and endurance; eager to perfect skills
2. Fully developed physical characteristics almost attained by boys; feminine body proportions achieved by girls
3. Outgrow awkward stage
4. Expend more energy than they normally possess and build up tremendous appetites
5. Suffer from skin disorders
6. Sleep and rest requirements about the same as for adults
7. Improved complex coordinations
8. Develop adult sex characteristics

Mental characteristics
1. Memory span much greater; more ability and desire to think for themselves
2. Mental growth almost mature; experience needed
3. Interested in ideals and sense importance of decisions in matters of education, vocation, sex, marriage, world affairs, and religion

Social and emotional characteristics
1. Aware of and sensitive to opposite sex
2. Most girls interested in diet and exercise because of weight and figure
3. Appreciation of need to choose a vocation
4. Getting away from adult protection

Text continued on p. 198.

ACTIVITY CHARTS
Grades 11 and 12
CURRICULUM DESIGN—AQUATICS

In schools with pools and organized swimming programs, the preliminary and fundamental tech-
wide range of skill in any given group, yet many will be ready for and desire proficiency in some of the

Developmental objectives		
Cognitive	**Affective**	**Physical and psychomotor**
Understand and apply principles of health related to swimming	Respect pool etiquette and rights of others	Are skillful in administering artificial respiration
Understand the principles of water safety	Appreciate and enjoy being in the water	Are skillful in handling rowboats, canoes, sailboats, and other small craft
Understand such factors as currents, tides, surf, wind, and water temperature and how they affect swimming	Appreciate the need and purpose of rules on beaches, pools, and locker rooms	Have recreational and special swimming skills
Understand the principles and purposes behind various strokes	Appreciate the skills involved in water safety	Develop endurance for required daily tasks and distance swims
Know basic terminology of small craft		Are skillful in certain competitive techniques, such as racing starts, turns

niques will have been mastered by pupils, and they will be ready for advanced skills. There will be a special skills of diving, lifesaving, scuba, snorkeling, and synchronized activities.

Suggested units	Suggested activities	Evaluation criteria
Lifesaving	Drills for water entry Reversal of direction Contact approaches Carries, breaks Disrobing in water Recovery from bottom Land carries Lift from water Artificial respiration	Have the Junior and Senior American Red Cross lifesaving tests been administered? Has the aquatic skill test sheet been used? Has classification by test series—beginners, swimmers, advanced swimmers, lifesavers—been done?
Games, stunts, relays	Water basketball Water polo (modified) Dodge ball Backward swimming Handspring dive Logrolling Leapfrog relays In and out relay Over and under relay	
Synchronized swimming	Basic strokes Somersaults Sculling Rolls and turns	
Marathon swim	Participants amass a total of laps between a starting date and a deadline date	
Swimming skills	Basic swimming Beginner swimming Advanced swimming Water safety aids	
Diving	Basic dives Scuba diving Skin diving Snorkeling	
Small craft	Sailing Canoeing Rowboating Powerboating Surfing	

Grades 11 and 12
CURRICULUM DESIGN—GAMES AND SPORTS

Since the physical education program, if offered, is often elective at these grade levels, the activities of lower organization, de-emphasizing team sports, and teaching advanced skills and strategies with often best given to interest groups organized into lifetime interest sections and individualization.

Developmental objectives		
Cognitive	Affective	Physical and psychomotor
Demonstrate knowledge of advanced sports	Learn to sacrifice their own personal "whims" or desires for the purpose of group or team success	Develop skills in the fundamentals of all sports activites
Know how to officiate in several sports	Learn to appraise and evaluate their own abilities	Develop desirable physiques
Know how to critically evaluate general team play	Learn to participate in large groups	Are especially efficient in at least one team and one individual or dual sport
Understand the rules, strategy, and techniques of various team and individual games and sports	Learn to control emotions in situations (games) highly charged with tension	Develop well-coordinated bodies
Understand the necessity for good equipment and its care	Learn to abide by rules and accept the official's decision as final	Develop the ability to pace themselves in competitive games
Understand the contribution of sports activities to the development of mind, body, and personality	Participate in wholesome leisure time activities	Gain poise and overcome awkwardness and self-consciousness
Understand their responsibilities to others	Enjoy the fun of using and testing their growing abilities and strengths in team situations	
Understand and respect the possibilities and limitations of the human body	Respect the skill and ability of others (opponents) with the realization that they furnish opportunities to test personal skill, endurance, and self-control	
Learn to think and act "on the spot" in game situations		

should appeal strongly to current needs and desires. This probably means minimizing of group games emphasis on sports such as golf, tennis, archery, handball, and bowling. Instruction at this level is

Suggested units	Suggested activities	Evaluation criteria
Team sports	Football-type games Touch football Soccer Speedball Field ball Field hockey Basketball-type games Basketball Volleyball Softball	Have the students had written tests on rules and strategy? Have they been given standard achievement tests? What are their attitudes toward their activity, selves, officials, teammates? Has a sportsmanship behavior checklist been made? Have they been evaluated for promotional team work and cooperation? To what extent are activities used for recreation?
Individual and dual recreational sports	Archery Badminton Golf Tennis Handball Fencing Deck tennis Table tennis Horseshoes Racquetball Bait and fly casting Track and field Snowskiing	

Grades 11 and 12
CURRICULUM DESIGN—RHYTHMICAL ACTIVITIES (dance)

Many girls take eagerly to modern dance skills and composition, whereas others show a natural
social dancing is willingly accepted by less than one half of the boys, and other forms of dancing
sures and attitudes. These can be changed, as some school programs have indicated.

Developmental objectives		
Cognitive	Affective	Physical and psychomotor
Are able to compose a simple modern dance Know a variety of social and American country dances Are able to interpret music Understand the origins of certain folk dances Understand the etiquette of the dance floor	Enjoy the self-expression that comes from participation in the rhythmical arts Learn to make new friends through dances Appreciate the social importance of dancing in our culture Have confidence in the acceptability of their own dancing skills Appreciate that dance is a form of language and communication Appreciate the long-lasting value of dancing skills Appreciate the artistic performances of others who use the body as a medium of expression in dance	Are able to express ideas through the medium of the body Skillful in performance of certain folk, social, or country (square) dances Develop sensory skills such as reactions to music, tones Develop timing and coordination Develop strong, well-coordinated, and flexible bodies Increase flexibility, agility, endurance Develop accurate cadence and rhythm that carries over to other activities Develop sensory skills, such as reactions to various cadences, patterns Develop social and physical poise

interest to carry on in square, tap, and social dance. Some surveys have shown that instruction in instruction only involve a small number of American boys. This is a result of American social pres-

Suggested units	Suggested activities	Evaluation criteria
Folk dancing	Tarentella (Italian) Czardas (Hungarian) Sailor's Hornpipe (English) Kamerinskaia (Russian)	Can the students demonstrate accuracy of phrasing, memory of dance sequences, correctness of rhythm, etc?
Tap dancing	Waltz Clog Soft shoe	Do they identify various steps, have knowledge of folklore, etc? Have they been judged for understanding and appreciation?
Ballroom dancing	Waltz Samba Fox trot Rhumba Cha-cha	Have their performance standards for grades 11 and 12 been checked in various units? Do they show evidence of joy in participation?
Modern dance skills and composition	Locomotor movements Axial movements Rhythm Composition of an original dance	Do they show leadership and interest in school and community dance opportunities (e.g., modern dance club, noon-hour dances, community square dance groups)?
American country dance	Docey Out as She Comes In Eight Hands Over The Dollar Whirl Swing Your Opposite All Alone	
Contemporary social dancing Jazz Ballet Aerobic dancing	Trends	

Grades 11 and 12
CURRICULUM DESIGN—GYMNASTICS ACTIVITIES

Gymnastics is a means for maintaining fitness, flexibility, poise, grace, and balance. It is an esthetic

Developmental objectives		
Cognitive	**Affective**	**Physical and psychomotor**
Know their own strengths and weaknesses and how to adjust to them	Appreciate the relation of self-improvement to their own self regarding attitude and social acceptance	Develop balance, agility, strength, endurance, and ability to relax in coordinated movement
Understand that through practice and effort they can accomplish much	Accept their own limitations and do the best they can within this framework	Develop pride in their abilities and accomplishments
Understand that different muscles serve different purposes	Accept personal responsibility for their own safety and the safety of others	Improve "form" in activity
Understand and observe safety precautions in activities and equipment use		Meet achievement standards in physical fitness and performance in stunts, tumbling, apparatus
Understand basic laws of mechanics applied to gymnastics		

activity in which the body performs graceful movements.

Suggested units	Suggested activities	Evaluation criteria
Tumbling	Basic tumbling Advanced tumbling Free exercise	Have the performance abilities been rated? Has their "form"—approach, execution, retreat, and other components with reference to body mechanics—been rated?
Stunts	Partners Pyramids	
Apparatus	Balance beam Side horse Uneven and even parallel bars Horizontal bar Rings Vaulting boxes Mini-trampoline Ropes Balls Wands Hoops Streamers	Have their accomplishments with regard to achievement standards for these grade levels been checked? Have their standings in class competitions been rated?
Development of routines	Free exercise Tumbling Apparatus	
Demonstrations	P.T.A. meeting School assembly	

Grades 11 and 12
CURRICULUM DESIGN—DEVELOPMENTAL ACTIVITIES
Instruction resulting in good body mechanics—the dynamic, graceful, and easy handling of the body developing and maintaining physical fitness.

Developmental objectives		
Cognitive	Affective	Physical and psychomotor
Understand the physical limitations confronting various individuals	Appreciate good body mechanics	Have ability to recognize and apply personally good body mechanics
Know the need for and value of various exercises	Develop personal pride in overcoming weaknesses	Are skillful in applying mechanical principles effectively in all movement
Understand why "an ounce of prevention is worth a pound of cure"	Overcome emotional difficulties	Are able to apply the principles of physical fitness in daily living
Know how to use the body at work and play with the minimum expenditure of energy	Appreciate individual differences	Develop and improve in strength, endurance, flexibility
Know how to develop and maintain fitness	Appreciate the value of healthy and physically fit bodies	
Know basic principles of kinesiology and exercise physiology		
Analyze the relative worth of commercial fitness clinics and devices		

in action, and body development—should, by this time, have resulted in knowledge and attitudes for

Suggested units	Suggested activities	Evaluation criteria
Basic exercise physiology and bio-mechanics	Laboratory testing Development of concepts Designing exercise programs Determine fitness status	Has a fitness test been administered? Has the 12-minute run-walk test been given? Have knowledge tests been administered? Are skin-fold measurements taken?

Physical fitness development	Weight training
	  Universal Gym
	  Isokinetics
	  Nautilus
	Interval training
	Circuit training
	Jogging
	Aerobics
	Stretching exercises	

Grades 11 and 12
CURRICULUM DESIGN—OUTDOOR EDUCATION

In this modern age of technology, we should not forget the deeply rooted, long-established, mental and physical health. There is a strong ecological movement that must be nurtured.

Developmental objectives		
Cognitive	**Affective**	**Physical and psychomotor**
Understand some of the principles of map making	Understand, appreciate, and make use of natural facilities	Develop some handicraft skills
Understand the importance of conservation, extinguishing outdoor fires, etc.	Are interested in supporting safety rules	Develop enough skill to plan and execute a camping trip with enjoyment
Sense and admire some of the wonders of nature	Become effective members of an outdoor activities group	Have ability to set up a camp on various terrains, including rocky
Are able to plan and carry out activities for a group of campers	Realize the heritage of camping and outdoor life	Develop self-confidence and assurance that helps to bring physical and mental relaxation
Understand the importance of good sanitation practice	Recognize and are willing to help correct improper and unsafe performances	Develop durable legs and the appreciation of a sense of physical adequacy
Know how nature provides many helpful things for the camper	Feel the thrill of catching game and fish or discovering new natural beauties	Are able to lead some camp activities
Understand weather conditions, their causes and effects	Seek permission to hike or camp on private property	Develop increased visual and auditory acuity
Understand utilization of materials and their application to the mastery of the environment and that preplanning helps activities to succeed	Appreciate both solitude and companionship	Are able to prepare and cook small game and fish
		Feel a little "rugged" and are equal to the task and proud of the ability to survive

far-reaching relationships between humans and nature. These cannot be ignored without loss of

Suggested units	Suggested activities	Evaluation criteria
Advanced camping	Planning an overnight camp Making and packing a bedroll Making and using primitive cooking devices Building a campfire Marking a trail Basic climbing Survival skills	Has a check list of a variety of camping and outdoor skills commensurate with leisure time enjoyment, safety and personal satisfaction been made? Has the degree to which students understand, appreciate, and make use of the natural resources and facilities in their fairly immediate respective communities been determined?
Small craft handling	Handling a rowboat: using oars, backing, turning, keeping a straight course Canoeing: how to get into a canoe, paddle in bow and stern, land, enter an overturned canoe, etc. Sailing: hoist sail, reef, let out a reef, steer, tack, come about Powerboats: safety	
Hosteling	Selecting shoes for hiking Making and carrying a pack Following a compass course and noting positions by sun or stars Demonstrating care of bicycle Demonstrating use of maps Planning a compact yet well-balanced diet for a 3-day trip	
Fishing	Bait fishing Proper angling Cleaning and cooking fish Fly casting under various conditions Surf fishing	
Winter sports	Skating, figure and speed Skiing, snow shoe hiking Sledding, ice hockey	

Grades 11 and 12
CURRICULUM DESIGN—RECREATIONAL ACTIVITIES

Young people, at this age, are heavily engaged in problems of human relationships, learning how to
may be gained through recreational settings.

Developmental objectives		
Cognitive	Affective	Physical and psychomotor
Understand the value of wholesome recreation	Appreciate dramatics and music	Develop skills in individual forms of recreation
Are able to plan and carry out activities for selves or group	Appreciate and apply social etiquette and approved conduct	Develop poise, personality, and attitudes of social sensitivity and awareness
Increase understanding of personal-social relationships with opposite sex	Enjoy the company of others and are interested in them	Are skillful in organizing and leading games or activities for spur-of-the-moment situations
Realize the full enjoyment of life depends on associations with others	Show willingness to include everyone in activities regardless of ability	Develop a sense of rhythm and timing through dancing
Become self-directive in choices of worthy leisure time activities	Work with others and plan activities with a minimum of conflict	Develop sustained effort through interest in physical and social activities

5. Great interest in social development
6. Desire excitement and adventure
7. Very conscious of dress and appearance
8. More independent
9. Great desire to succeed
10. Strong friendships developing
11. Restrictions on personal liberties by parents and teachers often resented
12. Greatly influenced by group opinion

A classification and percentage time allotment plan is presented for grades 11 and 12 from the charts on pp. 186 to 199.

ACTIVITY CLASSIFICATION AND TIME ALLOTMENT

Activity	Grade 11 (%)	Grade 12 (%)
Aquatics	10-20	10-20
Games and sports	25-30	25-30
Rhythmical (dance)	10-20	10-20
Gymnastics	10-15	10-15
Developmental	10-15	10-15
Outdoor	10-15	10-15
Recreational	10-15	10-15

manage friendships, and becoming adults. Healthy outlets for the development of these relationships

Suggested units	Suggested activities	Evaluation criteria
Mixers	Square dancing Contemporary dancing Ballroom dancing Group games	Has the sociometric test to determine increased range of acquaintance and friendship been administered? Has the individual ability on part of the pupils to plan been determined? What is the degree of participation on the part of individual students? Who are the "fringers"? The "actives"? How is their development of recreational skills?
Recreational skills	Cycling Horseshoes Deck tennis Badminton Archery Bowling Shuffleboard Croquet Table tennis Skateboarding Frisbee Dart games Paddle tennis Regional	

REACTORS

1. Many permanent interests and values are established by the eleventh and twelfth grades.
2. Physical activity interests now grow more specialized.
3. Elective programs require different curriculum models and strategies.
4. Competition at these grade levels is highly individual for both sexes and at the same time intensely cooperative.
5. Physical education programs should offer choice, selection, and election.

LEARNING ACTIVITIES

1. Conduct a survey of the recreational facilities in your community.
   a. List the ones used by adults only.
   b. List the ones available for high school students.
   c. State implications for curriculum planning and offerings.
2. Select one school program for this age group and analyze it, as to:
   a. Positive effects.
   b. Negative effects.
3. Select a major activity area.
   a. List the appropriate subactivities for each area.
   b. Indicate time allotments by percentage.
4. Select an activity for eleventh to twelfth graders.
   a. State the criterion reference to be achieved by eleventh and twelfth graders for each skill.
   b. Explain strategy for evaluation.

UNIT EVALUATIVE CRITERIA

Can you:
1. Characterize the interests and needs of eleventh and twelfth graders?

2. Design a program and select activities related to their interests?
3. Develop a curriculum model, instructional materials, and strategy that permits choice, selection, and election of activities?

RESOURCES

AAHPER. *Physical education for high school students.* Washington, D.C.: The Alliance, 1970.

Annarino, A. A. *Individualized instructional set: archery, bowling, badminton, golf, tennis.* Englewood Cliffs, N.J.: Prentice-Hall, Inc., 1973.

Annarino, A. A. *Developmental conditioning for women and men.* St. Louis: The C. V. Mosby Co., 1976.

Block, J. H. *Mastery learning.* New York: Holt, Rinehart & Winston, 1971.

Bucher, C. A., & Koenig, C. *Methods and materials for secondary school physical education* (5th ed.). St. Louis: The C. V. Mosby Co., 1978.

Daughtrey, G. *Effective teaching in physical education for secondary schools.* Philadelphia: W. B. Saunders Co., 1973.

Daughtrey, G., & Woods, J. B. *Physical education programs.* Philadelphia: W. B. Saunders Co., 1971.

Dowell, L. J. *Strategies for teaching physical education.* Englewood Cliffs, N.J.: Prentice-Hall, Inc., 1975.

Heitmann, H. M. *Organizational patterns for instruction in physical education.* Washington, D.C.: American Alliance for Health, Physical Education, and Recreation, 1971.

Heitmann, H. M., & Kneer, M. *Physical education instructional techniques: an individualized humanistic approach.* Englewood Cliffs, N.J.: Prentice-Hall, Inc., 1976.

Hellison, D., et al. *Personalized learning in physical education.* Washington, D.C.: American Alliance for Health, Physical Education, and Recreation, 1976.

Mackenzie, M. M. *Toward a new curriculum in physical education.* New York: McGraw-Hill Book Co., 1969.

Miller, A. G., & Massey, D. *Dynamic concept of physical education for secondary schools.* Englewood Cliffs, N.J.: Prentice-Hall, Inc., 1963.

Mosston, M. *Teaching physical education.* Columbus, Ohio: Charles E. Merrill Publishing Co., 1966.

Nixon, J. F., & Jewett, A. E. *Physical education curriculum.* New York: Ronald Press Co., 1964.

Siedentop, D. *Physical education—introductory analysis.* Dubuque, Iowa: William C. Brown Co., Publishers, 1972.

Siedentop, D. *Developing teaching skills in physical education.* Boston: Houghton Mifflin Co., 1976.

Singer, R., et al. *Physical education: foundations.* New York: Holt, Rinehart & Winston, 1976.

Singer, R., & Dick, W. *Teaching physical education: a systems approach.* Boston: Houghton Mifflin Co., 1974.

Straub, W. L. *The lifetime sports oriented physical education program.* Englewood Cliffs, N.J.: Prentice-Hall, Inc., 1976.

Thompson, J. C. *Physical education for the 1970's.* Englewood Cliffs, N.J.: Prentice-Hall, Inc., 1971.

Vannier, M., & Hollis, F. *Teaching physical education in secondary schools.* Philadelphia: W. B. Saunders Co., 1969.

Walker, J., et al. *Modern methods in secondary school physical education.* Boston: Allyn & Bacon, Inc., 1973.

Willgoose, C. E. *The curriculum in physical education.* Englewood Cliffs, N.J.: Prentice-Hall, Inc., 1969.

PART THREE

CURRICULUM ORGANIZATION

UNITS

The chief aim in curriculum construction should be to choose the right kind of experiences and to organize them in such a way that they may be taught and learned most effectively.

LESLIE L. CHISHOLM

Teachers are not mere purveyors of information, they are openors of doors, awakeness to reality.

DAN PRESCOTT

16 Organizational concepts

COMPETENCIES

After completing this unit, you should be able to:

Identify the general concepts for organizing learning experiences so that desirable changes of behavior—including ways of thinking and feeling—result.

Develop a physical education curriculum with the principles of growth and development as an organizing focus.

Illustrate how physical education experiences can provide for continuity and sequential development.

Develop a strategy so that physical education is an integral part of the total school curriculum.

Define the following:

Core

Integrated curriculum

Corrected curriculum

Sequence

Scope

Continuity

PERSPECTIVE

PRINCIPLE: The competent teacher knows how to organize learning experiences so that desirable changes in behavior—including ways of thinking and feeling—result.

As an individual faces a situation and endeavors to make some satisfactory adjustment to it, certain modifications take place in his/her total behavior pattern. We call these changes in behavior patterns learning. Therefore we may think of learning as the result of an experience.

The competent teacher knows how to organize learning experiences so that desirable changes in behavior—including ways of thinking and feeling—result. The good curriculum takes a great many hazards out of learning and reduces the waste of time and energy. A child learns from many experiences without the aid of either school or teacher. The business of the school, however, is consciously to select and arrange learning experiences, to give direction, and to avoid educational mismanagement.

The curriculum is the means by which the school provides the learner with desirable experiences, and the nature of these experiences and their organization are the most important problems in curriculum development.

After one has selected the content of the physical education curriculum, one faces the question of how to organize it for most effective learning. Without organization, learning experiences are unrelated, haphazard, and often meaningless. The development of the physical, psychomotor, cognitive, and affective objectives requires some consideration of sequence and continuity of experiences, time for their "digestion" and the possibility of integrating and relating them with other educational experiences, and identification of the best type of instruction. Hence organization is a primary task of curriculum development for achieving the specified objectives. The curriculum, in these terms, requires a more difficult type of planning. It involves the formulation of a general framework and development of specificities to accomplish the task.

In organizing the physical education curriculum, we seek answers to such questions as the following:

1. How can the physical education experiences of next spring or next week be planned so that they add to the meaningfulness and learning resulting from the experiences of this spring or this week?
2. How can each learning experience grow out of those preceding, so that they increase in complexity and lead to increased skill, increased understanding, and greater appreciation in subsequent experiences?
3. How can learning experiences in physical education be related to those in social studies, biology, English, and health so that the relationships are clarified and learning reinforced, so that the student senses some unity to life and learning?
4. How can learning experiences in physical education provide opportunities for student independence, creativity, self-reliance, and individual responsibility?
5. How can learning experiences in physical education compensate for the wide range of physiological, psychological, and sociological variances that exist in every teaching/learning setting?
6. How can learning experiences in physical education be organized so that equal oppor-

tunities and experiences are provided for both sexes?

7. How can learning experiences in physical education be offered so that there is choice, selection, and election by the student?

8. How can learning experiences for the handicapped child be integrated with those learning experiences for the nonhandicapped?

The curriculum planner, in seeking answers to these questions, must have an understanding of the basic concepts of curriculum organization, such as the organizing focus, sequence and continuity, seasonality, and correlation and integration. Information is needed as to the past, present, and future practices in the American school system relative to organizational patterns, operational and administrative procedures, and supervisory practices. In addition, the planner must have a knowledge and "feel" of the school and community's socialization process; in a democratic society, he/she must be able to interpret and implement local, state, and federal legislation as it pertains to the curriculum.

ORGANIZING FOCUS

Health, character, citizenship, and morale are generalized educational objectives. Every teacher in the school should be concerned with the student's physical and emotional well-being (health), his/her concepts and desirable standards of conduct (character), and his/her hopeful and energetic participation in programs to improve the effectiveness of the school as a social group (citizenship) and as an institution in accomplishing these things (morale). The collective attitude of the students and leaders toward health, character, citizenship, and morale will, in the last analysis, determine the degree to which health, character, citizenship, and morale are in the student rather than merely in the course of study.

Are we to teach "health" as a subject with definite and logical principles of organization, or is it possible to study personal health problems so that, in the end, a coherent and systematic picture of relevant biological principles is achieved? If we select the latter, the interests, needs, and purposes of boys and girls provide the appropriate organizing focus. Facts about health, growth, exercise, fitness, and nutrition become organized around the problems and concerns of students so that these are met, while at the same time other related ideas and facts are included as well. If the purposes of students are to be used as an organizing focus for learning experiences in physical education, it is most important that what is taught and how it is taught be considered with respect to this particular central organizing idea. Unfortunately, the techniques for organizing the curriculum or teaching for such values as attitudes, appreciations, purpose satisfaction, and similar valuable outcomes are still somewhat in the developmental stage; we still think of education as accretion of subject matter.

The present tendency is to attempt to make education functional, to help people meet needs and solve problems. This places in the forefront problems and issues that are of concern to students, rather than subjects that are central organizing ideas. The organization of the curriculum into subject matter areas, departments, and subjects is being reexamined and challenged by the current tendency to organize it into categories more directly related to the problems of life. Obviously, the organizational pattern of the curriculum will be strongly influenced by the choice made.

Physical education conceived of merely as games presents no problems related to some organizing focus around which learning experiences are centered. If, however, physical education is interested in motor skill development, fitness, health, growth, personal-social relations, and the interests, needs, problems, and concerns of students related to such problems, mere planning for games is not enough.

Although the problem of organization of learning experiences is the most important aspect of curriculum construction, it is also the most difficult to solve. It is much easier to plan a curriculum for the development of skill and fitness than it is to plan for ways of meeting the basic personality needs (recognition, achievement, security, and the like) of all pupils. The former approach merely requires the teacher's instructions; the latter demands pupil-teacher planning.

By organization we try to relate the various experiences within the school in such a way that the most desirable cumulative effect is produced in achieving not only the specific objectives of each subject area but also the general, ultimate purposes of the school. To this end physical education must avoid isolation and coordinate its efforts toward common ends.

SEQUENCE AND CONTINUITY

In educational areas such as reading, English, mathematics, or social studies, our school curricula reflect some fairly uniform attention to progression—sequence and continuity. Learning experiences are planned so that each grows out of the preceding one and prepares children for the experiences to follow. As a result, with our geographically mobile population, children may transfer from the fourth grade in Miami to the fourth grade in Seattle or from the sixth grade in Santa Barbara to the sixth grade in Albany without undue educational loss or confusion, due to the fact that in the educational areas mentioned, fairly similar principles of sequence and continuity have been employed. As a result, all children in the same grade have achieved fairly similar standards.

Unfortunately, the same cannot be said of physical education; one finds a great range of ability in children transferring from various towns and cities in various sections of the United States. The reasons are numerous. Although most states have laws requiring physical education in the curriculum, in many places the choices are minimal. Contributing factors are inadequate facilities, untrained teachers, inadequate time allotment, poor or no equipment and supplies, and educational mismanagement on the part of many physical education teachers who fail to provide for sequence and continuity. Very often the same activities are taught at several grade levels year after year. It will be a happy day for both teachers and pupils in physical education when we find, for example, that eighth-grade pupils transferring to one school, from anywhere else, can swim 50 yards, know the basic tumbling skills and stunts on the mats, and can participate with reasonable skill in certain basic team and individual sports.

Sequence and continuity are based on the fact that children grow in complexity and maturity—that they start with simple manipulations such as block building and sand modeling, proceed to games of low organization, and finally move to more complex games. Developmental sociopsychological factors, including needs, problems, concerns, social values, and a host of other motivational factors related to the learning process, are involved in the important questions of what follows what, and in what order should it follow.

Physical education experiences of the first grade must be effectively related to those of the second grade and be based on those of the nursery school. Experiences in the ninth grade should be related to those of the tenth grade and based on those of the eighth grade. It would be an ineffectual curriculum that provided the same experiences at each level. When we see the physical education curriculum of junior high school boys and girls consisting chiefly of basketball at the seventh, eighth, and ninth grade levels, we know that the principles of sequence have been violated.

Physical education has certain excellent organizational principles with scientific bases on which sequence and continuity can be made educationally defensible. As an example, the developmental principles that make us think generically in terms of free play, low organized games, and team games, proceed from activities involving simple reactions to those more complex. We do not start games with second-graders by explaining all the details of the rules and so forth before they begin to play. We give them concrete experience—trying the game—before we bring in the abstractions dealing with rules of conduct.

Children in the primary grades play naturally in small groups, numbering from three to six or more. The size increases with maturity. Children 3 to 4 years of age seem only vaguely aware of particular competitors if urged to see who can build the best house of blocks. With the present unfortunate tendency to push intensive competition for grades, for status, and for "getting ahead" down into the elementary grades through "beating someone else" in games, serious consideration should be given to this question of sequence. Obviously, the kind of competition that senior high school students may be able to handle satisfactorily would be very difficult for most sixth graders. Because of different levels of maturity, individual personality makeup, and the surrounding culture pattern (the group values that determine what constitutes

"success"), competition has a different meaning and significance to each boy or girl. Again, the sixth grader looks at the world through glasses that are a bit different from those of the eleventh grader.

We provide not only physical activities but also sociopsychological experience to correspond with the natural perceptions of children and youth at a given stage of development. Therefore we ask for serious research as to the physiological, social, and psychological effects of intensive competition among elementary schoolchildren in "Itsy-Bitsy" basketball, "Piggy-Bank Bowl" football, and similar debatable procedures in the name of education. When we ask the question, At what age and maturity levels should various activities be introduced and encouraged? we face the practical problem of sequence in the curriculum.

SEASONALITY

The seasonal rhythms of summer, autumn, winter, and spring and the climatic conditions in any given locality are factors of concern to anyone considering curriculum construction in physical education. Likewise, they affect sequence and continuity. In a part of the country where autumn weather lasts until late November, one might well plan in terms of large blocks of time labeled early autumn, late autumn, winter, and spring. These larger blocks are then divided into smaller time units depending on the type of instructional unit and the level of maturity of the students involved.

SCOPE AND CONTINUITY

If we recognize affective objectives such as the development of significant interests, appreciation, and attitudes as well as skill, we realize immediately that the problem of scope involves much more than mere teaching of motor skills. It also involves planning for learning experiences that will call forth the desirable attitudes and behavior patterns of thought, feeling, and involvement.

We must be realistic and recognize that when we often have students on the field or in the gymnasium for a meager half hour of activity we do face a problem. We do not want to take much of our limited time away from the possible achievement of the unique purposes of psychomotor development, for if we do not achieve biological fitness all else is lost. We do not want to spend a great portion of an already too short period in discussion and "chit-chat," yet if we are to relate the activities of physical education curriculum to our objectives, some means must be found for achievement in all the objective domains.

One major concern in curriculum construction is with the problem of scope. At times, imposed limitations hamper the range and depth of learning experiences.

To what extent is cognitive content, such as understanding of rules, care of equipment, safety measures, etiquette, and history of the activity, to be taught as well as motor skills? If the cognitive domain includes these learning experiences, they should be classified within the scope of the physical education curriculum. They should be included in the "subject matter" of physical education along with physical development and motor development.

CORRELATION AND INTEGRATION

If learning experiences are going to have the maximum relationship to life and living and become meaningful to people, we must seek for ways of developing interrelationships among simultaneous learnings.

It is true that physical education has a unique function to perform, but it also has a generalized educational function. If citizenship, sportsmanship, and character are generalized educational objectives—and they are—the several subjects in the curriculum must be coordinated with respect to these particular objectives of education. The principal objective is to have the student understand and recognize the interrelationships and extract principles that he/she may utilize in dealing with problems of living. By some cooperative faculty effort and coordinating scheme, ideas, attitudes, and ideals related to citizenship, sportsmanship, character, or health, "transfer of training" should be effected to a degree not possible when these outcomes are dealt with in "fatal disconnectedness" through single, isolated subjects. Here some effort is made to bring unity into life and to learn coordinated subjects with respect to particular objectives of education.

Correlation related to the physical education curriculum refers to the cross-reference of learning in this field to similar learnings in other fields. For example, if ninth-grade biology students are working on a unit entitled, "Maintaining a Healthy Body," certainly the elementary principles of the physiology of activity directly related to physical activities should be correlated with this unit. In this case the biology teacher and the physical education teacher should plan jointly.

A unit in world history on "Games and Sports in Ancient Greece" would provide many opportunities for correlation—the relating of certain aspects of physical education to related aspects of ancient Greek history. If fifth-grade children are studying a unit on life in the various countries of the United Nations and the music and physical education teachers join in planning corresponding folk songs and dances as a part of the culminating activities of this unit, we have another example of correlation. The establishment of relationship between two areas such as ancient history and physical education or the study of various national groups and their folk music and dances is correlation. The main purpose is to increase meaning and to improve learning.

Correlation as a process, particularly as it involves physical education, has developed few specific and widely used techniques and there is great need for intensive experimentation. Effective correlation of learning experiences depends, chiefly, on the serious cooperation of teachers concerned.

Integration refers to the process of relating the parts to a whole. Learning experiences are organized around a central theme or objective. An example is the integration of history and geography into the single broader division called "social studies," embracing a body of closely related materials and identifying the aims, methods, and content of these materials with the broader problems and purposes of social living in a complex industrial society.

The so-called "core," "unified studies," "common learnings," "general education," or "foundation" courses, as they are variously named, exemplify attempts at improving integration of learning. This is done by focusing attention on broad problems, which represent the persistent problems of living in a democratic society, which cut across subject matter lines, and which therefore involve aspects of the extended curriculum such as athletics, recreation, and personal-social relations in school club life.

Core topics usually represent "problems to be solved." Frequently, problem-solving techniques, pupil-teacher planning, and working in groups or committes are employed.

The chief characteristics of an integrated core program are as follows:

1. Requires a group of students to spend an important part of the school day with one teacher who has important coordinating and guidance functions
2. Cuts across subject matter lines and the unit or "broad field" of study has no subject matter label; however, it draws on many subjects, including science, art, and physical education, in the solution of problems
3. Requires special teachers in health, physical education, language, art, and so forth to cooperate in the planning and development of the unit; they are "resource" persons who aid the core teacher or at times work directly with the pupils
4. Provides for more extensive teacher-pupil planning and more opportunities for individual differences
5. Requires socialization, interaction among pupils, and group participation for planning and outlining appropriate action and for evaluation
6. Holds a high level of interest for pupils and staff
7. Takes the school program out of the realm of the strictly subject-centered approach and organizes learning experiences better to meet the developmental needs of youth

REACTORS

1. There should be a high correlation between the maturity levels of students and the proper sequencing of physical education experiences and activities.
2. At times, imposed limitations hamper the range and depth of activities in a curriculum.
3. A child learns from many experiences without the aid of either school or teacher.
4. The business of the school is consciously to arrange learning experiences, give direction, and avoid educational mismanagement.
5. The curriculum cannot be made up entirely

in advance or it would be merely a course of study.

6. Physical education conceived of merely as games presents no problems related to an organizing focus on which learning experiences are centered.

7. Research is still in the primary stage of development as to the total effects and relative values of innovative curriculum models and instructional strategies in physical education.

LEARNING ACTIVITIES

1. Throwing and catching skills used in various types of ball games comprise a portion of fundamental motor development. Select a grade division and illustrate for these skills the basic concepts of the following:
   a. Sequence and continuity
   b. Seasonal activities
   c. Scope and continuity
   d. Correlation and integration

2. Using the same skills:
   a. List specific activities to be offered for each grade level correlated with growth and development characteristics
   b. Outline the activities for one grade level

3. Select a subject matter area or unit (e.g., American Indian current trends) and propose correlated physical education activities.

UNIT EVALUATIVE CRITERIA

Can you:

1. Identify the growth and development characteristics of youth and correlate them with the proper progressive sequencing of experiences?

2. Explain the basic concepts of vertical and horizontal curriculum planning?

3. Differentiate between an integrated and a correlated curriculum?

4. List criteria for organizing physical education experiences and activities?

RESOURCES

AAHPER. *Curriculum improvement in secondary school physical education*. Washington, D.C.: The Alliance, 1973.

AAHPER. *Knowledge and understanding in physical education*. Washington, D.C.: The Alliance, 1969.

AAHPER. *Organizational patterns for instruction in physical education*. Washington, D.C.: The Alliance, 1971.

AAHPER. *Personalized learning in physical education*. Washington, D.C.: The Alliance, 1976.

AAHPER. *Tones of theory* (2nd ed.). Washington, D.C.: The Alliance, 1972.

Anderson, M. H., Elliot, M. E., & LaBerge, J. *Play with a purpose*. New York: Harper & Row, Publishers, Inc., 1972.

Annarino, A. A. *Fundamental movement and sport skill development*. Columbus, Ohio: Charles E. Merrill Publishing Co., 1973.

Arnheim, D. E., & Pestolesi, R. A. *Elementary physical education: a developmental approach* (2nd ed.). St. Louis: The C. V. Mosby Co., 1978.

Baley, J., & Field, D. *Physical education and the physical educator*. Boston: Allyn & Bacon, Inc., 1976.

Bookwalter, K., & VanderZwaag, H. J. *Foundations and principles of physical education*. Philadelphia: W. B. Saunders Co., 1969.

Brown, C., & Cassidy, R. *Theory in physical education—a guide to program change*. Philadelphia: Lea & Febiger, 1963.

Bucher, C. A. *Administration of health and physical education programs, including athletics* (6th ed.). St. Louis: The C. V. Mosby Co., 1975.

Bucher, C. A., & Koenig, C. *Methods and materials for secondary school physical education* (5th ed.). St. Louis: The C. V. Mosby Co., 1978.

Burton, E. C. *The new physical education for elementary school children*. Boston: Houghton-Mifflin Co., 1977.

Cassidy, R., & Caldwell, S. F. *Humanizing physical education*. Dubuque, Iowa: William C. Brown Co., Publishers, 1974.

Corbin, C. B. *A textbook of motor development*. Dubuque, Iowa: William C. Brown Co., Publishers, 1973.

Cowell, C. C., Schwehn, H. M., Walker, J., & Miller, A. G. *Modern methods in secondary school physical education*. Boston: Allyn & Bacon, Inc., 1973.

Cratty, B. J. *Movement behavior and motor learning*. Philadelphia: Lea & Febiger, 1974.

Dauer, V. *Essential movement experiences for preschool and primary children*. Minneapolis: Burgess Publishing Co., 1972.

Daughtrey, G. *Methods in physical education and*

health for secondary schools. Philadelphia: W. B. Saunders Co., 1967.

Davis, E. C., & Wallis, E. L. *Toward better teaching in physical education.* Englewood Cliffs, N.J.: Prentice-Hall, Inc., 1961.

Dowell, L. J. *Strategies for teaching physical education.* Englewood Cliffs, N.J.: Prentice-Hall, Inc., 1975.

Fait, H. F. *Physical education for the elementary school child.* Philadelphia: W. B. Saunders Co., 1976.

Felshin, J. *More than movement.* Philadelphia: Lea & Febiger, 1972.

French, E., & Lehsten, N. G. *Administration of physical education.* New York: Ronald Press Co., 1973.

Frost, R. B. *Shaping up to quality in physical education.* New London, Conn.: Croft Educational Series, 1968.

Frost, R. B., & Marshall, S. *Administration of physical education and athletics.* Dubuque, Iowa: William C. Brown Co., Publishers, 1977.

Gallahue, D. L. *Motor development and movement experiences for young children (3-7).* New York: John Wiley & Sons, Inc., 1976.

Gallahue, D. L., Werner, P. H., & Luedke, G. C. *A conceptual approach to moving and learning.* New York: John Wiley & Sons, Inc., 1975.

Kirchner, G. *Physical education for elementary school children.* Dubuque, Iowa: William C. Brown Co., Publishers, 1974.

Knapp, C., & Leonhard, P. H. *Teaching physical education in secondary schools.* New York: McGraw-Hill Book Co., 1968.

Lapp, D., Bender, H., Ellenwood, S., & John, M. *Teaching and learning: philosophical, psychological, curricular applications.* New York: Macmillan Publishing Co., Inc., 1975.

Larson, L. A. *Curriculum foundations and standards for physical education.* Englewood Cliffs, N.J.: Prentice-Hall, Inc., 1970.

Lockhart, A. S., & Slusher, H. S. *Contemporary read-* *ings in physical education.* Dubuque, Iowa: William C. Brown Co., Publishers, 1975.

Mackenzie, M. M. *Toward a new curriculum in physical education.* New York: McGraw-Hill Book Co., 1969.

Miller, A. G., & Massey D. M. *A dynamic concept of physical education for secondary schools.* Englewood Cliffs, N.J.: Prentice-Hall, Inc., 1963.

Miller, A. C., Cheffers, T. F., & Whitcomb, V. *Physical education: teaching human movement in the elementary schools.* Englewood Cliffs, N.J.: Prentice-Hall, Inc., 1974.

Nixon, J. F., & Jewett, A. E. *Physical education curriculum.* New York: Ronald Press Co., 1964.

Ohio State University. *How children develop.* Columbus, Ohio: The Ohio State University, 1946.

Saylor, J. G., & Alexander, W. M. *Curriculum planning for better teaching and learning.* New York: Rinehart & Co., Inc., 1958.

Singer, R. N. *Physical education: an interdisciplinary approach.* New York: Macmillan Publishing Co., Inc., 1972.

Singer, R. N., et al. *Physical education: foundations.* New York: Holt, Rinehart, & Winston, 1976.

Smart, M. S., & Smart, R. C., *Children development and relationships.* New York: Macmillan Publishing Co., Inc., 1967.

Straub, W. F. *The lifetime sports-oriented physical education program.* Englewood Cliffs, N.J.: Prentice-Hall, Inc., 1976.

Webster, R. W. *Philosophy of physical education.* Dubuque, Iowa: William C. Brown Co., Publishers, 1965.

Wells, K. F., & Luttgens, K. *Kinesiology—scientific basis of human motion.* Philadelphia: W. B. Saunders Co., 1976.

Wickstrom, R. L. *Fundamental motor patterns.* Philadelphia: Lea & Febiger, 1977.

Willgoose, C. E. *The curriculum in physical education.* Englewood Cliffs, N.J.: Prentice-Hall, Inc., 1978.

Daring ideas are like chessmen moved forward; they may be beaten, but they may start a winning game.

GOETHE

17 Organizational implications

CONTENTS

Perspective
Organization of schools
Operational and supervisory practices
Physical education requirements
Title IX
Mainstreaming
Accountability: competency-based education

COMPETENCIES

After completing this unit, you should be able to:

Differentiate between types of school organizational patterns.

Identify common staffing and supervisory practices.

Know the physical education requirements of your state.

Demonstrate a knowledge of the Title IX regulations and their implications for the physical education, intramural, and interscholastic programs.

Explain the concepts of mainstreaming and apply them in the physical education curriculum.

Identify the basic concepts of competency-based education.

Define the following:

Mainstreaming	Middle school
Handicapped	Auxiliary personnel
Title IX	
Nongraded	Team teaching
Open classroom	Accountability
Differentiated staffing	Trimester
	Quinmester
Hardware	Competency-based education
Software	

PERSPECTIVE

PRINCIPLE: Societal changes demand that educators periodically evaluate not only curriculum content but also the most effective organizational practices for transmitting this knowledge.

The purpose of this unit is to briefly describe implications of organizational and legislative changes affecting curriculum planning. Traditional and contemporary practices for organizing instruction include a variety of schedule and organizational patterns, changes in operational environmental procedures, differentiated staffing, expansion of learning resources, development of educational technology, and introduction of innovative instructional strategies.

Variations and modifications of traditional scheduling patterns are being used more extensively. (These will be discussed in the next unit.) The nongraded and open classroom concepts, although controversial, are being introduced particularly in elementary schools. Economic pressures are causing schools to consider extending the school year by adopting trimester and quinmester plans.

Operational procedures are permitting students more opportunities for selection, election, and choice of courses and activities. These include independent study options, minicourse offerings, extended curriculum, and individualized programs. Instructional staff members are being more effectively utilized by team teaching and the use of auxiliary personnel to assist teachers in instruction, class management, and clerical duties. State and federal legislation, such as Title IX and the Education of All Handicapped Children Act, is causing radical changes in class organization.

Instructional strategies and models have been introduced based on systems, competency-based, and mastery approaches. These strategies and models are using more extensive communication modes that include technological advances in hardware (teaching machines, computers, cassette recorders, television, videotape machines, and all types of projectors) and newly designed software (loop films, slides, videotapes, cassette tapes, sound pages, contracts, and individualized instructional packets).

The implications of these trends are having an impact on American elementary and secondary school education. The results of this impact are still not conclusive. A state of fermentation and distillation will always exist in a changing complex society. Societal changes demand that educators periodically evaluate not only curricular content but also the most effective organizational practices for transmitting knowledge.

ORGANIZATION OF SCHOOLS

American schools vary in their organizational patterns. The most basic organizational pattern is the 8-4 plan. In this plan, the 4-year senior high school is preceded by the 8-year elementary school. Another common pattern is the 6-2-4 plan, which consists of a 4-year high school, two grades in the junior high school, and six elementary grades. Variations of these basic patterns are the 6-6 or 7-5 plans, with the junior and senior high schools combined; the 6-3-3 with the junior high consisting of grades seven through nine; and, the middle school plan that is a 4-4-4 pattern that consists of the 4-year high school, four elementary grades, and grades five through eight grouped in a middle school.

Within these organizational patterns, an administrative device may be employed that rejects traditional grade designations and age grouping. This is a nongrading organization. Students are grouped by developmental age or achievement and given an opportunity to individually progress without being "locked-in" by a conventional organizational system.

OPERATIONAL AND SUPERVISORY PRACTICES

Elementary schools operate under two basic operational plans or modifications of these two. In the departmentalized classroom approach, the homeroom teacher will teach a certain number of subjects to his/her class and the remainder of the subjects will be taught by subject matter specialists. In the self-contained classroom approach, the students will be taught all subjects by the same homeroom teacher.

The teaching of physical education will vary in either of these plans or their modifications. Schools may employ a full-time or part-time physical education specialist, who is responsible for all instruction; physical education may be taught by the classroom teacher under the supervision of a physical education specialist, who may be responsible for supervising a number of schools; the classroom teacher may be solely responsible for the physical education instruction under the supervision of the principal; or physical education for the upper elementary grades may be taught by a specialist, who will supervise the instruction by a classroom teacher for the primary grades.

The practice in middle schools and junior and senior high schools is to employ physi-

cal education specialists. Depending on the size of the school, these specialists may also be involved in coaching responsibilities, intramural supervision, athletic training, health education, driver training education, and, in some cases, teaching other subject areas.

The introduction of team or cooperative teaching or differentiated staffing by many schools is initiating changes in class, staffing, and schedule organization. This concept is defined simply as the use of multiple teaching specialists for a given class in an instructional area. A team comprises not only certified teachers but may also include auxiliary personnel, such as paraprofessionals, teacher aides, teacher assistants, clerical assistants, technicians, or other qualified lay persons. All these practices have an effect on curriculum planning.

PHYSICAL EDUCATION REQUIREMENTS

It would be difficult to describe the variance in physical education requirements that exists for each state. The mandating of requirements is the responsibility of state departments of instruction or comparable legislative bodies. However, in this era of educational accountability, the concerted efforts of physical educators and professional organizations should ensure and justify a daily physical education experience for 12 years for every child.

TITLE IX

Title IX of the 1972 Amendments Act caused radical changes in physical education curriculum planning and instructional organization. This legislation prohibited discrimination on the basis of sex for all federally funded education programs and required institutions that were recipients of federal funds to conduct a self-evaluation on sex discriminatory practices. The results of this evaluation served as a basis for the development of a compliance plan that was to be completed by July 21, 1976, in all public elementary schools, and July 21, 1978, by all public secondary schools, colleges, and universities. This legislation affected all physical education, interscholastic, intercollegiate, and intramural programs from preschool through the college/university that were recipients of federal funds for their educational programs.

Basically, the interpretation of Title IX for physical education programs is that boys and girls have an equal opportunity to enroll in all program offerings. More specifically, classes must be coeducational. Ability grouping, not based on sex, may be used within a class for more effective instruction, with the exception of certain contact sports, such as football, wrestling, and basketball. In addition, varying standards of evaluation may be used in a physical education class if the standards used are not fair for either sex.

In the organization and administration of intramural, interscholastic, and intercollegiate athletic programs, Title IX guidelines should be followed. They are as follows:

1. Each institution must provide equal interscholastic/intercollegiate, club, recreational, and intramural athletic opportunity for both sexes.
2. If only one team is offered in a contact sport, both sexes must be permitted to try out for the team.
3. For interscholastic/intercollegiate and club sports, where team selection is based on competitive skills, there may be separate teams for boys/men and girls/women.
4. If only one team is offered in a bodily contact sport, members of the excluded sex need not be allowed to try out. However, schools are not prohibited from permitting both sexes to try out.
5. Where team selection is not competitive, noncontact intramural and recreational sports must be offered on a coeducational bases. Separate teams are not permitted except for contact sports.
6. Institutions must provide equal opportunities for both sexes as to:
    a. Facilities
    b. Equipment
    c. Supplies
    d. Equal practice and game time
    e. Medical services
    f. Coaching services
    g. Funding
    h. Academic tutoring
    i. Travel and per diem
    j. Housing and dining services
    k. Financial aid and/or scholarships

Each school system, college, and university should conduct a self-evaluation for achieving compliance in accord with Title IX regulations that will provide equal and increased opportunities for all students in physical education, intramural, interscholastic, and intercollegiate athletic programs.

MAINSTREAMING

Final rules and regulations for the Education of All Handicapped Children Act (PL 94-142) became fully effective October 1, 1977. It was designed to ensure that all handicapped children will be provided with a free appropriate public education that includes special education and related services to meet their unique needs.

This act has far-reaching implications for physical education, since physical education was listed as the only curriculum area included in the defined elements of special education and included special education; adapted physical education; motor development; fitness development; fundamental movement skills and patterns; body mechanics; individual and group games; and sport skills that include intramural, lifetime sports, and dance. It further specifies that each handicapped child must be afforded the opportunity to participate in the regular program available to the nonhandicapped child—"mainstreaming"—with the following exceptions:

1. The handicapped child is enrolled full-time in a separate facility.
2. The handicapped child needs a specifically designed physical education program as prescribed by the child's total individualized program.
3. The public education agency and parents mutually agree that the child should not participate in the regular physical education program.

In addition, provisions in the act ensured that handicapped children are provided with services comparable to the nonhandicapped not only in physical education but also for extracurricular activities that include athletics, health services, special interest groups or clubs, and recreation sponsored by a state or local educational agency.

Research pertaining to the effects of mainstreaming on the individual handicapped or nonhandicapped child and physical education instructional programs is still in early experimental stages. However, physical education teachers and/or curriculum planners must accept the challenges offered by mainstreaming through a systematic planning and programming process, the development of an individualized educational program (IEP) based on the assessed needs of the handicapped child, and monitoring and measuring the child's progress during instruction.

In the total organizational process, the physical education teacher is an integral part of a team working for more effective education through integration of learning by educating and aiding handicapped students in achieving self-actualization. Specific information for planning individu-alized education programs for the handicapped is described in Unit 20.

ACCOUNTABILITY: COMPETENCY-BASED EDUCATION

A controversial trend initiated by public demand is the "back to basics" movement. Due to this movement, an increasing number of states and school districts are requiring students to demonstrate minimal competencies for basic educational skills as one of many criteria for promotion and graduation. Educators are responding to this challenge by developing competency-based curricula incorporating competency-based instruction and assessment techniques that reflect the value, credibility, and accountability of their disciplines.

The implication of this trend for physical education curriculum planning is that more specific learning outcomes for any given grade level must be listed and information relative to the extent to which students have mastered particular skills, knowledges, and attitudes needs to be produced. As a result, competency-based curriculums are being developed that will result in accountability for physical education programs.

However, the decision to implement a competency-based program raises the following challenging questions for the physical educator:

1. What constitutes the minimal competencies for the physical education objectives at each grade level?
2. Are there valid and reliable ways to measure competency achievement?
3. Are competency testing programs fair and/or legal?
4. Will competency tests have curricular and instructional validity?
5. What do you do with students who do not achieve the minimal competencies?

6. When should competency testing be implemented?
7. Should we be accountable?

The answer to the last question should provide direction for future curriculum planning and instruction. As physical educators, we must be accountable—accountable to ourselves, to our students, and to the profession by ensuring that all students achieve a degree of competency for all the objectives stated in the curriculum. Efforts are being made in this direction by the development of physical education programs using a competency-based approach. These programs were initiated, in many cases, by federal Title IX funding or by state department support and have merit in providing leadership for the development of competency-based programs in physical education. Examples of these programs are shown in Units 18 and 19.

REACTORS

1. Societal changes demand that educators periodically evaluate not only curriculum content but also the most effective organizational practices for transmitting this knowledge.
2. The adoption of new organizational practices is a slow process.
3. Results as to the relative value and worth of many innovative organizational practices are not yet conclusive.
4. Equal opportunities should be provided for both sexes in all school activities.
5. Varying standards should be used for evaluation in physical education classes.
6. Research as to the effects of mainstreaming are still in early experimental stages.
7. Physical education requirements should be standardized for all states.

LEARNING ACTIVITIES

1. Conduct a survey of state physical education requirements for kindergarten through grade twelve. List the following:
   a. Minimal requirements
   b. Maximum requirements
   c. Most common requirement
2. Develop a rationale for offering daily physical education for kindergarten through twelfth-grade students.
3. Develop a chart with the following headings:
   a. Organizational practices
   b. Basic concepts
   c. Advantages
   d. Disadvantages
4. Design a checklist for determining if a school's physical education, intramural, and interscholastic programs are in compliance with Title IX regulations.
5. Critique the concept of mainstreaming:
   a. Pros
   b. Cons
   c. Your conclusions
   d. Your rationale
6. List the implications of a competency-based education for physical education.
   a. Pros
   b. Cons
   c. Your conclusions
   d. Your rationale

UNIT EVALUATIVE CRITERIA

Can you:
1. Identify traditional and newer organizational practices and their effect on curriculum planning?
2. Interpret Title IX regulations for the organization and administration of physical education, intramural, and interscholastic programs?
3. Interpret the basic concepts of mainstreaming and their implications for physical education and related services?

4. Justify required daily physical education for all grades?

5. Implement the basic concepts of competen-cy-based education for a physical education program?

RESOURCES

AAHPER. *Curriculum improvement in secondary school physical education*. Washington, D.C.: The Alliance, 1973.

AAHPER. *Organizational patterns for instruction in physical education*. Washington, D.C.: The Alliance, 1971.

Association for Supervision and Curriculum Development. *Curricular concerns in a revolutionary era*. Washington, D.C., The Association, 1971.

Brookwalter, K., & Vanderzwag, H. J. *Foundations and principles of physical education*. Philadelphia: W. B. Saunders Co., 1969.

Brown, C., & Cassidy, R. *Theory in physical education*. Philadelphia: Lea & Febiger, 1963.

Bucher, C. A. *Foundations of physical education* (7th ed.). St. Louis: The C. V. Mosby Co., 1975.

Bucher, C. A. *Administration of health and physical education programs, including athletics* (6th ed.). St. Louis: The C. V. Mosby Co., 1975.

Bucher, C. A., & Koening, C. *Methods and materials for secondary school physical education* (5th ed.). St. Louis: The C. V. Mosby Co., 1978.

Bush, R. N., & Allen, D. W. *A new design for high school physical education*. New York: McGraw-Hill Book Co., 1964.

Comes the revolution. *Time*. June 26, 1978, p. 54.

Dodson, C. How to comply with Title IX. In: *Proceedings: National Federation's Fifth Annual National Conference of High School Directors of Athletics*. Elgin, Ill.: National Federation of High School Directors of Athletics, Dec., 1974.

Dowell, L. J. *Strategies for teaching physical education*. Englewood Cliffs, N.J.: Prentice-Hall, Inc., 1975.

Fait, H. F. *Physical education for the elementary school child*. Philadelphia: W. B. Saunders Co., 1976.

Frost, R., & Marshall, S. *Administration of physical education and athletics*. Dubuque, Iowa: William C. Brown Co., Publishers, 1977.

Gunn, S. L. Mainstreaming is a Two-Way Street. *JOPER*, Sept. 1976, p. 48.

Hawkins, D. E., & Vinton, D. A. *The environmental classroom*. Englewood Cliffs, N.J.: Prentice-Hall, Inc., 1973.

Heidenreich, R. R. *Improvements in curriculum*. Virginia: College Readings, Inc., 1972.

Heitmann, H. M. *Organizational patterns for instruction in physical education*. Washington, D.C.: American Alliance for Health, Physical Education, and Recreation, 1971.

Jansema, P. Get ready for mainstreaming. *JOPER*, Sept. 1977, p. 50.

Knapp, C., & Leonhard, P. H. *Teaching physical education in secondary schools*. New York: McGraw-Hill Book Co., 1968.

Larson, L. A. *Curriculum foundations and standards for physical education*. Englewood Cliffs, N.J.: Prentice-Hall, Inc., 1970.

Mackenzie, M. M. *Toward a new curriculum in physical education*. New York: McGraw-Hill Book Co., 1969.

McKnight, D., & Hult, J. Competitive athletics for girls—we must act. *JOPER*, June 1974, p. 45.

Moyer, L. J. Women's athletics—what is our future. *JOPER*, January 1977, p. 52.

National Association of Sports and Physical Education. Title IX prospects and problems. *JOPER*, May 1976, p. 23.

National Association of Sports and Physical Education. Quality secondary physical education. *JOPER*, Jan. 1978, p. 42.

Nixon, J. F., & Jewett, A. E. *Physical education curriculum*. New York: Ronald Press Co., 1964.

Nixon, J. F., & Ulrich, C. *Tones of theory*. Washington, D.C.: American Alliance for Health, Physical Education, and Recreation, 1972.

University of the State of New York, The State Education Department. *Mainstreaming: Idea and actuality*. Albany, N.Y.: The University of the State of New York, 1975.

U.S. Department of Health, Education, and Welfare, Office for Civil Rights. *Final Title IX regulations implementing education amendments of 1972—prohibiting sex discrimination in education*. Washington, D.C.: U.S. Government Printing Office, 1975.

Singer, R. N., et al. *Physical education: foundations*. New York: Holt, Rinehart, & Winston, 1976.

Slusher, H. S., & Lockhart, A. S. *Anthology of contemporary readings*. Dubuque, Iowa: William C. Brown Co., Publishers, 1966.

Willgoose, C. E. *The curriculum in physical education*. Englewood Cliffs, N.J.: Prentice-Hall, Inc., 1979.

The heavens themselves, the planets, and this centre, observe degree,
priority and place; insisture, course, proportion, season, form,
office, and custom, in all line of order.

WILLIAM SHAKESPEARE

18 Organizational patterns and programs

COMPETENCIES

After completing this unit, you should be able to:

Identify the criteria for the selection of a schedule pattern.

Contrast and compare conventional and flexible schedule patterns.

Describe the advantages and disadvantages of a wide variety of schedule patterns.

Integrate the parts, elements, or components of a physical education curriculum into a meaningful pattern.

Define the following:

Conventional schedule	Seasonal plan
Flexible schedule	Election
Modular schedule	Selection
Basic weekly plan	Scope
Informal yearly plan	Sequence
Cyclic plan	Extended curriculum

PERSPECTIVE

PRINCIPLE: It is the responsibility of the physical educator/administrator to design and justify the best "game plan" that will benefit the greatest number of students.

The fusion of the parts, elements, and components of the curriculum into a meaningful whole is accomplished through program design and scheduling patterns. This is where the curriculum pieces "fit together" and are seen and better understood because of their relationship to the total curriculum.

In designing or selecting programs and scheduling patterns, the curriculum planner must consider the following criteria:

1. The needs and interests of students
2. The number and type of students
3. The preentry skills of the students
4. The terminal objectives to be achieved
5. The type, expertise, and number of instructional personnel
6. The grouping of students
7. The availability of equipment and supplies
8. The number of teaching stations
9. Time allotments
10. School and state requirements
11. Type of instructional strategy to be employed
12. Availability and types of instructional aids
13. Seasonality

In addition to meeting these criteria, a program and schedule pattern must be compatible with the philosophies of the school's administration and of the community.

The integration of the physical education schedule with the overall school's schedule of classes should be a joint effort of the physical education staff and school administrator responsible for scheduling the total curriculum. In many cases the school administrator may not be cognizant of the unique problems involved in the organization of physical education activities, and it is the responsibility of the physical educator/administrator to design and justify the best "game plan" that will benefit the greatest number of students.

This requires the curriculum planner to be familiar with the types of organizational patterns available and also to understand the characteristics, advantages and disadvantages, and specific purposes and uses of each. In addition, the curriculum planner must have the insight to modify and adapt existing patterns or create a new pattern that may be more feasible and effective for a specific situation and school level based on the aforementioned criteria.

CONVENTIONAL AND FLEXIBLE SCHEDULE PATTERNS

The two most widely used school organizational scheduling patterns are the conventional and flexible (modular) patterns. With the flexible pattern, more individualized-type programming permitting student choice and selection, such as competency-based, elective minicourses, and independent study, can be implemented. A comparative analysis of conventional and flexible scheduling patterns and their characteristics is shown in Table 4.

Generally, for a conventional scheduling pattern, there is a traditional six- or seven-period school day divided into 45- to 55-minute class periods. Each subject is allotted one class period, usually at the same

Table 4. General characteristics of scheduling patterns for instruction in physical education*

Characteristic	Conventional	Flexible		
		Competency-based	Elective mini-courses	Advanced courses
Time allotment	Each subject is allotted an equal amount of time. Class periods usually last 45 to 55 minutes, and each subject usually occurs at the same time each day.	Class periods are usually based on short time segments called modules, varying from 10 to 30 minutes. Modules are combined to provide appropriate time blocks for specific instruction. Activities may occur in various time slots throughout the day.	Time segments can vary from 6 days to 9 weeks and can fit into regular daily periods.	Courses may incorporate additional time for independent study along with regular class periods.
Number of students	Normally the class size remains constant, with 35 pupils a recommended maximum.	Class size may vary depending on the needs of the student, the type of activity, and the availability of staff.	Class size may vary, depending on interests of students, availability of facilities, and role of the staff.	Class size may vary, depending on interests and abilities of students, availability of facilities, and role of the staff.
Grouping patterns	Generally the class is heterogeneous. Individual needs are provided for through patterns of grouping that may include circuit teaching, small group activities, etc.	Students are grouped on the basis of specific needs and/or competencies. This provides a vehicle for dealing with both deficiencies and particular abilities and talents.	Students are grouped primarily on the basis of interest. Courses may be designed so as to provide electives on a restricted or open basis. They may also be phased in order to provide for different ability levels.	Students are grouped on the basis of interest and ability. A course design is based on prerequisites.

*From Cripe, J. In C. Nordholm et al. (Eds.), *Motion and direction: physical education curriculum guide, grades K-12*. Indianapolis: Indiana State Department of Public Instruction, 1976, p. 8. *Continued.*

Table 4. General characteristics of scheduling patterns for instruction in physical education—cont'd

Characteristic	Conventional	Flexible		
		Competency-based	Elective mini-courses	Advanced courses
Coeducational programs	Generally, classes may be coeducational except for the contact sport areas.	Classes are organized on the basis of an individual's skill ability.	Classes could be organized on the basis of the individual's interest.	Classes could be organized on the basis of the individual's interest and skill ability.
Teacher role	The teacher generally functions primarily as the leader or director of class activities.	The teacher assumes a variety of roles: serving as a diagnostician and prescriber, setting up activities designed to meet specific student needs, working in team situations with other teachers.	The teacher assumes a variety of roles: guidance counselor to students, course designer, director of activities, supervisor, etc. He/she may work in a team teaching arrangement, including the use of paraprofessionals.	The teacher assumes a variety of roles: guidance counselor to students, course designer, director of activities, supervisor, etc. He/she may work in a team teaching arrangement, including the use of paraprofessionals.
Student options	There is limited choice in terms of the type of activity available. Special provision may be made, however, for pupils with particular needs.	Activities are based on particular needs and/or abilities. Optional approaches may include small-group activities, independent study, or leadership responsibilities.	Activities may be based on an analysis of needs and interests. Choices may include out-of-school experiences, independent study, or small-group experiences.	Activities may be based on an analysis of needs, interests, skills, and leadership ability. Choices may include out-of-school experiences, independent study, or small-group experiences.
Student evaluation	Evaluation is usually based on group norms. However, provisions might be made for individual progress.	Evaluation is generally based on attainment of realistic competencies on an individual basis.	Evaluation strategies may vary. Assessment may be based on performance, interest, ability, etc., or a combination of factors.	Evaluation strategies may vary. Assessment may be based on performance, interest, ability, etc., or a combination of factors.

Table 5. Student's schedule in a conventional schedule pattern*

Time	Monday	Tuesday	Wednesday	Thursday	Friday
8:00-8:55	←		English		→
9:00-9:55	←		Mathematics		→
10:00-10:55	←		Study		→
11:00-11:55	←		Social studies		→
12:00-12:55	←		Lunch-homeroom		→
1:00-1:55	←		Physical education		→
2:00-2:55	←		Science		→
3:00-3:55	←		Industrial arts		→

*From Heitmann, H. M. (Ed.) *Organizational patterns for instruction in physical education.* Washington, D.C.: American Alliance for Health, Physical Education, & Recreation, 1971, p. 5.

time for the assigned days, regardless of what subject content is to be taught.

A student's schedule in a conventional schedule might look like that shown in Table 5.

A flexible scheduling pattern is not limited to a traditional time unit (period). A school day is divided into modules, generally 10 to 30 minutes in length. It is flexible in that the time modules may be used singly or in any of a number of combinations by each subject area. This is determined primarily by the instructional activity of that subject area and may vary for a given day, week, or semester. An example of a flexible schedule for a student is shown in Table 6.

Examples of programs, instructional materials and instructional strategies used for conventional, competency-based, elective mini-courses, and advanced courses schedule patterns are described in the last section of this unit and in Unit 19.

WEEKLY, SEASONAL, SEMESTER, AND YEARLY SCHEDULE PATTERNS

The weekly, seasonal, semester, and yearly organization of physical education experiences within a conventional or flexible scheduling pattern may be approached

for each school level in a variety of ways. In selecting or modifying one of these programming approaches, the curriculum planner must not only be aware of the previously mentioned criteria for designing and selecting programs but, in addition, consider the scope, range, sequence, and time allotments of curriculum content for the total K through 12 physical education program.

The concept of scope refers to the areas of content and the range of activity that we want children and youth to learn. Progression reflects a sequence. The idea of progression is still very important in programming activities. The curriculum is more than a hodgepodge of separate activities or units; it should be a patterned and continuous design. Continuity is needed so that one activity has some logical basis for leading to another. The child naturally learns to walk before running. Sequence of growth toward educational objectives requires a sequence of skills and activities as well as adequate time allotment. Some orderly programming of physical education experiences is imperative. The scope and sequence of curriculum content by grades and years based on the maturity levels of the learners and the levels of competency

Table 6. A sample student flexible schedule for 1 week with 30-minute modules and many variables (secondary)*

Time	Monday	Tuesday	Wednesday	Thursday	Friday
8:00	English	Independent Study	English	Social Studies	English
8:30					
9:00	Independent Study	Math	Guidance	Math	Social Studies
9:30			Social Studies		
10:00	Math	English	Math	English	
10:30	Industrial Arts	Typing	Industrial Arts	Typing	Math
11:00	Boys' Chorus		Boys' Chorus	Physical Education	
11:30	Independent Study		English		
12:00	Lunch	Lunch	Lunch	Lunch	Lunch
12:30	Social Studies	Social Studies	Independent Study	Independent Study	Guidance
1:00	Physical Education				
1:30		Industrial Arts		Industrial Arts	Physical Education
2:00			Physical Education		
2:30					English
3:00					Boys' Chorus

*From Heitmann, H. M. (Ed.). *Organizational patterns for instruction in physical education*. Washington, D.C.: American Alliance for Health, Physical Education, and Recreation, 1971, p. 13.

they should achieve are important factors for organizing experiences.

The most commonly used weekly, seasonal, semester, and yearly organizational patterns are described and analyzed in Table 7.

Table 7. Weekly, seasonal, semester, and yearly organizational patterns*

Organizational pattern	Description	Advantages	Disadvantages
Elementary			
Basic weekly programs	Activities are alternated according to certain days of the week. The same pattern is repeated every week.	Excellent for the primary grades when taught by a classroom teacher Helps ensure proper content balance in the program Helps when sharing equipment and facilities Students know what to expect and can dress in the proper clothing	Teacher may not allow for flexibility Not appropriate when physical education is not planned on a daily basis
Seasonal programs	Experiences are organized as a series of seasonal units. The unit may vary in time. In a daily program two units may be offered concurrently. This plan is best suited for the intermediate grades.	Provides for seasonal interest and motivation Provides for continuity of presentation More advantageous for the intermediate grades due to increased interest span Minimizes the need for sophisticated facilities	In many cases, a well-balanced program is not maintained and individual needs are not met
Informal yearly balance programs	An outline would provide only a single list of suggested activities for use if time permits. No definite sequence of units is set; no specific pattern for the weekly schedule is followed.	Physical education teacher can work with the classroom teachers individually to plan the most suitable program for that situation	Based on close evaluation and supervision of the physical education teacher May allow for too much program variability Requires constant evaluation and adjustment of daily lesson plans

*Adapted from Nixon, J., & Jewett, A. *Physical education curriculum.* New York: The Ronald Press Co., 1964, pp. 111-121. Used by permission.

Continued.

Table 7. Weekly, seasonal, semester, and yearly organizational patterns—cont'd

Organizational pattern	Description	Advantages	Disadvantages
Elementary—cont'd			
Cyclic programs	This plan is quite similar to a basic unit plan; however, time units are based on the administrative division of the school year.	Provides for continuity and progression Provides for strict budgeting of time Helps assure logical progression By budgeting the time between fewer activities, each year allows for more intensive instruction that can lead to greater skill development	Program flexibility is limited Is ineffective with short class periods
Middle/junior and senior high schools			
Prescribed single block programs	This sets up a basic sequence to be followed by all students. Units may vary in length. The students are classified according to grade level, and the curriculum is planned on a 3-, 4-, or 6-year basis, depending on the school organization.	The pattern encourages progression in the curriculum Provides for balance and planned sequence Allows dual activities to be presented Lends itself to the small school where grades are combined	Does not compensate for individual differences within any one grade level May involve overlap and repetition Requires a great deal of administrative scheduling
Concurrent programs	Two units of activities are scheduled for the same grade level concurrently. This plan is widely used in schools offering classroom work in physical education or when facilities such as swimming pools are shared.	Provides a higher level of interest and motivation Makes optimum use of facilities and personnel Allows for flexible pupil grouping and team teaching	Difficulty in mainstreaming continuity of instruction Increased scheduling difficulties
Elective and selective programs	Elective programs are possible with many pattern variations. The basic program can be carried through the ninth, tenth, or eleventh grade, allowing the student to elect in the last 2 or 3 years.	Meets individual differences Increases student's enthusiasm for participation in physical education	Is practical only for large schools with good instructional facilities Requires great care in scheduling and record maintenance

SAMPLE PROGRAMS

The sample programs that follow are examples of weekly, seasonal, semester, and yearly programs using the various organizational patterns. They are not to be considered as universally applicable to all schools and all climates. The selected programs are basically schools from midwestern or eastern climates. However, they do illustrate the implementation of a wide variety of basic and modified schedule patterns. Additional programs will be presented in Unit 19.

Basic weekly programs

BASIC WEEKLY SCHEDULE PLAN, GRADES 1 AND 2

(Developed for Frankfort Elementary Schools, Frankfort, Ind.)

Period	Monday	Tuesday	Wednesday	Thursday	Friday
Fall (9 weeks)	Low organization games	Rhythmical activity	Low organization games	Body conditioning	Low organization games
Early winter (9 weeks)	Rhythmical activity	Low organization games	Self-testing	Low organization games	Self-testing
Late winter (9 weeks)	Rhythmical activity	Low organization games	Self-testing	Low organization games	Self-testing
Spring (9 weeks)	Low organization games	Rhythmical games	Low organization games	Body conditioning	Low organization games

BASIC WEEKLY SCHEDULE PLAN, GRADES 1 AND 2

(Developed for Frontier School Corporation, Brookston, Ind.)

Week	Grade 2			Grade 1	
	Monday	Wednesday	Friday	Tuesday	Thursday
1	No school	Orientation, classification, and testing	Classification and testing	Orientation, classification, and testing	Classification and testing
2	Continue classification and testing	*Games* Sliding Hopping Twisting and turning	*Games* Hopping Skipping Galloping Stretching and bending	*Games* Walking Running	*Games* Walking Running Skipping
3	*Games* Walking Running Jumping Leaping	*Games* Hopping Skipping Rising and falling	*Self-testing* Playground apparatus Combatives	*Games* Walking Running Skipping Galloping	*Games* Walking Running Skipping Galloping

Continued.

BASIC WEEKLY SCHEDULE PLAN, GRADES 1 AND 2—cont'd

Week	Grade 2			Grade 1	
	Monday	Wednesday	Friday	Tuesday	Thursday
4	*Games* Walking Running Jumping Swinging and swaying	*Games* Tossing Throwing Dodging Tagging	*Self-testing* Outdoor apparatus Combatives	*Games* Running Skipping Galloping	*Self-testing* Combatives Playground apparatus
5	*Games* Rolling Catching Tossing	*Games* Rolling Catching Throwing	*Conditioning* Obstacle over and under Game type Marching	*Conditioning* Obstacle *Games* Sliding Skipping Galloping Hopping	*Self-testing* Apparatus Marching
6	*Games* Bouncing Throwing Catching Running	*Games* Dodging Tagging Turning Leaping	*Self-Testing* Apparatus *Conditioning* Circuit training Marching	*Games* Leaping Rising and falling Twisting and turning	*Self-testing* Apparatus Jumping *Conditioning* Obstacle
7	*Games* Relays—running and turning Marching	*Conditioning* Obstacle through and around Game-type Marching	*Games* Relays—rolling and turning, passing and running	*Games* Walking Running Jumping Dodging	*Games* Walking Running Jumping Tagging Dodging
8	*Conditioning* Circuit training Game-type	*Games* Bouncing Running Rolling	No school	*Self-testing* Relays—running and turning	No school
9	*Games* Bouncing Kicking Hitting	*Games* Bouncing Kicking Hitting Catching	*Self-testing* Combatives Relays—ballhandling	*Games* Sliding Jumping Hopping Leaping Turning	*Games* Rolling Catching Bouncing
10	*Games* Rolling Catching Hitting Throwing Kicking	*Conditioning* Circuit training *Self-testing* Combatives Marching	*Conditioning* Game-type *Relays* Kicking and running	*Games* Rolling Catching Bouncing	*Self-testing* Combatives Track—running and jumping
11	*Rhythms* Walking Running Skipping Jumping Sliding	No school	*Rhythms* Galloping Sliding Leaping Swaying Twisting	*Rhythms* Walking Running Tiptoeing Skipping	*Rhythms* Walking Running Skipping Jumping Galloping

Week	Grade 2			Grade 1	
	Monday	Wednesday	Friday	Tuesday	Thursday
12	*Rhythms* Walk-hop Run-fall Run-leap Run-hop-skip	*Rhythms* Folk dance	*Self-testing* Combatives *Conditioning* Circuit train- ing Game-type	*Rhythms* Walking Running Skipping Tiptoeing Jumping Hopping	*Rhythms* Singing games
13	*Rhythms* Folk dance	*Rhythms* Folk dance and mixers	No school	*Rhythms* Walking Running Skipping Galloping	No school
14	*Rhythms* Folk dance and mixers	*Rhythms* Creative dance	*Rhythms* Creative dance	*Rhythms* Sliding Galloping Hopping Skipping	*Rhythms* Folk dance
15	Evaluation	Evaluation	Evaluation	Evaluation	Evaluation
16	*Conditioning* Obstacle Circuit train- ing Game-type	*Rhythms* Marching *Self-testing* Rope activity *Games* Relays— passing and run- ning	*Games* Running Jumping Skipping	*Rhythms* Folk dance	*Rhythms* Folk dance
17	*Games* Hopping Skipping Bouncing Catching	*Games* Throwing Catching Running	*Self-testing* Combatives *Conditioning* Obstacle Circuit train- ing	*Conditioning* Obstacle Game-type *Rhythm* Marching	*Rhythms* Folk dance
18	*Games* Running and tag Hopping and skipping	*Games* Bouncing and kick- ing Throwing and run- ning	Evaluation	*Rhythms* Creative dance	*Rhythms* Creative dance
19	*Conditioning* Circuit train- ing	*Conditioning* Game-type Circuit train- ing	*Self-testing* Rope activity *Conditioning* Obstacle	*Self-testing* Combatives Rope activity Rhythms	*Conditioning* Circuit train- ing Obstacle Game-type

Continued.

BASIC WEEKLY SCHEDULE PLAN, GRADES 1 AND 2—cont'd

Week	Grade 2			Grade 1	
	Monday	Wednesday	Friday	Tuesday	Thursday
20	*Self-testing* Stunts and tumbling	*Self-testing* Stunts and tumbling	*Self-testing* Stunts and tumbling	*Conditioning* Game-type *Self-testing* Stunts and tumbling	*Conditioning* Game-type *Self-testing* Stunts and tumbling
21	*Games* Bouncing Catching Throwing	*Self-testing* Rope activity *Conditioning* Circuit training *Rhythms* Marching	*Self-testing* Stunts and tumbling	*Self-testing* Stunts and tumbling	*Self-testing* Stunts and tumbling
22	*Self-testing* Stunts and tumbling	*Games* Rolling Catching Bouncing	*Self-testing* Stunts and tumbling	*Self-testing* Stunts and tumbling	*Self-testing* Stunts and tumbling
23	*Rhythms* Singing games	*Self-testing* Stunts and tumbling Rope activity	*Self-testing* Stunts and tumbling Rope activity	*Self-testing* Stunts and tumbling	*Self-testing* Stunts and tumbling
24	*Games* Running Skipping Bouncing Catching	*Rhythms* Singing games	*Self-testing* Stunts and tumbling Rope activity	*Self-testing* Rope activity Stunts and tumbling	*Self-testing* Rope activity Stunts and tumbling
25	*Self-testing* Rope activity *Conditioning* Game-type	*Conditioning* Circuit training Game-type *Games* Relay—bending and hopping	*Games* Walking Running Jumping	*Games* Relays—running and turning Ball-handling	*Games* Running Catching Throwing Passing
26	*Games* Running Skipping Hopping	*Conditioning* Circuit training Obstacle *Self-testing* Combatives	*Rhythms* Singing games	*Games* Dodging Tagging Hitting Catching	*Games* Running Jumping Throwing Catching Hitting
27	*Conditioning* Obstacle *Self-testing* Rope activity Marching	*Conditioning* Circuit training Game-type *Relays* Running and jumping	*Games* Dodging Tagging Twisting Turning	*Games* Starting Stopping Twisting Turning Stretching	*Games* Dodging Jumping Leaping Starting Stopping Stretching
28	*Games* Rolling Bouncing Throwing Catching	*Games* Rolling Bouncing Throwing Catching Hitting	*Conditioning* Obstacle Circuit training Game-type	*Self-testing* Track and field Running Jumping	*Self-testing* Apparatus

	Grade 2			Grade 1	
Week	Monday	Wednesday	Friday	Tuesday	Thursday
29	*Games* Rolling Bouncing Throwing Catching Hitting	*Self-testing* Running track *Conditioning* Circuit training	*Self-testing* Running track and jumping	*Self-testing* Track and field Starting and running	*Self-testing* Track and field Starting, running, jumping
30	*Rhythms* Singing games	*Self-testing* Outdoor apparatus	*Self-testing* Track—running, jumping, throwing	*Self-testing* Rope activity *Conditioning* Game-type	*Games* Throwing Kicking Hitting
31	*Games* Skipping Hopping Jumping Bouncing	*Self-testing* Apparatus	*Self-testing* Track—running and jumping	*Self-testing* Outdoor apparatus	*Self-testing* Track and field— starting, running, jumping, throwing
32	*Games* Running Catching Throwing	*Conditioning* Obstacle Circuit training Relays—hopping and jumping	*Self-testing* Track—running, jumping, throwing	*Games* Hitting Striking Kicking	*Games* Hitting Striking Throwing Catching Kicking
33	*Games* Rolling Bouncing Catching Striking	*Self-testing* Outdoor apparatus	*Games* Hopping Skipping Chasing Fleeing	*Games* Hitting Striking Kicking Throwing Catching Pushing Pulling	*Games* Hitting Kicking Throwing Catching Batting
34	*Games* Catching Throwing Striking	*Games* Throwing Catching Kicking	*Relays* Jumping and running	*Conditioning* Obstacle Circuit training Game-type	*Conditioning* Game-type *Self-testing* Combatives *Games* Relays— kicking and running
35	*Conditioning* Circuit training Obstacle Game-type	*Games* Relays—running, jumping, turning	*Conditioning* Circuit training	*Conditioning* Obstacle Relays— kicking and running	Evaluation
36	Evaluation	Evaluation	Evaluation	Evaluation	Evaluation

BASIC WEEKLY SCHEDULE PLAN, GRADES 5 AND 6

Weeks	Monday	Tuesday	Wednesday	Thursday	Friday
First 6 weeks					
1	Organization	Organization	Softball funda-mentals	Flag football fundamentals	Group games
2	Talk on pool safety and health habits	Soccer funda-mentals			Relays
3	Review strokes		Softball	Touch football	Group games
4					Relays
5					Group games
6	Diving		Testing	Testing	Testing

Weeks	Monday	Tuesday	Wednesday	Thursday	Friday
Second 6 weeks					
1	Diving	Relays	Basketball fun-damentals	Stunts	Square dance
2	Practice strokes and diving	Group games			
3	Water games	Relays		Tumbling	Social dancing
4		Group games			
5		Relays			
6	Testing	Group games		Testing	Testing

BASIC WEEKLY SCHEDULE PLAN, GRADES 5 AND 6—cont'd

Weeks	Monday	Tuesday	Wednesday	Thursday	Friday
Third 6 weeks					
1	Circuit	Relays	Basketball fundamentals	Apparatus	Volleyball fundamentals
2	Weight training	Group games			
3	Track training	Relays	Testing		
4	Obstacle	Group games	Basketball	Tumbling	
5		Relays			
6	Testing	Testing			Testing

Weeks	Monday	Tuesday	Wednesday	Thursday	Friday
Fourth 6 weeks					
1	Badminton	Group games	Basketball	Stunts	Volleyball
2		Relays			
3		Group games			
4		Relays		Testing	
5		Group games		Apparatus	
6		Relays			

Continued.

BASIC WEEKLY SCHEDULE PLAN, GRADES 5 AND 6—cont'd

Weeks	Monday	Tuesday	Wednesday	Thursday	Friday
Fifth 6 weeks					
1	Badminton	Group games	Basketball	Tumbling	Folk dance
2		Relays			
3		Testing			
4		Group games		Stunts	
5		Relays			Recreational games
6	Testing	Group games	Testing	Testing	

Weeks	Monday	Tuesday	Wednesday	Thursday	Friday
Sixth 6 weeks					
1	Archery	Tennis	Track fundamentals	Softball	Relays
2					Group games
3					Relays
4					Group games
5			Track meet		Testing
6	Testing	Testing	Testing	Inventory for close of school	Inventory for close of school

Seasonal programs

SEASONAL ACTIVITY PROGRAM, NURSERY SCHOOL–KINDERGARTEN

(Courtesy Milwaukee Public Schools, Milwaukee, Wis.)

Fall

Outdoors—September-October
Formations
Locomotor activities (walking, running, skipping)
Exercises
Ball skills (throwing, catching, kicking, rolling, bouncing, striking)
Games (low organization)
NOTE: Use games employing the ball skills.

Winter I

Indoors—November-January
Formations
Exercises
Rhythmical activities
Basic movements
Games (low organization)

Winter II

Indoors—February-April
Formations
Exercises
Self-testing (stunts, tumbling, balance beams)
Rhythmical activities
Games (low organization)

Spring

Outdoors—May-June
Formations
Exercises
Locomotor activities
Self-testing (ropes, playground equipment)
Ball skills
Games (low organization)

SEASONAL ACTIVITY PROGRAM, GRADES 3 AND 4*

(Courtesy Evansville-Vanderburgh School Corporation, Evansville, Ind.)

Report period	Season	Physical fitness	Team sport	Games of low organization	Recreational activities	Gymnastics	Track and field	Rhythmical activities
I (6 weeks)	Fall	Self-testing Rope jump	Lead-up games for soccer, speedball, football	Active Ball-type Quiet Races-relays	Cageball	Playground apparatus		Basic rhythms Dances— folk, circle
II (6 weeks)	Fall	Self-testing Rope jump Physical fitness test	Lead-up games for speedball, soccer, volleyball	Active Ball-type Relays Quiet	Tetherball	Playground apparatus		Basic rhythms Dances— folk, circle
III (6 weeks)	Winter	Self-testing	Lead-up games for basketball	Active Circle Ball-type Quiet Relays	Deck tennis	Stunts Tumbling (elementary)		Basic rhythms Dances— folk, circle
IV (6 weeks)	Winter	Self-testing	Lead-up games for basketball	Active Circle Ball-type Quiet Relays	Shuffleboard Hopscotch	Stunts Tumbling (elementary)		Basic rhythms Dances— folk, circle
V (6 weeks)	Spring	Self-testing	Lead-up games for softball	Active Throw-catch Ball-type Quiet Relays	Four square	Playground apparatus		Basic rhythms Dances— folk, circle
VI (6 weeks)	Spring	Self-testing Rope jump Retest physical fitness	Spring break	Active Throw-catch Ball-type Relays	Sidewalk tennis	Playground apparatus	Track/field events (elementary)	Basic rhythms Dances— folk, circle

*Conditioning and warm-up exercises done daily; achievement tests periodically.

SEASONAL ACTIVITY PROGRAM, GRADES 5 AND 6

(Courtesy Crawfordsville Public Schools, Crawfordsville, Ind.)

Grade 5

Fall

Monday	Games—recreational
Tuesday	Games—athletic lead-up to speedball
Wednesday	Games—athletic lead-up to football
Thursday	Games—athletic lead-up to speedball
Friday	Conditioning—circuit training

Early winter

Monday	Games—athletic lead-up to basketball
Tuesday	Rhythmical activities
Wednesday	Self-testing—stunts, tumbling
Thursday	Rhythmical activities
Friday	Games—recreational and low organization

Late winter

Monday	Games—athletic lead-up to volleyball
Tuesday	Rhythmical activities
Wednesday	Self-testing—stunts and tumbling
Thursday	Rhythmical activities
Friday	Games—athletic lead-up to basketball

Spring

Monday	Games—athletic lead-up to softball, baseball
Tuesday	Self-testing—track and field
Wednesday	Self-testing—track and field
Thursday	Conditioning—circuit training
Friday	Games—athletic lead-up to softball, baseball

Grade 6

Fall

Monday	Games—athletic lead-up to football
Tuesday	Games—athletic lead-up to football
Wednesday	Games—athletic lead-up to soccer, speedball
Thursday	Games—recreational and low organization
Friday	Physical fitness and skill testing

Early winter

Monday	Games—athletic lead-up to basketball
Tuesday	Games—athletic lead-up to volleyball
Wednesday	Rhythmical activities
Thursday	Rhythmical activities
Friday	Physical fitness and skill testing

Late winter

Monday	Games—athletic lead-up to basketball
Tuesday	Games—athletic lead-up to volleyball
Wednesday	Rhythmical activities
Thursday	Rhythmical activities
Friday	Physical fitness testing and skill testing

Spring

Monday	Games—athletic lead-up to softball, baseball
Tuesday	Self-testing activities—track and field
Wednesday	Self-testing activities—track and field
Thursday	Games—recreational and low organization
Friday	Physical fitness and skill testing

SEASONAL ACTIVITY PROGRAM, GRADES 7 AND 8—FALL PROGRAM

(Suggested by Sayers J. Miller, Jr., physical education teacher, Blue Island High School, Blue Island, Ill.)

Weeks	Monday	Tuesday	Wednesday	Thursday	Friday
Weeks 1-3: Flag football					
1	Fundamentals and rules of flag football—forward passing and receiving; lead-up game Tuesday		Punting, kicking, and receiving kicks, plus lead-up games and review		Centering ball and receiving by backs, plus review
2	Ball-carrying tactics and fundamentals, plus lead-up games and review		Blocking tactics and fundamentals, plus lead-up games		Offensive and defensive group work and tactics
3	Continue offensive and defensive work, plus lead-up games	Review of fundamentals, tactics, rules, safety, etc., plus actual games of flag football			
Weeks 4-6: Soccer					
4	Fundamentals, rules, and scoring of soccer, plus fundamentals of kicking and passing; beginning of lead-up games Wednesday			Blocking and volleying, plus review and lead-up games	
5	Heading and running tactics and fundamentals, plus review and lead-up games		Goal shooting and practice of goalkeeper skills, plus review and lead-up games		Team tactics and play, both offensive and defensive
6	Continue offensive and defensive work, plus lead-up games	Review of fundamentals, tactics, rules, safety, etc., plus actual games of soccer			
Weeks 7-10: Gymnastics (indoors) OR Badminton and archery (outdoors)					
7	Advanced tumbling, including headstands, handsprings, somersaults, cartwheels, walking on hands, free exercise				
8	Fundamentals of rope climbing, with tests of speed and skill Tuesday		Fundamental stunts and work on the horse		Fundamental stunts on the horizontal bars
9	Continued work on the horizontal bars	Fundamental stunts on the parallel bars		Fundamental stunts from the springboard	
10	Fundamental stunts involving the buck, plus review of the springboard		Demonstration of stunts on the rings and trampoline	Obstacle course involving skills learned in previous gymnastic work	
OR 7-8	Fundamentals of badminton				
9-10	Fundamentals of archery				

SEASONAL ACTIVITY PROGRAM, GRADE 9

(Developed by Frank Kurth for Hobart High School, Hobart, Ind.)

Season	Monday	Tuesday	Wednesday	Thursday	Friday
Fall outdoor program (6 weeks)	Conditioning exercises Obstacle course Flag football	Warm-up relays Obstacle course Flag football	Army ball, speedball, box hockey "choice"	Conditioning exercises Obstacle course Touch football	Warm-up relays Speedball Box hockey or horseshoes
Fall indoor program (6 weeks)	Line games Volleyball	Swimming	Warm-up relays Circle games Boxing fundamentals	Swimming	Line games Volleyball
Early winter indoor program (6 weeks)	Line warm-up drills with basketball Passing Shooting Guarding	Selected tumbling and stunt activities	Warm-up relays Basketball fundamentals Shooting Basketball games	Selected tumbling stunt activities Pyramids	Selected games
Late winter indoor program (6 weeks)	Advanced basketball drills One-goal basketball Individual test	Basketball games Mat and weight activities Swimming	Mat work Wrestling Rhythmical activities	Basketball games Mat and rope activities Swimming	Basketball games Mat and weight activities Gymnasium meet
Spring indoor program (6 weeks)	Track activities		Tap dancing Rope skipping Shadow boxing		
Spring outdoor program (6 weeks)	Softball Track activities	Softball Track activities	Softball Track	Softball Track	Softball Track

SEASONAL ACTIVITY PROGRAM, GRADE 10

(Developed by Jane Stratman for Logansport High School, Logansport, Ind.)

Season	Monday	Tuesday	Wednesday	Thursday	Friday
Early fall	5 minutes of conditioning exercises	5 minutes of conditioning exercises	5 minutes of conditioning exercises	5 minutes of conditioning exercises	5 minutes of conditioning exercises
	Field hockey fundamentals and rules	Play Field hockey	Swimming	Beginning tennis fundamentals	Beginning tennis
Fall	5 minutes of conditioning exercises	5 minutes of conditioning exercises	5 minutes of conditioning exercises	5 minutes of conditioning exercises	5 minutes of conditioning exercises
	Team sports Volleyball Kickball	Stunts and tumbling	Swimming	Square and social dancing	Self-testing and achievement tests
Winter	5 minutes of conditioning exercises	5 minutes of conditioning exercises	5 minutes of conditioning exercises	5 minutes of conditioning exercises	5 minutes of conditioning exercises
	Basketball and relays	Basketball and volleyball	Swimming	Bowling fundamentals	Bowling competition
Early spring	5 minutes of conditioning exercises	5 minutes of conditioning exercises	5 minutes of conditioning exercises	5 minutes of conditioning exercises	5 minutes of conditioning exercises
	Recreational sports Badminton Shuffleboard Table tennis	Stunts and tumbling	Swimming	Square and social dancing	Recreational sports and relays
Spring	5 minutes of conditioning exercises	5 minutes of conditioning exercises	5 minutes of conditioning exercises	5 minutes of conditioning exercises	5 minutes of conditioning exercises
	Golf fundamentals	Golf	Swimming	Softball Tennis	Self-testing and achievement tests

SEASONAL ACTIVITY PROGRAM, GRADES 11 AND 12
Eleventh grade

Early fall—32 periods

Tennis	7 periods
Football	8 periods
Field hockey	8 periods
Archery	7 periods
Recreational activities	2 periods

Early winter—48 periods

Conditioning activities	3 periods
Tumbling	10 periods
Basketball	8 periods
Conditioning activities	3 periods
Dance	10 periods
Conditioning activities	4 periods
Wrestling	8 periods
Recreational activities	2 periods

Late winter—50 periods

Conditioning activities	3 periods
Basketball	10 periods
Tumbling	10 periods
Conditioning activities	7 periods
Volleyball	10 periods
Recreational activities	3 periods
Wrestling–figure control	7 periods

Early spring—30 periods

Softball	5 periods
Golf	7 periods
Track	7 periods
Speedball and soccer	11 periods

Twelfth grade

Early fall—32 periods

Tennis	7 periods
Speedball and soccer	12 periods
Archery	7 periods
Conditioning activities	2 periods
Recreational activities	4 periods

Early winter—48 periods

Dance	10 periods
Basketball	5 periods
Tumbling	8 periods
Volleyball	8 periods
Self-defense	3 periods
Conditioning activities	4 periods
Dance	10 periods

Late winter—50 periods

Dance	8 periods
Basketball	5 periods
Tumbling	8 periods
Volleyball	8 periods
Self-defense	5 periods
Conditioning activities	4 periods
Recreational activities	4 periods
Dance	8 periods

Early spring—30 periods

Conditioning activities	2 periods
Track	7 periods
Field hockey	8 periods
Golf	7 periods
Softball	6 periods

Informal yearly balance programs

INFORMAL YEARLY BALANCE PLAN, NURSERY SCHOOL–KINDERGARTEN

(Courtesy St. Patrick's Elementary School, Terre Haute, Ind.)

Module one: Sensorimotor activities

Behavioral objectives:
1. Students will demonstrate awareness of right and left, forward and back.
2. Students will successfully keep ball in air with paddle three times in succession.

Equipment: 10 Nerf balls and 10 paddles, 10 colored circles

Activities:
Angels in the snow—command movements
Command movements—standing
Creeping and crawling
Simon says—identifying body parts (if needed)
Game—colors

Module two: Body capabilities on tumbling mats

Behavioral objectives:
1. Children will become familiar with mat by lying, rolling, standing, and sitting on mat.
2. Children will perform various activities on mats that will involve space awareness,

body control, and skills such as curling, rolling, and pulling.
3. Students will have body control and balance on mats and will be able to work cooperatively with others on mat.

Equipment: 3 mats
Activities:

Sensory introduction to mats	Mat landing
	Partner pull
Touch and go	Mat balance
Mat maze	Partner and group
Stretch-o-mat	mat balancing
Curl-o-mat	Change-o-mat

Module three: Moving with balance

Behavioral objectives:
1. Students will do series of arm and leg movements in their individual spaces to develop static balance.
2. Students will participate in variety of activities that involve using balance and space awareness while working cooperatively with other students.
3. Students will be able to keep their balance in different body positions for at least 5 seconds.

Equipment: 10 bean bags, 20 carpet squares or paper plates
Activities:

Position balancing: move feet or legs, arms, or hands in sitting, standing, kneeling, on all fours, and lying-down positions.
Balance tag
Shadow balancing
Low steppingstones
Bean bag balancing
Partner bridging
Partners in balance

Module four: Ball handling

Behavioral objectives:
1. In gym, students will move progressively from bean bag to fleece ball to playground ball, performing progressively more difficult skills.
2. Students must successfully progress from tossing bean bag to oneself to successfully (without dropping it) tossing it to another person five times and also demonstrate these same skills with fleece ball.

3. Students will perform progressive skills with playground ball, moving from tossing ball to oneself and catching it, to bouncing ball in front of them and catching with both hands. Task is successful when five out of ten can do this.

Equipment: 10 bean bags, 10 yarn/fleece balls, 10 playground balls (8½″)
Activities:

Experiment with bean bag
Toss bean bag to partner
Experiment with fleece ball
Toss fleece ball to partner
Explore with playground ball
Toss playground ball to partner
Bounce playground ball
Bean bag relay

Module five: Tumbling and stunts

Behavioral objectives:
1. Children will demonstrate control over their bodies through balance and coordination, giving them a sense of achievement and accomplishment.
2. Success is achieved if students can hold their balance in three of different positions practiced for 5 seconds.

Equipment: 3 mats, 10 bean bags
Activities:

Rolling log
Forward roll
One-leg balance
Double-knee balance
Head balance—bean bag on head
Directional walk
Fluttering leaf
Elevator
End with progression type of course from mat to mat

Module six: Locomotor movement

Behavioral objectives:
1. Students will use skill and coordination of body parts involved in locomotor activities to help develop total body endurance.
2. Different locomotor activities such as walking, running, hopping, jumping, and leaping will be demonstrated by children.

3. Success is attained when students demonstrate control of body on the move, will stop with control, and will work cooperatively.

Equipment: 10 ropes, 10 Hula Hoops

Activities:

Walking in place	Hopalong Cassidy
Walking as if . . .	Jump still
Walk along	Jump along
Running in place	Rock-a-leap
Running wild	Obstacle leaping
Place hop	Leap the brook

Module seven: Creative movements and rhythmical expression

Behavioral objectives:

1. Students will demonstrate different movements with accompanying beat and will change their speed when beat changes.
2. Students will follow instructions of a record and move however they think particular animal named moves.

Equipment: Record—"Creative Movements and Rhythmic Expression" by Hap Palmer; Record—"Getting to Know Myself" by Hap Palmer; 10 hoops

Activities:

Teacher who couldn't talk
Percussion instruments
Moving game
Sammy
Circle game (if needed)
Turn around (if needed)
Game popcorn
Action drama—The Giant

Module eight: Physical fitness emphasis

Behavioral objectives:

1. Students will demonstrate different exercises as directed and be able to perform any given exercise.
2. Students will successfully complete miniobstacle course, using different walks and movements listed.

Equipment: 10 bean bags, 10 jump ropes, drum, cones for obstacle course, objects to go over, under, etc.

Activities:

Animal walks—alligator, bear, kangaroo	Jump and hop over ropes
Lifting	Finish with mini-
Rhythmical running	obstacle course

Module nine: Individual space

Behavioral objectives:

1. In gym, children will freely experiment with moves they can make with their body and/or equipment.
2. Students will participate in various activities that will help them become aware of space through exploration of body parts, body positions, and body management.
3. Children will be able to respond quickly and correctly, will have control of their body in desired position, and will correctly identify body parts.

Equipment: 10 bean bags, ropes, yarn balls, Hula Hoops

Activities:

Movement exploration—What can you do with each piece of equipment?
Tall-small
Can you?—with body positions and parts
Ducks fly
Follow the leader—do as I do
Statues
Simon says

Module ten: Rhythms

Behavioral objectives:

1. In gym, students will participate in three dances that stress following leader, following directions in beat to song, sliding, and socially participating with partner.
2. Students will perform dances, staying close to beat and movements of dance. They will perform correct steps of dance in time with music.
3. Dances will be successful when half of children can correctly follow steps and stay in beat with music.

Equipment: Records: "Dance of Greeting," "Chimes of Dunkirk," "The Thread Follows the Needle"

Activities:

Learn and perform "Dance of Greeting," "Chimes of Dunkirk," and "The Thread Follows the Needle"

INFORMAL 6-WEEK PLAN, GRADES 1 AND 2

(Developed by Jule Ann Collins and staff, Lafayette School Corporation, Lafayette, Ind.)

Week 1

Lesson 1
   Warm-up exercises
   Running and tagging game
   Movement fundamentals
   Evaluation
Lesson 2
   Warm-up exercises
   Running and tagging game
   Toy interpretations
   Evaluation

Week 2

Lesson 3
   Warm-up exercises
   Singing game (choose two)
   Movement fundamentals
   Evaluation
Lesson 4
   Warm-up exercises
   Self-testing activities
   Evaluation

Week 3

Lesson 5
   Warm-up exercises
   Movement exploration
   Running and tagging game
   Evaluation
Lesson 6
   Warm-up exercises
   Folk dances
   Singing game
   Evaluation

Week 4

Lesson 7
   Warm-up exercises
   Small equipment—balls
   Throwing and catching game

Lesson 8
   Warm-up exercises
   Balls–hoops–bean bags
   Evaluation

Week 5

Lesson 9
   Warm-up exercises
   Movement exploration
   Self-testing—stunts
Lesson 10
   Warm-up exercises
   Throwing and catching game
   Movement exploration

Week 6

Lesson 11
   Warm-up exercises
   Throwing and catching game
   Self-testing
Lesson 12
   Warm-up exercises
   Rhythms—interpretations
   Work with ropes
   Singing game

INFORMAL YEARLY PLAN, GRADES 3 AND 4

The master lesson chart (MLC) is designed to aid the teacher in the selection of daily physical education activities. The chart provides a variety of activities and is arranged to provide appropriate activities according to the seasons of the year. The chart is based on a 32-week school year, allowing for 4 weeks of vacation. Each week consists of two $1/2$-hour sessions. This allows for a total of 64 class periods $1/2$ hour in duration.

The order in which the activities are listed is the order in which they should be taught. Begin with lesson 1 and proceed through the entire chart. When vacations arrive, mark your spot on the chart and resume the lessons at this point when you return. If for some reason you complete all the lessons before the end of the school year, go back to the beginning of the chart and start over.

	Grade 3		Grade 4
Lesson	Activities suggested	Lesson	Activities suggested
1	Circle	1	Team
2	Fleeing and chasing	2	Team
3	Throwing and catching	3	Individual
4	Throwing and catching	4	Conditioning
5	Conditioning	5	Dance
6	Balance and stunts and tumbling	6	Dance—modern, folk, and square
7	Stunts and tumbling	7	Stunts and tumbling
8	Stunts and tumbling	8	Stunts and tumbling
9	Balance	9	Team
10	Relays and fleeing and chasing	10	Team
11	Conditioning	11	Individual
12	Relays and fleeing and chasing	12	Conditioning
13	Relays and circle	13	Team
14	Fundamental rhythms	14	Dance
15	Stunts and tumbling	15	Dance
16	Balance, optional—evaluation	16	Balance, optional—evaluation
17	Conditioning	17	Team
18	Relays and fleeing and chasing	18	Creative and fundamental rhythms
19	Relays and circle	19	Individual
20	Fleeing and chasing	20	Conditioning
21	Throwing and catching	21	Team
22	Relays and fleeing and chasing	22	Balance
23	Stunts and tumbling	23	Individual
24	Stunts and tumbling	24	Individual
25	Conditioning	25	Team
26	Circle and fleeing and chasing	26	Creative and fundamental rhythms
27	Balance and stunts and tumbling	27	Individual
28	Balance	28	Team
29	Fleeing and chasing	29	Conditioning
30	Fundamental rhythms	30	Balance
31	Fundamental rhythms	31	Stunts and tumbling
32	Balance and stunts and tumbling, optional—evaluation	32	Stunts and tumbling
33	Creative rhythms	33	Team
34	Throwing and catching	34	Team
35	Conditioning	35	Creative and fundamental rhythms
36	Conditioning	36	Conditioning
37	Circle and relays	37	Team
38	Circle and relays	38	Balance
39	Circle and fleeing and chasing	39	Individual
40	Circle and fleeing and chasing, optional—evaluation	40	Individual, optional—evaluation
41	Fundamental rhythms	41	Team
42	Circle and fleeing and chasing	42	Creative and fundamental rhythms
43	Folk and square dancing	43	Individual
44	Creative rhythms	44	Conditioning
45	Circle and throwing and catching	45	Team
46	Throwing and catching	46	Balance
47	Conditioning and fleeing and chasing	47	Stunts and tumbling

Continued.

Grade 3		Grade 4	
Lesson	Activities suggested	Lesson	Activities suggested
48	Stunts and tumbling	48	Stunts and tumbling
49	Fundamental rhythms and balance	49	Team
50	Throwing and catching	50	Team
51	Throwing and catching	51	Team, optional—evaluation
52	Circle and fleeing and chasing	52	Balance
53	Stunts and tumbling	53	Team
54	Stunts and tumbling	54	Conditioning
55	Fundamental rhythms	55	Individual
56	Folk and square dancing	56	Individual
57	Balance	57	Dance
58	Circle and fleeing and chasing	58	Dance
59	Conditioning	59	Team
60	Balance and stunts and tumbling	60	Team
61	Stunts and tumbling, optional—evaluation	61	Individual
62	Stunts and tumbling	62	Conditioning
63	Fundamental rhythms	63	Stunts and tumbling
64	Balance and stunts and tumbling	64	Stunts and tumbling, optional—evaluation

INFORMAL 6-WEEK PLAN, GRADES 5 AND 6

(Developed by Jule Ann Collins and staff, Lafayette School Corporation, Lafayette, Ind.)

	First 6 weeks	Second 6 weeks	Third 6 weeks	Fourth 6 weeks	Fifth 6 weeks	Sixth 6 weeks	Supplementary
Games and relays	X	X	X	X	X	X	X
Soccer	*						
Volleyball		*					
Basketball			*				
Softball						*	
Creative dance	X	X	X	*	X	X	
Folk dance	X	X	X	*	X	X	
Lummi sticks	X	X	X	*	X	X	
Marching	X	X	X	*	X	X	
Square dance	X	X	X	*	X	X	
Tinikling	X	X	X	*	X	X	
Small equipment	X	X	X	X	X	X	
Stunts and tumbling					*		
Track and field						*	
Tests—physical fitness	*					*	
Shuffleboard and table tennis							X

NOTE: Activities checked all across should be encompassed within the plan for *every* 6 weeks.
*Means concentration during this grading period.

Cyclic programs

CYCLIC PLAN, GRADE 4

(Courtesy Indiana Department of Instruction, Indianapolis, Ind.)

The semester is 18 weeks in length. Physical education is offered three times a week for 25-minute periods. About 7 minutes are used for management duties, leaving an 18-minute activity period. The semester is divided into three cycles each 6 weeks in length. Cycle I is planned for outdoor activities (fall semester), and cycles II and III are planned for an indoor program. The time devoted to activity is budgeted as follows: games, 50%; rhythms, 20%; self-testing, 20%; and conditioning, 10%. The figures on the time budget are calculated as follows:

$$3 \times 18 \text{ minutes} = 54 \text{ minutes of activity per week}$$
$$6 \times 54 \text{ minutes} = 324 \text{ minutes of activity per cycle}$$
$$3 \times 324 \text{ minutes} = 972 \text{ minutes per semester}$$

After the semester time budget is determined, weekly schedules can be planned and activities selected to fit the schedule.

Time budget, fall semester

	Cycle I (minutes)	Cycle II (minutes)	Cycle III (minutes)	Total (minutes)
Conditioning exercises and posture work (10%)	32	32	32	96
Rhythmical activities (20%)	0	97*	97	194
Self-testing activities (20%)	65†	65	65	195
Games—all types (50%)	227‡	130§	130	487
TOTAL	324	324	324	972

*About 1½ hours.
†Slightly over 1 hour.
‡A little less than 4 hours.
§About 2 hours.

MODIFIED CYCLIC PLAN FOR GRADES 7 TO 9

The physical education program is offered for 1 semester per year for seventh and eighth graders and 2 semesters for ninth graders. It is a modified cyclic plan, with those activities offered in grade 6 repeated at different levels in grade 8 and those in grade 7 repeated at different levels in grade 9. The coeducational classes are divided into two groups, with the activities being taught in blocks. The student remains in his/her assigned group for 1 or 2 semesters to ensure instruction in all activities.

Activity chart, grades 7 and 8

Week	Grade 7 Group A activities	Grade 7 Group B activities	Week	Grade 8 Group A activities	Grade 8 Group B activities
1	Conditioning and self-defense	Aquatics	1	Archery	Flag football
2			2	Soccer	Track and field
3	Handball		3		
4	Volleyball	Social and contemporary dance	4	Track and field	Soccer
5		Handball	5		
6	Aquatics	Volleyball	6	Flag football	Aquatics
7			7	Outdoor education	
8		Conditioning and self defense	8	Aquatics	Outdoor education
9	Social and contemporary dance		9		Archery
10	Outdoor education	Outdoor education	10	Paddleball	Square dance
11	Field hockey	Tennis	11	Square dance	Paddleball
12			12	Wrestling (boys) Modern dance (girls)	Wrestling (boys) Modern dance (girls)
13	Softball		13	Badminton	Folk dance
14	Tennis	Softball	14	Gymnastics	Basketball
15		Golf	15		
16			16	Folk dance	Badminton
17	Golf	Field hockey	17	Basketball	Gymnastics
18			18		

Activity chart, grade 9

Week	Group A activities	Group B activities	Week	Group A activities	Group B activities
1	Golf	Conditioning and self-defense	19	Aquatics	Social and contemporary dance
2			20		Square dance
3	Conditioning and self-defense	Golf	21	Square dance	
4			22		Basketball
5	Field hockey	Soccer	23	Aquatics	
6			24		
7			25		Aquatics
8	Flag football	Softball	26	Social and contemporary dance	
9	Soccer	Field hockey	27		
10			28	Track and field	Tennis
11			29		
12	Basketball	Volleyball	30		
13			31	Softball	Flag football
14			32	Outdoor education	Outdoor education
15	Handball	Handball	33		
16	Volleyball	Aquatics	34	Tennis	Track and field
17			35		
18		Social and contemporary dance	36		

Concurrent programs

CONCURRENT PROGRAM, GRADE 7
Implementation procedures

1. There are 18 weeks of physical education for each group, and each student has class twice a week.
2. The schedule is for the fall semester; the spring schedule just reverses the order of the indoor and outdoor activities.
3. There are three instructors—team teaching.
4. The three groups are coeducational, and students stay in the same group throughout the 18 weeks.
5. Instructors will each teach one outdoor activity, therefore students will have a different teacher for each area. Indoor teachers will teach different areas, with the exception of the aquatics instructor, who will teach only aquatics the last 6 weeks.

Duration (weeks)	Group 1	Group 2	Group 3
1	Orientation	Orientation	Orientation
3	Golf, tennis, archery	Soccer, flag football	Gymnastics
3	Gymnastics	Golf, tennis, archery	Soccer, flag football
3	Soccer, flag football	Gymnastics	Golf, tennis, archery
2	Volleyball, basketball	Dance	Badminton, bowling, table tennis
2	Aquatics	Volleyball, basketball	Dance
2	Badminton, bowling, table tennis	Aquatics	Volleyball, basketball
2	Dance	Badminton, bowling, table tennis	Aquatics

CONCURRENT PROGRAM, GRADE 8
Implementation procedures

1. The program is based on four 9-week terms, with each 9-week term subdivided into three 3-week sections.
2. All activities are conducted on a coeducational basis.
3. The aquatics instructor has been designated as an additional instructor during the outdoor segments.
4. Each instructor teaches the same 3-week course three times during each 9-week block.
5. Tournament I: 1 week will be basketball play; 1 week will be volleyball play; 1 week will be competitive swimming.

Week	Group 1	Group 2	Group 3
1-3	Field hockey	Tennis	Flag football
4-6	Flag football	Field hockey	Tennis
7-9	Tennis	Flag football	Field hockey
10-12	Aquatics	Volleyball	Dance
13-15	Dance	Aquatics	Volleyball
16-18	Volleyball	Dance	Aquatics
19-21	Gymnastics	Tournament I	Badminton
22-24	Badminton	Gymnastics	Tournament I
25-27	Tournament I	Badminton	Gymnastics
28-30	Softball	Track and field	Lacrosse
31-33	Lacrosse	Softball	Track and field
34-36	Track and field	Lacrosse	Softball

CONCURRENT PROGRAM, GRADE 9

Week	Class period 1	Class period 2	Class period 3
Semester I			
1	—	Fitness testing	Fitness testing
2	Field hockey	Field hockey	Field hockey
3	Field hockey	Field hockey	Field hockey
4	Field hockey	Field hockey	Field hockey
5	Field hockey	Field hockey	Field hockey
6	Soccer/wrestling/self-defense	Soccer/wrestling/self-defense	Soccer/wrestling/self-defense
7	Soccer/wrestling/self-defense	Soccer/wrestling/self-defense	Soccer/wrestling/self-defense
8	Soccer/wrestling/self-defense	Soccer/wrestling/self-defense	—
9	Soccer/wrestling/self-defense	Soccer/wrestling/self-defense	Conditioning
10	Dance	Dance	Dance
11	Dance	Dance	Dance
12	Dance	Dance	—
13	Badminton/floor hockey	Badminton/floor hockey	Badminton/floor hockey
14	Badminton/floor hockey	Badminton/floor hockey	Badminton/floor hockey
15	Badminton/floor hockey	Badminton/floor hockey	Basketball/volleyball
16	Basketball/volleyball	Basketball/volleyball	Basketball/volleyball
	CHRISTMAS VACATION		
17	Basketball/volleyball	Basketball/volleyball	Basketball/volleyball
18	Basketball/volleyball	Basketball/volleyball	Basketball/volleyball
Semester II			
1	Fitness testing	Fitness testing	Conditioning
2	Basketball/volleyball	Basketball/volleyball	Basketball/volleyball
3	Basketball/volleyball	Basketball/volleyball	Basketball/volleyball
4	Basketball/volleyball	Basketball/volleyball	Basketball/volleyball
5	Basketball/volleyball	Badminton/floor hockey	Badminton/floor hockey
6	Badminton/floor hockey	Badminton/floor hockey	Badminton/floor hockey
7	Badminton/floor hockey	Badminton/floor hockey	Badminton/floor hockey
8	Table tennis/horseshoes/skateboarding	Table tennis/horseshoes/skateboarding	Table tennis/horseshoes/skateboarding
9	Table tennis/horseshoes/skateboarding	Conditioning	Soccer/wrestling/self-defense
	SPRING VACATION		
10	Soccer/wrestling/self-defense	Soccer/wrestling/self-defense	Soccer/wrestling/self-defense
11	Soccer/wrestling/self-defense	Soccer/wrestling/self-defense	Soccer/wrestling/self-defense
12	Soccer/wrestling/self-defense	Soccer/wrestling/self-defense	Soccer/wrestling/self-defense
13	Softball/archery	Softball/archery	Softball/archery
14	Softball/archery	Softball/archery	Softball/archery
15	Tennis/golf	Tennis/golf	Tennis/golf
16	Tennis/golf	Tennis/golf	Tennis/golf
17	Tennis/golf	Tennis/golf	Tennis/golf
18	—	Fitness testing	Fitness testing

Prescribed single block programs

SINGLE BLOCK PLAN, GRADES 5 AND 6 (Each class meets twice a week.)

Week	Grade 5 Period 1	Grade 5 Period 2	Grade 6 Period 1	Grade 6 Period 2
1	Orientation — Introduction to soccer		Orientation — Introduction to soccer (if time)	
2	Conditioning (5-10 minutes) — Soccer: drills		Conditioning (5-10 minutes) — Soccer: drills	
3				
4	Conditioning (5-10 minutes) — Soccer: lead-up games		Conditioning (5-10 minutes) — Soccer: lead-up games	
5	Conditioning (5-10 minutes) — Speedball: lead-up games			
6				
7	Conditioning — Flag football		Conditioning — Soccer	
8			Conditioning — Obstacle course	
9			Conditioning for tumbling — Introduction to tumbling and balance beam	
10	Obstacle course		Conditioning — Tumbling and balance beam	
11	Conditioning for tumbling — Introduction to tumbling and balance beam			
12	Conditioning — Tumbling and balance beam			
13				
14				
15				
16			Circuit training — Recreational activities*	
17				
18	(½ week) Obstacle course			

*Shuffleboard, camping, table tennis.

Week	Grade 5		Grade 6	
	Period 1	**Period 2**	**Period 1**	**Period 2**
19	Conditioning Introduction to folk dance		Obstacle course	
20	Conditioning Folk dance		Conditioning Square dance	
21				
22				
23				
24				
25	Circuit training Recreational activi- ties†	Conditioning Folk dance		
26				
27			Conditioning Newcomb	
28		Circuit training		
29		Recreational activi- ties†		
30	Conditioning for softball			
31	Softball: drills, lead- up games	Conditioning for softball		
32		Softball: drills, lead- up games		
33	Conditioning Softball		Conditioning for track and field Introduction to track and field	
34			Conditioning Track and field	
35				
36	Last week duties		Last week duties	

†Bicycle safety, bowling, bait casting.

SINGLE BLOCK PLAN, GRADES 7 AND 8

(Developed for Rensselaer School Corporation, Rensselaer, Ind.)

Grade 7		Grade 8	
Week	Activity	Week	Activity
Semester I		**Semester I**	
1	Administrative-testing-recreational	1	Administrative-testing-recreational
2	Archery	2	Tennis
3	Archery	3	Tennis
4	Tennis	4	Archery
5	Tennis	5	Archery
6	Soccer	6	Flag football
7	Soccer	7	Flag football-soccer
8	Field hockey	8	Soccer
9	Field hockey	9	Swimming
10	Field hockey	10	Swimming
11	Basketball	11	Swimming
12	Basketball	12	Swimming
13	Swimming	13	Figure control-wrestling
14	Swimming	14	Figure control-wrestling
15	Swimming	15	Figure control-wrestling
16	Swimming	16	Volleyball
17	Dance	17	Dance
18	Administrative-testing-recreational	18	Administrative-testing-recreational
Semester II		**Semester II**	
19	Administrative-testing-recreational	19	Administrative-testing-recreational
20	Swimming	20	Basketball
21	Swimming	21	Basketball
22	Swimming	22	Conditioning
23	Gymnastics	23	Swimming
24	Gymnastics	24	Swimming
25	Gymnastics	25	Swimming
26	Dance	26	Volleyball
27	Dance	27	Gymnastics
28	Volleyball	28	Gymnastics
29	Volleyball	29	Gymnastics
30	Speedball	30	Track and field
31	Speedball	31	Track and field
32	Track and field	32	Softball
33	Track and field	33	Softball
34	Golf	34	Golf
35	Golf	35	Golf
36	Administrative-testing-recreational	36	Administrative-testing-recreational

SINGLE BLOCK PLAN, GRADES 9 AND 10

(Developed for Frontier High School, Brookston, Ind.)

Grade 9		Grade 10	
Activity	Periods*	Activity	Periods*
Organization	6	Organization	6
Conditioning	3	Conditioning	3
Tennis-recreation	10	Tennis–cross country–recreation	10
Soccer	5	Speedball	5
Speedball	5	Soccer	5
Field hockey	8	Field hockey	13
Rhythmical games	5	Weight training	5
Modern dance	17	Wrestling	12
Volleyball (power)	12	Volleyball	12
Conditioning	6	Conditioning	6
Basketball	12	Basketball	12
Gymnastics	30	Gymnastics	30
Indoor hockey	5	Rhythmical games	5
Badminton-recreation	10	Badminton-recreation	10
Bowling	5	Indoor hockey	5
Softball	5	Bowling	5
Tennis-recreation	5	Softball	5
Golf	10	Golf	10
Archery	5	Tennis-recreation	5
Testing	5	Testing	5
Clean-up	5	Clean-up	5

*Total of 174 days for each grade level.

Elective and selective programs

A SELECTIVE PROGRAM FOR MIDDLE SCHOOL

(Courtesy Bel Air Middle School, Bel Air, Md.)

Procedures

The physical education department offers a program of elective activities whereby students make course selections that meet their needs, interests, and abilities. At prescribed times students are given the opportunity to elect from a different list of available courses.

To assure that students elect a balanced program, teachers, using individual conferences, periodically review each student's program and progress. In addition, the developmental nature of certain activities requires that students meet selected prerequisite skills before participating in that activity. For such classes, beginning, intermediate, and advanced levels of activities are offered. The program contains individual, rhythmical, and team activities. Students select offerings at the end of each unit. Units vary in time modules.

Unit offerings

Unit 1
  Badminton
  Track and field
  Golf
  Archery
  Physical fitness test

Unit 2
  Lacrosse (girls)
  Field hockey
  Basketball
  Flag football
Unit 3
  Lacrosse
  Soccer
  Tumbling and vaulting
  Team handball
Unit 4
  Speedball
  Beginning volleyball
  Square dance
  Yoga/conditioning
  Wrestling
Unit 5
  Social dance
  Tumbling and vaulting
  Volleyball
  Riflery
  Fencing/conditioning
Unit 6
  Aerobic dance
  Riflery
  Weight training
  Gymnastics
  Wrestling
  Fencing
Unit 7
  Gymnastics
  Floor hockey
  First aid
  Square dance
  Advanced volleyball
  Modern dance
  Weight lifting
Unit 8
  Square dance
  Volleyball
  Floor exercise and dance
  Camping/backpacking
  Fencing
  First aid/fitness
Unit 9
  Team handball
  Target tennis
  Floor hockey
  Orienteering

  Soccer
  Lacrosse (boys)
  Physical fitness/ropes
Unit 10
  Softball
  Lacrosse (boys)
  Field hockey
  Indoor lacrosse
  Target tennis
  Golf
  Soccer
  Physical fitness test
Unit 11
  Softball
  Lacrosse (girls)
  Track and field
  Basketball
  Archery
  Badminton
Unit 12
  Softball
  Track and field
  Badminton
  Basketball
  Flag football
  Lacrosse (girls)
  Recreational games

AN ELECTIVE PROGRAM FOR JUNIOR HIGH SCHOOL

(Courtesy Don Jackson, Theodore Roosevelt Junior High School, Eugene, Ore.)

The entire school operates on an elective basis. Every 9 weeks students elect courses for the next quarter. There are no requirements in any area, including physical education; however, 85% of the student body does elect physical education every 9 weeks. Each course a student elects to take within the physical education curriculum has its own class requirements or behavioral objectives.

The physical education program is arranged to enable each student to become physically educated through participation in six major areas: team sports, individual sports, dance, fitness, recreational games, and swimming.

Each 9 weeks, 13 to 15 activities are offered. Students have an opportunity to elect a great variety of activities during their junior high school career. For each course, the physical education staff has established specific requirements, including performance or behavioral objectives. Students are expected to dress for activities each day, participate in all activities, pass a written test, and demonstrate cooperative behavior. Students are evaluated on improvement by skills and tests, are observed on their use of skills, and must pass written quizzes.

Teachers are motivated to be creative in their curriculum. They are able to teach from their expertise and to learn about new and different sports interests of the students, which many times develop new class offerings.

A MINI-COURSE ELECTIVE PROGRAM, GRADES 9 AND 10

(Developed for Lowell High School, Lowell, Ind.)

Procedures

1. The teacher should set certain criteria for giving a course (i.e., a minimum number of students must be enrolled in a course for it to be offered).
2. Testing will consist of diagnostic testing for fitness levels in order to individually prescribe a conditioning program.
3. This program is designed for team teaching (i.e., two physical education teachers and an aquatics specialist will be assigned).
4. Instructional materials consist of individualized instruction packets for each activity.
5. As students achieve predetermined competency levels, they are evaluated. This evaluation determines whether the student progresses to the next level or continues practice at that same level.
6. The emphasis in this program is on having the students learn skills and perform activities for enjoyment and lifetime value.
7. Every effort has been made to present a variety of activities to suit a range of interests among the students.

Week	Semester I	Semester II
1	Testing	Testing
2-4	Outdoor education (camping), handball, junior/senior lifesaving	Conditioning, synchronized swimming, physiology of exercises
5-7	Archery/golf, folk and square dance, junior/senior lifesaving	Modern dance, self-defense, junior/senior lifesaving
8	Testing	Testing
9-11	Diving, apparatus, conditioning	Table tennis/badminton, WSI, volleyball/basketball
12-14	Recreational swimming, tumbling, paddleball/bowling	Handball, conditioning, skin diving/water games
15-17	Physiology of exercise, table tennis/badminton, volleyball/basketball	Golf, tennis, outdoor education (camping)
18	Testing	Testing

A SELECTIVE PROGRAM, GRADES 9 AND 10

(Developed by Sally Combs and Carole Casten for West Lafayette High School, West Lafayette, Ind.)

Procedures

1. Class meets five times each week.
2. The same program is offered for grades 9 and 10.
3. Students select an activity for each block and meet proficiency requirements.
4. Blocks are team-taught and coeducational.

Week	Block	Location
Semester I		
1-3	I: Golf/tennis	Practice field
4-6	II: Speedball/flag football/archery	Football field
7-10	III: Swimming/badminton	Pool
11-14	IV: Volleyball/racquetball	Big gym—university gym handball court
15-18	V: Basketball/racquetball	Big gym—university gym handball court
Semester II		
1-4	I: Swimming/recreational activities	Pool
5-7	II: Dance/handball	Mini-gym
8-11	III: Tumbling/apparatus	Mini-gym
12-14	IV: Tumbling/apparatus	Mini-gym
15-18	V: Softball/track and field	Track-football field

AN ELECTIVE PROGRAM FOR GRADES 10 TO 12

(Developed for Benton Central High School, Oxford, Ind.)

Procedures

1. Students elect an activity every two weeks of each semester by indicating first, second, third, and fourth choices on an election card.
2. Cadet teachers are assigned to the junior high school physical education classes.
3. Students will receive a copy of their yearly program.

Week	Section 1	Section 2	Section 3	Section 4
Semester I				
1-2	Conditioning and administration*	Conditioning and administration	Water safety instruction	Cadet teacher group no. 1
3-4	Golf	Field hockey		
5-6	Track and field activities	Track and field activities	Advanced swimming and diving	
7-8	Archery	Tennis		Cadet teacher group no. 2
9-10	Gymnastic activities†	Gymnastic activities	Gymnastic activities	
11-12				
13-14	Volleyball	Handball		Cadet teacher group no. 3
15-16	Self-defense	Fencing		
17-18	Recreation and testing activities‡	Recreation and testing activities	Recreation and testing activities	

*This includes testing and group rating along with individual activities.
†This is offered on a station setup, with a wide range of activities being offered, including tumbling, ropes, rings, trampoline, side horse, vaulting, parallel bars, and mat exercise.
‡This 2-week period is to be used for all testing and administration. There will also be individual and dual recreational games—shuffleboard, deck tennis, paddleball, lawn tennis, and squash—offered at this time.

Continued.

Week	Section 1	Section 2	Section 3	Section 4
Semester II				
19-20	Conditioning and administration	Conditioning and administration	Conditioning and administration	Cadet teacher group no. 1
21-22	Wrestling	Modern dance	Modern dance	
23-24	Basketball	Badminton	Badminton	
25-26	Folk and square dancing	Folk and square dancing	Square dancing (week 25)	Cadet teacher group no. 2
27-28	Paddleball and bowling	Badminton	Advanced swimming and diving (weeks 26-29)	
29-30	Conditioning-weight training	Conditioning/interval running	Senior lifesaving (weeks 30-33)	
31-32	Outdoor education§	Outdoor education		Cadet teacher group no. 3
33-34	Speedball	Soccer	First aid (week 34)	
35-36	Recreation and testing activities	Recreation and testing activities	Recreation and testing activities	

§Activities offered are hiking, camping, cycling, and cave exploring.

AN EXTENDED AND ELECTIVE PROGRAM, GRADES 10 TO 12

(Courtesy Ralph V. Lord, Jr., Lexington High School, Lexington, Mass.)

Extended program

Definition

The extended physical education program offers the opportunity for students, in special situations, to gain credit in physical education through participation in approved and supervised physical activities outside of the on-campus physical education program.

Conditions

Students may be granted approval to participate in the extended physical education program and receive credit on completion of the following requirements:

1. Approval of the physical education department
2. Satisfactory attendance and participation in 1 hour of on-campus elective physical education
3. Off-campus participation consisting of a maximum of 1 hour of instruction by a professional teacher

Certification

Students meeting these conditions must, on a weekly basis, provide the physical education department with a signed certification form indicating that off-campus requirements have been met.

Elective program

Administration

1. The school year is divided into four quarters consisting of approximately 9 weeks each.
2. Students elect two different activities each quarter, one activity for each of the 2 days their class meets during the week.
3. Students are not allowed to repeat activities

over a single school year unless the nature of the activity requires repetition.

4. Students may choose from the following activities:

Fall (first quarter)	Winter (second and third quarters)	Spring (fourth quarter)
Archery I		Archery I
Archery II	Judo	Archery II
Tennis I	Volleyball	Tennis I
Tennis II	Table tennis	Tennis II
Golf I	Weight training	Golf I
Golf II	Dance	Golf II
Horseshoes	Fencing	Badminton
Tetherball	Basketball	Fishing
Badminton	Floor hockey	Fly casting
Flag football	Apparatus	Lacrosse
Soccer	Active games	Track and field
Field hockey	Wrestling	Softball
Speedball	Modern dance	
	Modern jazz	
	Movement for improvement	
	Self-defense	
	Basketball	
	Tumbling	
	Floor exercise	

Procedures

At the beginning of each quarter, students select their program. Two different activities are selected, each meeting once a week for an entire quarter. Two printed color-coded data processing cards are required for each student, one card for each period of physical education taken during the week. This card is given to the instructor of each activity the student elects. The card is used by the instructor to take attendance and keep cumulative evaluative records. At the end of each quarter, cards are reassigned to the instructors of each student's new activity. The cards are kept filed by activity and gym class. This enables easy accessibility in changing a student's gym class or activity. Also, in case of a substitute teacher, all necessary records are readily available.

AN ELECTIVE PROGRAM, GRADES 11 AND 12

(Developed for Attica High School, Attica, Ind.)

Implementation procedures

1. The elective program is based on an 18-week semester divided into six 3-week blocks.
2. Three activities are offered in each block.
3. All classes are coeducational.

Semester I	1	2	3
A	Field hockey	Tennis	Gymnastics apparatus
B	Soccer	Golf	Conditioning
C	Flag football	Track and field	Darts, shuffleboard, table tennis
D	Basketball	Lifesaving	Gymnastics
E	Volleyball	Water polo	Ballet
F	Bowling/badminton	Smallcraft	Folk and square dance
Semester II	**4**	**5**	**6**
A	Volleyball	Skin diving/swimming	Gymnastics, tumbling, free exercise
B	Basketball	Skin diving	Contemporary dance
C	Conditioning	Competitive swimming	Folk dance
D	Lacrosse	Golf	Horseshoes, archery, Frisbee
E	Softball	Tennis	Skateboarding, roller skating, shuffleboard
F	Speedball	Orienteering	Cycling, bait and fly casting

AN ELECTIVE PROGRAM, GRADES 11 and 12

(Developed for Rensselaer School Corporation, Rensselaer, Ind.)

The elective program is a 5-day per week, coeducational class. Students may elect either activity offered in a time block by completing the activity selection card.

Program of activity

1. Cadet teaching		1 semester	
2. Orientation-testing-lecture		3 weeks	(15 days)
3. Conditioning		2 weeks	(10 days)
4. Flag football	5. Archery	2½ weeks	(13 days)
6. Field hockey	7. Tennis	3 weeks	(14 days)
8. Basketball	9. Judo	2½ weeks	(13 days)
10. Volleyball	11. Indoor recreational games	1½ weeks	(7 days)
12. Testing			

CHRISTMAS VACATION

13. Conditioning			
14. Gymnastics		1 week	(5 days)
15. Dance	16. Badminton	5 weeks	(24 days)
17. Golf	18. Camp crafts	3 weeks	(15 days)
19. Softball-handball	20. Soccer-speedball	3 weeks	(15 days)
21. Testing		3 weeks	(15 days)
22. Outdoor recreational activities		1 week	(5 days)
		3 weeks	(15 days)

```
┌─────────────────────────────────────────────────────────────────────┐
│                      ACTIVITY SELECTION CARD                          │
├─────────────────────────────────────────────────────────────────────┤
│                                                                       │
│   Name _____ Phone no. _____        │
│                                                                       │
│   Address _____        │
│                                                                       │
│   Parent's name _____ Business phone no. _____   │
│                                                                       │
│   Circle activity desired              Circle one                     │
│       1           12                   Grade    11    12              │
│       2           13                                                  │
│       3           14                                                  │
│       4     5     15    16                                            │
│       6     7     17    18                                            │
│       8     9     19    20                                            │
│      10    11     21                                                  │
│                   22                                                  │
│                                                                       │
└─────────────────────────────────────────────────────────────────────┘
```

AN ELECTIVE LIFETIME ACTIVITY PROGRAM, GRADE 12

(Courtesy Prudence Penney and David R. Thompson, Plantation High School, Fort Lauderdale, Fla.)

Seniors may elect an elective course emphasizing lifetime leisure activities. The course is designed especially for the active young adult wishing to gain knowledge and skill in recreational leisure games. Some activities offered include risk activities and lifetime activities.

Activities*

1. Bowling
2. Golf
3. Tennis
4. Paddle tennis
5. Bicycling on track (R)
6. Gymnastics (R)
7. Table tennis
8. Small craft operation (R)
9. Sailing
10. Water skiing
11. Skish
12. Outdoor camping
13. Fly fishing
14. Scuba diving (R)

*R = Risk.

15. Badminton
16. Roller skating (R)
17. Weight training
18. Archery
19. Self-defense (unarmed) (R)
20. Deep-sea fishing (R)
21. Snorkling (R)

AN ELECTIVE PROGRAM FOR SECONDARY SCHOOLS

(Courtesy Ann Lockett, Gar-Field High School, Woodbridge, Va.)

The physical education program is divided into four phases. It is a planned curriculum that has been designed to meet the basic and diversified needs and interests of senior high school students.

The four phases of the program are phase one—required freshman health and physical education, phase two—required sophomore health and physical education, phase three—elective program for students who have completed phases one and two, and phase four—physical education aide program. In each phase, physical education consists of the following graduated skill development areas: team sports, individual and dual sports, rhythms, recreational activities, and class organization and testing.

Students begin with the required freshman and sophomore courses of study in health and physical education. These are phases one and two, which are based on the building of constructive concepts for healthful living and learning and placing into practice the skills needed for the enjoyment of individually selected activities.

Phase three, the elective program of studies, is for those students who have successfully completed, with a "C" average, phases one and two (freshman and sophomore courses) and who are interested in pursuing physical education. Significant emphasis has been placed on sports of carry-over value and leisure time activities in developing the phase three course of study.

The fourth phase of the physical education program, the physical education aide program, is designed for those students who are interested in learning more about the mechanics of health and physical education classes. This objective may be accomplished by assisting the teacher in the various aspects of instruction and by carrying out certain prescribed responsibilities within the class. In order to enter this fourth phase of the program, a student should have completed phases one, two, and at least 1 year in phase three.

All activities are taught in 3-week blocks. There are no grade levels, since the program is set up in various phases with a great emphasis on individual instruction and the use of the pre- and posttests in skill and cognitive areas. All activities are taught in 3-week blocks in a 45-15 year-round school plan. Teacher specialists are used in all areas.

A SELECTIVE PROGRAM FOR SECONDARY SCHOOLS

(Courtesy John E. Hayes, Lowville Academy and Secondary School, Lowville, N.Y.)

Administration

1. All activities are categorized into the three "FIT" areas—*f*itness units, *i*ndividual sports units, and *t*eam sports units.
2. Students must select one unit in each of the FIT categories each semester.
3. Students register for an entire semester, using the criteria given.
4. All units are 4 weeks in duration and are coeducational.
5. Students are graded on a pass/incomplete basis. An additional citizenship evaluation is used where such areas as appropriate dress, cooperation, and participation are evaluated by the teacher. If an "excellent" or "unsatisfactory" is given, parents are notified by special form. If satisfactory only, notices are not sent.

Following a unit, teachers submit their grades to the director, who then transposes them onto a master alphabetized list, grades 9 to 12.

Registration procedure

1. Students are handed a prenumbered registration form explaining the procedure, listing unit offerings, and requesting specific information such as grade, location during certain periods of the day, and whether the student is interested in volunteer service to the physical education department.
2. Four tables are arranged to coincide with the four 4-week blocks in the semester. Students register at a table that corresponds with their prenumbered sheet. Students then rotate from table to table until they have completed the process. A teacher then checks each sheet to see if criteria have been met.
3. These registration forms serve as the basis for unit class lists for the remainder of the semester. Class lists are posted prior to each unit so students know exactly which unit they have selected and who their teachers will be.

Physical education selective program, grades 9 to 12

Week	Group 1	Group 2	Group 3
1	REGISTRATION FOR FIRST SEMESTER/ORIENTATION		
2-5	Football (T)	Field hockey (T)	Water sports (F, I, T) Competitive swimming (F, I, T)
6-9	Soccer (F, T)	Team handball (T)	Aerobics (F, I)
10	←————————————— Gym and pool activities —————————————→		
11-14	Basketball (T)	Paddleball (I)	Weight training (F)
15-18	Basketball (T)	Badminton (I)	Cross-country skiing I (F, I)
19	REGISTRATION FOR SECOND SEMESTER/OPEN GYM/ICE SKATING		
20-23	Volleyball (T)	Floor hockey (T, F)	Cross-country skiing II (F, I)
24-27	Volleyball (T)	Skin diving (I)	Gymnastics (I, F)
28-30	11 and 12 graders mini-units/9 and 10 graders olympic program—fitness		
31-34	Softball (T)	Golf (I)	Tennis (I)
35-38	Softball (T)	Archery (I)	Recreational swimming and conditioning (I, F)

A SELECTIVE PROGRAM FOR SECONDARY SCHOOLS

(Courtesy Tom Lash and staff, Wheeling Park High School, Wheeling, W. Va.)

Implementation procedures

1. Each activity is taught for 4½ weeks.
2. Students make first, second, and third choices for each 4½-week session on schedule cards.
3. Students must have their first choices during the entire year from two team sports—football, soccer, softball, basketball, volleyball, field hockey; two individual/dual sports—archery, badminton, golf, track and field; two of the following—body management, wrestling, tumbling and gymnastics, dance; and any two electives.
4. The eight first choices must be different activities.
5. The physical education department will attempt to provide the students' first choices; however, this may be impossible in some situations. The student will be given one of the three choices.
6. If a student does not make a choice for each 4½-week session, the physical education department will place the student in a class.

Physical education schedule card

Name _____ Enrolled for:

☐ Male   ☐ Female   ☐ First quarter   ☐ Third quarter

Bus route _____   ☐ Second quarter   ☐ Fourth quarter   Period ____

Dates:	9-5 to 10-5	10-6 to 11-3	11-6 to 12-8	12-11 to 1-19
	☐ Soccer	☐ Soccer	☐ Volleyball	☐ Volleyball
	☐ Touch football	☐ Touch football	☐ Tumbling	☐ Tumbling
	☐ Field hockey (girls)	☐ Field hockey (girls)	☐ Dance—folk, square	☐ Dance—folk, square
	☐ Badminton	☐ Badminton	☐ Wrestling (boys)	☐ Wrestling (boys)
	☐ Archery	☐ Archery	☐ Body management	☐ Body management
	☐ Golf	☐ Golf		

Dates:	1-23 to 2-21	2-22 to 3-23	3-26 to 5-4	5-7 to 6-7
	☐ Basketball	☐ Basketball	☐ Softball	☐ Softball
	☐ Gymnastics	☐ Gymnastics	☐ Track and field	☐ Track and field
	☐ Dance—creative	☐ Dance—creative	☐ Badminton	☐ Badminton
	☐ Wrestling (boys)	☐ Wrestling (boys)	☐ Archery	☐ Archery
	☐ Body management	☐ Body management	☐ Golf	☐ Golf
			☐ Body management	☐ Body management

☐ *Medical excuse on file*   *Withdraw*   ☐ Class   *Schedule change*   ☐ In
                                          ☐ School   ☐ Out

AN ELECTIVE EXERCISE PHYSIOLOGY AND BIOLOGICAL AWARENESS COURSE FOR SECONDARY SCHOOLS

(Courtesy Edward L. Meyers, Penney High School, East Hartford, Conn.)

The special course in exercise physiology is open to juniors and seniors, both male and female, who have completed a high school course in biology. The course emphasizes functioning of body systems before, during, and after exercise. It is designed to develop understandings, abilities, attitudes, and appreciations related to exercise physiology, cardiovascular endurance, muscular strength, muscular endurance, and athletic conditioning as well as to develop an understanding of preventive and rehabilitative aspects of exercise in relation to disease and injury. The course lasts for one semester, with each student participating in two lectures and laboratory period or unit test each week. One-half credit is earned.

In addition to the in-depth elective program, all students participate in courses in exercise physiology held during unscheduled or so-called X-time blocks. The required physical education activity period is used as a laboratory for reinforcing biological awareness learned in the elective course or during X-block lectures. The use of X-block time and an elective course ensures that students do not lose time from learning skills, games, attitudes, and appreciations gained from actual participation. The staff merely reinforces what has been learned during X-block time and in the elective session. A resource center is maintained so that students can read materials related to exercise physiology, conditioning, nutrition, disease, and health.

Purposes

The purposes of the course are to develop:
- Understandings, abilities, and appreciations relative to exercise physiology, cardiovascular endurance, muscle strength, muscle endurance, and athletic conditioning
- Biological awareness of one's own body and how it responds to exercise
- Understandings of the preventive and rehabilitative aspects of exercise in relation to disease and injury

Methods of instruction

A combination of lecture, demonstration, illustration, and laboratory experiences is used in the instructional program.

Course content

The course is divided into eight major areas:
1. Review of musculoskeletal system
2. Muscle training
3. Provision of energy for muscular work
4. Role of oxygen in physical activity
5. Circulatory system and exercise
6. Body constitution and composition
7. Prophylactic and therapeutic effects of exercise
8. Females in training and athletics

Laboratory experiments

During the 20-week course, students participate in 12 laboratory sessions and have eight unit tests with either a laboratory period or test scheduled once a week.

REACTORS

1. The fusion of the parts, elements, and components of the curriculum is accomplished through program design and scheduling patterns.
2. The design and selection of schedule patterns are based on specific criteria.
3. A physical education program and schedule pattern must be compatible with the school's administrative philosophy and the community's philosophy.
4. It is the responsibility of the physical educator to design the best "game plan" that will benefit the greatest number of students.
5. The curriculum planner must have the insight to modify and adapt existing patterns for a specific situation.
6. Conventional scheduling patterns are more widely used because they "fit" most school organizational procedures.
7. The selection of an organizational schedule plan is determined by its purpose.
8. Elective and selective type programs should only be used for secondary schools.

LEARNING ACTIVITIES

1. Survey an elementary school as to the criteria listed in this unit.
   a. Devise a major activity classification chart with subclassifications and designate percentages and time modules
   b. Select a schedule pattern
   c. Design a physical education program
2. Do the same for a middle or junior high school.
3. Do the same for a secondary school.
4. Design an innovative election or selection program.

UNIT EVALUATIVE CRITERIA

Can you:
1. Identify the characteristics for conventional and flexible schedule patterns?
2. Design a program and select a schedule pattern based on specific school situational criteria?
3. Compare the advantages and disadvantages of a wide variety of schedule patterns?
4. Design and schedule an effective sequential physical education program?

RESOURCES

AAHPER. *Organizational patterns for instruction in physical education*. Washington, D. C.: The Alliance, 1971.

Barry, P. E. (Ed.). *Ideas for secondary school physical education*. Washington, D.C.: American Alliance for Health, Physical Education, and Recreation, 1976.

Bergen, E. V., & Pie, H. E. Flexible scheduling for physical education. *JOHPER,* March 1967, p. 29.

Bush, R. N., & Allen, D. W. *A new design for high school physical education*. New York: McGraw-Hill Book Co., 1974.

Hawkins, D. E., & Vinton, D. A. *The environmental classroom*. Englewood Cliffs, N.J.: Prentice-Hall, Inc., 1973.

Indiana State Board of Health. *Motion and direction*. Indianapolis: State Department of Instruction, 1976.

Nixon, J. F., & Jewett, A. E. *Physical education curriculum*. New York: Ronald Press Co., 1964.

Trump, J. L. Flexible scheduling. *Phi Delta Kappa,* May 1963, pp. 367-371.

Trump, J. L., & Baynham, D. *Focus on change*. Chicago: Rand McNally & Co., 1961.

Willgoose, C. E. *The curriculum in physical education* (3rd ed.). Englewood Cliffs, N.J.: Prentice-Hall, Inc., 1979.

Growth of individual identity in open relatedness; creation of being in vital experiences with other beings; ingestion of meaning, feeling, belief, value; within a unique self—this is the essential creativity of human life.

CLARK E. MOUSTAKAS

19 Instructional materials and strategies

COMPETENCIES

After completing this unit, you should be able to:

Identify and utilize various modes and models of communication for a teaching-learning environment that requires a high degree of student involvement.

Demonstrate and evaluate a variety of instructional strategies that do and do not involve the student in a responsible decision-making process.

Interpret the relationships between student characteristics, objectives, and instructional strategies.

Design and refine instructional strategies and materials with complementary media that permit each student to perform and learn continuously at an appropriate rate of progress.

Create a learning environment that will make discovery and learning an exciting and enjoyable experience.

269

Define the following:

Unit plan	Contingency management
Lesson plan	Competency-based instruction
Instructional strategy	Prescription learning
Hardware	Independent study
Software	IIP
Individualized instruction	Systems approach
Traditional instruction	Mastery learning
Personalized learning	Formative evaluation
Humanistic instruction	Summative evaluation

PERSPECTIVE

PRINCIPLE: The teacher must be able to conceptualize the relation of the specific tasks to the whole activity, to see things both in their genesis and in wider cause and effect relationships.

Educational method has to do with how learning experiences are organized. If we want to teach children to swim, we segment the total activity into more teachable specific tasks, such as learning to breathe, floating, and treading water. The tasks must be sequenced so that they lead to a definite goal—swimming.

The teacher must be able to conceptualize the relation of the specific tasks to the whole activity, to see things both in their genesis and in wider cause and effect relationships. In this process, the teacher must consider the elements that represent a series of worthwhile and progressive experiences that are bound together for achieving the ultimate goal of a major activity.

The teacher must consider:

1. That the central problem must be brought into focus—what is the instructional goal?
2. What the students know—preentry skills.
3. What is to be learned—performance objectives.
4. How it is to be taught—an instructional strategy.
5. What types of teaching aids supplement and complement instruction.

6. The development of instructional materials.
7. Measurement and evaluation techniques for measuring ongoing and final achievement—formative and summative evaluation.

The first step in the planning of learning experiences is to classify learning activities by areas, such as team sports, individual and dual sports, self-testing activities, dance activities, and fitness activities. These areas are further subdivided into subareas or specific sports (e.g., basketball, soccer, tennis). Well-planned functional units would then be developed for each of the subareas.

UNIT PLANNING

A unit has been defined in various ways, but all definitions imply an integration of teaching/learning experiences. Some generally accepted definitions are as follows:

A unit is an arrangement of content into meaningful wholes so that it functions in the life of the pupils.

A unit is a series of worthwhile experiences bound together around some project or theme of interest.

A unit of work organization is a plan for organizing and integrating the learning experiences of pupils around a central interest.

Learning units are organized around one or more "activity areas" and may be segmented into weeks, seasons, or years. Although we need research to determine more definitely the relative values of different types of unit structure, there is fairly uniform agreement that the following values are inherent in the unit idea:

1. Frees the teacher from the limitations of one textbook and makes for clearer objectives.
2. Permits the organization and integration of learning experiences into larger blocks of work contrasted with its assign-study-recite counterpart.
3. Has a psychological foundation in the "whole" method of learning contrasted with the method that conceives of learning as a piece-by-piece additive process; satisfies the principle that learning should be unitary, not fragmentary.
4. Encourages the planning of experiences that are meaningful and in keeping with some particular aspect of a broader field of study; for example, a lesson on base running becomes meaningful in relation to the game of baseball as a whole.
5. Contains within it some well-defined center of organization about which the activities, work, or subject-matter of the unit can be developed. Therefore it aids in the organization of data and makes for more and better understanding, hence more retention and greater permanence of learning.

TEACHING UNITS

Physical education at any given seasonal period is normally divided into major units to facilitate organization and evaluation of learning experiences. Each unit is an integral part of the whole course of physical education and related in sequence and scope to other units of the course. Each planned experience of the student is part of a unit, each unit a part of the course, and each course an integral part of the total educational program of the school.

Some curriculum specialists would say that where learning is organized systematically around basic skills such as music, swimming, typing, throwing, tumbling, or catching, we are not dealing with units in the usual sense. However, when skills become integrated into sports or dance, this involves additional conceptual content, such as historical relationships, understanding of principles of movement, and physiology of activity, or the additional development of attitudes, concepts, or understandings, and the name *unit* may be properly applied. The chief criterion is the extent to which the unit embraces a body of experiences closely related to some central purpose or theme.

A unit represents a plan for action. The following elements or component parts of a comprehensive unit plan are recommended:

1. Introduction
   a. Brief history and origin
   b. General description
      (1) Rules
      (2) Terms
      (3) Equipment and facilities
   c. Playing courtesies
   d. Safety measures
2. Performance objectives
   a. Physical domain
   b. Psychomotor domain
   c. Cognitive domain
   d. Affective domain
3. Skill content
   a. Progressive fundamentals
      (1) Beginning
      (2) Intermediate
      (3) Advanced
4. Instructional strategies
   a. Demonstration
   b. Explanation
   c. Execution
5. Teaching aids
   a. Type, name, source, date, price, and brief description

6. Culminating activity
7. Measurement and evaluation
   a. Physical tests
   b. Psychomotor tests
   c. Cognitive tests
   d. Affective evaluation
   e. Formative and summative evaluations
8. Resource bibliography
   a. Author, title, publisher, location, date, and price

In the development of a unit on soccer at the seventh grade level in early autumn, more detailed and specific information would be included for the recommended unit elements. Some examples of this information are given in the following section.

INTRODUCTION. Introducing the unit serves to get the unit started, gives the student a concept of the unit as a whole, and helps relate it properly to present needs, interests, and achievements. Students should sense the wholeness of the unit and be motivated to the point where they are ready to undertake it. The introduction is the "purposing" part of the unit, to be followed by planning, execution, and evaluation. Some ways of introducing the seventh-grade soccer unit are as follows:

1. Seeing a motion picture of two top-flight teams in action.
2. Watching two good teams play a match.
3. Having students discuss previous experiences in lead-up games involving the elements of soccer and perhaps leading into the history of soccer as a game and its international character.
4. Using a standardized soccer skill test as a pretest to find gaps and perhaps convince some that they are not as skillful as they thought they were.
5. Using a brief knowledge test on the rules to form the foundation for discussion of these bases and also of certain misconceptions that will appear.
6. Having pupils relate their past experiences to identify themselves with the unit.

7. Discussing with students the values inherent in soccer and establishing with them the objectives of the unit.
8. Presenting a broad overview or sketch of the unit as a whole.

ESTABLISHING PERFORMANCE OBJECTIVES. Objectives must be recognized by the pupils as early in the unit as possible. It is advisable that these be stated in terms of the pupil who can conceive objectives only in anticipation of the experience he/she expects to have and what is to be achieved related to the following:

1. Playing the game.
2. Playing specific positions such as goalie or center forward.
3. Learning the specific skills related to specific positions.
   a. Dribbling
   b. Trapping
   c. Kicking
   d. Heading
   e. Tackling
   f. Retaining the ball from tackler
   g. Making a "throw in"
4. Learning the rules and applying them.
5. Learning the strategy of the game.
6. Finding out what teamwork is, why it is necessary for a full game, and how one achieves it.

INSTRUCTIONAL STRATEGIES. There are advantages in the pupils' recognizing the unit in its entirety before the mastery of its parts is undertaken. This places each part of the unit in its proper perspective at the beginning and during the course of the unit. If unit teaching is functioning, the pupil comprehends the significance of the unit in its early stages.

In planning the *how,* many factors must be considered by the teacher. Strategy refers to how learning experiences are organized. A good strategy results in effective learning. Here the teacher is faced with such factors as the following:

1. Time.
2. Space.
3. Equipment and supplies (goals, balls).
4. Bases for groupings in class (squads, teams).
5. Number of groups.
6. Student leaders.
7. Sequence in daily lesson plans.
8. The specific day's lesson.

In a unit such as soccer, it is most important that skills are not taught in extended isolation from the game as a whole. Greater skill is achieved when the game is taught by strategies whereby game techniques or skills are practiced in relation to the felt need for improving these techniques, while playing the game as a whole. We all realize that a game as a whole is more than the sum of the separate skills we may be able to isolate.

Skills should be developed through situations in which the learner sees a real need for them and through situations similar to those in which he/she will use the skill again.

TEACHING AIDS

1. Demonstrations by skilled individuals.
2. Motion pictures, film strips, some films and slides.
3. Charts and pictures; use of the chalkboard.
4. Functional and well-illustrated books and magazines.
5. Visits to games between skilled teams.
6. Illustrated talks by skilled people—perhaps some Scotsman or Englishman who has played and loved the game for years.

CULMINATING ACTIVITY. A unit has a beginning and an end. A summarizing or culminating activity provides a climax or conclusion to what has been anticipated from the beginning of the unit. It represents the culmination of anticipated achievement.

In the introduction, the students had an overall view of the unit in prospect. The culminating activity gives this view in retrospect. It reinforces the permanence of learning by further integration of what has been learned. This may be done in several ways:

1. A round-robin intersquad tournament.
2. A Saturday morning soccer game with a neighboring school.
3. A soccer skills demonstration for the benefit of the fifth and sixth grades.
4. A game between two "all-star" teams chosen by class members.
5. The showing and analysis of videotapes taken during actual class activities in the autumn.

MEASUREMENT AND EVALUATION. Evaluation, naturally, relates to the objectives stated at the introduction of the unit. It is an appraisal or assessment procedure to determine what changes have taken place in boys and girls as a result of their learning experiences in the unit.

Some phases of the culmination of the unit provide opportunities for evaluating pupil achievement; for example, individual skills may be rated during intersquad matches. Self-appraisal of skill, personal relationships, and one's own needs are equally important.

Evaluation is not something that is done solely at the close of the unit; it takes place also during the course of the unit. Formative evaluation of pupil achievement begins as soon as the unit is initiated. Some brief suggestions follow:

1. Physical domain.
   a. Fitness batteries
   b. Fitness test items
2. Psychomotor evaluation—specific skill tests given at the preunit period may be given again to determine the degree of skill improvement or final status.
3. Cognitive evaluation.
   a. Tests on application of rules in various situations

b. Application of relevant tactics and strategy in various situations
4. Affective evaluation—subjective attitude tests or verbal interaction.
   a. The game as a whole
   b. Self-actualization
   c. Personal relations (new friendships, etc.)
5. Unit evaluation—the student's own suggestions as to the following:
   a. The things liked most about the unit
   b. The things liked least about the unit
   c. How to improve the unit

• • •

Different types of unit designs are presented by the following examples.

DEVELOPMENTAL UNIT PLANS, NURSERY SCHOOL–KINDERGARTEN

(Developed for St. Ann's Elementary School, Terre Haute, Ind.)

Unit one

Behavioral objectives:
1. On the playground, the students will demonstrate their knowledge of at least 10 parts of their body.
2. The students will demonstrate their ability to roll a ball accurately to another person at least three times.

Equipment: Records: "Shake Your Bootie" and "Hokeypokey"
Activities:
   Dayton Sensory Motor Awareness Test
   Hot Potato
   Simon Says
   Shake Your Bootie
   Balloons
   Call and Roll
   Hokeypokey

Unit two

Behavioral objectives:
1. In the gym, children will develop increased balance, agility, body control, and self-confidence.
2. Children will demonstrate the ability to walk a line at least two times without falling off.

Equipment: Balance beam or rope, chalk
Activities:

Balance beam	Footprint
Duck, Duck, Goose	Rocking Boat

Unit three

Behavioral objectives:
1. Through different activites, the students will perform at least three different animal sounds and at least five different animal motions outside on the playground.
2. In some activities, the students will show their ability to listen and to respond quickly to commands at least eight times.

Equipment: Yarn, record: "Chicken Fat"
Activities:
   Chicken Fat
   Cats and Dogs
   Squirrels in the Trees
   Follow the Leader
   Barnyard Symphony
   Simon Says
   Grunt, Piggy, Grunt

Unit four

Behavioral objectives:
1. In the gym, children will demonstrate ability to roll, bounce, and toss a ball.
2. Children will develop eye-hand coordination.
3. Children will successfully roll and catch a ball with hands in correct position a minimum of five times.

Equipment: 30 rubber balls, record for bouncing to music
Activities:
   Bounce ball individually
   Bounce ball with partner
   Toss ball up in the air and catch
   Toss ball to partner and catch
   Bounce ball to music
   Call and Roll
   Dodge ball

Unit five

Behavioral objectives:
1. In the gym, children will develop strength and endurance of the leg muscles.

2. Children will develop better perception of spatial relationships and alertness.
3. Children will jump a minimum of five consecutive times, remaining in the center of the long rope.

Equipment: Four ropes, record: "Popcorn"
Activities:
Jumping Over the River
Hopscotch
Popcorn
If You're Happy and You Know It
Jump rope
Birthday Surprise

Unit six

Behavioral objectives:
1. In the gym, children will learn to follow commands and to cooperate with each other while playing.
2. Children will acquire knowledge and awareness of their body.
3. Children will tap their feet accurately through at least one rhythm game.

Equipment: Two balloons
Activities:
Kneeling tag
Marching Ponies
Let Your Feet Go Tap, Tap, Tap
Snowball
My Fingers
Balloon volleyball

Unit seven

Behavioral objectives:
1. On the playground, children will develop body awareness, spatial awareness, and body control.
2. The activities will provide opportunity for individual participation.
3. Children will throw a bean bag to a partner and catch it a minimum of three times without dropping it.

Equipment: 27 streamers, six bean bags, 30 plastic eggs, record: "Bunny Hop"
Activities:

Colors	Bunny Hop
Streamers	Bean bag games
Six Little Ducks	Easter egg hunt

Unit eight

Behavioral objectives:
1. In the gym, the children will develop muscular coordination and strength, better posture, and physical endurance and efficiency in movement.
2. Children will explore to realize their physical potential and body control.
3. Children will be able to perform with minimal skill at least five different body exercises.

Equipment: Shoe polish or chalk, streamers, record: "Chicken Fat"
Activities:
Follow the Leader
Streamers, Big Circle, Little Circles
Chicken Fat
Stations
Numbers on the floor in boxes
Mickey Mouse

Unit nine

Behavioral objectives:
1. On the playground, children will develop ability to run fast and stop quickly.
2. Children will develop arm muscles, strength, endurance, and body awareness.
3. Children will respond accurately to signals at least three times in sequence.

Equipment: Blindfold, parachute, yarn balls, record: "Rock Around the Clock"
Activities:
Head, Shoulders, Knees, and Toes
Stop and Go
Blindman's Bluff
Mulberry Bush
Parachute
Tag
Rock Around the Clock

Unit ten

Behavioral objectives:
1. On the playground, children will improve their ability to follow instructions and take commands.
2. Children will successfully respond to commands 50% of the time.

Equipment: Records: "Hokeypokey" and "It's a Happy Feeling"

Activities:

Stop and Go	It's a Happy Feeling
Simon Says	Freeze tag
Midnight Mister Wolf	Hokeypokey

Unit eleven

Behavioral objectives:
1. Using different apparatus, children will develop body awareness, body control, sense of personal space, and agility.
2. Children will perform the activities of the obstacle course at least once without making a mistake.

Equipment: Wooden play equipment, Hula Hoops, scooters, record: "The Twist"

Activities:
Guess What I Am
Obstacle course
Hula Hoops
Scooters obstacle course
Twist exercises
Children's choice

Unit twelve

Behavioral objectives:
1. In the gym, children will develop body awareness, spatial awareness, and body control.
2. Children will display good rhythm.
3. Children will respond accurately to commands 50% of the time.

Equipment: 30 mats (carpet squares), 30 wands, 2 handkerchiefs, record: "Loopy Loo"

Activities:
Individual mats activities
Wands
Laughing Handkerchief
Loopy Loo
Let Your Feet Go Tap, Tap, Tap
Cats and Dogs

BADMINTON UNIT

(Developed by Carol Swindler, Lexington Public Schools, Lexington, Mass.)

Performance objectives

1. The student shall be able to demonstrate knowledge of the rules, terminology, safety, scoring, and basic strategy involved in the game of badminton.

2. The student shall be able to demonstrate with correct technique the forehand, backhand, overhead clear, and long and short serves.
3. The student shall be familiar with and be able to recognize, explain, and/or demonstrate the correct technique involved in the smash, drop shot, and net play.
4. The student shall be able to incorporate the skills, rules, methods of scoring, and basic strategy in order to successfully compete in doubles and singles play.
5. The student shall know the appropriate playing situations under which particular badminton strokes are used.
6. The student shall demonstrate ability to control emotions under stress, show good sportsmanship, exhibit team loyalty, accept responsibility, assume leadership, and respect decisions of officials.

Skills to be taught

Forehand
Backhand
Overhead clear
Long serve
Short serve
Smash
Drop shot
Hairpin (net play)

Equipment

8 nets
40 racquets
1 gross shuttles
8 badminton standards
2 badminton carts

Evaluation procedure

1. The student's knowledge of the rules, terminology, safety, scoring, and basic strategy involved in the game of badminton shall be measured by a written test.
2. The student's ability to perform with correct technique the forehand, backhand, overhead clear, and long and short serves shall be measured by a skills test or evaluated by teacher observation (suggested skills tests: French Short Serve Test, French Clear Test, Miller

Wall Volley Test, Lucey Badminton Rating Scale).

3. The student's ability to recognize, explain, and/or demonstrate the correct technique involved in the smash, drop shot, and net play will be measured by a written or verbal explanation or demonstration with teacher evaluation.

4. The student's ability to incorporate the skills, rules, and basic strategy and scoring in game situations shall be evaluated by teacher observation (suggested skills test: Lucey Badminton Rating Scale).

5. The student's ability to recognize certain playing situations and the appropriate stroke for each shall be evaluated by teacher observation.

6. The student's ability to control emotions under stress, show good sportsmanship, exhibit team loyalty, accept responsibility, and respect the decisions of officials shall be evaluated by teacher observation throughout the quarter.

GOLF UNIT

(Submitted by Elmer Freese and staff, Ohio County Public Schools, Wheeling, W. Va.)

Course description

Students will acquire a knowledge and understanding of golf through an opportunity to learn the basic fundamentals of the grip, full swing, short shots for accuracy, and putting. Basic rules, terminology, strategy, club selection, etiquette, and safety will be stressed. Through their participation and discussion, they should have an interest in a sport that has carry-over value to be utilized in leisure time.

Student competency

A. The student will be able to execute the full swing with ease and with 90% success of ball contact.

B. The student will be able to execute the short shots with 50% accuracy toward a target.

C. The student will be able to putt on an indoor green with 50% accuracy.

D. The student will play a required number of holes on an outdoor course using the funda-

mental swings, basic rules, etiquette, strategy, and club selection.

E. The student will score 60% on a written test that will include all aspects of golf covered in class through participation and discussion.

F. The student will score 50% on a skill test involving the full swing, swings for accuracy, and putting.

Activities

A. Demonstration and explanation of the following:
   1. Full swing
   2. Swing for accuracy
      a. Lob or stop shot
      b. Pitch and run
   3. Putting

B. Participation using the basic shots as just listed

C. Utilization of loop films, 16 mm films and filmstrips

D. Teacher explanation of the following:
   1. Rules
   2. Etiquette
   3. Club selection
   4. Strategy and scoring
   5. Uneven lies and trouble shots
   6. Handicap system
   7. Terminology
   8. Course design

E. Evaluation through written and skills tests

Objectives

The student will:

A. Acquire knowledge of golf through participation.

B. Identify the rules, terminology, etiquette, and equipment in golf.

C. Determine choice of golf club to be used in various situations.

D. Acquire an appreciation for the difficulty of golf.

E. Demonstrate muscular coordination and body awareness.

Content of course

A. Introduction—scientific analysis of the golf swing:
   1. Grip
   2. Etiquette
   3. Club selection
   4. Strategy and scoring

5. Putting
6. Difficulty of the sport
7. Value of practice
8. Handouts
B. Skills to be taught:
  1. Grip
     a. Overlapping
     b. Variations
     c. Pressure points
     d. Common errors and corrections
     e. Practice suggestions
  2. Stance
     a. Club alignment
     b. Body-feet alignment
     c. Square stance
     d. Closed stance
     e. Open stance
     f. Common errors and corrections
     g. Practice suggestions
  3. Distance or full swing
     a. Address position
     b. Backswing
     c. Forward swing
     d. Finish or follow-through
     e. Body movement through the swing
     f. Common errors and corrections
     g. Practice suggestions
  4. Short shots for accuracy (pitch and run, stop or lob shot)
     a. Body position
     b. Stance
     c. Backswing
     d. Forward swing
     e. Finish or follow-through
     f. Common errors and corrections
     g. Practice suggestions
  5. Putting
     a. Grip
     b. Stance
     c. Body alignment
     d. Club alignment
     e. Mental aspects
     f. Variations of ground contour
     g. Common errors and corrections

Materials

Woods 1 to 3
Irons 3, 5, 7, and 9
Putter

Indoor mat
Indoor net
Plastic balls
Regulation balls
Putting carpet
Putting disk

Resources

Andrews, Emily L., et al. *Physical education for girls and women.* Englewood Cliffs, N.J.: Prentice-Hall, Inc., 1963.

How to improve your golf. Chicago: National Golf Foundation.

Johnson, C., & Johnstone, A. *Golf—a positive approach.* Reading, Mass.: Addison-Wesley Publishing Co., Inc., 1975.

Official rules of golf. The Golf House. Far Hills, N.J.: United States Golf Association, 1976.

Physical education for high school students. Washington, D.C.: American Alliance for Health, Physical Education, and Recreation, 1965.

National Golf Foundation, Room 707, Merchandise Mart, Chicago, Ill. 60654.

Visual aids

A. 8 mm loop films—National Golf Foundation:
  1. Full Swing
  2. Grip—Address Position
  3. Short Approach—Pitch
  4. Pitch and Run
  5. Uneven Lies
B. 35 mm filmstrips—National Golf Foundation:
  1. The Game
  2. Getting Set to Swing
  3. Building Control into Your Swing
  4. Getting onto the Green
  5. Putting
  6. Courtesies and Etiquette
C. 16 mm motion pictures:
  1. Great tournaments—Shell Oil Company
  2. Education series—National Golf Foundation:
     a. Welcome to Golf
     b. Building Your Golf Swing
     c. Pitching, Pitch and Run, and the Sand Shot
     d. Putting
     e. Courtesy on the Course

D. Wall Chart of the Rules—National Golf Foundation
E. Games:
1. Galloping Golf Fame—book and game stores
2. Thinking Man's Game—a 3M Sport Game

SYNCHRONIZED SWIMMING UNIT

(Developed by Sue Lipnickey for the Attica School Corporation, Attica, Ind.)

Instructional goal

This unit is designed to provide the student with the opportunity to learn the basic stunts and modified strokes needed for synchronized swimming, to combine these skills and strokes to perform a routine, and to perform a routine with others to music.

Introduction of the activity

A. General description—Synchronized swimming is often considered to be a sport limited to females, as ballet once was. However, this is being disproven, as popularity for both men and women is increasing rapidly. A form of aquatics that requires skill, precision, creativity, strength, and stamina, synchronized swimming combines series of stunts with modified strokes. These stunts and strokes, when combined, form routines that are performed to music. Routines may be done by one person or by two or more in unison.
B. Equipment and facilities—See *Official Rules for Synchronized Swimming 1977.* Amateur Athletic Union, 3400 West 86th Street, Indianapolis, Ind. 46268.
C. Rules and modifications—See *Official Rules for Synchronized Swimming 1977.* Amateur Athletic Union, 3400 West 86th Street, Indianapolis, Ind. 46268.
D. Safety measures—Each student will have passed the intermediate level of swimming (Red Cross program) before entering the synchronized swimming unit.

Teaching suggestions

A. Try to combine stunts and modified strokes as early as possible (as soon as the students learn more than one of the fundamental skills, combine the two to form a mini-routine).
B. Use music in the background—even when just practicing.
C. Have students get used to working with others by always practicing stunts and strokes together.
D. At the beginning of each class, have students warm up by swimming to music.

Skill teaching content

A. Stunts
1. Tub
2. Waterwheel
3. Backward and forward rolls
4. Oyster
5. Corkscrew
6. Porpoise
7. Dolphin
8. Ballet leg
B. Sculling
1. Forward
2. Backward
3. To both sides
C. Modifications of strokes for synchronized swimming
1. Front crawl
2. Sidestroke
3. Breaststroke
4. Back crawl
D. Combination of stunts and modified strokes

Measurement and evaluation

A. Skills tests
1. There are no standardized tests, so teacher-made tests should be used here to evaluate stunts, strokes, and combinations.
2. Knowledge tests—There are no standardized written tests, so teacher-made tests should be used. These may be based on formations used, how certain stunts are performed, and stroke modifications.

Available teaching aids

A. Loop films
1. Available from the Amateur Athletic

Union, 3400 West 86th Street, Indianapolis, Ind. 46268.

2. Available for a wide variety of stunts and formations.

B. Films

1. *Silver Springs*—9 minutes, color, $60.00; available from Courneya Hyde Productions, 1566 North Gordon Street, Los Angeles, Calif. 90052.

2. *Ornamental Swimming*—9 minutes; available from Skibo Productions, 165 West 46th Street, New York, N.Y. 10019.

Resource bibliography

Gundling, B. *Exploring aquatic art*. Cedar Rapids, Iowa: International Academy of Aquatic Art, 1963.

Henderson, J. Synchronized swimming for men. *JOPER*, Oct. 1977, 48, 24.

Spears, B. *Fundamentals of synchronized swimming*. Minneapolis: Burgess Publishing Co., 1967.

Vickers, B. *Teaching synchronized swimming*. Englewood Cliffs, N.J.: Prentice-Hall, Inc., 1965.

SQUARE DANCE UNIT

(Developed by Deborah Flynn, Logansport High School, Logansport, Ind.)

Behavioral objectives

1. The student will be able to demonstrate the basic fundamental dance skills, positions, and patterns taught in class by the teacher and the specific skill level record, which will be a necessary foundation for more complicated dances at higher skill levels.

2. The student will be able to combine the dance fundamentals into any dance pattern as instructed by the teacher and the dance record, depending on the skill level of that student.

3. The student will be able to identify and/or explain the dance skills, positions, patterns, and terms on a written test chosen by the teacher, depending on the skill level of that student.

4. The student will be able to identify and/or explain on a written test the history and description of the type of square dances learned and executed in class.

5. The student will be subjectively assessed through some type of behavioral testing sheet, designed by the teacher, on the individual's ability to effectively work and cooperate in a group situation, learning to accept every other student as an individual to be respected.

6. The student will be able to explain the purpose of learning square dance, its social importance, and its carry-over value into later life, as explained by the teacher at the beginning of the dance unit.

7. The advanced student will be able to take the dance skills learned in class and construct his/her own square dance with certain limitations and requirements established by the teacher.

History and origin, description, equipment and facilities, and rules and courtesies

History and origin

Although square dance is usually considered American, it stems from European folk dances that preceded it by several hundred years. Square dancing in America first developed along two separate lines, eastern and western. Eastern dance was closely linked to New England country dances, which were transplants from France and England. Western square dance had its influence from Spain and Mexico. As our nation became more mobile, influences of the East and West combined to form what is now the American square dance.

Description

Square dance involves the use of a pattern caller who directs the entire figure, choosing materials without reference to any predetermined sequence. The pattern call, in addition to giving directions or commands for movement, is embellished with colorful phrases and "folksy" references to western life. The pattern call serves a real purpose in that it fills in the beats required for execution of a movement.

Equipment and facilities

1. A record player with adequate volume and good sound.
2. A large dance floor or gym floor.
3. A microphone (if a caller is used).

4. Records with written instructions, diagrams, and descriptions.

Rules and courtesies

1. Listen carefully to the teacher and the calls.
2. Practice social etiquette—act like a lady or a gentleman.
3. Dancing is a vigorous activity with close contact. Personal cleanliness is a must.
4. Be cooperative. There are others involved in the dances. Thus in order to have a successful dance, everyone has to work together.
5. Be a good mixer—do not form cliques. Try to avoid getting into the same set every time.
6. Enjoy yourself—get into the spirit of the dance.
7. It is a must to learn the fundamentals correctly in order to execute them in a dance situation.

Fundamentals (BASIC)

NOTE: For an explanation of these terms and skills, refer to the listed references at the end of this unit plan.

Terms

Square the set
Home position
Partner
Corner
Head couple—side couple

Skills

These are most common skills. Other skills may appear in the various dances on the record being used for a specific skill level. These new skills should be explained and diagrammed in the instructions attached to the record.

Basic step	Box the gnat
Balance	Allemande thar
Swing	Bend the line
Do-sa-do	Wheel around
Do paso	Promenade ending
Allemande left	Weave the ring
Grand right and left	See saw
	Circle 4-6-8
Right and left through	Split the ring
	Half-sashay (rollaway)

Pass through	Eight to the center
Ladies chain	Center back to back
Ladies grand chain	Right (left) hand star
Sashay	
Do-si-do	Star promenade
Backtrack (turn back)	Slip the clutch
Once and half	Ends turn in (turn out)
Courtesy turn	Swing through
Star through	Cast off
Square through	Circulate
Cross trail through	Wagon wheel
Grand square	Sides (or head) divide
Dive through	
Substitute	Alamo style
Ocean wave	Rip 'n' snort
All eight chain	Thread the needle
Catch all eight	Triple allemande
Double elbow	
Dixie chain	

Dances (most common)

Adam and Eve	Polka on a Banjo
Corners of the World	Birdie in the Cage
Bird in the Cage	and Seven Hands
Sashay Partners Half	Around
Way Around	Shoot the Owl
Star by the Right	Milagro Square
Texas Star	Square Through and
Take a Little Peek	Box the Gnat Hash
Inside Out and the	Sally Good'in
Outside In	Cowboy Loop
Swing at the Wall	Arkansas Traveler
Oh Johnny	Catch All Eight
Promenade the Ring	Yorkshire Pudding
Forward Up and	Sides Divide
Back	Four Gents Star
The "H"	Double Star
The Route	Inside Arch and the
Promenade the Out-	Outside Under
side Ring	Alabama Jubilee
Three Ladies Chain	Aloha to You
Ends Turn In	Are You from Dixie
Split the Ring	Cotton Pickin' Polka
Split Your Corners	Everywhere You Go
Right and Left	Hot Time
Hook	Yes Sir!
Moffits's Maneuvers	
Little Red Wagon	

Measurement and evaluation
Skill test

Ashton, D.: A gross motor rhythm test. *Research Quarterly,* October 1953, *24,* 253-260.

Benton, R.: The measurement of capacities for learning dance movement techniques. *Research Quarterly,* May 1944, *15,* 137.

Blake, P.: Relationship between audio perceptual rhythm and skill in square dance. *Research Quarterly,* May 1960, *21,* 229-231.

Written test

Jensen, C., & Jensen, M. B. Self testing and evaluation. In *Beginning square dance.* Belmont, Calif. Wadsworth Publishing Co., Inc., 1968, pp. 56-61.

Available teaching aids
Record companies

Blue Star Records, P.O. Box 7308, Houston, Tex.

Folkraft Record Co., 1159 Broad Street, Newark, N.J. 07102.

Health, physical education records, 1976-1977 edition. Educational Activities, Inc., P.O. Box 392, Freeport, N.Y. 11530.

Imperial Records, 137 Western Avenue, Los Angeles, Calif. 90052.

Physical education records, 1976-1977 edition. Kimbo Educational, P.O. Box 477, Long Branch, N.J. 07740.

Records, cassettes, filmstrips, transparencies, 1977 catalog. Educational Record Sales, 157 Chambers Street, New York, N.Y. 10007.

Sets In Order, 462 N. Robertson Blvd., Los Angeles, Calif. 90052.

Wagon Wheel Records, 9500 53rd Avenue, Arvada, Colo. 80002.

Reference books and bibliography

Durlacher, E. *Honor Your Partner.* New York: Berin-Adair Co., 1949.

Flood, J., & Putney, C. *Square dance U.S.A.* Dubuque, Iowa: William C. Brown Co., Publishers, 1963.

Hall, J. T. *Dance, a complete guide to social, folk, and square dance.* Belmont, Calif.: Wadsworth Publishing Co., Inc., 1963.

Harris, J. A., Pittman, A., & Walker, M. S. *Dance a while: handbook of folk, square and social dance.* Minneapolis: Burgess Publishing Co., 1968.

McNair, R. J. *Western square dance.* Dubuque, Iowa: Oran V. Siller Co., 1941.

Osgood, B. *Square dancing for beginners.* P.O. Box 89, Santa Barbara, Calif., 1949. (Also for intermediate and advanced.)

SCOPE AND SEQUENCE UNITS

Scope, sequence, and continuity were defined in Units 16 and 18 in terms of organizational concepts for total curriculum planning. These same concepts and their interpretations can be used for designing scope and sequence units or as additions to conventional units.

A scope and sequence chart indicates the specific unit fundamentals to be taught for various grade levels. This type of format ensures vertical sequencing and horizontal scoping for activities within the total curriculum. In addition, performance objectives are designed for each fundamental by grade level or grade divisions and can be used for accountability of student achievement in competency-based programs.

The following unit formats are variations of scope and sequence unit planning.

SCOPE AND SEQUENCE VOLLEYBALL UNIT

(Developed by the staff, Highline Public Schools, Seattle, Wash.)

Skill	K	1	2	3	4	5	6	7	8	9	10	11	12
Passing													
Overhead pass								I	E	E	E	E	
Forearm bounce pass								I	E	E	E	E	
Set													
Front sets								I	E	E	E	E	
Back sets								I	E	E	E	E	
Cross court and back court sets									I	E	E	E	
Setter's movement and function										I	E	E	
Play set—strategy											I	E	
Serves													
Underhand								I	E	E	E	E	
Overhand (floater)									I	E	E	E	
Overhand spins											I	E	
Roundhouse											I	E	
Net recovery									I	E	E	E	
Spiking									I	E	E	E	
Blocking									I	E	E	E	
Defensive tactics													
Defensive on serve reception									I	E	E	E	
Receiving nonspiked returns									I	E	I	I	
Setting two-player block											I	E	
Back court coverage behind block											I	E	
Covering the spiker											I	E	
Block or no-block choice											I	E	
Defensive adjustment according to set and spiker												I	
Defensive switching and strategy											I	E	
Offensive tactics													
Offensive basic pass pattern (pass, set, spike)									O	I	E	E	
Hitting the angles											I	E	
Dive and roll											I	E	
Use of spike option to counter the block												I	
Set variations to counter block												I	
Multiple offense and strategy											I	E	
Rules and court procedures								I	E	E	E	E	
Officiating techniques									O	I	E	E	

KEY: I, introduce; E, expand; O, optional.

Skill classification chart

Skills		Classification		
General	Specific	Beginning	Intermediate	Advanced
Form	Mechanical adjustment of bicycle			
	Seat height	X		
	Seat forward/backward	X		
	Seat tilt	X		
	Handlebar adjustment	X		
	Body position	X		
	Ankling with and without toe clips		X	
Cadence	Use of gears			
	Straight and level terrain		X	
	Uphill		X	
	Downhill		X	
	Braking		X	
	Speed riding			X
	Distance riding			X
Safety	Equipment	X		
	Signals	X		
	City riding		X	
	Country riding		X	
	Packing for trips			X

SCOPE AND SEQUENCE CYCLING UNIT

(Developed by the staff, West Hartford Public Schools, West Hartford, Conn.)

Course objectives

The student knows the definition of terms that relate to cycling.

The student knows the appropriate form for the skills required for riding a bicycle, including balancing, pedaling, steering, starting, and stopping.

The student is able to execute the skills necessary for bicycle riding, using the appropriate form.

The student knows that clothing for recreational cycling is selected for comfort, climate, and safety.

The student knows the equipment and the care of the equipment needed for cycling.

The student knows the safety concepts for recreational cycling, including obeying traffic laws, riding single file at side of streets and highways, keeping the bicycle mechanically efficient, and using proper lighting at night.

The student knows that recreational cycling can contribute to one's health.

The student is able to analyze and evaluate his/her performance in recreational cycling.

Safety precautions

Obey all signs and lights as though driving a car.

Use hand signals.

Check safety of bicycle.

Knowledges, understandings, and appreciations

Know the history of bicycling.

Understand how the bicycle operates.

Understand the techniques used in cycling.

Understand and execute the proper safety precautions.

Understand the opportunities available in bicycle tripping.

Appreciate bicycling as a lifetime activity that develops physical fitness.

Teaching emphases

Stress proper technique and use of the equipment.

Emphasize form and safety.

Encourage conditioning and taking trips.

Grade level	Skills		
	Beginning	Intermediate	Advanced
11-12	Required	Optional	Optional

SCOPE AND SEQUENCE BASKETBALL UNIT

(Developed by Jeffrey Meyer for Lafayette School Corporation, Lafayette, Ind.)

Introduction of the activity
Brief history and origin

Basketball was originated by Dr. James Naismith in 1891 at Springfield College (then YMCA affiliated) in Springfield, Massachusetts. Its original purpose was to provide an activity to condition athletes during the winter season. Peach baskets were used as goals at opposite ends of the gymnasium, with nine players making up each team. The first set of rules for women was devised in 1899.

The basic objective of the game was to put the ball into the basket while preventing the opposition from doing the same.

General description

Basketball is a full-court game played by two teams of five players each. The objective of the game is to score more points than the opposing team. Scores are made from the field (2 points) and from the free throw line (1 point).

Teaching content

A. Fundamentals
  1. Dribbling
    a. Right-hand and left-hand
    b. Changing hands
    c. Crossover and spins
    d. Changing speeds

  2. Passing
    a. Chest
    b. Bounce
    c. Overhead
    d. Baseball
    e. Lob
  3. Shooting
    a. Lay-up
    b. One-hand push shot
    c. Free throw
    d. Jump shot
    e. Hook shot
B. Offensive skills
  1. Cuts
    a. V cut
    b. diagonal cut
    c. L cut
  2. Pivoting
  3. Screening
    a. Screen and roll
    b. Weak side screen (lateral screens)
    c. Down screens
  4. Rebounding
    a. Pivot block-out
    b. Crossover block-out
C. Defensive skills
  1. Basic stance
  2. Footwork
    a. Sliding
    b. Approach step
    c. Swing step
    d. Retreat step
  3. Man without ball
  4. Man with ball
D. Team concepts
  1. Man-to-man
    a. Offense
    b. Defense
  2. Zones
    a. Offense
    b. Defense
  3. Delay offense
  4. Fastbreak offense
  5. Pressure defense
  6. Special plays

Evaluation

Skill tests—*AAHPER Basketball Skills Tests*
Written tests—teacher-created tests evaluating

knowledge of rules, skills, techniques, and strategies covered in class

Teaching aids

A. Films
   1. *Basketball Fundamentals*—30 minutes, 16 mm, rent $1.50; available from University of Wisconsin, Bureau of Visual Instruction, Madison, Wis.
   2. *Basketball*—16 mm, 15 minutes, rent $2.00; fundamentals of basketball by Branch McCracken; available from Coronet Films, Coronet Building, Chicago, Ill.
   3. *Basketball—Individual Skills*—10 minutes, sound, free; analyzes stance, footwork, and evasive tactics in slow motion, full-speed, and game action.
   4. *Fundamentals of Basketball*—76 minutes, five-reel series; available from Baily Film Service, Hollywood, Calif.

B. List of film distributors
   1. Association Film, Inc., 600 Madison Avenue, New York, N.Y. 10022
   2. The Athletic Institute, 805 Merchandise Mart, Chicago, Ill. 61606
   3. Coca-Cola Distributors (local)
   4. School Film Service, 549 W. 123rd Street, New York, N.Y. 10027

Bibliography

Barnes, M. J. *Women's basketball.* Boston: Allyn & Bacon, Inc., 1972.

Kirchner, G. *Physical education for elementary school children.* Dubuque, Iowa: William C. Brown Co., Publishers, 1972.

Stanley, D. K., Waglow, I. R., & Alexander, R. *Physical education activity handbook for men and women.* Boston: Allyn & Bacon, Inc., 1972.

Performance objectives for grades 8 to 10

Skill: Shooting

Grade 8: Students will score 12 points from a designated spot on the foul line. Two points are awarded for a successful attempt; one point is awarded for hitting the rim if the ball hits the rim before it touches the backboard. A total of 15 shots will be taken by each student.

Scope and sequence chart

	Grade level						
Skill	**4**	**5**	**6**	**7**	**8**	**9**	**10**
Dribbling							
Right-hand	X	X	X	X	X	X	X
Left-hand	X	X	X	X	X	X	X
Changing hands	X	X	X	X	X	X	X
Crossover		X	X	X	X	X	X
Spins			X	X	X	X	X
Changing speeds				X	X	X	X
Passing							
Chest	X	X	X	X	X	X	X
Bounce	X	X	X	X	X	X	X
Overhead			X	X	X	X	X
Baseball			X	X	X	X	X
Lob				X	X	X	X
Shooting							
Lay-up	X	X	X	X	X	X	X
One-hand push shot	X	X	X	X	X	X	X
Free throw		X	X	X	X	X	X
Jump shot					X	X	X
Hook shot						X	X
Cuts		X	X	X	X	X	X
Pivoting	X	X	X	X	X	X	X
Screening			X	X	X	X	X
Defensive skills							
Basic stance	X	X	X	X	X	X	X
Footwork	X	X	X	X	X	X	X
Team concepts							
Man-to-man	X	X	X	X	X	X	X
Zones					X	X	X
Delay offense					X	X	X
Fastbreak offense				X	X	X	X
Pressure defense				X	X	X	X
Special plays			X	X	X	X	X

Grade 9: Students will score 17 points from a designated spot on the foul line. Rules stated previously apply.

Grade 10: Using the same procedures, students will score 18 points.

Skill: Shooting

Grade 8: Students will score 11 points, taking 10 shots on each side of the court not less than 20 feet away from the basket. Two points are awarded for a successful attempt; 1 point is awarded for hitting the rim. A total of 20 shots will be taken by each student.

Grade 9: Students will score 19 points, taking 10 shots on each side of the court, using the same procedures as stated previously.

Grade 10: Same as grade 9.

Skill: Foul shooting

Grade 8: Students will score 4 points, taking 20 foul shots, scoring 1 point for each basket made.

Grade 9: Students will score 8 points using the same procedures as stated previously.

Grade 10: Students will score 9 points using the same procedures as stated previously.

Skill: Under the basket shooting

Grade 8: Students will score 7 points shooting any way desired continuously for 30 seconds from under the basket. Each basket made scores 1 point. Two trials will be given to each student.

Grade 9: Students will score 12 points using the same procedures as stated previously.

Grade 10: Students will score 14 points using the same procedures as stated previously.

Skill: Speed passing

Grade 8: Students will pass the ball continuously 10 times against a wall in 12.4 seconds or less. Each student will stand behind a line 9 feet from the wall. Time starts when the first pass hits the wall and stops when the tenth pass hits the wall. Each student will be given two trials. The ball must be caught and passed, not batted.

Grade 9: Students will perform the same task under the same conditions in 9.0 seconds or less.

Grade 10: Students will perform the same task under the same conditions in 8.7 seconds or less.

Skill: Jump and reach

Grade 8: Students will have their optimal reach measured from a flat-footed position. With both feet planted, students will jump 13 inches above their optimal reach.

Grade 9: Using the same procedures, students will jump 20 inches above their optimal reach.

Grade 10: Using the same procedures, students will jump 22 inches above their optimal reach.

Skill: Overarm pass for accuracy

Grade 8: Students will score 11 points standing behind a line 35 feet from a target and passing the ball at the target 10 times. The target with an 18-inch diameter center circle = 3 points; 38-inch diameter second circle = 2 points; 58-inch diameter outer circle = 1 point.

Grade 9: Using the same target and scoring procedures, students will score 18 points.

Grade 10: Using the same target and scoring procedures, students will score 19 points.

Skill: Chest pass for accuracy

Grade 8: Using the same target and scoring procedures, students will stand 25 feet from the target and execute 10 two-hand chest passes, scoring 9 points.

Grade 9: Executing the two-hand chest pass, students will score 20 points in their 10 attempts.

Grade 10: Students will score 22 points using the same target and scoring procedures.

Skill: Dribbling

Grade 8: Students will dribble in and out of six cones as fast as possible with either hand in 13.9 seconds or less. Cones will be placed 8 feet apart, with the first being 5 feet from a line. Each student will be given two trials.

Grade 9: Using the same procedures, students will dribble in and out of the cones in 11.3 seconds or less.

Grade 10: Students will perform this task in 10.9 seconds or less.

LESSON PLANNING

Developing an outline for a unit should not be confused with a "lesson plan." A unit may extend over a period of several weeks, whereas a lesson plan considers what will be done each day in the direction of achieving the objectives of a unit. The lesson plan segments the unit into a series of related lessons.

The criteria of age level, time allotment, days per week, size of classes, and needs of the teacher may affect the depth and breadth of a lesson plan. However, it should include the following:

1. The performance objectives to be achieved that day in all domains
2. A warm-up activity
   a. Exercises
   b. Procedures
3. Instructional content
   a. Fundamental skills
      (1) Task analysis
      (2) Instructional cues
   b. Knowledges
4. Instructional strategy
   a. Equipment, supplies, and facilities
   b. Selection and use of teaching style(s)
   c. Media
   d. Organizational procedures
   e. Formative and summative evaluation techniques
5. Culminating activity
   a. Lead-up game
   b. Tournament
6. Summary and preview
7. Announcements
8. Instruction and lesson evaluation

In a conventional lesson, time modules may be designated for each lesson segment. This ensures coverage of lesson material but may detract from any "teachable moment" that occurs. The teacher should be aware that rates of learning differ in individuals and between classes. Instruction and learning may vary, depending on the time of day. Therefore teachers are cautioned to be cognizant of predesignation time allotments but to use good judgment and perceive what is occurring in the teaching-learning environment.

Examples of two types of lesson plan formats are presented on pp. 289 and 290.

LESSON PLAN

Subject: _____ Time: From _____To _____

Location: _____ Number of students: _____

1. Equipment to be used:

2. Roll call (method):

3. Exercise program:

4. Performance objectives:

5. Instructional content:

6. Specific instructional strategies and materials:

7. Evaluation procedures:

8. Summary, preview, announcements:

LESSON PLAN

(Courtesy Jo Ann Price, Purdue University, West Lafayette, Ind.)

1. Unit topic
2. Situation
   a. Size of class
   b. Time available
   c. Lesson number
3. Performance objectives
   a. Psychomotor
   b. Cognitive
   c. Affective
4. Day's lesson
   a. Activities to be presented
   b. Materials needed
5. Plan for lesson procedure

Time (minutes)	Subject matter (activities)	Method (organization)	Input-output cues, possible errors, correction, teaching hints
5-10	Roll call Announcements Warm-ups		
20-25	Review New skills Explanation- demonstration Practice Evaluation		

2-3	Summary and/or
	  preview of next
	  lesson		

10	Showers and dressing		

6. Evaluation of the lesson
   a. Strong points
   b. Weak points
7. How could the lesson be improved?

INSTRUCTIONAL STRATEGY DEFINED

Method is defined as an orderly procedure or process. However, this definition limits its use in the total instructional process.

A strategy implies that there is an art and science for devising or employing a comprehensive plan toward an instructional goal. The term *instructional strategy* not only encompasses the art of teaching but also gives consideration to the science of teaching. In developing an instructional strategy, one must consider the learner (characteristics, needs, interests, and readiness), be familiar with the various learning theories (conditioning, informa-tion processing, and Gestalt), be able to identify kinds of learning (physiological, psychomotor, cognitive, and affective), understand the three phases of learning a motor skill (cognitive, fixation, and autonomous), be knowledgeable in various modes of communication (verbal, nonverbal, hardware, and software), and, last but not least, have a feeling as to what "turns students on" and what "turns them off."

An analysis of the most widely used instructional strategies as they relate to their basic concepts and principles, advantages and disadvantages, is shown in Table 8.

Table 8. An analysis of instructional strategies

Basic concepts and principles	Advantages	Disadvantages
Lecture—The lecture style consists of a teacher-centered presentation. The instructor presents the material, and the students record (write) the material for later reference and study.	The instructor can present more material in the given class period. Very systematic and organized approach and presentation for the instructor. Very few apparent advantages.	The students do not usually play an active part in the class presentation. Very little class interaction and discussion. If the class, or even one student has difficulty, the instructor is interested in feedback to correct errors in instruction.
Drill—The drill style centers on repetition of a skill. The instructor demonstrates the skill, and the students follow up with repeated practice of that skill.	Allows the student to work at a skill. The best way to learn a skill is by doing the skill. Very advantageous if the drill is in conjunction with a one-to-one situation or in a small group paced by the group's rate of learning.	Drills are usually conducted on a large-scale basis. They do not allow for individual problems of the underskilled and the overskilled. Drills can become very impersonal unless there is adequate interaction between the instructor and group and within the group itself.
Information processing—Primary attention is focused on the learning process. The student's learning capacity, ability to process information, and effectiveness in retrieving information accurately when required are fundamental to this process.	This enhances creativity. In the process of acquiring and processing useful information, students will vary the uses of the material in content and presentation that for the class as a whole will provide creativity and diversity in the subject matter and in the learning process. It also allows the student to pursue depth of content.	If a student moves in a tangential direction, time may be wasted. Motivation might become a problem if the student does not have an interest in the assignment. A very impersonal process if not contained within a group or if no interaction with the instructor.
Humanistic instruction—Humanistic instruction is personalized. The teaching-learning act is actually a personal relationship extending to the teacher, the student, and the student's peers. It requires genuineness, respect, and understanding from the teacher.	Human contact and feeling create a way of teaching possibly unsurpassed due to the close interaction and communication between the teacher and the learner. Inhibitions can usually be overcome and the one-to-one environment opened. Many possible advantages in the affective domain.	Difficult if class sizes are very large or there are too few instructors. Often the attention is focused on those who are underskilled and the other students may be neglected. Often a slow process in relation to other methods.
Mastery learning—Mastery levels are defined in terms of specific objectives. The time variable is manipulated to provide for different rates of learning. The stu-	Permits each student to learn at an individual rate. Ensures that a student acquires mastery of a specific level before proceeding to the next level. Provides	Students may not be able to handle the responsibility. Difficult to determine mastery levels. Students may not be exposed to all types of activities.

dent must achieve mastery before proceeding to the next level. Diagnostic feedback (formative evaluation) is provided during learning stages.	immediate feedback to the student. Alternative instructional corrections can be used for each student.	
Systems analysis—The systems approach is based on a systematic model that proceeds through goals, objectives, evaluation instruments, instructional strategies, and content and contains an instructional analysis. The approach moves step by step through the model and identifies all parts of the instructional process.	This method can be used to determine the best fit for a teaching situation. It forces the teacher to do more than just appear before the class. It is well-organized and exact in its presentation. It allows for revision of instruction by constant evaluation.	Does not seem very flexible during the process, and does not seem very easy to change or modify once the process has begun. Planning is very time consuming, but in general, the problems or disadvantages seem very few. It seems that problems can arise during specific teaching situations rather than during the procedure.
Competency-based strategy—This strategy is based on the premise that students must achieve certain objectives before proceeding to a goal. Students who do not achieve an objective cannot continue.	This process ensures that the student has gained the appropriate background to continue. The student is provided the necessary time to learn the material without holding back or leaving the other students behind. It also informs the students exactly what they must achieve before they can progress.	An instructor must always be available for student consultation. A seemingly impersonal approach unless the instructor takes an active part in the instructional process and is aware of individual learning plateaus.
Teacher directed—The center of instruction is the teacher. It is very similar to the lecture style. The teacher takes command of the class and conducts the instruction according to a specific plan of study.	The instructor can cover all the material for that day's presentation. Very systematic and organized. Does not have to deal with divergent questions from the group.	There is very little activity from the class. Similar to the lecture style. Without class interaction, it is difficult to determine what the students have learned and what they have missed.
Individualized instruction—This means to impart knowledge to an indivisible being who has a quality that distinguishes him/her from another . . . to treat or notice individually. It gives consideration to individual differences in learning ability and rate.	This permits the teacher to work with those who vary in learning rates. It also allows students to progress without being held back by the normal progress of the class.	If the class size is too large and there are too few instructors, this plan may not always be feasible. Problems may stem from certain teaching situations but in general there seem to be few faults with this type of approach.

TRADITIONAL INSTRUCTIONAL STRATEGIES AND MATERIALS

The term *traditional* as applied to physical education instruction has been defined and interpreted in many ways. Synonyms have been proposed, such as drill method, teaching by command, and cohort instruction.

The traditional instructional strategy that will be analyzed here, in the broadest interpretation, involves the more conventional instructional practices that are primarily teacher controlled. More specifically, the teacher makes all the decisions regarding what the student will learn, how the student will learn, and when the student will learn. These decisions are based on the assumptions that individual differences in learning abilities and rates do not exist in a class, that all students have the same needs and interests, that students cannot function as individuals in a teaching-learning environment, and that there is organizational efficiency and control.

The most common traditional strategy consists of the following:

Teacher	Demonstration—model
	Explanation—verbal
Teacher-directed	Practice—group
	Evaluation—summative

Instructional materials widely used for a traditional instructional setting are the unit and lesson plans. These are primarily for the teacher's use as instructional information and provide a format for instruction. In some cases, student handouts are devised to explain class policies, rules of the game, terminology, and other information not primarily related to learning tasks.

INDIVIDUALIZED INSTRUCTIONAL STRATEGIES AND MATERIALS

Curriculum planners in physical education have always been confronted with three major problems: to provide a teaching-learning environment that allows the learner a degree of independence and choice; to compensate for the physiological, psychological, and sociological variances that exist in every learning situation; and to manipulate the program time modules in order to permit individual rates of learning.

In the past, instructional materials for the student have not been widely used in physical education. There now is a need and demand for these materials for many of the "innovative" instructional strategies that have been devised based on the following propositions:

1. A student should be able to progress at his/her own rate of learning.
2. Achievement of minimal competencies should be ensured.
3. Instruction should personally and actively involve each student in the teaching-learning process.
4. Learning should not be restricted to a regularly scheduled class period or to a specific facility.

The implication of these propositions is that individual differences among learners do exist; therefore instructional strategies must be used that consider each student as an individual learner.

Various terms are being used for these "new" strategies—individualized instruction, personalized learning, humanistic instruction, contingency management or contracting, competency-based instruction, prescription learning, and independent study.

Since these strategies or approaches to instruction are designed to provide the best match for individual needs, interests, and characteristics, the term *individualized instruction* hereafter will be used to designate an instructional strategy that adapts the teaching-learning process to each student.

The implementation of an individualized

instructional strategy involves, in most cases, a change in the communication mode between teacher and student. Verbal instruction may be used if the tasks to be performed are very brief, for example:

Teacher verbal tasks

1. I will demonstrate a push-up.
2. See how many different ways you can do a push-up.
3. Select the most difficult way and see how many times you can do it.
4. Tomorrow, try to do more than you did today.

However, a more sophisticated approach to individualization utilizes written materials correlated with visual aids.

The unit plan and its format can still be used to provide resource information; however, the design and preparation of student instructional materials present some unique problems. The designer must have the ability to thoroughly task analyze skills, structure cognitive problems, and present the subject matter in a concise, systematic, progressive form considering the comprehension level of the student. In addition, visual aids can be used to complement the materials.

Instructional strategies, materials, and curriculum models have been designed around systems, competency-based, and mastery learning approaches. These strategies involve in varying degrees a wide variety of instructional communication modes that replace or supplement teacher demonstration and verbal instruction. These include hardware (teaching machines, computers, cassette recorders, television, videotape recorders, and all types of projectors) and software (loop film, slides, videotapes, cassette tapes, sound pages, contracts, individualized instructional packets, task cards and sheets, and self-instructional transactions).

The following programs illustrate examples of individualized strategies, materials, and communication modes that have been designed, refined, and implemented for different school divisions.

ELEMENTARY AND MIDDLE SCHOOL PROGRAMS

The function of elementary and middle school physical education is to combine the basic principles of movement and the common elements of a challenging activity as progressive subject matter for learning and instruction. The child is a progressively developing, integrating organism. Progressive development is from basic movement to more complex skills. Activities for the development of fundamental movement patterns are presented prior to those skills requiring a higher degree of refined and specialized learnings.

Many times we search for new activities to include in our program when the problem is not the activity, but rather its presentation. If our aims are as follows:

1. To develop a wide range of physical, perceptual, and motor abilities through the implementation of the best theories of learning
2. To provide experiences that are progressively more complex in order to establish a favorable environment for the development of imaginative and creative thinking
3. To structure a learning environment that will enhance students' self-concepts in the environment
4. To involve students in activities that are challenging and fun

Then we must critically analyze the relative worth of the activity and the instructional strategy regarding their contributions to these aims. The following principles were formulated for selecting and presenting elementary and middle school activities:

1. Fundamental movement activities are learned, not taught. Activity experiences should be structured so that learning takes place.

2. The selection of activities should be based on a specific desired outcome.
3. The activity experience should provide a creative challenge and movement response for the learner.
4. The flexibility of the activity should allow the learner to experiment with movement.
5. The basic method of teaching fundamental movement patterns is by providing experiences for experimentation and exploration.
6. Guiding corrections and cues should be given to the learner during the activity.
7. Sufficient amount of equipment and activity areas should be provided for maximum participation.

These principles served as guidelines for developing a series of progressive activities and instructional strategies for the elementary and middle school grades, as shown here in a program that included fundamental movements, ball-handling skills, and rope-jumping skills.

INDIVIDUALIZED PROGRAM FOR FUNDAMENTAL MOVEMENTS

The criteria for selection of the activities and design of instructional materials were their relative contributions to the following objectives of physical education:
1. Physical domain
   a. Leg strength and endurance
   b. Cardiovascular endurance
   c. Flexibility
2. Psychomotor domain
   a. Perceptual-motor abilities
      (1) Balance
      (2) Kinesthesis (body image, body awareness, laterality, and directionality)
      (3) Visual discrimination (tracking and figure-ground extraction)
      (4) Visual motor coordination (eye-hand coordination)
   b. Fundamental movement skills
      (1) Locomotor (running, hopping, and jumping)
      (2) Nonlocomotor (bending, stretching, twisting, and turning)
      (3) Locomotor combinations (skipping, landing, and changing directions)
      (4) Propulsive skills (throwing)
      (5) Receptive skills (catching)
3. Cognitive domain
   a. The use of judgment related to time, form, space, speed, and direction in the use of activity implements, balls, and self
   b. The solution of developmental problems through movement
4. Affective domain
   a. The ability to be challenged and have fun in an activity
   b. An awareness of what the body is capable of doing at a specific time
   c. The knowledge of what one is and the ability to accept this knowledge of one's capacity and potential

Activities

The following activities were selected:
1. Fundamental movement activities
   a. Locomotor skills
      (1) Running
      (2) Leaping
      (3) Jumping
      (4) Hopping
   b. Nonlocomotor skills
      (1) Stretching
      (2) Bending
      (3) Twisting
      (4) Turning
   c. Locomotor combinations
      (1) Skipping
      (2) Starting
      (3) Stopping
      (4) Changing direction
2. Ball-handling activities
   a. Throwing
   b. Bouncing
   c. Catching
3. Rope-jumping activities
   a. Individual
   b. Partner
   c. Group

Instructional strategy

1. Students should be given a thorough orientation as to the type of tasks and use of materials.

2. If necessary, instruction should be provided on the more complex tasks.
3. Sufficient equipment and supplies should be provided.
4. Students should complete all tasks in one level and check with the instructor before proceeding to the next level.

Instructional materials and evaluation

Individualized, partner, and group skill sheets were designed for the activities with progressive tasks categorized by levels of difficulty and number of participants involved.

An individual skill sheet may be distributed to all students as needed, used verbally by the teacher, or modified by designing a master wall chart for each class. Check-off space is provided for completion of a task by the student.

The assessment of a student's achievement in these activities should be based on skill performance, improvement, and effort. Individual progress can be indicated on a checklist through teacher observation. The sample checklist below is recommended for inclusion with all the skill sheets.

EVALUATION

Student _____ Teacher _____ Grade level _____

Activity areas	Level 1	Level 2	Level 3
Fundamental movements			
Rope jumping			
Ball handling			

Comments:

GRADING SYMBOLS: +, outstanding; √, average; −, needs improvement

Activity Skill Sheet 1: Fundamental movements

Name _____ Grade level _____ Class period _____

Level 1: Individual activities	Level 2: Partner activities	Level 3: Group activities

DIRECTIONS: Your body has five points: head, hand, hand, foot, and foot. Without moving, what can you do touching the floor with:

_____ 1. Five points?
_____ 2. Four points?
_____ 3. Three points?
_____ 4. Two points?
_____ 5. One point?

While moving, what can you do touching the floor with

_____ 6. Five points?
_____ 7. Four points?
_____ 8. Three points?
_____ 9. Two points?
_____10. One point?

DIRECTIONS: Select a partner. You and your partner have ten body points. Without moving and touching your partner, what can you and your partner do touching the floor with:

_____1. Two points?
_____2. Three points?
_____3. Four points?
_____4. Five points?
_____5. Six points?
_____6. Seven points?
_____7. Eight points?
_____8. Nine points?
_____9. Ten points?

DIRECTIONS: You and your partner join with another group. The four of you now have a total of 20 body points. Without moving and touching each other, what can your group do touching the floor with:

_____ 1. Two points?
_____ 2. Three points?
_____ 3. Four points?
_____ 4. Five points?
_____ 5. Six points?
_____ 6. Seven points?
_____ 7. Eight points?
_____ 8. Nine points?
_____ 9. Ten points?
_____10. Eleven points?
_____11. Twelve points?
_____12. Thirteen points?
_____13. Fourteen points?
_____14. Fifteen points?
_____15. Sixteen points?
_____16. Seventeen points?
_____17. Eighteen points?
_____18. Nineteen points?
_____19. Twenty points?

While moving and touching each other, what can your group do touching the floor with:

_____20. Two points?
_____21. Three points?
_____22. Four points?
_____23. Five points?
_____24. Six points?
_____25. Seven points?
_____26. Eight points?
_____27. Nine points?
_____28. Ten points?
_____29. Eleven points?
_____30. Twelve points?
_____31. Thirteen points?
_____32. Fourteen points?
_____33. Fifteen points?
_____34. Sixteen points?
_____35. Seventeen points?
_____36. Eighteen points?
_____37. Nineteen points?
_____38. Twenty points?

Activity Skill Sheet 2: Rope jumping

Level 1: Individual activities	Level 2: Partner activities	Level 3: Group activities

Level 1: Individual activities

DIRECTIONS: With the rope turning forward, can you:

_____ 1. Hop on both feet?
_____ 2. Hop on right foot?
_____ 3. Hop on left foot?
_____ 4. Alternate hopping on right and left foot?
_____ 5. Run forward?
_____ 6. Skip forward?
_____ 7. Hop on both feet, crossing the rope on alternate hops?
_____ 8. Turn the rope twice for each hop on both feet?
_____ 9. Hop forward on one foot and backward on the other foot in a rocker motion?

With the rope turning backward, can you:

_____10. Hop on both feet?
_____11. Hop on right foot?
_____12. Hop on left foot?
_____13. Alternate hopping on right and left foot?
_____14. Run forward?
_____15. Skip forward?
_____16. Hop on both feet, crossing the rope on alternate hops?
_____17. Turn the rope twice for each hop on both feet?
_____18. Hop forward on one foot and backward on the other foot in a rocker motion?

Now:

_____19. Hop for 30 seconds, rest for 10 seconds. Repeat three times.
_____20. How many good hops can you do in 1 minute?
_____21. Create a routine using different jumps.

Level 2: Partner activities

DIRECTIONS: Select a partner. Use one rope.

_____ 1. Face your partner. Hop on both feet turning the rope forward.
_____ 2. Same as No. 1, turn the rope backward.
_____ 3. Stand behind your partner, repeat No. 1.
_____ 4. Stand behind your partner, repeat No. 2.
_____ 5. Stand back-to-back, repeat No. 1.
_____ 6. Stand back-to-back, repeat No. 2.
_____ 7. Stand side-by-side, join inside hands; turning rope forward, hop on both feet.
_____ 8. Stand side-by-side, facing opposite directions; repeat No. 7.
_____ 9. Repeat No. 7 and 8, turning rope backward.
_____10. Face partner, hop on both feet. Partner makes quarter turns while hopping.
_____11. Stand back-to-back, hop on both feeet. Each turn a rope end with the right hand.
_____12. Create a routine with your partner using different jumps.

Level 3: Group activities

DIRECTIONS: Form groups of three. Use a long rope. Take turns in turning the rope. Turn rope forward slowly.

_____ 1. Run through the turning rope.
_____ 2. Run in, one jump, run out same side.
_____ 3. Run in, one jump, run out opposite side.
_____ 4. Run in, jump with full turn, run out.
_____ 5. Run in, jump with full turn, run out.
_____ 6. Run in, jump with a heel click, run out.
_____ 7. Run in, jump on all fours, run out.
_____ 8. Run in, jump by crossing and uncrossing feet on alternate turns.
_____ 9. Run in; how many different types of jumps can you do?
_____10. Jump with a short rope inside the turning long rope.
_____11. Run in and around the rope turners, forming a figure 8.
_____12. Repeat No. 11, skipping with a short rope.

With a partner:

_____13. Run through the turning rope.
_____14. Run in, one jump, run out same side.
_____15. Run in, one jump, run out opposite side.
_____16. Run in, jump with full turn, run out.
_____17. Run in, jump with full turn, run out.
_____18. Run in, jump with a heel click, run out.
_____19. Run in, jump on all fours, run out.
_____20. Run in, jump by crossing and uncrossing feet on alternate turns.
_____21. Run in, how many different types of jumps can you do?

Activity Skill Sheet 3: Ball handling

Level 1: Individual activities	Level 2: Partner activities	Level 3: Group activities
DIRECTIONS: Using an 8-inch playground ball, can you:	DIRECTIONS: Select a partner and using an 8-inch playground ball, can you two:	DIRECTIONS: Form a group of six. Use a long rope. Take turns in turning the rope. Use an 8-inch playground ball. Can you:

Level 1: Individual activities

DIRECTIONS: Using an 8-inch playground ball, can you:

____1. Toss ball up and catch with both hands?
____2. Toss ball up, let it bounce, and catch with both hands?
____3. Toss ball up ahead of you and walk forward to catch it?
____4. Toss ball up ahead of you and run to catch it?
____5. Toss ball up ahead of you and hop on both feet to catch it?
____6. Toss ball up, make a half turn, and catch it?
____7. Toss ball up, make a full turn, and catch it?
____8. Toss ball up, let ball bounce, make a full turn, and catch it?
____9. Bounce ball ahead, walk, and catch it?

Level 2: Partner activities

DIRECTIONS: Select a partner and using an 8-inch playground ball, can you two:

____1. Pass the ball to your partner 10 feet away?
____2. Bounce the ball to your partner 10 feet away?
____3. Pass the ball off a wall to your partner?
____4. Bounce the ball off the wall to the floor to your partner?

Using two balls, can you two:

____5. Pass the balls to each other, one high, one low?
____6. Pass the balls to each other at chest level?
____7. One pass the ball, the other bounce the ball?
____8. Each bounce the balls to the other at the same time?

Level 3: Group activities

DIRECTIONS: Form a group of six. Use a long rope. Take turns in turning the rope. Use an 8-inch playground ball. Can you:

____ 1. Run in, toss ball in air, and catch ball while jumping?
____ 2. Run in, bounce ball while jumping?
____ 3. Run in, alternate a toss in air, catch, and bounce while jumping?
____ 4. Run in, toss ball in air, let it bounce and catch while jumping?
____ 5. Run in with partner, pass ball back and forth while jumping?
____ 6. Run in with partner, bounce and pass ball back and forth while jumping?
____ 7. Form a triangle with two jumpers and student outside of rope, pass the ball clockwise while jumping?
____ 8. Repeat No. 7, using a bounce pass?
____ 9. Form a diamond with four students, pass ball clockwise while jumping?
____10. Repeat No. 9, using a bounce pass?

MULTIMEDIA APPROACH FOR TEACHING UPPER ELEMENTARY AND MIDDLE SCHOOL TUMBLING SKILLS AND CORRELATED ACTIVITIES

(Developed by A. A. Annarino, Roger Taulman, and Sharon Otto)

Can elementary school students assume more responsibility and be less dependent on the teacher in a physical education gymnastic experience? An analysis of the characteristics, needs, and interests of the contemporary child seems to indicate that they can.

Accepting this premise, a multimedia approach for teaching tumbling to upper elementary and middle school boys and girls was developed.

Developmental procedures

The developmental procedures were as follows:
1. Selecting the tumbling stunts
   a. Forward roll and variations
   b. Backward roll, extension, and variations
   c. Cartwheel and round-off
   d. Roll-back neckspring and neckspring
   e. Headspring
   f. Handspring
   g. Headstand and variations
2. Establishing performance objectives
3. Analyzing each specific stunt
4. Producing loop films and correlated descriptive cassette tapes for each stunt
5. Designing mini-individualized instructional packets (IIPs) to include both cognitive and psychomotor learnings to accompany each loop film and tape
6. Designing supplementary, progressive, individualized skill sheets for rope-jumping, conditioning, balance beam, and long jump skills

Instructional strategy

The program is for two fourth, fifth, and sixth grade classes or for a middle school. Each section averages 30 students, with approximately an equal number of boys and girls. Each class meets three times a week for 30 minutes.

The gymnasium is divided into three viewing and listening areas and four activity areas. Each viewing area includes a writing area, a loop film projector, a cassette recorder, a screen, and IIPs for one stunt. The activity areas are used for tumbling, rope skipping, balance beam, and conditioning and have the necessary activity equipment and posted individualized skill sheets.

Each class is given a thorough orientation as to the program procedures and equipment operation. The class is divided into seven groups and randomly assigned to the three viewing areas and three activity areas.

At a viewing station, the student reads the mini-IIP instructions, starts the cassette recorder, and at an indicated direction (by tape) starts the loop film projector. After viewing the film and listening to the tape, the student answers the IIP questions. An answer key is provided for reinforcement.

After viewing and listening, the student moves to a tumbling activity area and completes the IIP skill grade level assignments with instructor assistance. When the student achieves the competency level for that grade, he/she is evaluated by the instructor. Based on the evaluation, the instructor may recommend that the student continue practicing at that level, work on the next level, select a new activity area, or start a new IIP. New IIPs are periodically added to the viewing stations.

The same procedures are followed at the other activity areas, only the students work from a posted individualized skill sheet.

Instructional materials
Sample mini-individualized instruction packet (IIP): tripod-headstand-handstand

Independent written assignment
View the loop film and listen to the tape about the tripod, headstand, and handstand. Now try to answer the following questions without any help. Circle the letter of the correct answer for the question.

 __a__ 1. When doing a tripod, what figure is formed with the head and hands?
   a. Triangle
   b. Straight line
   c. Circle

___c___ 2. During the tripod, where are the knees placed?
   a. On the floor
   b. On the hands
   c. On the inside of the elbows

___b___ 3. When doing a headstand from a tripod, what do you do after forming the tripod?
   a. A forward roll
   b. Extend the legs
   c. Keep legs in a pike position

___b___ 4. What is the other method of going into a headstand besides starting from a tripod?
   a. A front support
   b. A kick-up
   c. An extension

___a___ 5. In the loop film some of the performers had trouble keeping their balance in the tripod and headstand. Do you know what they should have done to help keep their balance?
   a. Have a firm triangular base and keep hips and feet over their heads
   b. Go into the stunt more slowly
   c. Put their hands closer to their heads

___c___ 6. How should you come out of a headstand?
   a. Fall to the side
   b. Any way that you want to
   c. Tuck chin to chest, roll to neck and shoulders, pull knees to chest

___b___ 7. When doing a handstand what should you do after your hands are placed on the mat and one foot is extended into the air?
   a. Do a forward roll
   b. Push with the other foot
   c. Raise second foot slowly to the same height as the first one

Now that you have answered the questions, check your answers with the ones given.

When you understand the answers to all of the questions, go on to the next section of this packet and practice the tripod, headstand, and handstand skills.

Independent skill assignment

The following section of this packet is for you to use to practice the tripod, headstand, and handstand. Each skill you are to do is listed. Next to the skill is a column labeled "Reps." The number in that column tells you how many times you should repeat the skill. There is another column marked "Check-off." When you have done the skill the number of times listed, place a check in this column. Keep in mind what you have learned about safety and spotting:

1. *Safety:* The tripod, headstand, and handstand should be done on mats and with a spotter.

2. *Spotting:* The spotter stands at the side of the performer. Assist him/her in getting up by grasping the lower leg. When he/she finds the point of balance, release.

Skill	Reps	Check-off
1. Form a triangle on the mat with your head and hands.	2	☐
2. Do a tripod. After forming a triangle with your head and hands, put your knees on the inside of the elbows and keep hips over the head.	2	☐
3. Hold a tripod for 10 seconds.	2	☐
4. From a tripod position, extend legs into the air.	3	☐
5. Form a triangle on the mat with head and hands, extend one leg into the air and kick up with the other leg into a headstand.	3	☐
6. From a tripod, do a headstand and hold it for 10 seconds.	2	☐
7. Using the kick-up method, do a headstand and hold it for 10 seconds.	2	☐
8. Do a handstand with a spotter helping you. a. Hands on mat shoulder distance apart b. One foot extended in the air c. Push with other foot	3	☐
9. Do a handstand against a wall.	3	☐
10. Hold a handstand for 10 seconds.	3	☐

Evaluation

Please see your teacher for a skill evaluation.

Individualized skill sheets

Rope-jumping skills

_____ 1. Jump with feet together using an intervening hop (20 times).

_____ 2. Jump with feet together with no intervening hop (20 times).

_____ 3. Jump on right foot with an intervening hop (20 times).

_____ 4. Jump on left foot with an intervening hop (20 times).

_____ 5. Jump on right foot with no intervening hop (20 times).

_____ 6. Jump on left foot with no intervening hop (20 times).

_____ 7. Alternate right and left with an intervening hop (20 times).

_____ 8. Run in place (no hop between steps) (15 seconds).

_____ 9. Run in place, keeping legs stiff and lifting them forward (15 seconds).

_____10. Do rocking step, one foot in front of other (20 times).

_____11. Run forward jumping rope.

_____12. Skip and jump rope.

_____13. Do double or triple turn (turn rope under feet two or three times with one jump).

_____14. Do backward any five of these items.

Conditioning skills

_____ 1. Jog the length of the gymnasium and back without stopping between lengths.

_____ 2. At half speed, run the length of the gymnasium and back without stopping between lengths.

_____ 3. Run two lengths of the gymnasium at full speed and do five sit-ups afterward.

_____ 4. Run three lengths of the gymnasium at half speed and do five sit-ups afterward.

_____ 5. Run three lengths of the gymnasium at full speed and do ten sit-ups afterwards.

_____ 6. Run three lengths of the gymnasium at full speed and do ten sit-ups and five push-ups after you run.

_____ 7. Run four lengths of the gymnasium at half speed and do ten sit-ups and ten push-ups.

_____ 8. Run four lengths of the gymnasium at full speed, do ten sit-ups and ten push-ups.

_____ 9. Run four lengths of the gymnasium at full speed, do ten jumping jacks, ten push-ups, and five sit-ups.

_____10. Run five lengths of the gymnasium at three quarter speed, do fifteen jumping jacks, ten push-ups, and ten sit-ups.

Balance beam skills

_____ 1. Walk forward, backward, and sideward with arms held at different positions.

_____ 2. Walk to the center of beam and perform a stunt (kneeling, walk under or over wand, one leg balance, etc.)

_____ 3. Hop on one foot, moving across beam.

_____ 4. Walk to middle of beam, do a right-side or left-side support, rise, and walk to the end.

_____ 5. Walk to middle of beam and do a balance stand on one foot, arms held sideward from trunk and free leg extended horizontally.

_____ 6. Walk beam forward, backward, sideward, left or right, eyes closed.

_____ 7. Partners start at opposite ends, walk to middle, pass each other, and continue to end of beam.

_____ 8. Place hands on beam; have partner hold legs (as in the wheelbarrow), and walk to the end of the beam. _Variation:_ Both partners on beam.

_____ 9. Do a V-sit.

_____10. Bounce a ball across on the beam. Repeat but bounce the ball on the floor as you walk on the beam.

_____11. Dribble the ball across the beam as you walk. Repeat dribbling ball on floor as you walk on the beam.

_____12. Pass and receive from a partner (one on beam and one off beam, then both on beam).

_____13. Forward roll.

_____14. Roll back to pike position.

Long jump skills

_____1. Run a short distance—five steps and take-off.

_____2. Increase the distance to 10 steps and take-off.

_____3. Start slowly and increase your speed to maximum before takeoff.

_____4. Start fast, slow down for a few steps, and go back to the original fast speed before take-off.

_____5. Try your own variations of speed.

TRACK AND FIELD PROGRAM FOR UPPER ELEMENTARY GRADES

(Developed by Jane Foley, Central Elementary School, Valparaiso, Ind.)

Instructional strategy

1. Organization of practice stations with a task card available for each student
2. Orientation of student to program
3. Assignment of groups to each station
4. Student completion of tasks
5. Teacher evaluation
6. Student moving to another station

Instructional materials
Task card

RUNNING EVENTS TASK CARD 2: 50-YARD DASH

Name _____ Grade _____

Performer _____ Observer _____

OBJECTIVE: Run the 50-yard dash at least at beginner's level for your grade.

	Grade 4		Grade 5		Grade 6	
	Boys	Girls	Boys	Girls	Boys	Girls
Beginner	8.0	8.2	7.8	8.1	7.6	8.0
Intermediate	7.4	7.5	7.4	7.5	7.0	7.5
Advanced	7.0	7.0	7.0	7.0	6.8	7.0

DIRECTIONS: Do each task and check off when completed.

	Completed	Incomplete
Task 1: Get a partner. Have your partner time you for 50 yards. Record time: _____	☐	☐
Task 2: Jog 50 yards. Concentrate on arms. *Cues:* (1) Arms go back and forth opposite legs and (2) arms reach forward, not across, body.	☐	☐
Task 3: Jog 50 yards. Concentrate on legs. *Cues:* (1) Run on balls of feet, (2) legs and toes go straight forward, and (3) legs reach with knees up.	☐	☐
Task 4: Sprint 50 yards. Concentrate on finish. *Cues:* (1) Look at finish, not feet and (2) do not slow down until 10 yards past finish line.	☐	☐
Rest	☐	☐
Task 5: Get a partner. Have your partner time you as you sprint 50 yards. Record time: _____	☐	☐

Were you faster the second time?

Are you ready for the finals? If so, have the teacher time you for the finals. If not, have a partner time you until you are ready.

COMPUTER-MONITORED INDIVIDUAL PROGRAM FOR JUNIOR HIGH SCHOOL

(Developed by the staff, C. F. Simmons Junior High School, Aurora, Ill.)

The variety of activities offers both familiar and new experiences in fulfillment of objectives through any one of many possible avenues of instruction, such as listening to and looking at a sound page, viewing a wall chart, viewing a transparency, listening to a cassette, signing out and using equipment in school facilities, using appropriate off-campus facilities such as a bowling alley, reading a book, or getting help from a teacher, student teacher, or even a student assistant (peer).

Basic requirements

1. All students must work on physical fitness at their own level, every day, all year.
2. All students must work on tumbling. They must pass, successfully, 19 lessons.
3. All students must complete or make reasonable progress in two team sports units.
4. All students must complete or make reasonable progress in three different individual sports.
5. All students must complete 12 units in the Young Boatman's Safety Course (state requirement).

Activities

The following 34 different activities are presently offered from which students may select sports to fulfill their requirements:

Archery	Parallel bars	Vaulting (boys
Badminton	Physical fit-	and girls)
Balance beam	ness	Volleyball
Basketball	Shuffleboard	Weight lifting
Boat safety	Side horse	UNIVERSITY
Bowling	Soccer	GYM
Cageball	Softball	Cycling
Camping and	Table tennis	Handball
outdoor education	Tennis	Horsemanship
First aid	Touch football	Jogging
Floor exercise	Trampoline	Paddleball
Golf	Tumbling	Swimming
Modern dance	Uneven bars	Wrestling

Organizational and instructional strategy

1. The students have their schedules arranged so that physical education is either their first class or their last class of the day.
2. The class period begins with each student completing an 8-minute circuit program.
3. The students select activities and individualized materials for activities called teaching-learning units (TLUs).
4. Each unit describes the performance objective to be achieved, what to use, and what to do.
5. The students work on the TLU, either individually or in small groups, using a resource center and teacher or peer assistance.
6. After completing the task, the students are evaluated. Results are indicated on individual computer cards. Student progress is indicated by a computer printout.

Instructional materials

Teaching-learning unit: bowling—approach and stance

PERFORMANCE OBJECTIVE: To demonstrate proper form for the approach. Select the most comfortable footwork for you.

Use	Do
1. Physical education handbook	1. Read specific section on bowling
2. *Basic Skills in Sports for Men and Women*	2. Read specific section on bowling
3. Sound page	3. Listen and view approach
4. Sound page	4. Listen and view stance
5. Bowling alley, ball, shoes	5. Practice
6. Teacher	6. Demonstrate

SECONDARY SCHOOL PROGRAMS

The first program illustrated is designed not only to provide election, selection, and choice of activities for the student, but also to ensure that each student achieves a mastery level.

Learning for mastery is not a new educational concept. Mastery learning is defined in terms of specific criterion—referenced standards to be achieved by students. However, for this to occur, the time variable for learning must be manipuled in order to permit individual rates of learning. Systematic and progressive segments of learning levels must be provided, and students are required to achieve mastery of a specified learning level before proceeding to the next lesson or level. Diagnostic feedback (formative evaluation) is provided to the student during the learning stages, and evaluation (summative) is given at the completion of a unit to determine achievement.

MASTERY LEARNING INDIVIDUALIZED PROGRAM FOR SECONDARY SCHOOLS
Developmental procedures

1. Develop psychomotor and cognitive criterion-referenced competencies for every learning unit.

2. Identify the competencies to be measured for formative and summative evaluation.
3. Design individualized instructional materials for each of the learning units, consisting of a systematic and progressive series of psychomotor tasks (closed through open) and cognitive tasks requiring written, verbal, and motor responses by the student.
4. Select or construct psychomotor and cognitive tests for preentry assessment, formative evaluation, and summative evaluation.

Operational environmental procedures

1. Modify the physical education facilities to include:
   a. Multiple indoor and outdoor skill practice areas
   b. Film viewing areas
   c. Listening areas
   d. Reading areas
   e. Testing areas
   f. Interview areas
2. Secure the following software and hardware:
   a. A sufficient amount of sports equipment
   b. Activity teaching films and slides
   c. Activity listening tapes
   d. Film and slide projectors
   e. Cassette recorders
   f. Videocamera, recorder, playback unit, and monitors
   g. Charts, posters, and diagrams
   h. Reading resource materials

Instructional strategy

1. A thorough orientation as to the nature and type of program is given to all students enrolled in a class section.
2. The student selects an activity unit (e.g., golf or tennis).
3. Specific activity instructional and learning procedures are described by each instructor.
4. The student may use the diagnostic psychomotor and cognitive tests or, through a personal interview, determine a starting level of competency.
5. The student achieves the prescribed psychomotor and learning tasks by using the available media, resource material, instruc-

tor assistance, and individual or group practice. The instructor is always available at the practice area for assistance and formative evaluation.
6. When a student completes the required minimal tasks in a lesson, the instructor formatively evaluates the student on a predetermined minimal competency level for that lesson.
7. A student who achieves the minimal tasks proceeds to the next lesson. If the student does not achieve, the instructor diagnoses the problem and provides instructional correctives. Alternatives to the original mode of instruction are used (e.g., if the original demonstration was by a loop film, the instructor could use as alternatives a live model demonstration, or a videotape replay).
8. After a student achieves all the minimal psychomotor and cognitive competencies for the learning activity, final (summative) psychomotor and cognitive tests are administered.
9. Psychomotor and cognitive grades for the activity are determined by the student's performance on the summative evaluation that is based on predetermined standards for mastery.
10. The results of summative evaluations may also be used to determine whether the student may elect to achieve a higher level for the activity, select another activity, or remain in the activity to achieve the minimal standard.
11. If a new activity is selected, the student is assigned to the new activity area and instructor. The procedures just outlined are followed.

Instructional materials

Individualized instructional packet for tennis (a sample lesson)
SKILL: The serve

Serving is a very important part of your tennis game. In many cases, a good service will win the match for you. It can be a method of attacking your opponent's weaknesses.

The purpose of this lesson is to develop the skill ability for placing a hard serve in your opponent's service court during a tennis match. The ball toss and racquet arm movement require coordination that can only be achieved through practice. After individual practice, have a partner evaluate your form.

Independent written assignment

The written assignment is based on the following resource materials:

Text:_____ Pages:_____

TRUE-FALSE QUESTIONS: Indicate a true statement with a +. If the statement is false, mark it 0 and correct it.

_____ 1. If you leave the ground with both feet while serving, it is illegal.

_____
_____

_____ 2. It is legal to step on the baseline while serving.

_____
_____

_____ 3. The serving grip is a pure eastern grip.

_____
_____

_____ 4. The slice service is less accurate than a flat serve.

_____
_____

_____ 5. The ball should be contacted by the racquet on its downward flight.

_____
_____

_____ 6. In preparing to serve, stand with your right side toward the net.

_____
_____

Independent skill assignment

INSTRUCTIONAL CUES
1. Ball toss
   a. Toss the ball with little or no spin.
   b. Toss the ball slightly higher than the height of the extended arm and racquet.
2. Backswing
   a. Start the arc in front of the body.
   b. Rotate the trunk and shoulders away from the net.
   c. Shift the weight to the right foot.
3. Forward swing
   a. As the ball starts down, shift the weight forward.
   b. At the point of impact, the racquet should be at its highest point.
   c. For a flat serve the ball is hit "on center."
   d. For a slice serve the ball is hit on the right side.
4. Follow-through
   a. Recover your balance by stepping forward with the right foot.
   b. The racquet should continue its swing across the left side of the body.

Skills	Reps	Date completed
1. Toss the ball up for the serve	15	_____
2. Toss the ball up, draw back the racquet and extend the arm; do not hit the ball	10	_____
3. Repeat No. 2, contact the ball	10	_____

Partner skills
4. Repeat No. 2; partner   5   _____
   checks:
   a. Ball tossed slightly higher than the extended arm.
      Evaluation*: P F G
   b. Little or no spin on the ball
      Evaluation*: P F G
5. Repeat No. 3; partner   5   _____
   checks:
   a. Weight shift to back foot on backswing
      Evaluation: P F G
   b. Trunk and shoulders rotated away from the net
      Evaluation: P F G
   c. Weight shifted forward on forward swing
      Evaluation: P F G
   d. Arm and racquet fully extended at ball impact
      Evaluation: P F G
   e. Proper ball height
      Evaluation: P F G
   f. Step foward on follow-through
      Evaluation: P F G
   g. Foot fault
      Evaluation: P F G

	Reps	Date completed
6. Good flat serves into the left service court	20	_____
7. Good flat serves into the right service court	20	_____
8. Good slice serves into the left service court	20	_____
9. Good slice serves into the right service court	20	_____

*P, Poor; F, fair; G, good.

Curriculum design

In designing an individualized physical education curriculum for a secondary physical education mastery learning program, the following guidelines were formulated:

1. Instruction should be the primary objective, with the emphasis on lifetime activities.
2. There should be maximum utilization of instructional staff and resources.
3. The teaching-learning environment should be structured, but within the structure freedom of choice by the student should be permitted.

4. The design should permit manipulation of the time variable for learning an activity so that a student regulates and controls not only his/her individual rate of learning but also the amount.
5. A team teaching approach should be utilized with instructors who are highly proficient in the designated activities, individualized methodology, and use of formative evaluation techniques.
6. Activities should be selected based on their feasibility for coed instruction.
7. The designs should include time modules for program orientation; activity selection;

MODEL A

Duration (weeks)	Option 1	Option 2	Option 3	Option 4
Semester I				
2	Program orientation, fitness diagnostic testing, and prescription	Program orientation, fitness diagnostic testing, and prescription	Program orientation, fitness diagnostic testing, and prescription	Program orientation, fitness diagnostic testing, and prescription
5	Golf	Tennis	Cadet teaching	Aquatics I
5	Archery	Badminton and handball	Cadet teaching	Aquatics II
5	Power volleyball	Gymnastics	Cadet teaching	Aquatics III
1	Fitness evaluation	Fitness evaluation	Fitness evaluation	Fitness evaluation
Semester II				
2	Program orientation, fitness diagnostic testing, and prescription	Program orientation, fitness diagnostic testing, and prescription	Program orientation, fitness diagnostic testing, and prescription	Program orientation, fitness diagnostic testing, and prescription
5	Power volleyball	Gymnastics	Cadet teaching	Aquatics I
5	Archery	Badminton and handball	Cadet teaching	Aquatics II
5	Golf	Tennis	Cadet teaching	Aquatics III
1	Fitness evaluation	Fitness evaluation	Fitness evaluation	Fitness evaluation

Alternate activities	Fitness activities	Aquatic activities
Fencing	Self-testing	Swimmer levels
Angling and casting	Conditioning	Advanced lifesaving
Dance		Water safety aide instruction
Bowling		Instructor: basic swimming, water safety, handicapped swimming
		Scuba diving and snorkeling
		Small craft
		Synchronized swimming

and physical fitness testing, evaluation, and individualized fitness prescriptions.

8. The designs can be modified as to the number and type of activity of instructional personnel and resources.
9. The time modules for the aquatic option should be determined by American Red Cross standards.
10. A pass/fail grading system is recommended. A student earns a passing grade by completing the minimal competencies for one activity. If a grading scale is used, variable grades may be given for completion of two or more activities.

11. Cadet teachers can be assigned to other physical education classes.

These curriculum design guidelines were used to design two models (A and B) for a secondary elective program. The major difference between the two models is the variance in the activity time module. Modifications in the models can be made for specific situations. Alternate activities can be substituted for fewer options offered, based on the criteria of facilities, equipment, supplies, and teaching personnel.

MODEL B

Duration (weeks)	Option 1	Option 2	Option 3	Option 4	Option 5
Semester I					
1	Program orientation, fitness diagnostic testing, and prescription	Program orientation, fitness diagnostic testing, and prescription	Program orientation, fitness diagnostic testing, and prescription	Program orientation, fitness diagnostic testing, and prescription	Program orientation, fitness diagnostic testing, and prescription
8	Archery	Golf	Tennis	Cadet teaching	Aquatics I
8	Gymnastics	Bowling	Badminton and handball	Cadet teaching	Aquatics II
1	Fitness evaluation	Fitness evaluation	Fitness evaluation	Fitness evaluation	Fitness evaluation
Semester II					
1	Program orientation, fitness diagnostic testing, and prescription	Program orientation, fitness diagnostic testing, and prescription	Program orientation, fitness diagnostic testing, and prescription	Program orientation, fitness diagnostic testing, and prescription	Program orientation, fitness diagnostic testing, and prescription
8	Gymnastics	Bowling	Badminton and handball	Cadet teaching	Aquatics I
8	Archery	Golf	Tennis	Cadet teaching	Aquatics II
1	Fitness evaluation	Fitness evaluation	Fitness evaluation	Fitness evaluation	Fitness evaluation

SECONDARY SCHOOL PROGRAMS PHYSICAL EDUCATION PERFORMANCE OBJECTIVES BANK

(Developed by Mary Anne Whited and Patricia E. Barry for Montgomery County Public Schools, Rockville, Md.)

The bank was designed as a basic guide and reference for teachers of junior and senior high girls' physical education. It serves as a resource from which a teacher can add or delete objectives based on the needs of the program or individual learner.

Instructional strategy

The type of strategy using the materials listed here is decided by the teacher. Individualized instruction, programmed instruction, contracting, or a traditional strategy are just a few of the limitless strategies that may be used with the performance objective bank.

Instructional materials

The bank is divided into 13 units with cards designed and color coded as follows:

White	Introductory information
Yellow	Psychomotor domain objectives
Blue	Cognitive domain objectives
Pink	Affective domain objectives
Green	Measurement techniques

The following is an example of a yellow card used in a basketball unit.

Bb/B73: Dribbling

Performance objective: Execute a dribble using proper form.

Assessment task:
1. Form: Body, footwork, coordination, finger and wrist control, changing of hands, body positioning
2. Conditions: While moving around stationary objects for instructor's observation

Criteria for student evaluation: The instruction should evaluate, through objective and/or subjective testing, the above skill.

INSTRUCTOR USE: □ B □ I □ A
ACCEPTABLE STUDENT MINIMAL LEVEL: _____% or _____times
NOTES:

COMPETENCY PACKAGES (COMPAC)

(Courtesy Florida Department of Education, Tallahassee, Fla.)

Competency packages (COMPACs) were developed to meet instructional assessment and organizational needs of the middle/junior and senior high school physical education teachers in Florida. The 44 COMPACS consist of 10 clusters that include the following areas:
1. The body
2. Physical development and conditioning
3. Lifetime sports
4. Team games
5. Gymnastics
6. Track and field
7. Movement and dance concepts
8. Aquatics
9. Recreational sports
10. Combatives

Each COMPAC contains:
1. An introductory overview of the activity
2. A scope and sequence chart with specific objectives for beginner, intermediate, and advanced levels, and the learning domains for each
3. Performance criteria for the objectives and teacher suggestions
4. Comprehensive tests for the following:
   a. Measuring entrance ability
   b. Measuring terminal performance
5. Enrolling activities for meeting the goals of the entire COMPAC
6. Resource materials
7. Student progress charts

These clusters can assist in program development and are designed to dictate the entire nature of the activity. The sequence of objectives as well as criteria can be modified to meet varying situations and standards.

College/university basic instructional program

The same developmental procedure, instructional materials, and instructional strategies described in the mastery learning program for secondary schools are used in the implementation of a mastery model for a college/university basic instructional program (Unit 21).

CONTRACT TEACHING

Contract teaching is based on widely accepted laws of learning, principles of human behavior, and understanding that the quality and quantity of learning are not equal for all students. It refers to an instructional strategy whereby reinforcement (points or grades) is given to a student upon the completion of selected contractual assignments. Contracts may be designed for psychomotor learnings, cognitive learnings, or both. The degree and quantity of learning are determined by the student.

There are various types of contract designs. The basic concept in contract design is to specifically state the learnings to be achieved and to allow students to select from the contract for the determination of a grade. They can be used in competency-based programs.

Sample contracts

SOFTBALL CONTRACT

(Courtesy Sheryl L. Gotts, Physical Education Department, University of Tennessee, Knoxville, Tenn.)

Contract 1 (10 points)

Perform an overarm softball throw at a velocity of at least 60 feet per second.

Contract 2 (10 points)

Demonstrate correct batting form as rated by the instructor.

Contract 3 (10 points)

Be able to bat 5 out of 10 well-pitched balls.

Contract 4 (10 points)

Field 20 batted balls successfully—10 fly balls and 10 ground balls.

Contract 5 (10 points)

Successfully pass a written test on rules.

Contract 6 (5 points)

Figure out offensive strategy for two different base-running situations. Tell the instructor.

Contract 7 (5 points)

Determine defensive strategy for two different situations. Report to the instructor.

Contract 8 (5 points)

Make up base-running signals. Coach third base and use these signals for at least two innings. Have two class members verify this.

Contract 9 (10 points)

Play one infield and one outfield position for at least five innings each. Have this verified by your team captain.

Contract 10 (10 points)

Score officially and correctly one full game. Turn in score sheet to the instructor.

Contract 11 (5 points)

Field in a game a minimum of four balls with no errors. Have this verified by two teammates.

Contract 12 (5 points)

Bat over 400 for four games. Keep own record and figure percentage. Give data to instructor.

Grades

A = 75 points or more
B = 65-74 points
C = 50-64 points
D = 40-49 points
F = 39 or below

TRACK AND FIELD CONTRACT FOR UPPER ELEMENTARY GRADES AND MIDDLE SCHOOL

(Developed by Geneen Soper, Purdue University, West Lafayette, Ind.)

TO THE STUDENT: The following contracts are for you to work on and complete at your own pace. You choose the contracts that *you* want to work on. Each contract is worth a certain number of points. There are 100 points in all. Below is the point scale that will be used:

86-100	A
66-85	B
50-65	C
Below 50	Unsatisfactory

Your contract will be due on _____.

Contract 1 (Level 2 = 10 points)

On a plain piece of paper draw a diagram of a track field. Draw a start and a finish line for the 50-yard dash. Using the same start line, draw a finish line for the 220-yard run. You may use colors if you wish.

Contract 2 (Level 3 = 15 points)

On a piece of paper list all the field events that you can think of. Next to each event write a few sentences about what you do in that event.

Contract 3 (Level 3 = 15 points)

Make four batons for your relay team. You choose the materials you would like for the batons.

Contract 4 (Level 2 = 10 points)

Write a short paper on how the sport of track and field began. The librarian will show you how to find the books that you will need.

Contract 5 (Level 3 = 15 points)

The inside of the track oval is where the field events take place. On a plain piece of paper draw in where you would put all the field events that you can think of. Be sure to label each event.

Contract 6 (Level 2 = 10 points)

Go to one of the high school track meets and write a short paper on what you saw while you were there.

Contract 7 (Level 2 = 10 points)

Go to one of the middle school track meets and act as a helper in two events of your choice.

Contract 8 (Level 1 = 5 points)

Go to one of the middle school track meets and act as a helper in one event of your choice.

Contract 9 (Level 2 = 10 points)

Pick one event in either track or field and show one of the fourth graders how to do it. Work together and help this person as much as you can. Write down which event you picked and what you did to help that person learn more about that event.

I received _____ points on my written contract. My grade for the written contract is _____.

Skill contract for track and field

TO THE STUDENT: The following contracts are for you to work on and complete at your own pace. You choose the contracts that *you* want to work on. Each contract is worth a certain number of points. There are 100 points in all. Below is the point scale that will be used:

86-100	A
66-85	B
50-65	C
Below 50	Unsatisfactory

Your contract will be due on _____.

Contract 1: 50-yard dash

Boys and girls will each have their own dashes. They will run the 50-yard dash three times.

BOYS   **Points**

If you run it in 8.0 seconds, give   _____
  yourself 5 points.

If you run it in 7.8 seconds, give   _____
  yourself 10 points.

If you run it in 7.6 seconds, give   _____
  yourself 15 points.

If you run it in 7.4 seconds, give   _____
  yourself 20 points.

GIRLS

If you run it in 8.4 seconds, give   _____
  yourself 5 points.

If you run it in 8.0 seconds, give   _____
  yourself 10 points.

If you run it in 7.9 seconds, give   _____
  yourself 15 points.

If you run it in 7.6 seconds, give   _____
  yourself 20 points.

Contract 2: Hurdles

You have 33 tries.   **Points**

If you can jump three hurdles 15   _____
  inches high, give yourself 5
  points.

If you can jump six hurdles 15   _____
  inches high, give yourself 10
  points.

If you can jump three hurdles 18 inches high, give yourself 15 points.   _____

If you can jump six hurdles 18 inches high, give yourself 20 points.   _____

Contract 3: Standing broad jump

Boys and girls will each have their own jumps. You have three tries.

BOYS   **Points**

If you can broad jump 5 feet 2 inches, give yourself 5 points.   _____

If you can broad jump 5 feet 6 inches, give yourself 10 points.   _____

If you can broad jump 5 feet 7 inches, give yourself 15 points.   _____

If you can broad jump 5 feet 10 inches, give yourself 20 points.   _____

GIRLS

If you can broad jump 4 feet 10 inches, give yourself 5 points.   _____

If you can broad jump 5 feet 2 inches, give yourself 10 points.   _____

If you can broad jump 5 feet 4 inches, give yourself 15 points.   _____

If you can broad jump 5 feet 8 inches, give yourself 20 points.   _____

Contract 4: Long jump

You have three tries.   **Points**

If you can jump at least 5 feet, give yourself 5 points.   _____

If you can jump between 6 and 7 feet, give yourself 10 points.   _____

If you can jump between 8 and 10 feet, give yourself 15 points.   _____

If you can jump between 11 and 13 feet, give yourself 20 points.   _____

Contract 5: High jump

You have three tries.   **Points**

If you jump over the bar at 2 feet 6 inches, give yourself 5 points.   _____

If you jump over the bar at 3 feet, give yourself 10 points.   _____

If you jump over the bar at 3 feet 6 inches, give yourself 15 points   _____

If you jump over the bar at 4 feet, give yourself 20 points.   _____

I received _____ points on my skill contract.

My grade for the skill contract is _____.

TRACK AND FIELD CONTRACT

(Developed by Shirley Hoff Krintz, Twin Lakes High School, Monticello, Ind.)

You are required to complete one contract on a running event and two contracts on a field event.

Contract 1 (Levels 1 to 5 = 3 to 20 points)

In a shot put skill test, you are given three trial throws, and you are to measure each throw. Record the best throw in the space provided for you in this contract. If you throw any of the following distances, award yourself the points indicated:

Level	Distance (feet)	Points
1	1-15	3
2	16-20	5
3	21-25	10
4	26-30	15
5	31+	20

Best trial: _____ Date: _____ Points: _____

Contract 2 (Levels 1 to 4 = 3 to 15 points)

In a running long jump skill test, you are given three trial jumps, and you are to measure each jump. Record the best jump in the space provided for you in this contract. If you jump any of the following distances, award yourself the points indicated:

Level	Distance (feet)	Points
1	1-10	3
2	11-12	5
3	13-14	10
4	15+	15

Best trial: _____ Date: _____ Points: _____

Contract 3 (Levels 1 to 5 = 3 to 20 points)

In a standing long jump skill test, you are given three trial jumps, and you are to measure each jump. Record the best jump in the space provided for you in this contract. If you jump any of the following distances, award yourself the points indicated:

Level	Distance	Points
1	0-4 feet	3
2	4 feet 1 inch-5 feet	5
3	5 feet 1 inch-6 feet	10
4	6 feet 1 inch-7 feet	15
5	7+ feet	20

Best trial: _____ Date: _____ Points: _____

BADMINTON CONTRACT

(Developed by Karen Emery, Northmont Senior High School, Clayton, Ohio)

Name _____ Period _____ Days _____

1. Serves
   a. Doubles—five good services in each court ☐
   b. Singles
      (1) Understanding of how executed and when used ☐
      (2) Do five good serves ☐
2. Backhand
   a. Know how to execute and when it is used ☐
   b. Hit against the wall, alternating backhand to forehand, 10 times ☐
   c. With a partner, hit five good backhand shots ☐
   d. Make up a drill to practice the backhand ☐
3. Using 2, 3, or 4 people, make up a drill to practice hitting and placing the clear ☐
   shot
4. Drives—forehand and backhand
   a. Execution and use ☐
   b. With a partner, practice drives across the net ☐
5. Scoring for doubles—learn and use in a game situation ☐
6. Wrist action: acceptable ☐
7. Foot work and balance: acceptable ☐

I accept responsibility for completing this contract and understand that if lost, it must be started over.

GOLF CONTRACT

(Developed by Sheryl Luneke Gotts, University of Tennessee, Knoxville, Tenn.)

Purpose

By writing a contract, I hope that you will clarify for yourself the goals you have in regard to golf. This should enable you to seek the appropriate help and provide you with information feedback. You may revise or change your contract at any time. You do not have to contract for all items. You and I can discuss and come to an agreement on what you need to do for a grade.

Some suggested measures are (you may use other means as well):
1. Videotape recording
2. Super 8 film
3. Rating scale
4. Distance
5. Accuracy
6. Ball flight characteristics
7. Number of strokes

The persons who will evaluate me are:

1. _____

2. _____

Goals

1. My goal for my basic golf swing is: _____

   _____

   I plan to evaluate my basic golf swing by: _____

   _____

2. My goals for my approach shots are:_____

   _____

   I plan to evaluate my approach shots by: _____

   _____

3. I will develop a putting technique that is comfortable and accurate for me.
   My goal will be: _____

   _____

4. I will demonstrate my knowledge of rules and etiquette before going on the course by:

   _____

5. I would like to work on the following special shots and show mastery of these by:

   _____

   _____

6. My scoring goals are as follows: _____

   _____

7. I will attend _____ class periods. (I expect all!)
8. I plan to help other students in the class by: _____

   _____

9. My particular style of learning in this course will be: _____

Continued.

GOLF CONTRACT—cont'd

Goals—cont'd

10. Goals I have that have not already been stated are: _____
    _____

11. For each item that I have contracted for I will present evidence supporting achievement of that goal. I feel that what I have agreed to accomplish is worth _____ grade.

_____   _____
Signature of student   Date

_____   _____
Signature of instructor   Date

CONCLUSION

The adoption of these "new" instructional approaches is a slow process. Many times, it is difficult for parents, administrators, teachers, and students to adapt to these instructional changes or innovations. Therefore a word of caution to the curriculum planner: Innovation is the act of introducing something new or novel. The newness or novelty of a program should be determined by the "why," not just the "how." Programs labeled "traditional" should not be completely discarded. Programs labeled "new or innovative" should not be completely accepted. Each must be critically analyzed as to advantages and disadvantages to determine what is best for the student and teacher and to provide the most effective instruction.

REACTORS

1. The teacher must be able to conceptualize the relation of the specific tasks to the whole activity.
2. A unit represents a plan for action.
3. A unit satisfies the principle that learning should be unitary, not fragmentary.
4. A unit outline should not be confused with a lesson plan.
5. In a traditional instructional strategy, the teacher makes all the decisions.
6. The time for learning a motor skill is not the same for all individuals.
7. Learning should not be restricted to a regularly scheduled class or facility.
8. The implementation of an individualized instructional strategy involves, in most cases, a change in the communication between teacher and student.
9. Teaching by contracting is "another way."
10. The adoption of new or innovative instructional approaches is a slow process.

LEARNING ACTIVITIES

1. Select an activity unit:
   a. Design a comprehensive unit plan.

b. Design five sequential lesson plans for a specific grade level.
2. Using the unit plan as resource material:
   a. Design a sample IIP lesson.
   b. Design a task card.
   c. Create your own design for individualized instruction.
   d. Briefly outline the instructional strategy to be employed.
3. Design contracts for:
   a. Physical achievement.
   b. Psychomotor achievement.
   c. Cognitive achievement.
   d. Affective achievement.

4. Develop a rationale for implementing an individualized instructional program.

UNIT EVALUATIVE CRITERIA

Can you:
1. Develop functional unit and lesson plans?
2. Segment the "whole of subject matter into small progressive learning tasks?"
3. Develop contracts for a wide variety of instructional strategies and materials?
4. Design and implement instructional strategies and materials that consider individual differences in learning rates?

RESOURCES

Annarino, A. A. Individualized Instructional Packets. *JOPER,* Iowa JOHPER Journal, Nov. 1971, p. 6.

Annarino, A. A. IIP. *JOPER,* Oct. 1973, p. 20.

Annarino, A. A. *Individualized instructional set: archery, bowling, badminton, golf, tennis.* Englewood Cliffs, N.J.: Prentice-Hall, Inc., 1973.

Annarino, A. A. Another way to teach. *JOPER,* Oct. 1974, p. 43.

Annarino, A. A. University basic instructional program—a new approach. *The Physical Educator,* Oct. 1974, 3, 31.

Annarino, A. A., Taulman, R., & Otto, S. A multimedia approach to teaching elementary school gymnastics. *JOPER,* April 1977, p. 64.

Bishop, L. K. *Individualizing educational systems.* New York: Harper & Row, Publishers, Inc., 1971.

Block, J. H. *Mastery learning.* New York: Holt, Rinehart & Winston, 1971.

Clark, D. E. *Physical education: a program of activities.* St. Louis, The C. V. Mosby Co., 1969.

Cogan, M. Innovative ideas in college physical education. *JOHPER,* Feb. 1973, 2, 44.

Dowell, L. J. *Strategies for teaching physical education.* Englewood Cliffs, N.J.: Prentice-Hall, Inc., 1975.

Driscoll, S., & Mathieson, D. A. Goal-centered individualized learning. *JOHPER,* Sept. 1971, p. 26.

Gustafson, J. Making programmed instruction practical. *The Physical Educator,* May 1973, 2, 30.

Heitmann, H., & Kneer, M. *Physical education instructional techniques: an individualized humanistic approach.* Englewood Cliffs, N. J.: Prentice-Hall, Inc., 1976.

Hellison, D., et al. *Personalized learning in physical education.* Washington, D.C.: American Alliance for Health, Physical Education, and Recreation, 1976.

Homme, L. *How to use contingency contracting in the classroom.* Champaign, Ill.: Research Press, 1972.

Hough, J. B., & Duncan, J. *Teaching: description and analysis.* Reading, Mass.: Addison-Wesley Publishing Co. Inc., 1970.

Johnson, P., et al. *Problem-solving approach to health and fitness.* New York: Holt, Rinehart & Winston, 1966.

Mosston, M. *Teaching physical education.* Columbus, Ohio: Charles E. Merrill Publishing Co., 1966.

Mosston, M. *Teaching: from command to discovery.* Belmont, Calif.: Wadsworth Publishing Co., Inc., 1972.

The new physical education. *JOHPER,* Sept. 1971, 42(7).

The new physical education. *JOHPER,* Sept. 1973, 44(7).

Piscopo, J. Videotape laboratory: a programmed instructional sequence. *JOHPER,* March 1973, 44(3).

Popham, J. W., & Baker, E. L. *Establishing instructional goals.* Englewood Cliffs, N.J.: Prentice-Hall, Inc., 1970.

Popham, J. W., & Baker, E. L. *Planning an instructional sequence.* Englewood Cliffs, N.J.: Prentice-Hall, Inc., 1970.

Popham, J. W., & Baker, E. L. *Systematic instruction.* Englewood Cliffs, N.J.: Prentice-Hall, Inc., 1970.

Programmed instruction in health education and physical education. Washington, D.C.: American Alliance for Health, Physical Education, and Recreation, 1970.

Russell, J. *Modular instruction, a guide to the design, selection, utilization and evaluation of modular materials*. Minneapolis: Burgess Publishing Co., 1974.

Siedentop, D. *Developing teaching skills in physical education*. Boston: Houghton Mifflin Co., 1976.

Singer, R., & Dick, W. *Teaching physical education: a systems approach*. Boston: Houghton Mifflin Co., 1974.

Smith, B. C., & Lerch, H. A. Contract grading. *The Physical Educator*, May 1972, 2, 29.

Staff, Simmons Junior High School (Aurora, Ill.) Computer monitored physical education. *JOPER*, May 1973, p. 24.

Thompson, J. C. *Physical education for the 1970's*. Englewood Cliffs, N.J.: Prentice-Hall, Inc., 1971.

Trump, J. L., & Baynham, D. *Focus on change*. Chicago: Rand McNally & Co., 1961.

When you reach out to help another person, you are reaching out not just to one, but to all, including yourself. When you abandon, reject or neglect one other human being, you are rejecting all, including yourself.

H. GERTHON MORGAN

20 Individualized physical education for special children and youth

COMPETENCIES

After completing this unit, you should be able to:

Interpret the implications of the Education for All Handicapped Children Act of 1975 (Public Law 94-142) for physical education.

Function as a contributing member of an individualized education program (IEP) planning group.

Identify and classify students on the basis of developmental or functional characteristics.

Define and interpret the basic concepts and principles for individualizing instruction.

Interpret the relationship between IEP components and physical education curriculum and instructional planning.

Be knowledgeable in techniques for assessing preentry performance, monitoring a student's progress, and evaluating achievement.

Develop and design an individualized physical education program.

Modify and adapt activities and instruction to meet individual needs.

Define the following:

Education for All Handicapped Children Act of 1975 (Public Law 94-142)	Special education
	Supportive services
	Individualized education program
Mainstreaming	Adapted physical education
Handicapped	
Special children	Education in separate facilities
Exceptional children	

PERSPECTIVE

PRINCIPLE: Handicapped children and youth have the same basic activity needs as normal individuals.

Individualized instruction has been defined as an instructional strategy that adapts the teaching-learning process for each student. It is designed to provide the best instructional match to individual needs, interests, and characteristics.

This broad definition has more specific significance and meaning due to the enactment of the Education for All Handicapped Children Act of 1975 (Public Law 94-142). This act assures a free and appropriate public education for all children regardless of their handicap. Specifically, it provides each handicapped child with a "special education" or specially designed instruction, which includes classroom instruction, physical education instruction, home instruction, instruction in hospitals and institutions, and opportunities for related recreational services—all at no cost. Physical education, in this act, is defined in terms of developmental and instructional areas, including physical and motor fitness, fundamental motor skills and patterns, aquatics, dance, individual and group games, and sports (including intramural and lifetime sports).

The implication of this legislation for curriculum and instructional planning in physical education is that every handicapped child must be provided with physical education services by participating in a regular physical education program (mainstreaming) unless the child is enrolled in a separate facility or the child needs specially designed physical education instruction.

The selection of the most appropriate educational setting for the handicapped child is determined by designing an individualized education program for each child. These written programs are planned, designed, and annually reviewed cooperatively by a representative of the local education agency (one qualified to provide or supervise the provision of special education); the child's teacher (special and/or regular teacher); parents or guardian; and, when appropriate, the child.

INDIVIDUALIZED EDUCATION PROGRAM

The individualized education program (IEP) must include the following components:

1. A statement of the child's current level of educational performance
2. A statement of yearly goals that include short-term objectives
3. A statement of specific special education and related services to be provided for the child
4. The projected dates for supportive services
5. The extent to which the child will be able to participate in regular programs
6. Evaluation procedures with criteria and time lines for determining whether short-term educational objectives are being achieved by the child

An example of a form used to develop an IEP is illustrated in Fig. 6.

Since the IEP components are related, directly or indirectly, to physical education curriculum and instructional planning, the involvement of the physical education teacher in IEP planning is essential. The implications for physical education are shown in Table 9.

INDIVIDUALIZED EDUCATION PROGRAM FORM

1. Child's name _____ Date prepared by committee _____

   School _____ Class _____

2. Summary of present levels of performance

3. Prioritized long-term goals

4. a. Short-term objectives
   b. Special education, regular education, and related services
   c. Person responsible
   d. Beginning and ending dates
   e. Review date

5. Placement decisions

6. Percent of time in regular classroom

7. For the committee recommendations for specific procedures/techniques, materials, information about learning style, etc.

8. Criteria for evaluation of annual goals

9. Committee members present

10. Dates of meetings

Fig. 6. Sample individualized education program form.

Table 9. Implications of IEP Development for Physical Education[*]

IEP components	Implications for physical education
Statement of student's present level of performance	A statement of the student's level of performance is written when an IEP is first developed. This statement helps to formulate annual goals and short-term instructional objectives. It is obtained by formal and/or informal assessment techniques that provide the clearest possible picture of the student's present levels of performance, including physical and motor development. This is the foundation for the child's IEP.
Statement of annual goals	In physical education as well as in other curricular areas, annual goals are designed to habilitate or rehabilitate a pupil's weaknesses after they have been assessed. Annual goals are *broad* in nature and give direction for the individual's educational program (e.g., a child is classified as a nonswimmer and his/her annual goal might be to swim the length of the pool without aid).
Statement of short-term instructional objectives	These give specific objectives and are in reality intermediate steps in reaching the annual goals of the IEP. They may be a specific game, fitness activity, movement pattern, or aquatics activity. These objectives should have a content-referenced base that permits analysis of pupil progress from day to day (e.g., the nonswimmer might have as short-term objectives [1] acquire knowledge of 7 out of 10 safety rules in the pool and [2] kick one complete width of a 50 by 25 meter pool, using a kickboard and the scissors kick).
Statement of specific media, materials, and supportive personnel	The handicapped student may need specific audiovisual aids to help in being successful in learning experiences. Media in physical education could include movies, videotapes, slides, or transparencies of an activity being taught. Specific materials refer to the adaptation of equipment or the use of special testing devices to meet the needs of a handicapped individual (e.g., in swimming one may need to purchase bubbles or flippers for the orthopedically handicapped). Specific supportive personnel include teacher aides, speech therapists, physical therapists, occupational therapists, and special physical educators, among others. These extra personnel may make all the difference in the type of educational placement chosen and the ultimate success of the handicapped child (e.g., the only help a primary student may need to participate successfully in a mainstreamed physical education setting is a teen leader).
Specific date services will begin and their duration	A statement must be provided to designate when the supportive services (e.g., special physical education consultant) will start and when they will end. The dates are applicable to both annual goals and short-term instructional objectives. It does not mean the instructor is responsible if the goals are not achieved at the end of a specified time period.
Specific statement of participation in regular education programs	The handicapped student should be placed in a class that is best suited to meet his/her needs. Common examples in physical education include a situation where the student may be totally mainstreamed without support or assisted by a full-time aide in a mainstreamed setting. In another situation, the student can be taken out of the mainstreamed setting when additional help is needed and brought back when participation can be successful (flexible schedule).

[*]Adapted by permission of Furnal, L. The individualized education program. In J. P. Winnick and P. Jansma (Eds.), *Physical education inservice resource manual for the implementation of the Education for All Handicapped Children Act.* Brockport, N.Y.: State University College, 1978, pp. 21-24. *Continued.*

Table 9. Implications of IEP Development for Physical Education—cont'd

IEP components	Implications for physical education
Specific evaluation requirements (criteria, procedures, scheduling)	Postevaluation is conducted to assess the handicapped student's progress. The scheduling is usually done on a quarterly basis, and specific accountability-based objective criteria are stressed, using exact numbers (e.g., sink *two* out of every *five* free throws on request, using a junior-sized basketball). There are different evaluation procedure options: 1. A content-referenced type deals with the individual's progress from day to day. In this type, progress is continually recorded (e.g., standing long jump distance improved 1 inch every day this week). 2. Standardized instruments compare the handicapped student's progress with peers of the same age and sometimes the same characteristics (e.g., the 25th percentile on a 600-yard run-walk for a 15-year-old, visually impaired girl might be 5:15). 3. A criterion-referenced procedure is evaluation based on an external variable, such as a grade. 4. Informal evaluation techniques are also used frequently in physical education. These consist of observations, anecdotal records, case studies, rating scales, and self-evaluations. These latter techniques are not as scientific, but are realistic, simple, and sometimes helpful.
The physical educator's involvement in the IEP planning conference	The physical educator may or may not be asked to help in planning a handicapped student's IEP. The physical educator should, however, make sure that he/she is at least consulted in reference to present level of performance data and reasonable objectives that should be established in the area of physical education. The idea of the IEP is to establish a written guide (not a contract) in order to give the handicapped child the best possible education. The physical educator is the expert in physical education and should be the best qualified to develop the program for the handicapped student in that *required* area.
Mandated physical education for the handicapped	Physical education is the *only* special education curricular area that is specifically mentioned in PL 94-142's definition of special education. It becomes, therefore, an obvious part of every IEP.

ASSESSMENT AND EVALUATION

The effectiveness of an IEP, as for any type of educational program, is based on assessment techniques that provide data relative to the student's preentry skills, monitor progress, and evaluate achievement. Basic measurement concepts and principles used for determining preentry, formative, and exit evaluations apply in these programs as for any type of educational program.

Preentry assessment results are used for formulating the child's long-range goals, and short-term instructional objectives are developed for attaining these goals. Formative evaluation monitors the child's progress in the program, and summative evaluation indicates achievement.

IEP planners are referred to professional test and measurement texts for valid and reliable tests with norm-referenced, criterion-referenced, and content-referenced scales in the areas of physical fitness, motor fitness, fundamental motor skills, perceptual motor skills, aquatics, dance, sports, and games. Specific tests for impaired, disabled, and handicapped individuals are described in a publication, *Testing for Impaired, Disabled, and Handicapped Individuals,* by the American Alliance for Health, Physical Education, and Recreation.

INDIVIDUALIZED EDUCATION PROGRAMS IN PHYSICAL EDUCATION

The bases for individual or class program planning are the results of preassessment. These results will indicate specific entry levels of performance and are used to classify students into general ability groups, to determine type of program placement, to set long-range goals, and to formulate short-term instructional objectives for each goal.

Identified goals should be directly related to the general goals of the school, community, and physical education program. They provide focus and direction for total program planning. Instructional objectives must meet the same criteria described in Unit 6 for designing instructional or performance objectives. They must have an identifiable terminal behavior that is observable and measurable. They must indicate the situation or conditions under which the behavior will be performed, and they must state the criteria or criterion as a standard of performance for achievement of the objective. In addition, instructional objectives should be designed for the four objective domains—physical, psychomotor, cognitive, and affective for each activity area. These short-term instructional objectives are used as guidelines for total program planning, more specifically, to determine the scope, sequence, duration, and levels of instruction.

A model IEP in physical education for a visually handicapped girl is shown in Fig. 7.

PROGRAMMING FOR THE HANDICAPPED

Public Law 94-142 mandates that every handicapped child must be assessed and programmed in the least restrictive learning environment with nonhandicapped classmates to the maximum degree possible. These environments include regular physical education programs (mainstreaming), special physical education programs, and educational programs in separate facilities. It further defines a handicapped individual as one who (1) has a physical or mental impairment that substantially limits one or more life activities, (2) has a record of such impairment, or (3) is regarded as having such an impairment. Handicapped individuals are specifically categorized as visually handicapped, mentally retarded, deaf and hard of hearing, multihandicapped, deaf-blind, orthopedically handicapped, seriously emotionally disturbed, specific learning disabled, speech impaired, and health impaired.

Programming for the handicapped is not determined by these handicapped categories but based on identifiable needs of the individual. The individuals must be accepted or rejected for programs and activities according to the same qualifications and standards applicable to other students in the same programs and activities. It is the responsibility of the school to modify the curriculum and instructional methods in

Text continued on p. 332.

Pupil's name: __Jane__   DB: __1/16/61__   Classification: __Blind__

Data:

   Jane is a fifteen-year-old pupil with visual acuity only at the level of light perception. She is socially well-adjusted, emotionally stable, and intellectually keen. Her height and weight are within normal limits for her age. Recently she has been removed from the State school for the blind and placed in a regular public school at the tenth grade level. Her fitness scores in the modified AAHPER fitness test battery (Buell) were all at the achievement level, except in the 600-yard run-walk. Her 600-yard run-walk score was at the 25th percentile for blind girls at Jane's age. Jane and her parents have an interest in learning archery and they request that she be taught this lifetime, leisure-time sport in her mainstreamed physical education class.

Present level of performance:

1. Over-all level of physical fitness is average for blind girls at age 15 using Buell's modified American Alliance for Health, Physical Education and Recreation (AAHPER) fitness test.

2. Jane's time in the 600-yard run-walk is 5:15 (25th percentile using Buell's fitness test).

RATIONALE FOR USING TEST: Appropriate for age and visual handicap

Annual goals:

1. Improved cardiorespiratory endurance in the 600-yard run-walk
2. Development of ability in lifetime activities, including archery

RATIONALE FOR SELECTION: Based on the present level of performance of the student
           and parent interest

Short-term objectives:

1. Jane will learn the skill of safely stringing a bow, notching an arrow, and shooting an arrow upon every attempt.
2. Jane will be able to safely and effectively use a bow and arrow to hit a target from 15 yards away a minimum of five times in ten attempts; an audible goal locator will be used.
3. Jane will improve to at least the 35th percentile in the 600-yard run-walk (4:45) on the Buell modification of the AAHPER fitness test.
4. Jane will learn all of the beginning level psychomotor and safety aspects of a lifetime sport of her choice that is offered in the curriculum. Short term skill objectives will be determined by Jane's initial level of skill in the chosen sport.

RATIONALE FOR SELECTION: Objectives are appropriate to Jane's individual
           characteristics and capabilities. Objectives were based
           on input from Jane and her parents.

Fig. 7. Individualized education program in physical education for a visually handicapped girl. (From Jansma, P. A model IEP for a visually handicapped girl. In J. P. Winnick & P. Jansma [Eds.], *Physical education inservice resource manual for the implementation of the Education for All Handicapped Children Act.* Brockport, N.Y.: State University College, 1978, pp. 31-33.)

Evaluation (criteria, procedures, scheduling):

Criteria: Objective levels of performance as specified within list of short-term objectives

Procedures: Use of Buell's fitness test; a checklist of skills in archery and other lifetime sports

Scheduling: At least twice comprehensively during class time on a quarterly basis; daily checks on specific points; year-end check on attainment of all annual goals

RATIONALE FOR SELECTION: These methods of evaluation will determine on at least an annual basis the appropriateness of set objectives.

Educational services and media/duration of services:

1. Purchase of Buell's modified fitness test
2. Purchase of audible goal locator
3. Mobility training for first two weeks of school year
4. Purchase of Braille materials when necessary
5. Access to the district's special physical education consultant during the school year

Participation in regular program:

A totally integrated program in physical education is recommended with up to two weeks of mobility training at the start of the school year. Within the program, adaptations such as the "buddy system" and audible and tactile teaching aids will be utilized when necessary.

RATIONALE: It has been determined that Jane functions normally and needs minimal supportive services. Safe and successful participation in most physical education activities is expected.

Fig. 7, cont'd. For legend see opposite page.

Mentally retarded:

1. Pitch activities to mental rather than chronological age—this is a rule of thumb that may be followed until the child attains a chronological age of 15.

2. Select games that require little memorization of playing rules or strategy.

3. A majority of the retarded, especially those moderately retarded or below, will not respond well to highly competitive sports.

4. The retarded generally enjoy music, dance, and other rhythmic activities.

5. Emphasize activities that hold the children's enthusiasm.

6. Favorite activities of the retarded include swimming, trampolining, tumbling, rhythms, badminton, bowling, tennis, table tennis, fishing, dancing, playground activities, relays, weight lifting (for older boys), catching, skipping, archery, and nature activities.

7. Activities least liked are calisthenics, marching, volleyball, certain positions in football and baseball.

8. Activity by deviancy analysis:

   a. Mildly retarded—very little difference in programming from the nonretarded. Some difficulty in team games (take a little more time to learn them). May need to emphasize fitness, motor, and perceptual activities.

   b. Moderately retarded—children in this category who are young (less than 9 years old) will function at about normal preschool level. Activities appropriate for this group approximate those of preschoolers. They are not ready for highly organized games or group activities. Need to emphasize physical, perceptual, and motor development. At age level 9-15 children begin to show interest in group games, will play team games but enjoy individual activities.

   c. Severely retarded—significantly retarded in physical and motor proficiency, do not play spontaneously, do not play group games with enthusiasm. Stress sensorimotor activities, basic movement activities, fitness activities, games with uncomplicated objectives.

Visually handicapped:

1. Stress activities to develop:

   a. Perceptual abilities
   b. Body awareness
   c. Knowledge of spectator sports
   d. Posture and body mechanics
   e. Auditory discrimination
   f. Orientation and mobility
   g. Fundamental movements and physical conditioning
   h. Balance
   i. Spatial concepts
   j. Leisure time skills

2. Create opportunities for movement.

3. "Blue chip" activities are rowing, hiking, trampolining, bowling, shuffleboard, swimming, wrestling, weight lifting, snowshoeing, tobogganing, certain gymnastic events, and certain track and field activities.

Fig. 8. Unique activity needs for special pupils in physical education. (From Winnick, J. P. Methods and activity needs for special pupils in physical education. In J. P. Winnick & P. Jansma [Eds.], *Physical education inservice resource manual for the implementation of the Education for All Handicapped Children Act.* Brockport, N.Y.: State University College, 1978, pp. 58-64.)

Deaf:

1. Activities to be emphasized:

    a. Physical fitness and motor development activities.
    b. Balance activities.
    c. Activities to enhance spatial concepts.
    d. Listening and auditory perceptual activities—when residual hearing exists.
    e. Activities to stimulate social interaction are of vital importance, and include:
        (1) Lifetime sports
        (2) Group games
        (3) Informal play
        (4) Leisure time activities

Remember: The greatest need for the deaf is social in nature and the greatest problem of teaching is in communication.

Learning disabled:

1. Motor activities involving academic concepts

2. Activities the child can perform successfully

3. Activities to enhance

    a. Body image
    b. Spatial orientation
    c. Balance
    d. Gross motor skills
    e. Coordination

4. Perceptual-motor activities

    a. Visual
    b. Auditory
    c. Haptic

Emotionally disturbed:

1. Since the emotionally disturbed are a very heterogeneous population, programs need to be individualized.

2. Physical conditioning, balance, and basic movement activities must often be stressed.

3. Attention should be given to the development of basic coordination and skill activities.

4. Relaxation and swimming activities are generally important.

5. Provide activities that allow for the release of aggression—except where such aggression is directed at another person.

6. Remember activities to "let off steam" will generally excite rather than calm the emotionally disturbed child.

7. Stress socialization activities.

8. Stress play and leisure-time activities.

9. Include activities for self-expression and interpretation—dance, mimetics.

10. Highly competitive activities may be contraindicated.

11. Nondirected or unstructured activities may be contraindicated at times.

12. Some children may have particular difficulty in group or team games.

Continued.

Fig. 8, cont'd. For legend see opposite page.

Cerebral palsy:

1. General goals

   a. Facilitate muscular functioning
   b. Develop voluntary muscular control
   c. Secure muscular relaxation
   d. Facilitate motor development
   e. Develop basic motor skills

2. Stretching exercises to increase flexibility, to prevent muscular contractures, and to inhibit bone deformity

3. Activities to counter spinal deviations to enhance body alignment

4. Muscle reciprocation exercises to facilitate the action of contralateral muscles

5. Activities to reduce muscular tension, to facilitate controlled movement, to promote body awareness, and to perform basic movements

6. Swimming

7. Spasticity

   a. Activities to lengthen spastic muscles and strengthen contralateral muscles
   b. Balance activities
   c. Swimming
   d. Relaxation
   e. Locomotor activities

8. Rigidity

   a. Involvement of agonistic and antagonistic muscles
   b. Balance
   c. Exercises to prevent contractures and induce relaxation

9. Ataxia

   a. Balance exercises
   b. Body awareness activities
   c. Body mechanics
   d. Strength training
   e. Locomotor activities

10. Athetosis and tremor

    a. Purposeful movement
    b. Relaxation activities
    c. Balance and water activities

11. Perceptual-motor activities

12. Fun activities

Fig. 8, cont'd. For legend see p. 328.

Other physical or neuromuscular handicaps:

1. Amputees: Balance activities to counter disruption in equilibrium due to limb loss, stretching and flexibility exercises to inhibit contractures, strengthening exercises to prevent atrophy of the unaffected limb, exercises to promote stump circulation, exercises to reduce weight, gross motor activities, and sports modified to their abilities.

2. Disorders of the hip: There is often a need for conditioning activities to overcome muscle weakness, atrophy, and loss of range of motion. Activities to improve skills of ambulation and posture, swimming, and perceptual abilities are often recommended. Since motor abilities lag, there may be a need to provide activities to enhance motor proficiency. Motor development lags are generally associated with coxa plana, since this condition generally occurs between the ages of 4 and 10. There may need to be modification in activities so that weight-bearing is prohibited. Since patients with coxa vara frequently are often obese, a program of weight training may be indicated. In view of postural deviations, activities to improve posture and body mechanics are often indicated.

3. Spina bifida: No single program of activities can be prescribed for all cases. Frequently mentioned needs include weight-reducing activities; exercises and activities to prevent contractures; activities to maintain or increase strength and endurance of unaffected parts of the body; and activities conducted on a regular basis (to enhance bowel and bladder control).

4. Muscular dystrophy: Activities are needed to help children stretch muscles, delay onset of contractures, and help maintain strength, endurance, coordination, balance, and cardiovascular functioning. Body weight should be kept at proper levels. Develop skills so that the children can participate in childhood games.

5. Epilepsy: Physical activity is very important to the epileptic and should be encouraged. Be cautious about activities that would lead to injury if seizure occurred during participation. It may be necessary to limit participation in highly competitive activities and contact sports. The sedentary existence of some epileptics may lead to muscle weakness, lack of stamina, poor body mechanics, and generally a low tolerance for exercise.

6. Diabetics: Activities to stress include weight control activities and circulatory activities. Activities that may need to be controlled include contact sport activities, highly competitive activities (in severe cases only), and activities involving circulatory restriction.

7. Multiple sclerosis: Exercises and activities particularly appropriate include those in which participants move through the maximum range of motion, those that serve to develop and maintain strength and endurance, activities to enhance coordination and balance abilities, and activities to prevent and contain spasticity and contractures. Ambulation and self-care activities are constantly encouraged for the maintenance of muscle tone and muscle stretching exercises are recommended to prevent or reduce the effects of contractures. Change in body position is important for victims confined to bed and/or wheelchairs.

8. Cystic fibrosis (mucoviscidosis): Breathing exercises are recommended (under medical supervision). Also, activities to maintain or improve posture, those that increase physical proficiency, and those that give the child the skills to participate in play and movement as normally as possible are recommended.

9. Asthma: Emphasize activities that improve physical and motor development—especially those that increase the strength of the abdomen, trunk, and shoulder muscles. Select activities to improve vital capacity and aerobic capacity. To prevent and lessen reactions to stress, use relaxation activities. Activities that contribute to proper body alignment are also recommended. Swimming is a favorite activity—keep water temperature warm. Allow rest periods—emphasize "short burst" activities.

10. Cardiopathic: Arrange and select activities according to the severity of the condition. In some cases (severe), bed rest is prescribed and activities may only be permitted while in bed. In mild cases, activity periods may be cut down and only extremely vigorous activities would be eliminated. In some cases it may be necessary to restrict participation in highly competitive activities.

Fig. 8, cont'd. For legend see p. 328.

order to provide maximum participation by the handicapped individual.

Handicapped children and youth have the same basic activity needs as normal individuals. They want to swim, throw and catch a ball, play sports and games, be physically fit, and develop all those physical skills to their individual potential so that they can enjoy the world of play. Therefore all those activities included in a regular physical education are appropriate. However, programmatic and instructional considerations must be given to limiting levels of participation due to the children's impairments. These levels of participation are classified as follows:

1. Unrestricted activity—full participation
2. Moderate restriction—participation in designated activities
3. Severe restriction—limited participation and a low level of activity
4. Reconstructive or rehabilitative activity—participation in a prescribed program of corrective exercises or adapted activities

In addition, unique program and instructional needs of special handicapped populations must be considered. Guidelines for program planning for these unique needs are outlined in Fig. 8.

INSTRUCTIONAL MODIFICATIONS

The limitations as to levels of participation and unique needs of the handicapped, whether they are integrated in a regular physical education program or in a special program, require modification and adjustment of conventional instructional strategies. Activities can be modified for equal participation by the following:

1. Decreasing the duration of the activity
2. Changing the rules for equal participation
3. Adjusting the heights of nets, baskets, standards, etc.
4. Shortening distances

5. Using different types of signals
6. Using partners, groups, or objects (wires, hand rails, ropes)
7. Using minimal contact activities
8. Limiting the size of play areas
9. Increasing or decreasing the size of game objects or implements
10. Increasing the size of target areas
11. Minimizing the use of elimination-type activities

These are just a few general examples for modifying instructional techniques. Different handicapping conditions may require more specific adaptations. A creative and sensitive teacher will be aware of the capacities and limitations of children and youth with disabilities who may not safely or successfully participate in the full range of physical education activities without some degree of adaptation or modification in order to experience satisfaction through participation.

SAMPLE PROGRAMS FOR SPECIAL CHILDREN AND YOUTH

I Can is a comprehensive individualized instructional system developed and field tested by the Field Service Unit in Physical Education and Recreation for the Handicapped at Michigan State University under the direction of Janet A. Wessel.*

The system consists of eight activity notebooks, with correlated films, for four skill areas: fundamental skills, health and fitness, body management, and aquatics. Each skill area is covered by two activity notebooks describing performance objectives, assessing activities, giving instructional activities, and listing game activities. The program was developed for the trainable mentally impaired, but the materials can be adapted for any physical education setting and learner.

*Distributed by Hubbard Scientific Co., Northbrook, Illinois 60062.

Project Active is designed to provide individualized—personalized—physical activity programs for all handicapped children. It was developed by The Township of Ocean School District, Oakhurst, New Jersey under the direction of Thomas M. Vodola. Publication and materials are available to assist teachers in testing, assessing, prescribing, and evaluating students with various handicapping conditions in terms of their physical and motor needs.

Personalized Physical Education consists of a physical education assessment checklist for assessing youngsters developmentally rather than in terms of handicapping condition. It was developed by the Special School District of St. Louis County, Town and Country, Missouri, under the supervision of Matthew E. Sullivan. The checklist is divided into five domains: foundation skills; physical fitness; developmental games and activities; lifetime, team, and recreation activities; and affective/effective activities. These domains are described in general objective terms. Specific performance indicators are listed for each objective to aid the teacher in selecting and conducting appropriate activities; recording the progress of individual students; and evaluating students in terms of objectives generally associated with physical education.

Perceptual Motor Training Program, designed for the Crown Point Community School Corporation, Crown Point, Indiana, under the direction of Russell Keller, consists of 40 lessons for educationally handicapped students (ages 6 to 12) in the areas of tumbling, balance boards, barrel roll, visual perceptual activities, simple obstacle courses, throwing, special ball-handling skills, and basic locomotor skills. The program utilizes 40-minute periods with two instructors and an aide in class sizes of 30 to 45 students.

RESOURCES FOR SPECIAL CHILDREN AND YOUTH

MATERIALS

Facts About the Menninger Foundation
The Director of Development
The Menninger Foundation
P.O. Box 920
Topeka, Kan. 66601

How to Deal with your Tensions
National Association for Mental Health
1800 North Kent Street
Arlington, Va. 22209

Mental Health Films
NAMH Film Service
P.O. Box 7316
Alexandria, Va. 22307

The National Society Is
Executive Secretary, NTRS
National Recreation and Park Association
1601 North Kent Street
Arlington, Va. 22209

PCMR is for People
President's Committee on Mental Retardation
Washington, D.C. 20201

Swimming for the Handicapped
The American National Red Cross
Washington, D.C. 20006

To Serve Children
Association for Childhood Education International
5615 Wisconsin Avenue, N.W.
Washington, D.C. 20016

What Is the National Federation of the Blind?
National Federation of the Blind
218 Randolph Hotel Building
Des Moines, Iowa 50309

ORGANIZATIONS

American Academy for Cerebral Palsy
1255 New Hampshire Avenue, N.W.
Washington, D.C. 20036

American Alliance for Health, Physical Education, and
    Recreation
1201 16th Street, N.W.
Washington, D.C. 20036

American Congress of Rehabilitation Medicine
30 North Michigan Avenue
Chicago, Ill. 60602

American Epilepsy Society
Box 341
University of Minnesota
Minneapolis, Minn. 55455

American Foundation for the Blind, Inc.
15 West 16th Street
New York, N.Y. 10011

American Occupational Therapy Association, Inc.
600 Executive Building
Rockville, Md. 20852

American Society of Allied Health Professions
Suite 300, 1 DuPont Circle
Washington, D.C. 20036

Association for Education of the Visually
   Handicapped
1604 Spruce Street
Philadelphia, Pa. 19103

Bureau of Education for the Handicapped
Department of Health, Education, and Welfare
Office of Education
Washington, D.C. 20202

Epilepsy Foundation of America
1828 L. Street, N.W.
Washington, D.C. 20036

Foundation for Child Development
345 East 46th Street
New York, N.Y. 10017

National Association for Music Therapy, Inc.
Box 610
Lawrence, Kan. 66044

REACTORS

1. Handicapped children and youth have the same basic activity needs as normal individuals.
2. The inclusion of a handicapped child in a regular physical education program is not harmful to the well-being of any individual.
3. The IEP components are directly or indirectly related to curriculum and instructional planning in physical education.
4. The effectiveness of an IEP is based on assessment.
5. Programming for the handicapped is not determined by the individual's handicap but based on identifiable developmental needs.
6. The unique needs of specific types of handicaps require modifications and adaptions in curriculum and instructional areas.

LEARNING ACTIVITIES

1. List implications as to the advantages and disadvantages of the "mainstreaming concept."

2. Design a chart identifying the different types of handicaps and list all types of activities in which they may participate (a) without modifications, (b) with modifications.
3. Devise hypothetical data for a handicapped student and design an IEP based on the components listed in the unit.

UNIT EVALUATIVE CRITERIA

Can you:
1. Explain the Education for All Handicapped Children Act of 1975 (Public Law 94-142) and its implications for curriculum planning?
2. Identify the different types of handicaps, list their characteristics and unique needs, and provide an activity program for them?
3. Administer various assessment instruments and analyze the results for the design of an IEP and for monitoring student progress and final achievement?

RESOURCES

AAHPER. *Adapted physical education guidelines: Theory and practices for the 1970's and 1980's.* Washington, D.C.: The Alliance, 1978.

AAHPER. *Annotated listing of films: physical education and recreation for impaired, disabled and handicapped persons.* Washington, D.C.: The Alliance, 1978.

AAHPER. *Annotated research bibliography in physical education, recreation and psychomotor function of mentally retarded persons.* Washington, D.C.: The Alliance, 1978.

AAHPER. *Aquatic Recreation for the blind.* Washington, D.C.: The Alliance, 1978.

AAHPER. *Dance for physically disabled persons: a manual for teaching ballroom, square and folk dances to users of wheelchairs and crutches.* Washington, D.C.: The Alliance, 1978.

AAHPER. *Early intervention for handicapped children through programs of physical education and recreation.* Washington, D.C.: The Alliance, 1978.

AAHPER. *A guide for programs in recreation and physical education for the mentally retarded.* Washington, D.C.: The Alliance, 1968.

AAHPER. *Guide to information systems in physical education and recreation for impaired, disabled, and handicapped persons.* Washington, D.C.: The Alliance, 1978.

AAHPER. *Integrating persons with handicapping conditions into regular physical education and recreation programs.* Washington, D.C.: The Alliance, 1978.

AAHPER. *Involving impaired, disabled and handicapped persons in regular camp programs.* Washington, D.C.: The Alliance, 1978.

AAHPER. *Making workshops in physical education and recreation for special populations.* Washington, D.C.: The Alliance, 1978.

AAHPER. *Motor fitness testing manual for the moderately mentally retarded.* Washington, D.C.: The Alliance, 1978.

AAHPER. *Physical activities for impaired, disabled and handicapped individuals.* Washington, D.C.: The Alliance, 1978.

AAHPER. *Physical activities for the mentally retarded/ideas for instruction.* Washington, D.C.: The Alliance, 1978.

AAHPER. *Physical education for cerebral palsied individuals.* Washington, D.C.: The Alliance, 1978.

AAHPER. *Physical education for individuals with multiple handicapping conditions.* Washington, D.C.: The Alliance, 1978.

AAHPER. *Physical education for the visually handicapped.* Washington, D.C.: The Alliance, 1978.

AAHPER. *Physical education, recreation and related programs for autistic and emotionally disturbed children.* Washington, D.C.: The Alliance, 1978.

AAHPER. *Physical education, recreation and sports for individuals with hearing impairments.* Washington, D.C.: The Alliance, 1978.

AAHPER. *Practical guide for teaching the mentally retarded to swim.* Washington, D.C.: The Alliance, 1978.

AAHPER. *Programming for the mentally retarded in physical education and recreation.* Washington, D.C.: The Alliance, 1978.

AAHPER. *Special fitness program for the mentally retarded.* Washington, D.C.: The Alliance, 1978.

AAHPER. *Special Olympics instructional manual—from beginners to champions.* Washington, D.C.: The Alliance, 1978.

AAHPER. *Testing for impaired, disabled, and handicapped individuals.* Washington, D.C.: The Alliance, 1978.

Adams, R. C., Daniel, A., & Rullman, L. *Games, sports and exercises for the physically handicapped.* Philadelphia: Lea & Febiger, 1975.

Amary, I. B. *Creative recreation for the mentally retarded.* Springfield, Ill.: Charles C Thomas, Publisher, 1975.

Arnheim, D. D., Auxter, D., & Crowe, W. C. *Principles and methods of adapted physical education and recreation* (3rd ed.). St. Louis: The C. V. Mosby Co., 1977.

Beter, T., & Cragin, W. E. *The mentally retarded child and his motor behavior.* Springfield, Ill.: Charles C Thomas, Publisher, 1972.

Clarke, H., & Clarke, D. *Developmental and adapted physical education.* Englewood Cliffs, N.J.: Prentice-Hall, Inc., 1978.

Cratty, B. *Developmental sequences of perceptual-motor tasks: movement activities for neurologically handicapped and retarded children and youth.* Freeport, N.Y.: Educational Activities, Inc., 1967.

Crowe, W. C., Auxter, D., & Arnheim, D. *Laboratory manual in adapted physical education and recreation: experiments, activities, and assignments.* St. Louis: The C. V. Mosby Co., 1977.

Daniels, A., & Davis, E. *Adapted physical education.* New York: Harper & Row, Publishers, Inc., 1975.

Drowatzky, J. N. *Physical education for the mentally retarded.* Philadelphia: Lea & Febiger, 1971.

Fait, H. *Special physical education.* Philadelphia: W. B. Saunders Co., 1978.

Geddes, D. *Physical activities for individuals with handicapping conditions.* St. Louis: The C. V. Mosby Co., 1978.

Hirst, C., & Michaelis, E. *Developmental activities for children in special education.* Springfield, Ill.: Charles C Thomas, Publisher, 1972.

Kelly, E. *Adapted and corrective physical education.* New York: John Wiley & Sons, Inc., 1965.

McClenaghan, B., & Gallahue, D. *Fundamental movement, a developmental and remedial approach.* Philadelphia: W. B. Saunders Co., 1978.

Moran, J. M., & Kalakian, L. H. *Movement experiences for the mentally retarded or emotionally disturbed child*. Minneapolis: Burgess Publishing Co., 1977.

Newman, J. *Swimming for children with physical and sensory impairments*. Springfield, Ill.: Charles C Thomas, Publisher, 1976.

Rarick, G., Dobbins, D., & Broadhead, G. *The motor domain and its correlations in educationally handicapped children*. Englewood Cliffs, N.J.: Prentice-Hall, Inc., 1976.

Sherrill, C. *Adapted physical education and recreation: a multi-disciplinary approach*. Dubuque, Iowa: William C. Brown, Co., Publishers, 1976.

Vannier, M. *Physical activities for the handicapped*. Englewood Cliffs, N.J.: Prentice-Hall, Inc., 1977.

Vodola, T. *Individualized physical education program for the handicapped child*. Englewood Cliffs, N.J.: Prentice-Hall, Inc., 1973.

Wehman, P. *Helping the mentally retarded acquire play skills*. Springfield, Ill.: Charles C Thomas, Publisher, 1977.

Wessel, J. A., et al. *Planning individualized education programs*. Northbrook, Ill.: Hubbard Scientific Co., 1977.

Winnick, J. P., & Jansma, P. (Eds.). *Physical education inservice resource manual for the implementation of the Education for All Handicapped Children Act*. Brockport, N.Y.: State University College, 1978.

Any psychology or learning theory, to be complete, must include the body—what we eat, how we move, how we live. Eventually, what we now call physical education, reformed and refurbished, may well stand— as it did in ancient times—at the center of the academy.

GEORGE LEONARD

21 The college and university basic instructional program

COMPETENCIES

After completing this unit, you should be able to:

Justify physical education in a college or university curriculum.

Construct and compare the advantages and disadvantages of a required versus an elective program.

Formulate organizational and procedural policies for administering a program.

Select activities and design instructional strategies that are most appropriate for today's college/university student.

Define the following:
Basic instructional
Elective
Service program
Required program

PERSPECTIVE

PRINCIPLE: Course offerings in the basic instructional program
should be designed to achieve specific outcomes that recognize
the physical, recreational, athletic, and leisure time needs
of the student in today's culture.

The primary purpose of attending college is to reinforce our intellectual powers, yet we realize that education is useless without physical and mental health. A basic instructional program in physical education should result in a "wholeness" or "oneness" of students so that without physical and emotional discord, they will be at peace with their own bodies and therefore able to optimize their intellectual efforts. With current American life-styles, now more than ever, "mans sano in corpore sano" is not an outmoded cliché. It is a contemporary pragmatic description of the individual as a total person functioning in today's society. Now, more than any other time, it is unacceptable to assume a posture of dualism. Indeed it is less than human.

Even if all American youth were exposed to excellent programs of physical education from nursery school through the twelfth grade, a basic instructional program at the college and university level could still be justified. As the main period of physical growth has taken place in the progress toward maturity, the functions of a general instructional program are threefold: (1) maintenance of physical fitness, (2) refinement of skills, (3) introduction of new skills, and (4) development of a healthy lifestyle.

The problems of our culture are more varied and intense than ever before. Leisure time is a serious concern. Extended vacations, unemployment, shorter workweeks, and early retirements have vastly intensified the need for Americans to be educated for a worthy, fulfilling utilization of leisure time. Our educational system must recognize this future need, and its resolution cannot be left to chance.

There are other future problems with which today's college and university students must cope—problems dealing with the type of occupations and daily living that provide physical and mental stress. Present-day literature is replete with research and professional guidance concerning the need for a greater, more intense effort to safeguard our most important resource—ourselves. The following are a few summarizing statements taken from research:

1. Physical activity has an effect on the reduction of coronary disease and minimizes problems of cardiovascular capacity and degeneration.
2. Physical activity is a satisfactory social outlet that constantly seeks expression.
3. There is a need for the development of physical skills that can be applied throughout life in the constructive and wholesome use of leisure time.

These statements should provide justification for the inclusion of physical education in a student's academic life.

Many leaders in physical education understand and firmly believe in the value of physical education for college and university men and women. However, the "requirement" issue is highly controversial. Philosophical and economic decisions have caused changes in basic instructional programs, often from "required" to "elective"; requirements have been increased or decreased. Other changes are occurring in activity offerings and the development of innovative curricular models and instructional strategies. The implementation of Title IX is causing major revisions in traditional program orientation. Presently, programs are being critically examined because instruction must be improved, and we must be reasonably certain that what we claim for physical education is justified by information based on specific data.

Further consideration must be given to the fact that young people enter higher education deficient in skills, attitudes, and interests with respect to physical fitness, sports, aquatics, recreation, physical education, and dance activities. There is a need for guidance and orientation under competent and friendly leadership with respect to their physical, social, and emotional needs as far as these may be satisfied by physical education course offerings. The limitation of facilities, equipment, and the supply of instructors is an additional reason for determining the greatest good for the greatest number with the greatest economy of money, personnel, time, and space.

In 1977, a national survey conducted by Joseph Oxedine and Jean Roberts* indicated that institutions with more than 5,000 undergraduates included physical education in the curriculum. Further findings indicated that the requirement of physical education in 4-year institutions is continuing to decline. One interesting change resulting from the effect of Title IX, for the institutions reporting in the survey, is that 89% of all courses are offered on a coeducational basis.

*Oxedine, J., & Roberts, J. A general instructional program in physical education at four year colleges and universities: 1977. *JOHPER,* 1978, pp. 21-23.

With all the pressures being exerted on the basic instructional program, specifically the loss of required physical education, large numbers of students (men and women) are electing physical education courses. Enrollments in elective courses are maintaining about an 80% level compared to those for required physical education. This may be due, in part, to students becoming more "fitness and lifetime sport skill conscious," but there are other facts to consider. One of the characteristics of education at this level, for the majority of students, is that it is taking place away from home. Students are experiencing an independence in living a 24-hour day that calls for personal judgments, decisions, and adjustments that are new and confusing to many. Whereas the core of the college or university setting is and should be the academic curriculum, they are concerned about the physical, social, and emotional phases of college and university life. There is a campus culture as definite as any social pattern. The typical student wants to fit into this pattern or have an outlet through another opportunity. Physical activity may be this outlet, since it provides the student with recreation and a familiarity with an activity in which there can be some type of social acceptability.

Physical activity courses in a college or university therefore should be designed to enrich the understanding of the students, to provide for thoughtful administration of their lives, and to aid in the development of the ability to accept themselves as total persons.

THE BASIC INSTRUCTIONAL PROGRAM

Course offerings in the program should be designed to achieve specific outcomes that recognize the physical, recreational, athletic, and leisure time needs of the student in today's culture. These specific outcomes are as follows:

1. To develop understanding and optimum skill in a variety of physical education, sport, dance, and leisure activities
2. To develop an understanding of individual abilities as related to the acquisition of skill
3. To develop an understanding of the principles, rules, and values related to specific activities
4. To develop an awareness of individual leisure-time needs and how these may be met in future years
5. To provide an opportunity for students to have regular physical activity
6. To advance skills beyond the beginning level
7. To develop an appreciation and skill in the performing arts through esthetic and creative experiences in dance
8. To develop appreciation and skill in a variety of movement activities
9. To understand basic exercise physiology and biomechanical principles and their relationship to leading a fuller, healthy life.

These outcomes indicate and reflect the relationships between physical, psychomotor, cognitive, and affective achievements.

If the dual role of the institutions of higher learning is to meet the continuous need of the individual student and also, at the same time, to develop professional skills and competencies for service in a very complex, constantly changing society, then these roles are not seen to be mutually exclusive. One does not exclude one for the other in an institution that purports to carry out its commitment to the education of the whole person and for total excellence.

The basic instructional program can meet these standards of excellence and have academic respectability if a physical education course can meet the following criteria:

1. It should be compatible with the university, school, and departmental philosophy.

2. It should be structured so as to meet the needs and interests of a diverse population who have varying levels of skills and capacities and myriad attractions and concerns competing for their time and energy.
3. It should contribute to personal life skills. These skills include the ability to think critically, to be receptive to new and varied information in problem solving, to bring clarity out of confusion, to cope with difficulty in a positive manner, to respect the abilities of others, and to know and accept one's own capacity and abilities.
4. The grading of students should reflect an assessment of the cognitive and motor skills achieved according to the specified objectives.
5. The university image portrayed by the courses should be one that exemplifies standards associated with quality educational experiences and contemporary systems of delivery.

Many of the experiences within a university are designed to impart knowledge, consumption, use, and interpretation. But others also deal more with the life of the student. Physical education courses serve in this last category. Admittedly, they are organized differently and operate with some uniqueness in a college or university setting; nevertheless, true to their heritage in early Greek tradition, their aims are to enrich the self-understanding of the student, to provide students with the means for a thoughtful "administration" of their lives, and to aid students in the development of a healthy self-concept.

Physical activity courses are nonetheless "academic." There is nothing in any definition of the term that would categorize such efforts expended by a modern program of physical education as "nonacademic." Only if instructional efforts in the "classical, literary, or mathematical pursuit" ignore the student completely and eliminate entirely the human equation in their teaching would physical education disclaim relationship to the best in the academic world. The play fields, gymnasiums, and pools are not laboratories where bridges are planned or formulas tested. Nor do we seek in them new strains of bacteria or new spectral phenomena. They are laboratories where changes in human personality take place, where human resources are cultivated.

The availability of the courses—their staffing, facilities, and program—and the predictable atmosphere attract students. They mingle. They learn from each other.

SHOULD THE PROGRAM BE REQUIRED OR ELECTIVE?

As previously indicated, economic pressures, philosophical decisions, and other factors have created a controversial issue related to a required or elective physical education program. One other factor to be considered is the development of campus recreational facilities such as those constructed at Purdue University, Michigan University, University of Milwaukee, University of Illinois, and many other institutions. This concept has also given impetus to the development of sports clubs. One argument presented is that these facilities and activities provide for the needs of students, therefore there is no longer a need for physical education, and its requirement is no longer a realistic expectation.

Presently, some colleges and universities are reinstating the requirement and there is some indication that this trend will be increasing. So, the controversy will continue to be a viable issue.

Some of the pros and cons of required programs on which this issue may one day be settled are herewith presented.

Required program

Pros
1. A guidance program is favored for all participants.

2. Scheduling makes for best use of facilities, instructors, activities, class size, and so forth. Furthermore, student schedules are apt to be so heavy that there will be no systematic participation unless it is scheduled.
3. An adequate program of screening and testing is relatively easy to administer, for example, "sinkers" from swimmers or skilled from unskilled.
4. Needs of individual students may be better met; students failing to participate cannot be helped.
5. Those students needing physical education are sure to get it.
6. Studies indicate that the weakest and most poorly skilled students tend (under an elective program) not to elect physical education and, if given a "free choice," choose activities that maintain their present developmental patterns.
7. Achievement is recognized with a grade and credit.

Cons
1. A required program is less democratic in principle.
2. It encourages excuses, fictitious or otherwise.
3. Leadership may be indifferent; there is more opportunity for student leadership on a "club" basis among students with common interests.
4. Programs often are not adapted to individual interests.
   a. With required attendance, instructors may not stress individual needs and interests.
   b. If a desired activity has reached its registration limit, the student is forced to choose anything that "fits in."

ADMINISTRATIVE POLICIES

Administration is the process of directing organized efforts toward the accomplishment of chosen objectives. It paves the way so that the program of activities may be carried on. It is involved with such noninstructional activities as providing equipment, supplies, facilities, play space, and leadership. Its function is to provide an effective curriculum.

Policies are basic agreements made after considering all the most valid evidence available. Policies represent some recognizable attitudes, purposes, or sets of values that result from careful examination of the data. Once policy is established, the function of administration is to translate the policy into action, by implementing or giving effect to it.

ATTENDANCE, SCHEDULING, GRADES, AND CREDIT

Administrative items such as attendance, scheduling, grades, and credit are treated more extensively in textbooks on administration. Brief summary mention is made here of some general policies under each heading.

Attendance
1. Generally, four semesters or six quarters constitute the required program.
2. Usually a limited number of class cuts (four to five a semester) are permitted. Absences are normally dealt with in the same manner as cuts in the general academic program.
3. In the case of members of varsity athletic teams, they are usually excused during the season of the sport engaged in.
4. Excuses from participation in the required program are issued by the institutional physician, but theoretically no one is excused. If a person is able to attend classes, he/she should be able to profit by participation in some activity adapted to his/her needs.

Scheduling
1. Students should be scheduled for physical education in the same manner and at the same time as for academic courses. They should not be simply assigned to any activity that happens to fit in their schedules.
2. Two double periods twice per week is most desirable, but only a few colleges and universities have been so fortunate in the intricate task of schedule making.

Instructional quality
The best teachers should be assigned to college service classes. Too often, institutions with teacher education programs assign undergraduate student teachers or inexperienced graduate assistants to teach these classes without adequate supervision.

Grades
1. A, B, C, D, F or numerical symbols are usually employed, and these appear on the student's official transcript. Some courses are offered on a pass-fail or credit-no credit basis.
2. Various combinations of factors are involved in assigning grades. Grades should be based on achievement of the course objectives:
   a. Attendance
   b. Physical domain
   c. Psychomotor domain
   d. Cognitive domain

Credit
1. Credit to the extent of one per semester is usually given and is required for graduation.
2. "Negative" credit is sometimes given, that is, physical education is required for graduation but grades do not figure into the "point-hour ratio" of the cumulative scholastic index.
3. One semester hour or quarter hour credit is given.

All these administrative aspects of the curriculum are important. Unfortunately, they still represent institutional and educational "issues" in some institutions. Their proper solution is imperative for the development of a sound curriculum, good teaching, and desirable student attitudes.

COEDUCATIONAL PROGRAMS

Since the implementation of Title IX, almost 90% of physical education courses are coeducational. Because of specific sex interests, variances in certain physiological factors, and the amount of physical contact involved, certain courses such as wrestling, lacrosse, and field hockey may still be offered on a segregated basis.

Teaching personnel should be assigned to classes based on their proficiency rather than the sex makeup of the class.

COURSE OFFERINGS

Geographical and climatic conditions; community and regional mores and customs; presence or absence of facilities, such as swimming pools, indoor ice skating rinks, or handball, squash, and racquetball courts; indoor tennis courts; ski jumps; teaching expertise; and so forth are all factors that determine the nature of offerings in the general instructional program.

Students' changing interests and needs require institutions to periodically examine course offerings. In recent years, the trend is toward individual and dual sports, outdoor education, fitness activities, and dance activities. Television and the development of community and private sport clubs have created strong demands for tennis, golf, racquetball, squash, bowling, and aquatics. Fitness concerns have initiated courses in jogging, aerobics, aerobic dancing, and conditioning courses. A renewed interest in ecology has created a demand for outdoor skills in backpacking, orienteering, survival camping, and mountain climbing. Easy access to mountains, oceans, and lakes requires offerings in skiing, skin and scuba diving, snorkeling, surfing, sailing, powerboating, kayaking and canoeing. Students are interested in all types of dancing from square to contemporary. The movies have created an interest in the martial arts and primarily self-defense (judo, aikido, kung fu, karate). Other courses being offered are fencing, billiards, belly dancing, weight control, movement awareness education,

jazz dance, trap and skeet shooting, horseback riding, skydiving, yoga, and hatha yoga.

Many institutions are offering lecture or foundation courses in exercise physiology, kinesiology, philosophy, sport sociology, and fitness testing.

SAMPLE PROGRAMS

The programs presented in this unit were selected to illustrate the trends in basic instruction programs using different approaches in curriculum design and instructional strategies. Each program meets the interests and needs of the college/university student but in different ways. An example of an effective, more "conventional" type of elective program is the program offered at Indiana University, Bloomington, Indiana.

INDIANA UNIVERSITY ELECTIVE PHYSICAL EDUCATION

(Courtesy Department of Physical Education)

The Department of Physical Education offers a wide range of elective physical education courses. Credit hours in the elective program count toward graduation in the University Division, The School of Business, The School of Education, The School of Music, as well as other schools and the College of Arts and Sciences at the university's Bloomington campus.

The classes are designed for students to learn beginning skills in activities in which they have not participated. Intermediate and advanced courses assist a student to become more highly proficient in activities about which they have some knowledge. Courses are coeducational in all but a few instances, primarily swimming classes in which only women may be accommodated due to facility limitations.

The levels of skill and knowledge necessary for success in the courses are progressive from beginning through intermediate and advanced courses. Students should be advised that unless they have adequate beginning skills, they should not consider enrolling in intermediate or advanced sections. Abbreviations in the schedule of classes are as follows: "Beg." refers to the beginning level, "Int." to the intermediate level, and "Adv." to the advanced level.

The size of a class is based on the nature of the activity and the space available for teaching. As an example, swimming classes usually do not exceed 25 in enrollment because safety demands a limited number so that an instructor is able to assist all students in an uncrowded situation.

Students enrolled in elective physical education courses are evaluated on both objective and subjective appraisals. Written and practical examinations are administered in most of the courses. In many of the courses, readings and lectures provide knowledge regarding history, rules, and etiquette in addition to the teaching and refining of skills. In the intermediate and advanced courses, skill analysis and strategies are stressed. In cources such as jogging and aerobics, lectures regarding the physical processes involved and the results of such activity are presented. Visual aids, demonstrations, and master lessons are also used to assist students in perfecting skills.

A student may enroll in elective courses in any of the following areas:

Archery	Judo
Billiards	Karate
Body dynamics	Modern dance
Bowling	Racquetball
Conditioning	Riflery
Conditioning and weight training	Soccer
	Squash
Diving	Swimming
Fencing	Scuba diving
Field hockey	Synchronized swimming
Folk and square dance	Aquatic conditioning
Fitness and jogging	Water polo
Golf	Advanced lifesaving
Gymnastics	Water safety instructors
Handball	(prerequisite: advanced lifesaving)
Horsemanship (class meets for double period once a week for a full semester)	Team handball
	Tennis
	Trap and skeet shooting
Martial arts	Volleyball
Aikido	Weight training

The schedule of classes will identify seasonal

courses that meet only the first 8 weeks, 4 days per week. Otherwise, classes meet 2 hours per week of scheduled class time for a full semester.

• • •

An innovative approach to a required basic instruction program that reflects an institution's philosophy of developing the whole person with equal emphasis on mind, spirit, and body is the "fitness for life" program designed for 3,000 full-time undergraduate students at Oral Roberts University, Tulsa, Oklahoma.

ORAL ROBERTS UNIVERSITY

(Courtesy Department of Health, Physical Education, and Recreation)

The program adopted Kenneth H. Cooper's aerobics concept as a basis for its total fitness. All students at the university are required to enroll in and pass a physical education activity course each semester. Each student is also required to participate in an individualized aerobics program as part of the activity curriculum.

During the first semester, a new student undergoes a series of comprehensive medical tests administered by the Human Performance Laboratory and Health Services. The results of individual tests indicate the special needs of the student.

In the first semester, each student is required to take Aerobics I, Scientific Foundations of Physical Activity. The course meets 1 day per week for 2 hours with 30 students per section and is a lecture-laboratory class. The student views the lectures on closed circuit television and completes a study guide on the material. The lecture is discussed, and the laboratory exercise is introduced. During the second semester, all students are enrolled in Aerobics II. It is an extension of the first course. Grading for the Aerobics II course is based on 40% knowledge, 30% aerobic points, 20% field test, and 10% effort and participation.

After the first year, the students select physical activity courses from the curriculum. They must select two team sports and four individual sports.

Initial feedback reported from students in the program is positive, and many reports received from graduates indicate that they continue to be active in some type of aerobic program. The collection of other data from well-controlled research studies should yield some information as to the relative worth and merit of this type of program.

• • •

A shift from required to elective programs has caused institutions to develop alternative curriculum models and instructional strategies that would appeal to students. The following examples of curriculum and instruction approaches were designed for a segment of the elective program offered at Purdue University, West Lafayette, Indiana. The programs were designed based on the following principles:

1. Today's college/university student wants choice and selection of activities.
2. Students differ in rates of learning.
3. Learning should not be restricted to a regularly scheduled class period or space.
4. An opportunity should be provided to each student for broader and in-depth learning.
5. Proficiency levels can be determined by the student.
6. There should be maximum utilization of instructional resources.

These principles, to be effectively implemented, necessitated changes in traditional program developmental procedures, operational environmental procedures, curriculum design, and instructional strategies.

PURDUE UNIVERSITY

(Developed by Anthony A. Annarino)

Instructional strategy

1. A thorough orientation as to the nature and type of program is given to all students enrolled in a class section.
2. The student selects an activity unit (e.g., golf or tennis) and an individual instructional packet for that activity.
3. Specific activity instructional and learning procedures are described by each instructor.
4. The student may use the diagnostic psychomotor and cognitive tests or, through a personal interview, determine a starting level of competency.
5. The student achieves the prescribed psychomotor and learning tasks by using the available media, resource material, instructor assistance, and individual or group practice. The instructor is always available at the practice area for assistance and formative evaluation.
6. When a student completes the required minimal tasks in a lesson, the instructor formatively evaluates the student on a predetermined minimal competency level for that lesson.
7. A student who achieves mastery of the minimal task proceeds to the next lesson. If the student does not achieve mastery, the instructor diagnoses the problem and provides instructional correctives. Alternatives to the original mode of instruction are used. (For example, if the original demonstration was by a loop film, the instructor could use as an alternative a live model demonstration or a videotape replay.)
8. After a student achieves mastery of all the minimal psychomotor and cognitive competencies for the learning activity, final (summative) psychomotor and cognitive tests are administered.
9. Psychomotor and cognitive grades for the activity are determined by the student's performance on the summative evaluation that is based on predetermined standards for proficiency.
10. The results of summative evaluations may be also used to determine whether the student may elect to achieve a higher mastery level for the activity, select another, or remain in the activity to achieve the minimal mastery standard.
11. If a new activity is selected, the student is

PHYSICAL EDUCATION MASTERY LEARNING CURRICULUM (COLLEGE/UNIVERSITY): DESIGN A*

Duration (weeks)	Option 1	Option 2	Option 3	Option 4
Semester I				
1	Program orientation, fitness diagnostic testing, and prescription	Program orientation, fitness diagnostic testing, and prescription	Program orientation, fitness diagnostic testing, and prescription	Program orientation, fitness diagnostic testing, and prescription
7	Archery	Golf	Tennis	Badminton
7	Handball	Bowling	Conditioning	Squash-racquetball
1	Fitness evaluation	Fitness evaluation	Fitness evaluation	Fitness evaluation
Semester II				
1	Program orientation, fitness diagnostic testing, and prescription	Program orientation, fitness diagnostic testing, and prescription	Program orientation, fitness diagnostic testing, and prescription	Program orientation, fitness diagnostic testing, and prescription
7	Handball	Bowling	Conditioning	Squash-racquetball
7	Archery	Golf	Tennis	Badminton
1	Fitness evaluation	Fitness evaluation	Fitness evaluation	Fitness evaluation

*Semesters I and II; laboratory, 3 hours; credit, 1 hour. Meets 3 days a week for 50-minute periods.

assigned to the new activity area and instructor. The same aforementioned procedure is followed.

The implementation of this mastery learning strategy necessitated the design of two curriculum models (designs A and B). The basic difference between the two models is the expansion of time modules in model B.

This same program may be used in the professional preparation program for proficiency development. One of the major problems in physical education teacher preparation programs is the minimal amount of qualitative and quantitative time devoted in an overcrowded curriculum to the acquisition of sport fundamentals, knowledges, and abilities by the student. To minimize this problem, the implementation of proficiency testing programs has been a suggested alternative. The models

just described, with some modifications, can be used to incorporate the basic concepts and procedures for a proficiency testing program in a professional preparation curriculum. The offering of a variety of courses, based on the models, can provide students with opportunities to demonstrate or acquire proficiencies in a variety of activities. The number and types of activities, the required levels of proficiency, and the specific tests for evaluating proficiencies are determined by the philosophy and objectives of a school and department.

Contracting

Another type of instructional strategy implemented in course offerings is contracting. This is a method of teaching whereby points or grades are determined by the student, based on selection and completion of various contractual tasks. These tasks are designed for quantitative and

PHYSICAL EDUCATION MASTERY LEARNING CURRICULUM (COLLEGE/UNIVERSITY): DESIGN B*

Duration (weeks)	Option 1	Option 2	Option 3	Option 4
Semester I				
1	Program orientation, fitness diagnostic testing, and pre-scription	Program orientation, fitness diagnostic testing, and pre-scription	Program orientation, fitness diagnostic testing, and pre-scription	Program orientation, fitness diagnostic testing, and pre-scription
14	Archery	Golf	Tennis	Badminton
1	Fitness evaluation	Fitness evaluation	Fitness evaluation	Fitness evaluation
Semester II				
1	Program orientation, fitness diagnostic testing, and pre-scription	Program orientation, fitness diagnostic testing, and pre-scription	Program orientation, fitness diagnostic testing, and pre-scription	Program orientation, fitness diagnostic testing, and pre-scription
14	Handball	Bowling	Conditioning	Squash-racquetball
1	Fitness evaluation	Fitness evaluation	Fitness evaluation	Fitness evaluation

*Semesters I and II; laboratory, 3 hours; credit, 1 hour. Meets 3 days a week for 50-minute periods.

qualitative psychomotor and cognitive learnings. Completion of the tasks is not restricted to the regularly scheduled class period or space.

The following sample contract is used for a course in golf at Purdue University.

GOLF CONTRACT

(Developed by Gregory Morgan and Anthony A. Annarino)

Before beginning this individualized program on golf, determine what grade you would like to receive by examining the following tasks. In order to receive a "C," you must satisfactorily complete *all* the tasks under "'C' work." If you do not satisfactorily complete a task the first time, then you may repeat the task until you do. If you wish to receive an "A" or "B," then you must complete all the tasks under that grade *plus all the tasks for the lower grades.* After you have determined what grade you want, you may go to the instructor to sign your contract. Once you have signed your contract, you may change the contract only to a higher grade.

"C" work

1. Complete the golf individualized instructional minimal skill competencies.
2. Score 60% or better on the summation written test at the end of the program.
3. Write a one- to two-page paper on the history of golf.
4. Be able to define 15 golf terms correctly on a quiz.
5. Complete a score card correctly from the enclosed sheet for Jane/John Doe, including the penalty strokes, and submit this to the instructor.

"B" work

1. Complete all of the "C" work plus the following.
2. Score 70% or better on the summation written test at the end of the program.
3. Write a paper analyzing the correct stance and swing or select a partner and analyze his/her swing (good and bad points).
4. Discuss orally with the instructor the difference between match and medal play.
5. Shoot 18 holes of golf at a local golf course, have your scorecard signed by the club pro, and turn it in to the instructor.

6. Watch a golf match on TV and write a one-page report.

"A" work

1. Complete all of the "B" and "C" work plus the following.
2. Score 85% or better on the summation written test at the end of the program.
3. Write a paper analyzing the causes of a slice, a hook, pulling the ball, pushing the ball, and a fade.
4. Shoot 18 holes of golf with a friend using match play, have your scorecard signed by the club pro, and turn it in to the instructor.

5. Give a 5-minute oral report to the class on any subject relating to golf, for example, correct golf attire and equipment.

This is only one type of contract design. Contracts described in Unit 19 can be adapted for college/university classes. Whatever design is used should specify the learning objectives, learning activities, and evaluation criteria. Students react favorably to "contract teaching," since it provides options.

REACTORS

1. If all Americans were exposed to excellent programs from nursery school through the twelfth grade, a required college/university program could still be justified.
2. Physical activity courses are nonetheless "academic."
3. A shift from "required" to "elective" has caused institutions to develop programs and instructional strategies that would attract more students.
4. Learning should not be restricted to a regular scheduled class period or facility.
5. Contracting is "another way" to teach.
6. Proficiency testing can be used to meet physical education requirements.

LEARNING ACTIVITIES

1. List arguments not stated in this unit that are against requiring physical education at the college/university level.
2. Compile a list of activities that could be offered in a basic instructional program.
   a. Do not be limited by facilities, equipment, etc.

   b. Indicate for men only
   c. Indicate for women only
   d. Indicate coeducational
3. Design a proficiency testing program that could be used by your undergraduate institution for the basic instructional program.
4. List the disadvantages and advantages of a coeducational program.

UNIT EVALUATIVE CRITERIA

Can you:
1. State a rationale with documentation for including physical education in a college/university curriculum?
2. Explain the benefits of either a required or elective program.
3. Identify the needs and interests of the college/university student related to physical education?
4. Translate policies into action?
5. List the type of activities that appeal to the present-day student?

RESOURCES

Annarino, A. A. *Individualized instructional programs: archery, badminton, bowling, golf, tennis.* Englewood Cliffs, N.J.: Prentice-Hall, Inc., 1973.

Annarino, A. A. Another way to teach. *JOPER,* Oct. 1974, pp. 43-44.

Annarino, A. A. University basic instructional program—a new approach. *The Physical Educator,* Oct. 1974, pp. 131-133.

Brody, H. S. *Paradox and promise.* Englewood Cliffs, N.J.: Prentice-Hall, Inc., 1961.

Bryteson, P. Fitness for life: aerobics at Oral Roberts University. *JOPER,* Jan. 1978, pp. 37-39.

Drews, F. Statement to the general faculty. *College Physical Education Packet,* American Alliance for Health, Physical Education, and Recreation, 1974.

Esslinger, A. A. In support of the requirement. In *College Physical Education Packet,* American Alliance for Health, Physical Education, and Recreation, 1974, p. 32.

Leonard, G. *The ultimate athlete.* New York: The Viking Press, 1975.

Lockhart, A. S., & Slusher, H. S. *Contemporary readings in physical education.* Dubuque, Iowa: William C. Brown Co., Publishers, 1975.

Michener, J. A. *Sports in America.* New York: Random House Inc., 1976.

Nixon, J., & Jewett, A. *Introduction to physical education.* Philadelphia: W. B. Saunders Co., 1974.

Oxedine, J., & Roberts, J. The general instructional program in physical education at four year colleges and universities: 1977. *JOPER,* Jan. 1978, pp. 21-23.

Rivenes, R. *Foundations of physical education.* Boston: Houghton Mifflin Co., 1978.

Steinhaus, A. The role of exercise in physical fitness. *JOPER,* June 1963, pp. 299-300.

Ward, L. R. *Philosophy of education.* Chicago: Henry Regnery Co., 1963.

PART FOUR

THE EXTENDED CURRICULUM

UNITS

Games are situations contrived to permit simultaneous participation of many people in some significant pattern of their own corporate lives.

MARSHALL McLUHAN

22 Intramural and recreational sports programs

COMPETENCIES

After completing this unit, you should be able to:

Organize and administer an intramural program for all educational levels.

Differentiate between an intramural and an interscholastic program.

Identify the relationships of the intramural program to the basic instructional program.

Define the most desirable organizational units for participation in the intermediate grades, junior and senior high school, and college and university.

Define the following:
Basic instructional
Interscholastic
Intramurals
Extended curriculum
Extraclass
Extramural
Recreational sports

PERSPECTIVE

PRINCIPLE: The intramural program is an extension of the physical education program. It is an opportunity for students to "try out" what they have learned.

What is commonly known as the intramural (within the walls) or, in a larger context, recreational sports programs in physical education applies to those sports, games, and dance activities taking place on school property and at some time other than the instructional physical education period. These activities are frequently referred to as extracurricular activities, but since our definition of a curriculum includes all activities of the school under the supervision of school authorities, this term is no longer valid. The term *extraclass activities* is the one currently accepted and includes all experiences or activities in the curriculum that are not usually provided for in typical classes. These activities include intramural and interscholastic athletics, glee clubs, bands, dances, school publications, and many other activities under school supervision.

Intramural and recreational sports programs are integral parts of the curriculum and not questionable accessories. As such, they should receive the same attention in planning, execution, and evaluation by teachers and pupils as the regular class work. However, one of the problems facing schools in conducting extensive intramural programs is the "facility crunch." The development of a comprehensive athletic program for girls comparable to the programs for boys has placed intramural programs in serious jeopardy. A school must philosophically decide that there must be a balance in the three areas of basic physical education instruction, intramurals, and athletics.

There is a definite need for each but not at the expense of the others. The basic program provides skill instruction for all students; the intramural program is an opportunity to utilize and refine these skills; and the athletic program is for a selected group of highly skilled students. Attention, in the future, must be given to the design of school facilities so that comprehensive programs can be provided for all three areas.

It is not the purpose of this volume to detail the organization and administration of school intramural programs at the various levels; there are several excellent books that already do that. The purpose here is to point out that the aims of the intramural program are a living part of the aims of education. This program supplements and complements the regular physical education program and contributes strongly to the common purposes that should permeate all school experiences.

A survey of 3,525 secondary school pupils indicated the following chief values that these students felt they achieved by participation in the extraclass activities of their respective schools:

1. Facilitated development of new friendships
2. Made school seem more interesting
3. Helped in learning how to win and lose in a sportsmanlike manner
4. Created a greater loyalty to the school
5. Gave something worthwhile to do in leisure time
6. Resulted in more friendly relations with teachers

7. Developed willingness to accept criticisms from others
8. Made available valuable information that would not have been received in a regular course

Parents tended to mention values similar to those of the students but mentioned more frequently that participation created a greater interest in regular school subjects.

In considering the curriculum and its enrichment and expansion at all levels in the interests of better meeting the needs of individuals, the extraclass activities in physical education should be examined with the following criteria:

1. To what extent do they satisfy pupils' interests and needs for
   a. Adventure, new experiences, excitement?
   b. Recognition, acceptance, and approval by peers?
   c. Group status, a feeling of "belonging," being part of a group to which they can give loyalty?
   d. Mastery and achievement?
   e. Affection, close friendships?
   f. Autonomy, self-realization, self-direction, individual integrity?
2. To what extent do they help bridge the gap between school and community by the arranging of games and having parents participate actively in school affairs?
3. Are boys and girls learning to play together, manage their friendships, and prepare for family living by the coeducational intramural activities?
4. Does the intramural program enrich the opportunities of students to participate in the policy-making and administrative aspects of the program?
5. Is the program open to all regardless of race, socioeconomic status, or absence of proficiency in activities?
6. Are the guidance possibilities based on the observance and appraisal of students in extraclass activities used to a high degree?
7. Are the activities such that they contribute positively to physical, cognitive, psychomotor, and affective development?
8. Is some effort made to evaluate the extent to which desirable educational outcomes have resulted from the intramural program?
9. Is participation in extraclass activities engaged in by a large number of different people or is it confined to some few participating in many activities?
10. To what extent is there adequate supervision under trained leadership of the activities of the intramural program?

The intramural program in its activities possesses qualities and potentialities that make it uniquely effective in meeting the needs and interests of youth, thereby contributing markedly to their wholesome growth and development.

THE INTERMEDIATE GRADES (4 to 6)

There is a definite tendency toward supervision of play periods at noon recess and after school hours for children of the intermediate age levels. In most schools the regular classroom teachers either supervise these activities for their respective classroom groups or take charge of several groups in rotation. The desirable goal is a program in which both the instructional activities in the gymnasium and the supervised play periods are directed by competent and well-trained teachers of physical education. Where such teachers are available, as in many junior and senior high schools, we see more adequate intramural activities in operation. Realistically, we must be aware that some assistance from teachers other than physical education or recreation specialists is both necessary and desirable for programs to effectively function.

At this level, athletic teams, "clubs," or "homerooms" within a given grade seem best for forming the basis of the intramural program. These may be given names—

"Explorers" and so forth or the names of colors, such as Blues, Greens, and so forth. Children can be assigned so that all may know the fun and value of being members of a particular club, team, or squad. The purpose, of course, is to introduce to participation as large a percentage of pupils as possible.

Purposes to be achieved and needs to be met by trained supervision

1. Supervision of play is fundamental.
   a. In addition to being a "teacher" and a "referee" in all sorts of social situations, the leader is also responsible for identifying and leading the solitary child into participation and for controlling the child who is overactive and disorganizes the play of others.
   b. Where children play together in large numbers, some classification in terms of maturity and ability is desirable.
   c. Because of their immaturity and inexperience, children need help in organizing their play activities. This fact is discernible even among college students.
   d. Safety and avoidance of injury from accidents demand the supervision and organization of playing groups and of use of equipment.
2. Children in these intermediate grades in an industrial age of limited play space and traffic hazards need safe places in which to play. They also need additional play activity, not only for maintaining optimum biological health but also for adequate social and emotional development.
3. The regular physical education period should be thought of not simply as a "relief" period but also as an "instructional" period. The after school programs provide opportunity for functional practice of skills in total game situations for motor development as well as leadership skills.
4. Education is conscious planning and control of experiences leading to certain objectives.

Organizational units

By the time boys and girls reach the fourth grade, some modified form of intramural organization is quite possible and should supply numerous opportunities for student participation in planning, execution, and, of course, appraisal. Much of the organization can, and should be, worked out in close collaboration with the classroom teacher.

If in a given small school there is, for example, only one fourth grade, one fifth grade, and one sixth grade, it would be possible to suggest an organization as follows:

1. Each class would have two units or teams, called Blue and Maroon (named after the two school colors), for example.
2. Each child would belong to one of the two, and every effort would be made to keep these two groups equal in general playing ability.
3. Theoretically assuming a class of 30 (15 boys and 15 girls), teams for the "Blues" and for the "Maroons" would be available in grades four, five, and six.
4. Each grade would have its own participating units; activities could be planned in terms of the interests and maturity level of each class, yet each student would feel a sense of affiliation with students in the other two grades of the school.
5. A boy would become interested in what the girls do since he would have common membership on the team (either Blue or Maroon) with certain of his girl classmates as well. Specific coeducational activities would be planned so that the Blues (boys and girls) would be participating in activities against the Maroons (boys and girls).

MIDDLE–JUNIOR HIGH SCHOOL

Schools that are organized on the 6-3-3 or middle school administrative plans will have an opportunity for setting up an intramural program for the seventh through ninth grades that tends to be more like the high school programs than programs of grades 4 to 6. With the increasing tendency to push intensive competition into the lower grades, there is all the more need to provide a broad intramural program that is available to all students. The characteristic tendency of intensive, league-scheduled games is to provide competition for more advanced players, therefore neglecting the average or below-average child.

Physical education in the middle and junior high school should be essentially an orientation period to the many opportunities and resources in games, sports, and dance, with emphasis on all-around general athletic ability rather than on specialized skill. The organization of the intramural program, therefore, should be flexible and informal enough that many games and sports can be played and so that experimentation can be made in playing different positions in the various games. For example, boys and girls should be encouraged to try out all positions in baseball or basketball as a basis for deciding whether or not they wish later to perfect the special skills required of a pitcher or shortstop in softball or a forward or guard in basketball. Track and field should be emphasized as an intramural sport at the middle–junior high school level because of the fundamental skills involved in running, jumping, and throwing that are basic to so many other activities.

As described for the intermediate grades, color teams, other teams, or clubs within the whole school may be used. However, with the middle–junior high school organization, the homeroom becomes an excellent and natural unit, especially if the homeroom includes students of the same grade levels.

Other possible unit groupings for participation are grades (classes), study rooms, physical education class sections, clubs, and residential districts. Perhaps the two most important factors in unit organization that make for successful programs are these:

1. There should be natural units that already have some normal social integration. The homeroom is such a unit. In contrast, the residential district usually has relatively little social integration.
2. The teams should be well-equated for competition, with no very strong or weak teams participating in the same leagues.

Program activities

The program should be flexible enough to take individual differences into considerations, that is, it should offer enough variety to attract, stimulate, and hold the interest of each student. A small number of well-administered activities are better than too many. Furthermore, the program of activities should be well-balanced between team and individual sports and between strenuous and nonstrenuous activities.

SUGGESTED SEASONAL ACTIVITIES

Fall	Winter	Spring
Archery	Badminton	Archery
Soccer	Basketball	Horseshoes
Touch football	Table tennis	Softball
Speedball	Handball	Baseball
Tennis	Indoor track	Track and
Recreational	Bowling	field
games	Volleyball	Handball-
Volleyball	Wrestling	racquetball
Swimming	Swimming	Golf
Field hockey		Tennis

SENIOR HIGH SCHOOL

There is every reason to expect an interesting and well-organized intramural program at the high school level whenever one finds a good physical education program. The extent and success of the elective intramural or recreational program will depend in part on the size of the school, its location, the interest and ability of the physical education teacher, the facilities available, the cooperation of the school administrator, the interests of high school boys and girls, and the competing attractions of home and community.

In general, the intramural program is carried on immediately after classes are over in the afternoon in a large city school, during the noon hour if the school is a consolidated school with a large proportion of the pupils transported by buses, or during a period in the school day set aside for club or school activities, usually referred to as the activity period. The activities in the intramural program will usually parallel those being taught in the physical education period. If, in the fall, soccer or speedball is being taught as a physical education class activity, it is desirable to plan for intramural competition in soccer or speedball after school in the fall. Likewise, intramurals in volleyball would coincide with instruction given in that activity in the early winter or winter season.

Most high schools are limited in their facilities for individual and dual sports such as bowling, tennis, golf, and swimming. However, there are often community facilities that can be used, particularly for the intramural program. It is highly desirable and often possible to teach the fundamental skills in these activities in the physical education class period and then arrange for the use, under supervision, of such community resources as the park tennis courts, the YMCA or YWCA swimming pool, or a commercial bowling establishment. For example, one can teach the basic techniques of bowling, including the scoring and etiquette of the game, in class and make arrangements for bowling as an intramural activity in a local bowling establishment.

SUGGESTED ACTIVITIES

Fall	Winter	Spring
Flag football	Basketball	Track and
Soccer	Swimming	field
Speedball	Wrestling	Softball
Cross-country	Indoor track	Baseball
Swimming	Handball-	Tennis
Tennis	racquetball	Archery
Golf	Volleyball	Horseshoes
Six-man foot-	Bowling	Swimming
ball	Apparatus	Golf
Archery	stunts	Badminton
Horseshoes	Skating	
Golf	Water basket-	
Field hockey	ball	
	Table tennis	

An organizational pattern for secondary schools is presented in Fig. 9.

COLLEGE AND UNIVERSITY

Recreational sports programs today include many activities of a physical-recreational nature as well as the traditional competitive sports. Increasingly more attention is being given to the educational experiences in recreational sports participation by supervision of practice periods, consideration of safety factors, more expert instruction, improved organization, better officiating, and excellent facilities. One need only examine the numerous fine recreational sports handbooks and observe programs in dozens of our institutions of higher education to realize the progress that has been made.

Organizational units

The number and type of units will depend on the nature and size of the institution. Purdue University is representative of the type of comprehensive recreational sports program being offered in large universities.

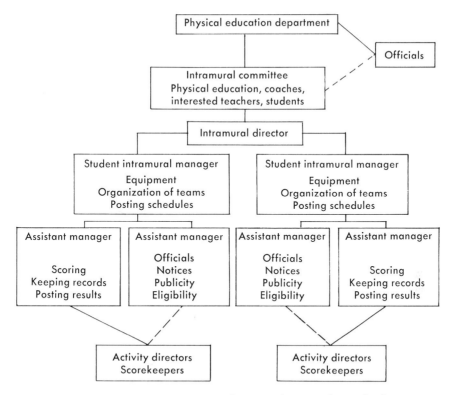

Fig. 9. Intramural organizational pattern for secondary schools.

PURDUE UNIVERSITY PROGRAM

(Courtesy George Haniford and staff, Division of Recreational Sports, Purdue University, West Layayette, Ind.)

Purdue offers three major types of programs—club sports, informal recreation sports, and intramural sports.

The recreational gymnasium is the primary facility designed specifically to serve as a home base for all the indoor recreational sports programs. Additional indoor campus facilities are also utilized. The outdoor facilities and areas include outdoor pools, the outdoor ice skating rink, 24 lighted tennis courts, 90 acres of grass-covered playing fields, horseshoe courts, volleyball courts, basketball courts, and a picnic area. The intramural sports program offers the students and staff extensive opportunities for competitive intramural activities within a structure of several divisions: residence halls and housing units, all-campus, graduate men, graduate women, coeducational, independent men, independent women, staff men, and staff women. Each unit has an intramural chairman. The chairman serves as the liaison between the professional staff and the unit. A student advisory council assists the staff in the promotion and development of the total program.

INTRAMURAL ADMINISTRATIVE ORGANIZATION

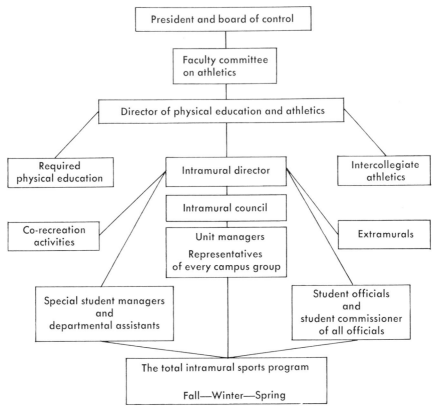

Fig. 10. Organizational plan for administering a college/university intramural program.

Activities

All-campus tournaments and/or leagues are conducted in the following:

12 inch softball	Miniature	Handball
Archery	golf	Free throw
Tennis	Squash	Bowling
Golf	Racquetball	Volleyball
Cross-country	Multimara-	Horseshoes
Badminton	thon	Touch foot-
Riflery	Weight	ball
Wrestling	lifting	Ice hockey
Inner tube	Basketball	Swimming
water polo	Soccer	Billiards
Table tennis	Turkey pull	

Facilities for informal recreational sports are also available for these activities. In addition, direct supervision and information instruction are provided for archery, gymnastics, riflery, roller skating, student/student spouse exercise programs, square and round dancing, swimming, and weight lifting.

The desire of students to participate in specialized sport activities through the function of a sports club is recognized, and such clubs are encouraged by the Division of Recreational Sports. Most of the sport clubs are or have been organized for the primary purpose of engaging in extramural/intercollegiate competition. Each club has a president. The presidents comprise the Club Sports Presidents Council, which advises the staff in all aspects of the club sports program and serves as an action committee. The organized clubs are listed next.

Archery   Canoeing   Crew
Fencing   Handball   Hockey
Ice skating   Judo   Lacrosse
Outing   Racquetball   Riflery
Rugby   Sailing   Soccer
Softball   Squash   Table tennis
Tae Kwon Do   Volleyball   Water polo
Weight lifting

Administrative organization

There are numerous types of administrative organizations for college and university recreational sports. Examination of the recreational sports handbooks for these institutions or references to one of the several good books on intramural activities will provide effective samples for institutions of varying sizes. Fig. 10 illustrates one type of organizational plan.

REACTORS

1. Students should be encouraged to organize and administer their own intramural programs.
2. The intramural program is an extension of the basic instructional program. The interscholastic program is an extension of the intramural program.
3. Intramurals are an integral part of the school curriculum, not questionable accessories.
4. One of the problems facing schools in conducting extensive intramural programs is the "facility crunch" caused by the expansion of the athletic program.
5. The intramural program in its activities possesses qualities and potential that make it uniquely effective in meeting the needs and interests of youth at all ages.
6. There is every reason to expect an interesting and well-organized intramural program at the high school level whenever one finds a good physical education program.
7. The terms, recreational sports and intramurals, differ in definition, scope, and interpretation.

LEARNING ACTIVITIES

1. Evaluate the intramural program at your own institution by applying the 10 criteria listed in this unit.
2. Examine the age characteristics of boys and girls listed in the previous units.
   a. Select a school division (e.g., intermediate, middle–junior high, senior high).
   b. Illustrate how a good intramural program can meet their needs and interests.
3. Devise a comprehensive list of activities that could be offered in an intramural program for:
   a. Intermediate level
   b. Middle–junior high school
   c. Senior high school
   d. College/university
4. Formulate administrative, organizational, and participation policies for conducting an elementary, middle–junior high school, or secondary program.
5. If you were designing a new physical education facility, what would you specifically request in order to conduct comprehensive basic instructional, intramural, and interscholastic programs?

UNIT EVALUATIVE CRITERIA

Can you:
1. Describe various types of organizational units for conducting an intramural program for different school levels?
2. Devise an effective set of administrative organizational and participation policies for an intramural program?
3. Design a functional structure for administering an intramural program at any school level?
4. Develop an effective intramural program for any school level based on the limitations of time, personnel, and facilities?
5. Design a facility that would meet the needs of a basic instructional, intramural, and interscholastic program?

RESOURCES

AAHPER. *Physical education for high school students*. Washington, D.C.: The Alliance, 1970.

Bucher, C. A., & Koenig, C. R. *Methods and materials for secondary school physical education* (5th ed.). St. Louis: The C. V. Mosby Co., 1978.

Danford, H. G., & Shirley, M. *Creative leadership in recreation*. Boston: Allyn & Bacon, Inc., 1970.

Gabrielsen, M. A., & Miles, C. M. *Sports and recreation facilities: for school and community*. Englewood Cliffs, N.J.: Prentice-Hall, Inc., 1958.

Hall, J. T. *School recreation: its organization, supervision and administration*. Dubuque, Iowa: William C. Brown Co., Publisher, 1966.

Hormachea, M. N., & Hormachea, C. R. *Recreation in modern society*. Boston: Holbrook Press, Inc., 1972.

Kando, T. M. *Leisure and popular culture in transition*. St. Louis: The C. V. Mosby Co., 1975.

Kraus, R. G. *Recreation and the schools: guides to effective practices in leisure education and community recreation sponsorship*. New York: Macmillan Publishing Co., Inc., 1964.

Means, L. E. *Intramurals, their organization and administration*. Englewood Cliffs, N.J.: Prentice-Hall, Inc., 1963.

Miller, A. G., & Massey, M. D. *A dynamic concept of physical education for secondary schools*. Englewood Cliffs, N.J.: Prentice-Hall, Inc., 1963.

Mitchell, E. D. *Intramural sports*. New York: A. S. Barnes & Co., Inc., 1939.

Resick, M. C., Seidel, B. L., & Mason, J. G. *Modern administrative practices in physical education and athletics*. Reading, Mass.: Addison-Wesley Publishing Co., Inc., 1970.

Roskosz, F. M. *Structured intramurals*. Philadelphia: W. B. Saunders Co., 1975.

Straub, W. F. *The lifetime sports-oriented physical education program*. Englewood Cliffs, N.J.: Prentice-Hall, Inc., 1976.

Vannier, M., & Fait, H. F.: *Teaching physical education in secondary schools*. Philadelphia: W. B. Saunders Co., 1969.

Willgoose, C. E. *The curriculum in physical education* (3rd ed.). Englewood Cliffs, N.J.: Prentice-Hall, Inc., 1979.

Sometimes in the process of a game a man or woman will experience a moment of almost shattering revelation, about either him/herself or the opponent, or even about the nature of life.

JAMES A. MICHENER

23 Interscholastic and intercollegiate sports programs

CONTENTS

COMPETENCIES

After completing this unit, you should be able to:

Translate philosophical beliefs, standards, and policies for an athletic program that contributes to the educational purposes of the school.

Compare the differences in philosophy between the instructional, intramural, and interscholastic programs.

Interpret Title IX regulations and conduct a self-evaluation of an athletic program regarding conformance to the regulations.

Identify the strengths and weaknesses of an athletic program and rectify the weaknesses.

Identify and explain the structure and function of the various organizations responsible for the governance of athletic programs for both sexes at all levels.

Formulate and explain your philosophy of athletics.

Define the following:
Platform
Standard
Policy
Interscholastic
Intercollegiate

PERSPECTIVE

PRINCIPLE: There is so much educational value in properly conducted interschool athletic programs that the challenge is there to see that they are conducted in such a way that their true educational resources may be encouraged and fostered.

Since, by definition, the curriculum is the life and program of the school and consists of all experiences pupils have that are under the supervision of the school authorities, interscholastic and intercollegiate athletic programs as well as intramural programs are part of the "extended curriculum." Supposedly, the primary criterion for the acceptance of any activity in the curriculum of an educational institution is, Does the activity contribute to the educational purpose of the institution? The answer to this question can only be sought be each institution conducting a self-evaluation based on the philosophical statements, guidelines, platforms, standards, and policies provided in this unit and by the governing bodies of athletic programs.

The fact is recognized that in too many interinstitutional athletic situations a sense of balance has been lost. The educational process has been confused with "show" business to the detriment of the athletes and the school. Competition has been carried to the point of hostility and the threads of kinship and fellowship are often broken as a result. These, and many other less

favorable outcomes of interschool athletic competition, are the results of educational mismanagement.

One of the functions of good educational management is the establishment of sound policies based on sound principles. Policies are basic agreements made after considering all the most valid evidence available. A policy should result in a statement of agreements reached, a platform, a code, or a charter listing the purposes and objectives of the interscholastic or intercollegiate athletic programs, and a listing of definite rules for their operation. Furthermore, some council or representative body should be delegated to interpret aspects of the code or policy that are not fully understood or clearly written.

Usually a school, college, or university has policies for self-discipline in its own local administration under the faculty committee on athletics or the athletic association. Furthermore, membership in the state high school athletic association or some collegiate athletic association or conference implies adherence to certain policies and procedures.

There is so much educational value in properly conducted interschool athletic programs that the challenge is there to see that they are conducted in such a way that their true educational resources may be encouraged and fostered. Unless this is done, movements to decry and suppress them will continue.

INTERSCHOLASTIC ATHLETIC PROGRAMS

There is a tremendous need for valid data leading to clarification of administrative thinking and policy concerning athletic competition at all levels, especially below the senior high school level. It might be helpful to examine claims and counter-claims with a clear realization that interschool athletics per se are neither good nor bad. The values inherent in them depend on the quality of leadership, the total environmental setting, and numerous other factors.

Strengths and weaknesses of interscholastic athletics

Strengths

1. Games and sports have long been recognized as a means to group unity, to "team spirit."
2. They offer appropriate opportunities for self-testing, important in the development of adolescent boys and girls.
3. They offer experience in recognizing that the group can achieve where the individual cannot, that the achievement of goals depends on using the contribution of each member, and that each team member needs to be in a position where he/she can make a unique contribution.
4. Young people like to share difficult undertakings because of the personal bonds that are established; they develop a sense of belonging.
5. Games give some common experiences so that students contact with students from other schools. Sports activities meet a need where other activities fail.
6. Young people are sensitive to judgments of other adolescents; they desire not to be odd or different. Lack of an athletic program makes them feel strange in a sports-conscious community.
7. The school team is a unifying agent that brings all cliques and factions into a common loyalty and community of interests.
8. Exceptionally skillful young people need competition on a high level. Interschool competition provides the needed opportunities.
9. Participation encourages correct health practices and self-sacrifice in training, practicing, and similar routines.
10. Basic ethics are taught concerning rules of conduct, that is, good sportsmanship and self-control in situations in which players are under tension.
11. Interscholastic teams motivate intramural and other participation by examples of excellence, raising the levels of aspiration of younger and less skilled youth.

Weaknesses

1. Interscholastic athletic programs emphasize the physical development of a few skillful performers and neglect the ordinary student.
2. Participation disrupts regular school routine at times, such as basketball tournaments and games in the middle of the week.
3. Rivalry encourages various types of "gang warfare" between students of different schools.
4. Competition places undue pressure on some coaches, who would like to be regarded in the same category as other teachers.
5. Booster clubs and outside interests, such as radio, press, and television, often gain control of the program and persuade players to become "professional" in attitude.
6. Too often, many schools have to compete out of their class.
7. "All-star" and/or postseason contests tend to prolong the season unduly.

8. There is not enough adequate medical supervision.
9. Facilities and equipment are often inadequate for the sports attempted.
10. Varsity programs are given an importance that preempts the value of facilities and the proper use of budgets, especially to the detriment of the intramural programs.
11. The need for financing programs leads to commercialism and "ballyhoo."
12. There is undue attention in the form of expensive awards, banquets, etc., which gives immature youth a distorted sense of values and estimation of their own importance and makes them seek special privileges.
13. There is a tendency to belittle the intramural program.
14. Severe demands on endurance and overfatigue may slow up students' growth processes.

As long as athletics are handled as entertainment rather than education, the financial aspects will be a source of trouble. We do not expect education in the industrial arts or fine arts laboratories to make a profit or depend on admissions to exhibits to finance the educational program. As long as many physical education classes and intramural activities depend on athletic gate receipts for supplies and equipment, we cannot solve the athletics-education problem satisfactorily.

PLATFORMS, STANDARDS, AND GUIDING POLICIES FOR INTERSCHOLASTIC ATHLETICS

As one reviews the historical evolution and development of interscholastic programs, the same problems and issues seem to be evident today as were cited in the early stages of their development. Platforms, standards, and policies stated from the 1930s to the 1970s still have significance and meaning to the critical issues and problems of today.

A platform

In 1937, the late Dr. Thurman B. Rice, formerly Chief, Bureau of Health and Physical Education of the Indiana State Board of Health, was requested to prepare a brief formal statement of Indiana's platform with regard to physical education and athletics. Even though the platform was stated in the late 1930s, it should be critically analyzed as to its relevance to the problems and issues we face today in conducting a well-balanced school program that includes physical education, intramurals, and interscholastic athletics.

1. We are interested in the physical education and development of all children.
2. We are more interested in the development of skill, speed, strength, endurance and health than in winning games and trophies.
3. We are willing to grant interschool sports the star role, but are not willing to make them the whole show.
4. We are interested in development and training in "carry-over" sports and games which may be useful in leisure time in later life, during periods of convalescence and in old age.
5. We believe that the leadership and control in matters pertaining to physical education (including athletics) should be in the hands of those trained and accredited in the principles and practices of physical education.
6. We believe that the tenure of a coach should depend upon his effectiveness (by precept and example) in teaching health, character, and sportsmanship, rather than upon the ability of his teams to win games.
7. We insist that since physical education is a required subject in the secondary school curriculum, it shall include all children in such schools, and that it shall include in particular those who need it most.
8. We are opposed to the exploitation and commercialization of athletes and athletic teams. The first consideration must be the welfare of the student.
9. We are opposed to those influences which place excessive emphasis upon a particular

sport, game, or athlete and do not take into consideration the full well-rounded school program as a whole.*

Standards

Athletics are vital in the program of education for youth and adults. Athletics should be used to develop and promote worthwhile educational goals. If athletics are to serve useful ends, they must be wisely guided, thoroughly supported, and wholeheartedly accepted. Participants, parents, and educators must understand the dynamic character of athletics—a force for good or a force for evil. All who are involved must insist that athletics conducted for our school youth shall be organized, developed, and administered as a vital and effective aspect of American culture. The responsibility of the school, its administrator, its staff, and its membership begins when a boy or girl becomes a member of the school and continues until he/she has graduated or withdrawn from it. This responsibility involves the student's way of living, his/her attitudes toward life, his/her views of human relationships, and the ways of promoting desirable changes in his/her behavior. This responsibility rests primarily with the school. It cannot be shirked or taken lightly. Will we as educators—as leaders of youth—assume this obligation and responsibility?

There are a number of controversies and misunderstandings in the present-day school athletic program that are causing grave concern:

1. The purpose of athletics. This involves such questions as, Are athletics for competition and to develop cooperation? Should one play to win and be judged only on such results? Are there other vital educational values?
2. Leadership. To clarify the issues here, there should be standards for the selection of lead-

*Reprinted from the *Monthly Bulletin,* Indiana Division of Public Health, June 1937, p. 107.

ers, their preparation, and the procedures in carrying out leadership duties.
3. Nature and scope of the administration and supervision of athletics. This involves sanction of contests, all-star games, bowl games, alumni administrative participation, procurement and use of facilities, financing, athletic schedules, conference and association tournaments, preseason and postseason games and practices, player and spectator control, recruiting, proselytizing, subsidization of players, public relations, and exploitation.
4. The participants. Involved here are considerations and standards of eligibility, parity of competition, traditional rivals, protection of participants, amateurism, and awards.
5. Activities. Are the activities selected, organized, and adapted to the needs of the participants?
6. Values and outcomes proposed and realized through interscholastic athletics. The need for standards and criteria for determining the worthiness of our interscholastic athletic programs is evident.

The National Federation of State High School Athletic Associations, the National Association of Secondary School Principals, and the American Alliance for Health, Physical Education, Recreation, and Dance are cooperating through a joint committee to recognize the fine progress that has already been made in the establishment of athletic standards, the indication of the best practices and interpretations, so that every secondary school may look critically at itself and, as a result, provide an effective educational athletic program. Basic to any consideration of acceptable standards in interscholastic athletics for secondary schools is the following statement of guiding policies for the organization, administration, and the development of a program of athletics for the youth of our schools.

Guiding policies

The guiding policies stated here are expressed in more complete detail in the *Offi-*

cial Handbook of the National Federation of State High School Athletic Associations as "Cardinal Athletic Principles"*:

1. Be closely coordinated with the general instructional program and properly articulated with other departments of the school.
2. Be sure that the number of students accommodated and the educational aims achieved justify the use of tax funds for its support and also justify use of other sources of income, provided the time and attention which is given to the collection of such funds is not such as to interfere with the efficiency of the athletic program or of any other department of the school.
3. Be based on the spirit of non-professionalism so that participation is regarded as a privilege to be won by training and proficiency and to be valued highly enough to eliminate any need for excessive use of adulatory demonstrations or of expensive prizes or awards.
4. Confine the school athletic activity to events which are sponsored and supervised by the proper school authorities so that exploitation or improper use of prestige built up by school teams or members of such teams may be avoided.
5. Be planned so as to result in opportunity for many individuals to explore a wide variety of sports, and in reasonable season limits for each sport.
6. Be controlled so as to avoid the elements of professionalism and commercialism which tend to grow up in connection with widely publicized "bowl" contests, barnstorming trips and interstate or intersectional contests which require excessive travel expense or loss of school time or which are bracketed with educational travel claims in an attempt to justify privileges for a few at the expense of decreased opportunity for many.

7. Be kept free from the type of contest which involves a gathering of so-called "all-stars" from different schools to participate in contests which may be used as a gathering place for representatives of certain colleges or professional organizations who are interested in soliciting athletic talent.
8. Include training in conduct and game ethics to reach all non-participating students and community followers of the school teams in order to insure a proper understanding and appreciation of the sports skills and of the need for adherence to principles of fair play and right prejudices.
9. Encourage a balanced program of intramural activity in grades below the ninth to make it unnecessary to sponsor contests of a championship nature in these grades.
10. Engender respect for the local, state and national rules and policies under which the school program is conducted.

We have here a series of sound principles and rules that compose a charter—a statement of fundamental philosophy that may be used as a guideline to determine whether a particular plan or act that is under consideration or in operation is in accord with the best principles of education.

INTERCOLLEGIATE ATHLETIC PROGRAMS

Athletics are an integral part of the physical education program as well as part of the American educational process. Their place in the curriculum should depend on their contribution to the better education of students and the absence of anything that impedes the educational process. In this position, athletics are not ends in themselves but means. When gate receipts, the prestige of the coach, and other factors become ends, the concern for the best development of the individual is apt to be lessened to the detriment of the cause of education.

This is no place to review the history of

*From National Federation of State High School Associations. *1974-1975 official handbook.* Elgin, Ill.: The Federation, 1974, pp. 9-10.

intercollegiate athletics in the fabric of American life, into which it is so deeply woven. For this purpose, several excellent references appear in the Bibliography of the text. Rather, a brief comment will be made concerning the efforts to integrate intercollegiate athletics into the program of general education so that they are not "sideshows" but a genuine part of the educational curriculum of the colleges and universities.

PLATFORMS AND GUIDING POLICIES FOR INTERCOLLEGIATE ATHLETICS

In facing the task of integration in a school's mission, we are inevitably drawn into the problem of policy-making. If the curriculum is the life and program of the institution and represents efforts to translate a social and educational philosophy into practices, we might start with a few basic assumptions. The first logical assumption is that athletics per se are neither good nor bad. Second, their "goodness" or "badness" will be determined by the standards of value established and the policies under which they are administered and taught. We can never escape from the educational mission of a college or university and the contribution of athletics to the achievement of this mission. The late President Guerry of Sewanee, in an address before the National Collegiate Athletic Association, touched on the question of subsidization:

To give its students a sense of values is one of the main and one of the essential objectives of education and an educational institution. When, however, a college or university places such undue emphasis upon the importance of a winning subsidized team as compared with its apparent emphasis upon the real qualities of an educational institution, and when a college or university pays its top teachers and scholars, the men upon whom the college or university rests,

far less than its football coach, the result is a distortion of values. The actual result is that colleges and universities are destroying a sense of values for the students and the public. . . .

These institutions undermine the very objectives they are created to achieve. They fail in the mission they were established to fulfill.

A platform

At its Board of Governors meeting in 1976, the American Alliance for Health, Physical Education, and Recreation approved the following statement as a platform for intercollegiate athletics:

COLLEGIATE SPORT MANIFESTO

(A Subscription to Sanity)

Athletics is a unique phenomenon. Its conduct in colleges and universities reflects diversity and emphasizes a multitude of values. Primarily, athletics provides students an opportunity to be involved in sport. In addition, athletic contests may be a part of university/college public relations and used for community enrichment.

The university/college must be attentive to the worth of the assets and the risk of each liability afforded by sport. Institutional values in establishing priorities for the conduct of athletic programs must be weighed carefully. The autonomy of the university/college in such decision making is absolute. The institutional autonomy conveys social responsibility.

Within the conduct of athletics there are certain moral absolutes. Responsible people are of the ethical persuasion that: The welfare of the athlete must be basic to all decisions regarding sport. The conduct of athletic programs must have an educational orientation. Athletic programs must afford equality of opportunity for all who desire to participate.

The concept of "fairness" must undergird the ethical code employed in the governance of athletics.

The financing of athletic programs must reflect patterns used by other educational components of the institution.

All who are involved in sport programs must

assume responsibility for societal welfare, individual integrity and a moral subscription to the betterment of sport.

Guiding policies

Obviously, the intercollegiate athletic practices of some institutions are entirely incompatible with the aims and ideals of true education. Since this book deals with curriculum planning and development, it can only suggest certain policies and procedures that a number of thoughtful individuals and groups have found to be helpful:

1. A sound philosophy of education regards athletics as sport, not as business. Therefore financial policies should be determined with the welfare of the student, not financial profit, in mind.
2. All athletic monies should be considered as school funds and concentrated with the other institutional funds under one financial officer, the college or university treasurer.
3. A budget or complete financial plan carefully based on needs, expenditures, and probable income for a definite period should be provided for intercollegiate athletics.
4. A financial statement showing the exact status of accounts of the athletic department should be made annually.
5. A faculty advisory committee on athletics should be appointed by the president or faculty to act in an advisory capacity in the shaping of athletic policies.
6. Athletic coaches should have academic training commensurate with their teaching responsibilities and be accorded corresponding faculty rank.
7. Athletic coaches are teachers, should be employed on a full-time basis, and should render capable assistance in other phases of education besides coaching, such as physical education "service" classes, intramural athletics, and (if a professional "major" exists) in physical education major classes.
8. All athletic training should be under the direct supervision of a medical doctor, preferably the director of student health services.
9. All students participating in intercollegiate athletics should be physically fit and insured for adequate care and treatment of athletic injuries; whatever policy exists pertaining to injuries should be definitely made known to the participants.
10. Intercollegiate games should be played only on the grounds of educational institutions.
11. Postseason, including charity, and bowl games should be limited.
12. Institutions should prohibit intensive preseason practice in intercollegiate sports.
13. Absences from classes by athletes for intercollegiate contests should be limited to a specific number of days.
14. Academic standards for eligibility should be rigidly adhered to.
15. Athletic contests should be engaged in only with other educational institutions, preferably those of similar size and athletic ideals, for instance, standards of admission, eligibility, and training practices.

Policies are basic agreements arrived at after considering all the pros and cons—all the valid evidence available. Policies are guiding rules for action toward desired goals. Athletic policies, then, are based on certain facts and principles and represent what is best under the circumstances.

Many colleges and universities are restudying their athletic policies. They are finding that participation in some competitive sports that require elaborate and expensive facilities for public entertainment are not in accord with the purposes of higher education, and furthermore, they find the financial outlay prohibitive. There is a definite trend toward the formulation of clear-cut policies to clarify for students, faculty, and alumni the philosophy guiding the conduct of intercollegiate sport and why certain policies have been followed.

INTERSCHOLASTIC AND INTERCOLLEGIATE ATHLETIC PROGRAMS FOR GIRLS AND WOMEN

Programs for girls and women are treated separately in this unit because of the "newness" and rapid growth of these programs due to the impact of Title IX regulations, a part of the Education Amendment Act of 1972 that relates to discrimination on the basis of sex in education programs receiving federal financial assistance.

In the area of interscholastic and intercollegiate competition, the same inherent values that were ascribed to the program for boys apply also to girls. In the past, girls in general have been overprotected and boys underprotected, particularly during the adolescent period. However, the drive for competitive sport is as strong in most girls as in most boys, so that the need for an intensive and extensive program of extramural competition is as great for girls as for boys.

The value of the whole experience depends on the leadership. The leaders in the field of girls' and women's athletics have been determined to try to avoid the dangers and evils that too often accompany the boys' interscholastic and intercollegiate program. They have been conservative in their approach to the problems inherent in varsity competition, whether on the high school or college level, knowing that trained leadership among the women must guide the course of development, and competent leadership comes gradually. Presently, this leadership is being provided by the organizations that govern interscholastic and intercollegiate athletic programs, either as advisory or regulatory groups. These are the National Association for Girls and Women in Sport (NAGWS), the Association for Intercollegiate Athletics for Women (AIAW), College Women in Sport (CWS), and the National Federation of State High School Associations (NFSHSA).

The critical issues and problems confronting girls' and women's programs are similar to those identified for the boys' and men's programs. Therefore the same platforms, standards, and guiding policies previously recommended are tenable for the organization and administration of interscholastic and intercollegiate athletic programs for girls and women. Further readings are recommended related to the basic beliefs, policies, procedures, and purposes stated by the organizations and institutions directly responsible for the conduct of these programs.

REACTORS

1. The primary criterion for the acceptance of any activity in the curriculum of an educational institution is, Does the activity contribute to the educational purposes of the institution?
2. Unfavorable outcomes of interschool athletic competition are the results of educational mismanagement.
3. There is a need for more valid data-based information regarding the effect of athletic competition on youth below the senior high level.
4. As long as many physical education and intramural activities depend on athletic gate receipts, we cannot solve the athletic-educational problem satisfactorily.
5. The same problems and critical issues exist in athletic programs today as were present decades ago.
6. In athletic competition, should one play to win and be judged only on such results, or are there other vital educational values?
7. Athletics is a unique phenomenon.
8. The conduct of athletics must have an educational orientation.

9. The same inherent values that were ascribed to the athletic programs for boys apply also to girls.

LEARNING ACTIVITIES

1. Synthesize from available evidence the pros and cons of interscholastic athletics below senior high school.
   a. State your conclusions.
   b. State a rationale.
2. Devise a set of oranizational and administrative policies for a school system's athletic program, specific to the following topics:
   a. Administrative structure
   b. Budget
   c. Requisition of equipment and emphasis
   d. Travel
   e. Number of games
   f. Practice sessions
   g. Facility practice scheduling
   h. Coaches' responsibilities
   i. Players' eligibility
   j. Medical examinations
   k. Legal liability
   l. First aid and accident procedures
   m. Maintenance and storage of equipment
3. Develop a checklist for Title IX regulations.
   a. Select a school, college, or university.
   b. Administer the checklist.
4. Formulate your personal athletic philosophy.

UNIT EVALUATIVE CRITERIA

Can you:
1. Explain the implications of Title IX for athletic programs?
2. Translate the educational purposes of the school into beliefs, standards, and policies for the organization and administration of an athletic program?
3. Compare and construct the philosophy between the instruction, intramural, and athletic programs?
4. Develop a policy handbook for the governance and regulation of an interscholastic/intercollegiate athletic program?

RESOURCES

Association for Intercollegiate Athletics for Women. *AIAW handbook of policies and operating procedures. 1974-1975.* Washington, D.C.: American Alliance for Health, Physical Education, & Recreation, 1974.

Bucher, C. A. *Administration of health and physical education programs, including athletics* (6th ed.). St. Louis: The C. V. Mosby Co., 1975.

Bucher, C. A., & Koenig, C. *Methods and materials for secondary school physical education* (5th ed.). St. Louis; The C. V. Mosby Co., 1978.

Coakley, J. J. *Sport in society: issues and controversies.* St. Louis: The C. V. Mosby Co., 1978.

Deatherage, D., & Reid, C. P. *Administration of women's competitive sports.* Dubuque, Iowa: William C. Brown Co., Publishers, 1977.

Division for Girls and Women's Sports. *Philosophy and standards for girls and women's sports.* Washington, D.C.: American Alliance for Health, Physical Education, & Recreation, 1973.

Dodson, C. How to comply with Title IX. In *Proceedings of the National Federation's Fifth Annual National Conference of High School Directors of Athletics.* Elgin, Ill.: Dec., 1974.

Frost, R., & Marshall, S. J. *Administration of physical education and athletics, concepts and practices.* Dubuque, Iowa: William C. Brown Co., Publishers, 1977.

Gerber, E. W., Felshin, J., Berlin, P., & Wyrick, W. *The American woman in sport.* Reading, Mass.: Addison-Wesley Publishing Co., Inc., 1974.

Hart, M. *Sport in the sociocultural process.* Dubuque, Iowa: William C. Brown Co., Publishers, 1976.

Michener, J. A. *Sports in America.* New York: Random House, Inc., 1976.

National Federation of State High School Associations. *1970-71 NFSHSAA handbook.* Elgin, Ill.: The Federation, 1971.

National Federation of State High School Associations. *1974-1975 official handbook.* Elgin, Ill.: The Federation, 1974.

School athletics—problems and policies. Washington,

D.C.: The Educational Policies Commission of the National Education Association of the United States and the American Association of School Administrators, 1954.

Shea, E. J., & Wieman, E. W. *Administrative policies for intercollegiate athletics.* Springfield, Ill.: Charles C Thomas, Publisher, 1976.

The sports and recreational programs of the nation's universities and colleges, report No. 4. Kansas City, Mo.: The National Collegiate Athletic Association, n.p., 1974.

PART FIVE

THE CURRICULUM
synthesis and assessment

UNIT

24 Curriculum evaluation and appraisal

High sounding objectives filed away in our course of study have value only when we appraise the progress that we make toward them.

HENRY SMITH

Evaluation is a process by which changes in young people are appraised. Appraisal in the last analysis, is a value judgment about the goodness of change.

IRVING LORGE

24 Curriculum evaluation and appraisal

COMPETENCIES

After completing this unit you should be able to:

Identify the elements and processes in the development of a grade K through 12 physical education curriculum guide plan.

Translate the procedures for curriculum evaluation into action research.

Select valid and reliable methods for appraising a physical education program regarding its effect on stated objectives and purposes.

Revise a curriculum formulated from valid and reliable data-based evaluative information.

Define the following:
Measurement
Evaluation
Action research
Outcomes
Assessment
Appraisal
Interaction analysis

PERSPECTIVE

PRINCIPLE: Curriculum evaluation is a continuous process.

Different opinions and theories related to curriculum organization present problems to the administrator and physical education teacher. Even more important than the specific design or plan, perhaps, is the existence of a procedure that will lead to constant appraisal and improvement of the curriculum. Most important is the realization that curriculum improvement must consist of more than just published statements. The examination of the relative value and worth of the curriculum demands continuous appraisal and evaluation. This evaluation process should be engaged in by administrators, teachers, students, and parents in order to fully assess what is happening to students as a result of curricular experiences. For this, appropriate evidence must be collected regarding the quality and quantity of student change and outcomes.

Evaluation should result in an ever-increasing clarification, specification, and integration of objectives. It should result in greater consideration of the individuals to be educated as well as the instructional methods employed. It should provide insight as to the performances and achievement of students and their growth and development in the direction of realizing objectives. It should be concerned with both process and product.

Since children and youth must be educated for both individual competency and active useful participation in societal groups, an effective curriculum evaluation identifies outcomes. Some of these outcomes to be identified are as follows:

1. Knowledge and information
2. Principles and concepts
3. Understandings and meanings
4. Motor skills
5. Cognitive skills
6. Values
7. Appreciations
8. Interests
9. Attitudes
10. Ideals
11. Fitness qualities

If we firmly believe in the worth of the individual, then the curriculum must be concerned with the immediate needs and interests of the individual as well as the needs of society. There is an underlying principle of balance, trying to reconcile the rights and duties of oneself, other individuals, and society as a whole.

If we are to use the *latent* interests of children and youth, rather than follow their whims, the curriculum must be developed and examined in order to determine the extent to which we build on their immediate interests and capacities. These interests should guide them through enriching experiences that will lead to new and more significant contributions.

Good education requires progressive planning from the nursery school through the high school and college/university. The curriculum guide becomes the medium or basic instrument of the articulated educative process. It is in reality a guide for teachers and students of physical education and indicates how philosophy, with respect to physical education, is translated into action. It is an important administrative instructional aid and necessity for every school.

The final "learning activity" for the

teacher or student of physical education is to design and develop a curriculum guide plan for the school, implement it, and measure and evaluate its effect as to process and product.

The difference between measurement and evaluation is primarily a matter of scope, extent, and mental attitude. Quantitative measurement thrives best where factors of the educational process can be isolated as in learning facts (information) and specific skills (swimming, jumping, etc.). In measurement, the isolation of variables is very basic to scientific control. The more interdependent these variables become, the more difficult it is to isolate or measure them. Exact quantitative determination of educational results requires repetition and uniformity, but children and youth have individual differences. No two are exactly alike. The judgment of growth and achievement where growth is incomplete and ongoing is different from measurement of a finished product. Measurement is always quantitative, never qualitative. We are interested in determining not only present status but also the student's potential for future growth and development.

The terms "evaluation" and "appraisal" indicate that we are concerned with the consequences of educational efforts. Whenever we try to determine what is happening to boys and girls as a result of their physical education experiences, whenever we seek to determine how they are growing, developing, and achieving in terms of whatever values we accept, we are engaged in the process of evaluation. Therefore in contrasting measurement and evaluation, the central theme in evaluation is, What values do the individuals obtain from these learning experiences? Evaluation implies that direction is as important as progress. One deals here, not with single values, but with a multiplicity of values. Appraisal of all

the outcomes of learning, both quantitative and qualitative, is included in the concept of evaluation.

CURRICULUM RESEARCH

The function of evaluation and appraisal is closely related to the function of teaching. Therefore the problem of curriculum research is essentially one of appraising teaching. We evaluate or appraise a curriculum in terms of the accepted purposes of education. More difficult and just as important would be the task of appraising the effects of school programs on American society as a whole. There is a need for measurement and evaluation of the possible results of changed curricula and the changed conditions of learning aimed at objectives such as the following:

1. Personal and social development
2. Initiative and cooperation
3. Ability to find, interpret, and apply information in solving problems
4. Power to express creative impulses and experiences in the shop, in the art room, in the English classroom or gymnasium, or on the athletic field
5. Development of wholesome and constructive interests, attitudes, and ideals

Systematic gathering of data regarding the effectiveness of the physical education curriculum is essential to a dynamic physical education program. Maximum use of measurement and evaluation in curriculum development calls for teamwork and mutual understanding of purposes and procedures among all teachers in a school, and is an integral part of the total school evaluation program, which should aim at the common goal of providing the best possible instruction for the pupils.

Research and sound philosophy of physical education go hand in hand. Both are necessary and important to curriculum improvement. Research is as important in deriving objectives as in determining the extent to which the objectives have been achieved. Therefore in any attempt at overall appraisal of the curriculum of a school, one is forced to inquire into the following:

1. The degree to which the curriculum is keeping up with a changing society
2. The extent to which it is trying to change conditions for the better
3. The extent to which the products of the school are happier, wiser, better adjusted socially, more moral, healthier, stronger, more skillful, and more cooperative than under previous curricula
4. The extent to which one type of curriculum organization is more effective than another
5. The extent to which maturation, growth, and development should determine the scope and sequence of activities and curriculum policies
6. The effects of having pupils, parents, and other citizens participate in curriculum development
7. The extent to which radio, television, and other learning materials should affect and suggest curriculum relationships
8. The extent to which the curriculum should consider the supplementary and complementary effects of community programs

Research in all these areas is important for the fullest development of the physical education curriculum. The conception of what constitutes scientific procedure in curriculum construction is vague. Since we seek cause and effect relationships in research, the task is a difficult one. We lack refined procedures, not only for gathering data but also for interpreting it after we have it.

RESEARCH PROCEDURES

Since research is "simply a systematic and refined technique of thinking," the following steps are but a refined formulation of what has been implied previously:

1. Check the present status of offerings in terms of objectives, activities taught, instructional strategies, and evaluation techniques.
2. Glean and evaluate critically all available research reports having to do with physical education curricula at various levels.
3. Determine what constitutes the objectives of the school in terms of the advancing of democratic ideals through physical education (social philosophy).
4. Clarify and establish what constitutes the biological conception of education—that education is a dynamic process in response to inner needs and by means of self-activity (educational philosophy).
5. Consider carefully and list the physical, social, psychological, emotional, and mental characteristics of the age level or levels to be considered in the curriculum.
6. Examine and list the cultural needs of the group or groups under consideration. What does society require or expect of, for example, tenth graders?
7. Consider the organismic needs of the pupils for which curriculum plans are being made (recognition, approval, appreciation, status, new experience, excitement, adventure, affection, being wanted, a sense of "belonging," power, a sense of mastery and achievement, a sense of protection, and security).
8. Suggest tentatively the means and conditions that should be provided so that the "needs" in No. 7 may be satisfied (playing on a team, increasing skill and strength, learning to swim, and so forth).
9. State the objectives for the direction in which you are trying to change students: physical, psychomotor, cognitive, and affective domains.
10. Analyze curriculum content. What is taught to achieve objectives (here some direct comparison should be made between what is taught in the present curriculum and what should be taught)?
    a. Games, sports, athletics, including "lead-up" games of low organization
    b. Aquatic activities
    c. Dance (fundamental rhythms, folk,

modern, square, social dancing) activities
  d. Self-testing activities
  e. Developmental activities
  f. Outdoor education activities
  g. Recreational activities
11. Determine how the desired experiences are to be organized for teaching and learning or how to do what is needed.
12. Develop instructional strategies and materials.
13. Involve teachers in the development of curriculum guides for their assistance.
14. Try out the curriculum experimentally. (Needless to say, the entire school system would not be involved at first. Curriculum research might deal with one experimental school, with other schools being used as controls.)
15. Establish valid and inclusive evaluative criteria.

CURRICULUM EVALUATION

Unless objectives really make a difference to what we do as teachers, their formulation is simply a waste of time. Objectives as goals of achievement represent preferences, choices of values. As we change our objectives or values, we must develop new strategies for teaching. Furthermore, we must eliminate the discrepancy between our objectives and our practices by relating our goals more closely to the methods of reaching and testing them.

Goals or objectives in physical education represent plans of action for orienting and changing the behavior and developmental growth of individuals in certain desirable directions. These have all been discussed. Teachers and administrators cannot stop with the formulation of goals. The most urgent next step is to implement or translate them into concrete and specific curricula. Here, we face the important task of evaluating or appraising the extent to which we make good what our curriculum

objectives promise in the way of changes in pupils.

If we examine a large number of physical education curricula and find that our own practices do not differ from those examined, can we assume that our practices are necessarily sound? This would be similar to solving important social and economic problems by a "show of hands" instead of applying valid principles related to sociology and cultural anthropology (the nature and needs of society), developmental physiology (how the individual grows, develops, and learns), and psychology (the nature and needs of the individual).

EVALUATION PROCEDURES

Curriculum-making and evaluation are two closely related aspects of an educational program in physical education. A truly comprehensive evaluation should provide evidence of the effectiveness of the educational process in attaining the purposes of physical education. New evidence should lead to new curriculum policies and practices and, perhaps, even to new objectives.

Designs for the evaluation of an educational program or curriculum have broadened in scope and now include related measurements of a comprehensive range of major objectives. Evaluation of larger and more complex aspects of behavior is now possible and desirable, since the conception of education is concerned with related aspects of affective development as well as skill and information.

Since it is virtually impossible to teach what we are unable to evaluate, and we can direct or redirect the course of learning only by evaluation, the following procedural steps are important:

1. Specifying in an understandable fashion the objectives set up by the curriculum. The

kinds of changes in behavior in the variety of aspects of pupil development must be considered. This statement would include specific skills, knowledges, attitudes, and ideals. It is assumed that the objectives themselves have been evaluated against certain criteria.

2. Classifying objectives under major types of categories. The categories are physical, psychomotor, cognitive, and affective domains.

3. Selecting the pupils in whom these objectives are to be realized, in whole or in part.

4. Defining objectives in terms of behavior. Whether we appraise change in behavior (learning) in French, swimming, or art appreciation, the most valid criterion is direct observation of what students do. The ability to resist fatigue as shown in the results of a 12-minute run is an aspect of behavior that we identify with the objective of cardiovascular endurance (classified under the physical domain).

5. Sportsmanship as an objective must be broken down into specific behaviors. The ascertainable degrees of change in behavior are the data for evaluation. These come from the careful inspection of the performances and achievement of individuals.

   a. Finding life situations where the kinds of behavior being evaluated may be directly observed. We must seek a comprehensive series of situations in which types of responses from pupils may be observed.

   b. Devising means—techniques or instruments—for obtaining a record of the pupils' behavior in these situations. This is a data-collecting task that involves the use of both qualitative and quantitative techniques. More subjective, yet valuable, appraisals would employ rating scales, observation time samples (for example, for number of social contacts, if one were studying socialization), personal-distance scales, similar sociometric devices, achievement scales, and numerous other devices.

6. The concept of change naturally requires at least two, and generally more, inspections;

therefore a cumulative record is important for curriculum evaluation.

   a. Putting the techniques or instruments to work by recording the pupil's behavior and evaluating it in the light of the standards formulated in step 1 (objectives).

   b. Practices must be evaluated in terms of their consequences. This demands a physical education curriculum with a purpose, directed by teachers who have a conscious educational philosophy and can translate this philosophy into teaching procedures and into the lives of boys and girls.

It is imperative to learn to appraise the effects of the educational processes in physical education in terms of the degree to which its purposes are being achieved. Essentially, this is the function of curriculum evaluation.

EVALUATION TECHNIQUES

Evaluation procedures provide answers to the question, Why do we evaluate? The next problem is, How do we evalute? What are the best techniques or instruments available for collecting relevant data that represent development aspects of individuals, or data that concern the environmental settings that affect their development? Techniques are "things that we do." Techniques or instruments are evaluating and measuring tools, tests, or devices.

The application of one technique does not supply all the necessary information needed to evaluate the effectiveness of the total program. There are many variables that influence and determine its worth. If evaluation is a process by which changes in individuals are appraised and appraisal is a value judgment about the goodness of change, then data must be obtained from a number of sources, using a variety of techniques, in order to make these value judgments.

Student evaluations

Many techniques can be used that measure a student's achievement or ability in quantity and quality amounts for the four objective domains—physical, psychomotor, cognitive, and affective. The selection of a technique should be determined by its appropriateness for a particular group, its relationship to the program objectives, its ability to supply data that can be interpreted in terms of both the process and product, and its feasibility of administration. One technique for measuring student outcomes would be to select and administer appropriate instruments that are available, such as physical and youth fitness tests, motor fitness tests, perceptual-motor tests, specific skill tests, knowledge tests, social behavioral tests, and personality tests. Other types of available instruments include rating scales, checklists, scorecards, questionnaires, affective behavior inventories, anecdotal reports, cumulative records, time sampling observations, critical incident analyses, and appraisal devices for clarifying one's values, self-concepts, and attitudes.

Newer techniques that provide immediate and summative feedback for student evaluation are the competency-based, mastery, and contracting instructional strategies. Established norms and data-based information from other sources can be used to identify criterion-referenced program objectives for these strategies. The qualitative and quantitative degrees of achievement for these objectives can be used for evaluation.

Evaluation of student/teacher interactions

Any curriculum appraisal must consider the variables of student/teacher relationships, interactions, and interventions in an instructional setting. The old adage "the curriculum is only as effective as the teacher" has strong implications for total curriculum evaluation.

Various coding and observational systems have been developed to identify, analyze, dissect, and categorize teaching behaviors, instructional management skills, student/teacher interactions, and teacher interventions.

Data-based information yielded by observational experiences, descriptive analytical studies, and interaction analyses, through in-class observations or by analyzing videotapes, can be used as bases for making value judgments regarding the relative influence and effect of the teacher in the learning process. These techniques show promise for identifying teaching behaviors, instructional management skills, and interactions that positively and negatively affect the curriculum.

Evaluation of the total program

The total physical education program can only be improved when it is viewed as a whole comprised of functioning parts. Evaluation of its parts gives some indication as to the effectiveness of its parts, but for curriculum evaluation to have meaning, it must include techniques that provide a more global evaluative perspective of the total program. A variety of techniques are available as tools for assisting elementary and secondary schools in assessing and improving the quality of their total physical education programs.

One of the earliest and most extensively used instruments is the LaPorte Health and Physical Education Score Card No. II developed by William Ralph LaPorte. It was designed to evaluate the total health and physical education program for elementary and secondary schools. State departments of instruction, in most states, and various national educational associations have either developed instruments or formulated criteria and standards for appraising physical education programs. Available instruments consist of scorecards, checklists, surveys, rating scales, and questionnaires. They may be used by an outside professional survey team or for self-evaluation. Instruments are presently available through state departments of education in California, Florida, Georgia, Illinois, Indiana, Michigan, New York, Ohio, Pennsylvania, Texas, Utah, and Wisconsin. Evaluative criteria and standards are available from the American Alliance for Health, Physical Education, and Recreation, the National Education Association, and the American Council on Education.

Cumulative data from the application of a variety of these techniques should indicate the extent to which the students' needs are met, the strengths and weaknesses of the program objectives, the quality of instruction, the qualitative and quantitative degree of students' achievement, and whether there is effective utilization of staff, facilities, and equipment. The result of a com-

prehensive and periodic assessment program should be the basis for curriculum revision and improvement.

SAMPLE EVALUATION INSTRUMENTS

ASSESSMENT GUIDE FOR SECONDARY SCHOOL PROGRAMS

(Developed under the auspices of the National Association for Sport and Physical Education, American Alliance for Health, Physical Education, and Recreation, Washington, D.C.)

This is a functional, easily administered assessment instrument that permits a self-study and evaluation of four secondary school program areas:

1. Administration
2. Instructional program
3. Intramural program
4. Athletic program

It consists of program or criterion statements requiring a *Yes* or *No* answer. A negative response is indicative of program problem areas.

The table below and on p. 385 illustrates 3 of the 15 criteria statements for the instructional program.

Instructional program

Criteria	Response (circle)	Notes
1. Cooperation and communication with presecondary physical education units in curriculum development is evidenced by a sequential school district physical education curriculum that avoids unnecessary repetition of subject matter.	Yes No	
2. A written statement of program goals and objectives for the instructional physical education program is available. The following areas are included in the statement:	Yes No	
a. Evaluation and remedial development of fundamental motor capabilities	Yes No	
b. Organization, development, and refinement of skillful movement in sport, dance, and exercise	Yes No	
c. Organization and performance of creative and inventive movement patterns designed to serve the individual purposes of the learner	Yes No	

Instructional program—cont'd

Criteria	Response (circle)		Notes
d. Knowledge of the basic theoretical concepts of gross motor behavior as it relates to sport, dance, and physical fitness	Yes	No	
e. Development of social, intellectual, and emotional objectives congruent with general educational goals through physical education experiences	Yes	No	
3. Instructional program areas that are designed to meet objectives focusing on the evaluation and remedial development of effective movement fundamentals include the following units as *required* courses or unit objectives:			
a. Evaluation of motor ability of incoming students	Yes	No	
b. Basic conceptual knowledge of motor efficiency	Yes	No	
c. Remedial fundamental movement instruction	Yes	No	

In addition to the criteria checklist is an evaluative summary sheet for indicating area weaknesses, strengths, and future direction. The value of this instrument is that it assesses not only the physical education program but the intramural and athletic programs as well.

PHYSICAL EDUCATION SCORECARD FOR ELEMENTARY AND SECONDARY SCHOOLS

(Courtesy Indiana State Board of Health and State Department of Instruction, Indianapolis, Ind.)

A physical education scorecard for evaluating elementary and secondary schools in Indiana was the result of a cooperative effort by the state board of health and the state universities. It was originally designed to be administered by a state survey team but later revised and expanded to be used as a self-evaluative instrument.

The total scorecard consists of five major areas divided into subareas with scoring and weighting values. Norms are available for determining the effectiveness of each area. The final major areas and their subareas are:

1. *Administration (15%)*—managerial procedures, standards, and policies
2. *Program activities (25%)*—selected learning experiences and activities
3. *Facilities and materials (20%)*—available instructional areas, equipment, and supplies
4. *Class management (15%)*—organizational and routine administrative factors controlled by the teacher in an instructional setting
5. *Instruction (25%)*—methods, techniques, teaching procedures, and teacher characteristics in a learning situation (This area is not to be used for self-evaluation.)

Separate scorecard booklets are available for grades 1 to 6 and grades 7 to 12. Norms are available for secondary schools, so that more meaningful comparisons can be made with results achieved by comparable Indiana schools.

REACTORS

1. Educational "lag" means that good curriculum theory is about 20 years ahead of actual practice.

2. The curriculum translates philosophy into action.

3. The curriculum is based on the latent inter-

ests of young people rather than their whims.
4. Good education requires progressive planning from the nursery school through the high school and college/university.
5. Systematic gathering of data regarding the effectiveness of the physical education curriculum is essential to a dynamic program.
6. Curriculum evaluation and development form a continuous process.
7. When is curriculum revision not research?
8. Measurement is always quantitative, never qualitative.

LEARNING ACTIVITIES

1. Educational "lag" means that good curriculum theory is about 20 years ahead of actual practice. Examine the programs of physical education in several schools of your state. Compare their actual practices with the basic assumptions on which a good program of physical education should be built. Compare assumptions versus actual practice under the following:
   a. Philosophical point of view
   b. Aims
   c. Instructional content (activities)
   d. Organization
   e. Procedures
   f. Recording and appraising student progress
2. You and your high school faculty colleagues have accepted as some of the overall purposes of the school the following series of abilities in which the school seeks positive change in students:
   a. To think effectively
   b. To observe, collect information, and organize data
   c. To infer and generalize from data and to apply principles
   d. To develop social sensitivity and social awareness
   e. To acquire a wide range of abiding and significant interests
   f. To develop better personal-social adjustment, make satisfactory heterosexual adjustments, and cooperate with others
   g. To initiate action, direct oneself, and develop a sense of responsibility

h. To develop an increased appreciation of esthetic values through music, art, literature, and use of the body as a medium of expression
   i. To develop, improve, and maintain physical and mental health by being at peace with the "self," having a positive and wholesome self-regarding attitude and a sense of serenity—"feeling at home" in one's own skin
   j. To develop a consistent system of values, a philosophy of life
   In terms of curriculum research, how would you attempt to determine the extent to which the physical education curriculum is contributing to these worthwhile objectives that permeate every area (science, home economics, mathematics, physical education, social studies) of the school?
3. Your superintendent is faced with budgeting problems. You are asked to indicate what the minimum essentials in a public school physical education curriculum are. Reply.
4. Survey a community:
   a. What social pressure groups strongly influence the physical education curriculum?
   b. What affects the athletic programs?
   c. How?
5. Formulate a continuous evaluation process that could be an integral part of the curriculum.
6. List valid and reliable measurement techniques for curriculum evaluation.
7. Design a research proposal to determine the effects of the physical education and intramural and interscholastic programs on high school graduates.

UNIT EVALUATIVE CRITERIA

Can you:
1. Translate your philosophy (education and physical education) into action through the development of a functional and effective curriculum?
2. Design and implement a curriculum research proposal?
3. Identify valid and reliable techniques for curriculum evaluation?

RESOURCES

AAHPER. *Assessment guide for secondary school physical education programs.* Washington, D.C.: The Alliance, 1977.

AAHPER. *Curriculum improvement in secondary school physical education.* Washington, D.C.: The Alliance, 1973.

AAHPER. *Evaluating the high school athletic program.* Washington, D.C.: The Alliance, 1973.

American Educational Research Association. Curriculum. *Review of Educational Research,* 1969, *39*(2), 283-375. (Also in June, 1960, 1963, and 1966 issues.)

American Educational Research Association. *Perspectives of curriculum evaluation* (Monograph Series on Curriculum Evaluation. O. Smith, Ed.). Chicago: Rand McNally & Co., 1967.

Beauchamp, G. A., & Beauchamp, K. E. *Comparative analysis of curriculum systems.* Wilmette, Ill.: Kagg Press, 1967.

Berman, L. M., & Roderick, J. A. *Feeling, valuating, and the art of growing: insights into the affective.* Washington, D.C.: Association for Supervision & Curriculum Development, 1977.

Carr, W. G. *Values and the curriculum: a report of the Fourth International Curriculum Conference.* Washington, D.C.: NEA Center for the Study of Instruction, 1970.

Cheffers, J., Amidor, E. J., & Rodger, K. D. *Interaction analysis: an application of nonverbal activity.* Minneapolis: Minnesota Association for Productive Teaching, 1974.

Flanders, N. A. *Analyzing teaching behavior.* Reading, Mass.: Addison-Wesley Publishing Co., Inc., 1970.

Foshay, A. W. Curriculum. In R. L. Ebel (Ed.), *Encyclopedia of educational research* (4th ed.). London: Macmillan London Ltd., 1969.

Huebner, D. (Ed.). *A reassessment of the curriculum.* New York: Teachers' College, Columbia University, 1964.

Indiana State Board of Health. *Indiana physical education score card for elementary and secondary schools.* Indianapolis: The Board, 1969.

Nixon, J. E., & Locke, L. F. Research on teaching physical education. In R. M. W. Travers (Ed.), *Second handbook of research on teaching.* Chicago: Rand McNally & Co., 1973.

Parker, J. C., & Rubin, L. J. *Process as content: curriculum design and the application of knowledge.* Chicago: Rand McNally & Co., 1966.

APPENDIX A Selected bibliography

CURRICULUM

AAHPER. *Professional preparation in dance, physical education, recreational education, safety education, and school health education.* Washington, D.C.: The Alliance, 1974.

AAHPER. *Curriculum design: purposes and processes in physical education teaching-learning.* Washington D.C.: The Alliance, 1977.

AAHPER. *Knowledge and understanding in physical education.* Washington, D.C.: The Alliance, 1978.

ASCD. *Curricular concerns in a revolutionary era.* Washington, D.C.: The Association, 1971.

Baley, J. E., & Field, D. A. *Physical education and the physical educator.* Boston: Allyn & Bacon, Inc., 1970.

Behee, J. *Hail to the victors.* Ann Arbor, Mich.: Swenk-Tuttle Press, Inc., 1974.

Blanchard, V. S. *Curriculum problems in health and physical education.* New York: A. S. Barnes & Co., Inc., 1942.

Brown, C., & Cassidy, R. *Theory in physical education—a guide to program change.* Philadelphia: Lea & Febiger, 1963.

Bucher, C. A., & Goldmann, M. *Dimensions in physical education,* St. Louis: The C. V. Mosby Co., 1974.

□ A very special thanks to Sharon Otto and Stephanie Korschot for their invaluable assistance in compiling these materials.

Bucher, C. A., & Koening, C. R. *Methods and materials for secondary school physical education* (5th ed.). St. Louis: The C. V. Mosby Co., 1978.

Cassidy, R. *Curriculum development in physical education.* New York: Harper & Row, Publishers, Inc., 1954.

Cassidy, R., & Caldwell, S. F. *Humanizing physical education.* Dubuque, Iowa: William C. Brown Co., Publishers, 1974.

Cheffers, J., & Evaul, T. *Introduction to physical education: concepts of human movement.* Englewood Cliffs, N.J.: Prentice-Hall, Inc., 1978.

Christine, C. T., & Christine, D. V. *Practical guide to curriculum and instruction.* West Nyack, N.Y.: Parker Publishers Co., Inc., 1971.

Corbin, C., Dowell, L., Lindsey, R., & Tolson, H. *Concepts in physical education with laboratories and experiments.* Dubuque, Iowa: William C. Brown Co., Publishers, 1974.

Cowell, C. C. *Scientific foundations of physical education.* New York: Harper & Row, Publishers, Inc., 1953.

Cowell, C. C., & Hazelton, H. W. *Curriculum designs in physical education.* Englewood Cliffs, N.J.: Prentice-Hall, Inc., 1955.

Cowell, C. C., & Schwehn, H. *Modern principles and methods in high school physical education.* Boston: Allyn & Bacon, Inc., 1958.

Cratty, B. J. *Social dimensions of physical education.* Englewood Cliffs, N.J.: Prentice-Hall, Inc., 1967.

388

Cratty, B. J. *Psychology and motor activity*. Englewood Cliffs, N.J.: Prentice-Hall, Inc., 1970.

Daugherty, G. *Methods in physical education and health for secondary schools*. Philadelphia: W. B. Saunders Co., 1967.

Davis, E. C., & Wallis, E. L. *Toward better teaching in physical education*. Englewood Cliffs, N.J.: Prentice-Hall, Inc., 1962.

Duncan, R. O., & Watson, H. B. *Introduction to physical education*. New York: The Ronald Press Co., 1960.

Edwards, N., & Richey, H. G. *The school in the American social order*. Boston: Houghton Mifflin Co., 1963.

Fabricius, H. *Physical education for the classroom teacher*. Dubuque, Iowa: William C. Brown Co., Publishers, 1971.

Felshin, J. *More than movement: an introduction to physical education*. Philadelphia: Lea & Febiger, 1972.

Frost, R. B. *Shaping up to quality in physical education*. New London, Conn.: Croft Educational Series, 1968.

Harrow, A. J. *A taxonomy of the psychomotor domain*. New York: David McKay Co., Inc., 1972.

Heidenreich, R. R. *Improvements in curriculum*. Va.: College Readings Inc., 1972.

Heitmann, H. M. *Organizational patterns for instruction in physical education*. Washington, D.C.: American Alliance for Health, Physical Education, and Recreation, 1971.

Holland, G., & Davis, E. *Values of physical activity*. Dubuque, Iowa: William C. Brown Co., Publishers, 1975.

Insley, G. S. *Practical guidelines for the teaching of physical education*. Reading, Mass.: Addison-Wesley Publishing Co., Inc., 1973.

Irwin, L. W. *The curriculum in health and physical education*. Dubuque, Iowa: William C. Brown Co., Publishers, 1960.

Ismail, A., & Gruber, J. *Motor aptitude and intellectual performance*. Columbus, Ohio: Charles E. Merrill Publishing Co., 1967.

Jewett, A. E., & Mullan, M. R. *Curriculum design: purposes and processes in physical education teaching-learning*. Washington, D.C.: American Alliance for Health, Physical Education, and Recreation, 1977.

Kane, J. E. *Movement studies in physical education*. Boston: Routledge & Kegan Paul Ltd., 1977.

Kruger, H., & Myers, J. *Movement education in physical education*. Dubuque, Iowa: William C. Brown Co., Publishers, 1977.

Kryspin, W., & Feldhusen, J. *Writing behavioral objectives*. Minneapolis: Burgess Publishing Co., 1974.

LaPorte, W. R. *The physical education curriculum*. Los Angeles: University of Southern California Press, 1968.

Larson, L. A. *Curriculum foundations and standards for physical education*. Englewood Cliffs, N.J.: Prentice-Hall, Inc., 1970.

Lockhart, A., & Slusher, H. *Contemporary readings in physical education*. Dubuque, Iowa: William C. Brown Co., Publishers, 1975.

MacKenzie, M. M. *Toward a new curriculum in physical education*. New York: McGraw-Hill Book Co., 1969.

Metheney, E. *Connotations of movement in sport and dance*. Dubuque, Iowa: William C. Brown Co., Publishers, 1965.

Metheney, E. *Movement and meaning*. New York: McGraw-Hill Book Co., 1968.

Michigan Department of Education. *Elementary and secondary minimal performance objectives for physical education*. Ann Arbor, Mich.: The Department, 1973.

Nagel, C. *Methods guidebook in physical education and recreation*. Palo Alto, Calif.: The National Press, 1959.

Nash, J. B. *Physical education: interpretations and objectives*. New York: A. S. Barnes & Co., Inc., 1948.

Netcher, J. R. *A management model for competency-based HPER programs*. St. Louis: The C. V. Mosby Co., 1977.

Nixon, J. F., & Jewett, A. E. *Physical education curriculum*. New York: John Wiley & Sons, Inc., 1964.

Nixon, J. F., & Jewett, A. E. *An introduction to physical education*. Philadelphia: W. B. Saunders Co., 1974.

Nixon, J. F., & Ulrich, C. *Tones of theory*. Washington, D.C.: American Alliance for Health, Physical Education, and Recreation, 1972.

Oxendine, J. B. *Psychology of motor learning*. New York: Appleton-Century-Crofts, 1968.

Penman, K. A. *Physical education for college students*. St. Louis: The C. V. Mosby Co., 1968.

Russell, J. *Modular instruction, a guide to design, selection, utilization and evaluation of modular materials*. Minneapolis: Burgess Publishing Co., 1974.

Siedentop, D. *Physical education—introductory analysis*. Dubuque, Iowa: William C. Brown Co., Publishers, 1976.

Singer, R. *Psychomotor domain: movement behaviors*. Philadelphia: Lea & Febiger, 1972.

Singer, R. *Readings in motor learning.* Philadelphia: Lea & Febiger, 1972.

Singer, R., & Dick, W. *Teaching physical education (instructor's manual and study guide).* Boston: Houghton-Mifflin Co., 1974.

Slusher, H. S., & Lockhart, A. S. *Anthology of contemporary readings.* Dubuque, Iowa: William C. Brown Co., Publishers, 1966.

Smith, H. M. *Introduction to human movement.* Reading, Mass.: Addison-Wesley Publishing Co., Inc., 1968.

Straub, W. F. *The lifetime sports–oriented physical education program.* Englewood Cliffs, N.J.: Prentice-Hall, Inc., 1976.

Thompson, J. C. *Physical education for the 1970's.* Englewood Cliffs, N.J.: Prentice-Hall, Inc., 1971.

Willgoose, C. E. *The curriculum in physical education* (3rd ed.). Englewood Cliffs, N.J.: Prentice-Hall, Inc., 1979.

Williams, J. F. *The principles of physical education.* Philadelphia: W. B. Saunders Co., 1948.

PHILOSOPHY AND PRINCIPLES

AAHPER. *Tones of theory.* Washington, D.C.: The Alliance, 1972.

AAHPER. *Concepts and convictions.* Washington, D.C.: The Alliance, 1978.

AAHPER. *Vital issues.* Washington, D.C.: The Alliance, 1978.

Allen, D., & Fahey, B. *Being human in sports.* Philadelphia: Lea & Febiger, 1977.

Baley, J., & Field, D. *Physical education and the physical educator.* Boston: Allyn & Bacon, Inc., 1976.

Barrow, H. M. *Man and his movement: principles of his physical education.* Philadelphia: Lea & Febiger, 1977.

Bookwalter, K., & Zanderzwag, H. J. *Foundations and principles of physical education.* Philadelphia: W. B. Saunders Co., 1969.

Brauner, C. J., & Burns, H. W. *Problems in education and philosophy.* Englewood Cliffs, N.J.: Prentice-Hall, Inc., 1965.

Brown, C., & Cassidy, R. *Theory in physical education.* Philadelphia: Lea & Febiger, 1963.

Bucher, C. A. *Foundations of physical education* (7th ed.). St. Louis: The C. V. Mosby Co., 1975.

Cobb, R., & Lepley, P. *Contemporary philosophies of physical education and athletics.* Columbus, Ohio: Charles E. Merrill Publishing Co., 1973.

Cowell, C. C., & France, W. L. *Philosophy and principles of physical education.* Englewood Cliffs, N.J.: Prentice-Hall, Inc., 1963.

Cratty, B. J. *Social dimensions of physical activity.* Englewood Cliffs, N.J.: Prentice-Hall, Inc., 1967.

Cratty, B. J. *Career potentials in physical activity.* Englewood Cliffs, N.J.: Prentice-Hall, Inc., 1971.

Davis, E. C. *Philosophies fashion.* Dubuque, Iowa: William C. Brown Co., Publishers, 1964.

Davis, E. C., & Miller, D. M. *The philosophic process in physical education.* Philadelphia: Lea & Febiger, 1967.

Felshin, J. *Perspectives and principles for physical education.* New York: John Wiley & Sons, Inc., 1967.

Fordham, S. L. *Physical education and sports.* New York: John Wiley & Sons, Inc., 1978.

Frost, R., & Sims, E. J. *Development of human values sports.* Washington, D.C.: American Alliance for Health, Physical Education, and Recreation, 1974.

Gerber, E. W. *Innovators and institutions in physical education.* Philadelphia: Lea & Febiger, 1971.

Gerber, E. W., Felshin, J., Berlin, P., & Wyrick, W. *The American woman in sport.* Reading, Mass.: Addison-Wesley Publishing Co., Inc., 1974.

Hackensmith, C. W. *History of physical education.* New York: Harper & Row, Publishers, Inc., 1966.

Hall, J. *Fundamentals of physical education.* Englewood Cliffs, N.J.: Prentice-Hall, Inc., 1969.

Harper, W., Miller, D. M., Park, R. J., & Davis, E. C. *The philosophic process in physical education.* Philadelphia: Lea & Febiger, 1977.

Hellison, D. *Humanistic physical education.* Englewood Cliffs, N.J.: Prentice-Hall, Inc., 1973.

Kalakian, L., & Goldman, M. *Introduction to physical education: A humanistic approach.* Boston: Allyn & Bacon, Inc., 1976.

Kane, J. E. *Readings in physical education.* London: Ling House, 1966.

Kane, J. E. *Psychological aspects of physical education and sport.* Boston: Routledge & Kegan Paul Ltd., 1975.

Lockhart, A. S., & Slusher, H. S. *Contemporary readings in physical education.* Dubuque, Iowa: William C. Brown Co., Publishers, 1975.

Lowe, B. *The beauty of sport.* Englewood Cliffs, N.J.: Prentice-Hall, Inc., 1977.

McCloy, C. H. *Philosophical bases for physical education.* New York: F. S. Crofts & Co., 1940.

McGlynn, G. *Issues in physical education and sports.* Palo Alto, Calif.: Mayfield Co., 1974.

Methany, E. *Movement and meaning,* New York: McGraw-Hill Book Co., 1968.

Neilson, N. P., & Bronson, A. O. *Problems in physical education: an introductory course.* Englewood Cliffs, N.J.: Prentice-Hall, Inc., 1965.

Nixon, J. F., & Jewett, A. E. *An introduction to physical education.* Philadelphia: W. B. Saunders Co., 1974.

Oberteuffer, D., & Ulrich, C. *Physical education: a*

textbook of principles for professional students. New York: Harper & Row, Publishers, Inc., 1970.

Read, D., & Simmons, S. The humanistic education sourcebook. Englewood Cliffs, N.J.: Prentice-Hall, Inc., 1975.

Rice, E., Hutchinson, J., & Lee, M. A brief history of physical education. New York: John Wiley & Sons, Inc., 1969.

Rivens, R. S. Foundations of physical education. Boston: Houghton Mifflin Co., 1978.

Rushall, B., & Siedentop, D. The development and control of behavior in sport and physical education. Philadelphia: Lea & Febiger, 1972.

Sanborn, M. A., & Hartman, B. C. Issues in physical education. Philadelphia: W. B. Saunders Co., 1970.

Siedentop, D. Physical education introductory analysis. Dubuque, Iowa: William C. Brown Co., Publishers, 1972.

Singer, R. N. Physical education: an interdisciplinary approach. New York: Macmillan Publishing Co., Inc., 1972.

Singer, R. N. Physical education: foundations. New York: Holt, Rinehart & Winston, 1976.

Steinhaus, A. Toward understanding of health and physical education. Dubuque, Iowa: William C. Brown Co., Publishers, 1963.

Thompson, J. C. Physical education for the 1970's. Englewood Cliffs, N.J.: Prentice-Hall, Inc., 1971.

Updyke, W. F., & Johnson, P. B. Principles of modern physical education, health and recreation. New York: Holt, Rinehart & Winston, 1970.

VanDalen, D., & Bennett, B. World history of physical education: cultural, philosophical, and comparative. Englewood Cliffs, N.J.: Prentice-Hall, Inc., 1971.

Vanderzwaag, H. J. Toward a philosophy of sport. Reading, Mass.: Addison-Wesley Publishing Co., Inc., 1972.

Webster, R. W. Philosophy of physical education. Dubuque, Iowa: William C. Brown Co., Publishers, 1965.

Weston, A. The making of American physical education. New York: Appleton-Century-Crofts, 1962.

Zeigler, E. History of physical education and sport. Englewood Cliffs, N.J.: Prentice-Hall, Inc., 1964.

Zeigler, E. Problems in the history and philosophy of physical education. Englewood Cliffs, N.J.: Prentice-Hall, Inc., 1968.

Zeigler, E. Philosophical foundations for physical, health, and recreation education. Englewood Cliffs, N.J.: Prentice-Hall, Inc., 1977.

Zeigler, E. Physical education and sport philosophy. Englewood Cliffs, N.J.: Prentice-Hall, Inc., 1977.

INSTRUCTIONAL METHODOLOGY

AAHPER. Organizational patterns for instruction in physical education. Washington, D.C.: The Alliance, 1971.

AAHPER. Personalized learning in physical education. Washington, D.C.: The Alliance, 1978.

AAHPER. Programmed instruction in health education and physical education. Washington, D.C.: The Alliance, 1978.

AAHPER. T.V.: production and utilization in physical education. Washington, D.C.: The Alliance, 1978.

Airasian, P., Bloom, B., & Carroll, J. Mastery learning. New York: Holt, Rinehart & Winston, 1971.

Anderson, R. C. Current research on instruction. Englewood Cliffs, N.J.: Prentice-Hall, Inc., 1969.

Annarino, A. A. Individualized instructional set: archery, bowling, badminton, golf, and tennis. Englewood Cliffs, N.J.: Prentice-Hall, Inc., 1973.

Berenstain, S. Education impossible. New York: Dell Publishing Co., 1970.

Bishop, L. K. Individualizing educational systems. New York: Harper & Row Publishers, Inc., 1971.

Catterall, C. D., & Gazda, G. M. Strategies for helping students. Springfield, Ill.: Charles C Thomas, Publisher, 1977.

Clark, D. E. Physical education: a program of activities. St. Louis: The C. V. Mosby Co., 1969.

Cougan, H. Physical education—individualized instruction of badminton and track & field. Punta Gorda, Fla.: A & R Publishing Co., 1971.

Cowell, C., Schwehn, H. M., Walker, J., & Miller, A. G. Modern methods in secondary school physical education. Boston: Allyn & Bacon, Inc., 1973.

Daugherty, G. Methods in physical education and health for secondary schools. Philadelphia: W. B. Saunders Co., 1967.

Davis, E. C., & Wallis, E. L. Toward better teaching in physical education. Englewood Cliffs, N.J.: Prentice-Hall, Inc., 1961.

Dowell, L. J. Strategies for teaching physical education. Englewood Cliffs, N.J.: Prentice-Hall, Inc., 1975.

Felfner, D. Building positive self-concepts. Minneapolis: Burgess Publishing Co., 1974.

Fisk, L., & Lindfgen, H. C. A survival guide for teachers. New York: John Wiley & Sons, Inc., 1973.

Flanders, N. A. Analyzing teaching behavior. Reading, Mass.: Addison-Wesley Publishing Co., Inc., 1970.

Flanders, N. A., Kryspin, W., & Feldhusen, J. Analyzing verbal classroom interaction. Minneapolis: Burgess Publishing Co., 1974.

Full, H. Controversy in American education. New York: Macmillan Publishing Co., Inc., 1967.

Hazard, W. *The tutorial and clinical program.* New York: Northwestern University Press, 1967.

Healey, J. H., & Healey, W. H. *Physical education teaching problems for analysis and solution.* Springfield, Ill.: Charles C Thomas, Publisher, 1975.

Heitmann, H. M., & Kneer, M. E. *Physical education instructional techniques: an individualized humanistic approach.* Englewood Cliffs, N.J.: Prentice-Hall, Inc., 1976.

Hellison, D. *Humanistic physical education.* Englewood Cliffs, N.J.: Prentice-Hall, Inc., 1973.

Homme, L. *How to use contingency contracting in the classroom.* Champaign, Ill.: Research Press Co., 1972.

Hoover, K. H. *The professional teachers handbook.* Boston: Allyn & Bacon, Inc., 1976.

Hyman, R. T. *Teaching: vantage points for study.* Philadelphia: J. B. Lippincott Co., 1974.

Hyman, R. T. *Ways of teaching.* Philadelphia: J. B. Lippincott Co., 1974.

Insley, G. S. *Practical guidelines for the teaching of physical education.* Reading, Mass.: Addison-Wesley Publishing Co., Inc., 1973.

Johnson, P., et al. *Problem-solving approach to health and fitness.* New York: Holt, Rinehart & Winston, 1967.

Keach, E. T., Fulton, R., & Gardner, W. *Education and social crisis.* New York: John Wiley & Sons, Inc., 1967.

Knapp, C., & Leonhard, P. H. *Teaching physical education in secondary schools.* New York: McGraw-Hill Book Co., 1968.

Kozman, H. C., Cassidy, R., & Jackson, C. O. *Methods in physical education.* Dubuque, Iowa: William C. Brown Co., Publishers, 1967.

Lapp, D., Bender, H., Ellenwood, S., & John, M. *Teaching and learning, philosophical, psychological, and curricular applications.* New York: Macmillan Publishing Co., Inc., 1975.

Lindeburg, F. *Teaching physical education in the secondary school.* New York: John Wiley & Sons, Inc., 1978.

Madsen, C., & Madsen, C. *Teaching/discipline—a positive approach for educational development.* Boston: Allyn & Bacon, Inc., 1974.

Miller, A., & Massey, D. *A dynamic concept of physical education for secondary schools.* Englewood Cliffs, N.J.: Prentice-Hall, Inc., 1963.

Mosston, M. *Teaching: from command to discovery.* Belmont, Calif.: Wadsworth Publishing Co., 1972.

Mosston, M. *Teaching physical education.* Columbus, Ohio: Charles E. Merrill Publishing Co., 1966.

Netcher, J. *A management model for competency-based HPER programs.* St. Louis: The C. V. Mosby Co., 1977.

Palardy, M. *Teaching today.* New York: Macmillan Publishing Co., Inc., 1975.

Penman, K. A. *Programmed instruction: physical education for college students.* St. Louis: The C. V. Mosby Co., 1964.

Petrequin, G. *Individualizing learning through modular-flexible programming.* New York: McGraw-Hill Book Co., 1968.

Popham, W. J., & Baker, E. L. *Establishing instructional goals.* Englewood Cliffs, N.J.: Prentice-Hall, Inc., 1970.

Popham, W. J., & Baker, E. L. *Planning an instructional sequence.* Englewood Cliffs, N.J.: Prentice-Hall, Inc., 1970.

Read, D. A., & Simon, S. B. *Humanistic education sourcebook.* Englewood Cliffs, N.J.: Prentice-Hall, Inc., 1975.

Rothman, E. *The angel inside went sour.* New York: David McKay Co., Inc., 1972.

Russell, J. *Modular instruction, a guide to the design, selection and evaluation of modular materials.* Minneapolis: Burgess Publishing Co., 1974.

Ryan, K., & Cooper, J. M. *Those who can teach.* Boston: Houghton Mifflin Co., 1972.

Sarason, S. B., Davidson, K., & Blatt, B. *The preparation of teachers.* New York: John Wiley & Sons, Inc., 1962.

Scheffler, I. *Reason and teaching.* Indianapolis: Bobbs-Merrill Co., Inc., 1973.

Siedentop, D. *Physical education—introductory analysis.* Dubuque, Iowa: William C. Brown Co., Publishers, 1976.

Singer, R., & Dick, W. *Teaching physical education: a systems approach.* Boston: Houghton Mifflin Co., 1974.

Taber, J., Glaser, R., & Schaefer, H. *Learning and programmed instruction.* Reading, Mass.: Addison-Wesley Publishing Co., Inc., 1965.

ORGANIZATION AND ADMINISTRATION

Ashton, D. *Administration of physical education for women.* New York: John Wiley & Sons, Inc., 1968.

Athletic Institute. *Planning facilities for health, physical education, and recreation.* Chicago: The Institute, 1962.

Bucher, C. A. *Administration of physical education and athletic programs* (7th ed.). St. Louis: The C. V. Mosby Co., 1979.

Colgate, J. A. *Administration of intramural and recreational activities: everyone can participate.* New York: John Wiley & Sons, Inc., 1978.

Cook, T. E., & Brown, C. L. *Organizational and administrative problems in physical education, intramurals and athletics.* Dubuque, Iowa: Kendall/Hunt Publishing Co., 1972.

Daugherty, G., & Woods, J. B. *Physical education and intramural programs.* Philadelphia: W. B. Saunders Co., 1976.

Deatherage, D., & Reid, P. *Administration of women's competitive sports.* Dubuque, Iowa: William C. Brown Co., Publishers, 1977.

Forsythe, C., & Keller, I. *Administration of high school athletics.* Englewood Cliffs, N.J.: Prentice-Hall, Inc., 1977.

French, E., & Lehsten, N. *Administration of physical education: for schools and colleges.* New York: John Wiley & Sons, Inc., 1973.

Frost, R., & Marshall, S. *Administration of physical education and athletics: concepts and practices.* Dubuque, Iowa: William C. Brown Co., Publishers, 1977.

Gerou, N. *Complete guide to administrating the intramural program.* Englewood Cliffs, N.J.: Prentice-Hall, Inc., 1976.

Hall, J. *Administration: principles, theory and practice with applications to physical education.* Englewood Cliffs, N.J.: Prentice-Hall, Inc., 1973.

Healey, J. N., & Healey, W. *Administrative practices in boys and girls interscholastic athletics.* Springfield, Ill.: Charles C Thomas, Publisher, 1976.

Hixon, C. *The administration of interscholastic athletics.* Columbus, Ohio: Charles E. Merrill Publishing Co., 1967.

Howard. G. W., & Masonbrink, E. *Administration of physical education.* New York: Harper & Row, Publishers, Inc., 1963.

Humphrey, J. H., et al. *Principles and techniques of supervision in physical education.* Dubuque, Iowa: William C. Brown Co., Publishers, 1972.

Hyatt, R. W. *Intramural sports: organization and administration.* St. Louis: The C. V. Mosby Co., 1977.

Manjone, J. A., & Bowen, R. T. *Co-rec intramural sports handbook.* West Point, N.Y.: Leisure Press, 1978.

Means, L. *Intramurals: their organization and administration.* Englewood Cliffs, N.J.: Prentice-Hall, Inc., 1973.

Nash, J. B., Moench, F. J., & Saurborn, J. B. *Physical education: organization and administration.* New York: A. S. Barnes & Co., Inc., 1951.

Parker, B. V. *The dynamics of supervision.* New York: McGraw-Hill Book Co., 1971.

Penman, K. A. *Planning physical education and athletic facilities in schools.* New York: John Wiley & Sons, Inc., 1977.

Pestoleski, R., & Sinclair, W. *Creative administration in physical education and athletics.* Englewood Cliffs, N.J.: Prentice-Hall, Inc., 1978.

Peterson, J. *Intramural administration: theory and practice.* Englewood Cliffs, N.J.: Prentice-Hall, Inc., 1976.

Peterson, J., & Preo, L. S. *Intramural director's handbook.* West Point, N.Y.: Leisure Press, 1978.

Puckett, J. *Guide to an effective physical education program.* Englewood Cliffs, N.J.: Prentice-Hall, Inc., 1976.

Purdy, R. *Successful high school athletic programs.* Englewood Cliffs, N.J.: Prentice-Hall, Inc., 1973.

Voltmer, E., & Esslinger, A. *The organization and administration of physical education.* Englewood Cliffs, N.J.: Prentice-Hall, Inc., 1978.

Zeigler, E., & Spaeth, M. *Administrative theory and practice in physical education and athletics.* Englewood Cliffs, N.J.: Prentice-Hall, Inc., 1975.

ELEMENTARY PHYSICAL EDUCATION

AAHPER. *The significance of the young child's motor development.* Washington, D.C.: The Alliance, 1971.

AAHPER. *Children's dance.* Washington, D.C.: The Alliance, 1978.

AAHPER. *Echoes of influence for elementary school physical education.* Washington, D.C. The Alliance, 1978.

AAHPER. *Preparing the elementary specialist.* Washington, D.C.: The Alliance, 1978.

AAHPER. *Trends in elementary school physical education.* Washington, D.C.: The Alliance, 1978.

Aitken, M. H. *Play environment for children: play space, improvised equipment and facilities.* Bellingham, Wash.: Educational Designs & Consultants, 1972.

Anderson, M. H., Elliot, M. E., & LaBerge, J. *Play with a purpose.* New York: Harper & Row, Publishers, Inc., 1972.

Andrews, G., Saurborn, J., & Schneider, E. *Physical education for today's boys and girls.* Boston: Allyn & Bacon, Inc., 1960.

Annarino, A. A. *Fundamental movement and sport skill development.* Columbus, Ohio: Charles E. Merrill Publishing Co., 1973.

Arnheim, D. *Developing motor behavior in children.* St. Louis: The C. V. Mosby Co., 1973.

Arnheim, D., & Pestolesi, R. A. *Elementary physical education: a developmental approach* (2nd ed.). St. Louis: The C. V. Mosby Co., 1978.

Arnheim, D., & Sinclair, W. *The clumsy child: a program for motor therapy.* St. Louis: The C. V. Mosby Co., 1975.

Barlin, A. *Teaching your wings to fly: the non-special-*

ist's *guide to movement activities for young children.* Englewood Cliffs, N.J.: Prentice-Hall, Inc., 1978.

Block, S. *Me and I'm great; physical education for children three through eight.* Minneapolis: Burgess Publishing Co., 1977.

Boorman, J. *Creative dance in the first three grades.* New York: David McKay Co., Inc., 1969.

Boyer, M. H. *The teaching of elementary school physical education.* New York: J. Lowell Pratt & Co., 1965.

Bryant, R., & Oliver, E. *Complete elementary physical education guide.* Englewood Cliffs, N.J.: Prentice-Hall, Inc., 1974.

Bucher, C. *Physical education and health in the elementary school.* New York: Macmillan Publishing Co., Inc., 1971.

Bucher, C., & Reade, E. *Physical education in the modern elementary school.* New York: Macmillan Publishing Co., Inc., 1964.

Burton, E. C. *The new physical education for elementary children.* Boston: Houghton Mifflin Co., 1977.

Clarke, H. H., & Haar, F. B. *Health and physical education for the elementary school classroom teacher.* Englewood Cliffs, N.J.: Prentice-Hall, Inc., 1964.

Cochran, N. A., Wilkinson, L. C., & Furlow, J. J. *A teacher's guide to elementary school physical education.* Dubuque, Iowa: Kendall/Hunt Publishing Co., 1971.

Corbin, C. B. *Inexpensive equipment for games, play and physical activity.* Dubuque, Iowa: Wm. C. Brown Co., Publisher, 1972.

Corbin, C. B. *Becoming physically educated in the elementary school.* Philadelphia: Lea & Febiger, 1976.

Cratty, B. J. *Active learning: games to enhance academic abilities.* Englewood Cliffs, N.J.: Prentice-Hall, Inc., 1971.

Cratty, B. J. *Remedial motor activity for children.* Philadelphia: Lea & Febiger, 1975.

Dauer, V. P. *Fitness for elementary school children.* Minneapolis: Burgess Publishing Co., 1962.

Dauer, V. P. *Essential movement experiences for preschool and primary children.* Minneapolis: Burgess Publishing Co., 1972.

Dauer, V. P., & Pangrazi, R. P. *Dynamic physical education for elementary school children.* Minneapolis: Burgess Publishing Co., 1975.

Delcato, C. H. *The elementary school of the future.* Springfield, Ill.: Charles C Thomas, Publisher, 1965.

Ellis, M., & Scholtz, G. *Activity and play of children.* Englewood Cliffs, N.J.: Prentice-Hall, Inc., 1978.

Fabricius, H. *Physical education for the classroom teacher.* Dubuque, Iowa: William C. Brown Co., Publishers, 1971.

Fait, H. F. *Physical education for the elementary school child.* Philadelphia: W. B. Saunders Co., 1976.

Farina, A., Furth, S. H., & Smith, J. M. *Growth through play.* Englewood Cliffs, N.J.: Prentice-Hall, Inc., 1956.

Flinchum, B. M. *Motor development in early childhood: a guide for movement education with ages 2-6,* St. Louis: The C. V. Mosby Co., 1975.

Fraser, E. D., Bransford, J. B., & Hastings, M. *The child and physical education.* Englewood Cliffs, N.J.: Prentice-Hall, Inc., 1956.

Gallahue, D. L. *Motor development and movement experiments for young children.* New York: John Wiley & Sons, Inc., 1976.

Gallahue, D. L., Werner, P., & Luedke, G. *Moving and learning: a conceptual approach.* New York: John Wiley & Sons, Inc., 1975.

Gerhardt, L. *Moving and knowing: the young child orients himself in space.* Englewood Cliffs, N.J.: Prentice-Hall, Inc., 1973.

Gilbert, A. G. *Teaching the three R's through movement experiences.* Minneapolis: Burgess Publishing Co., 1977.

Gillion, B. C. *Basic movement education for children.* Reading, Mass.: Addison-Wesley Publishing Co., Inc., 1970.

Hacket, L. C., & Jenson, R. G. *A guide to movement education.* Palo Alto, Calif.: Peck Publications, 1967.

Halsey, E., & Porter, L. *Physical education for children.* New York: Dryden Press, 1958.

Humphrey, J. *Elementary school physical education.* New York: Harper & Row, Publishers, Inc., 1958.

Humphrey, J. *Child learning—through elementary school physical education.* Dubuque, Iowa: William C. Brown Co., Publishers, 1965.

Jackson, A., & Randall, J. *Activities for elementary physical education.* Englewood Cliffs, N.J.: Prentice-Hall, Inc., 1971.

Jones, E., Morgan, E., & Stevens, G. *Methods and materials in elementary physical education.* New York: World Book Co., 1957.

Kirchner, G. *Physical education for elementary school children.* Dubuque, Iowa: William C. Brown Co., Publishers, 1978.

Kirchner, G., Cunningham, J., & Warrell, E. *Introduction to movement education.* Dubuque, Iowa: William C. Brown Co., Publishers, 1978.

Kruger, H., & Kruger, J. M. *Movement education in physical education: a guide to teaching and planning.* Dubuque, Iowa: William C. Brown Co., Publishers, 1977.

LaSalle, D. *Guidance of children through physical education*. New York: Ronald Press Co., 1957.

Latchaw, M. *Pocket guide of movement activities for the elementary school*. Englewood Cliffs, N.J.: Prentice-Hall, Inc., 1970.

Logsdon, B. J., et al. *Physical education for children*. Philadelphia: Lea & Febiger, 1977.

Metzger, P. A. *Elementary school physical education readings*. Dubuque, Iowa: William C. Brown Co., Publishers, 1972.

Miller, A. C., Cheffers, J., & Whitcomb, V. *Physical education: teaching human movement in the elementary schools*. Englewood Cliffs, N.J.: Prentice-Hall, Inc., 1974.

Morris, G. S. D. *How to change the games children play*. Minneapolis: Burgess Publishing Co., 1976.

Murray, R. *Dance in elementary education*. New York: Harper & Row, Publishers, Inc., 1975.

Nagel, C. *Play activities for elementary grades* (2nd ed.). St. Louis: The C. V. Mosby Co., 1964.

Neilson, N. P., et al. *Physical education for elementary schools*. New York: John Wiley & Sons, Inc., 1966.

O'Keefe, P. R., & Aldrich, A. *Education through physical activities*. St. Louis: The C. V. Mosby Co., 1959.

O'Quinn, G. *Gymnastics for elementary school children*. Dubuque, Iowa: William C. Brown Co., Publishers, 1967.

Richardson, H. *Games for the elementary school grades*. Minneapolis: Burgess Publishing Co., 1962.

Salt, B. E., Fox, G. I., & Stevens, B. K. *Teaching physical education in the elementary school*. New York: John Wiley & Sons, Inc., 1960.

Schurr, E. *Movement experiences for children: a humanistic approach to elementary school physical education*. Englewood Cliffs, N.J.: Prentice-Hall, Inc., 1975.

Smith, J. A. *Creative teaching of the creative arts in the elementary school*. Boston: Allyn & Bacon, Inc., 1967.

Vannier, M., Foster, M., & Gallahue, D. *Teaching physical education in elementary schools*. Philadelphia: W. B. Saunders Co., 1978.

Vick, M., & McLaughlin, R. *A collection of dances for children*. Minneapolis: Burgess Publishing Co., 1970.

Wallis, E. L., & Logan, G. A. *Exercise for children*. Englewood Cliffs, N.J.: Prentice-Hall, Inc., 1965.

Werner, P. H. *Inexpensive physical education equipment for children*. Minneapolis: Burgess Publishing Co., 1976.

Wickstrom, R. L. *Fundamental motor patterns*. Philadelphia: Lea & Febiger, 1977.

Winters, S. J. *Creative rhythmic movement for children of elementary school age*. Dubuque, Iowa: William C. Brown Co., Publishers, 1975.

Young, H. L. *A manual-workbook of physical education for elementary teachers*. New York: Macmillan Publishing Co., Inc., 1963.

SECONDARY PHYSICAL EDUCATION

AAHPER. *Physical education for high school students*. Washington, D.C.: The Alliance, 1970.

AAHPER. *Assessment guide for secondary school physical education programs*. Washington, D.C.: The Alliance, 1978.

AAHPER. *Guidelines for secondary school physical education*. Washington, D.C.: The Alliance, 1978.

AAHPER. *Ideas for secondary school physical education*. Washington, D.C.: The Alliance, 1978.

Bookwalter, K. W. *Physical education in the secondary schools*. New York: The Center for Applied Research in Education, 1963.

Bossing, N. L. *Teaching in secondary schools*. Boston: Houghton Mifflin Co., 1952.

Bucher, C. A., & Koenig, C. R. *Methods and materials for secondary school physical education* (5th ed.). St. Louis: The C. V. Mosby Co., 1978.

Cassidy, R., & Caldwell, S. *Humanizing physical education: methods for the secondary school movement program*. Dubuque, Iowa: William C. Brown Co., Publishers, 1974.

Cowell, C. C., Walker, J., Schwehn, H., & Miller, A. G. *Modern methods in secondary school physical education*. Boston: Allyn & Bacon, Inc., 1973.

Daugherty, G. *Methods in physical education and health for secondary schools*. Philadelphia: W. B. Saunders Co., 1967.

Daugherty, G. *Effective teaching in physical education for secondary schools*. Philadelphia: W. B. Saunders Co. 1973.

Dexter, G. *A teachers guide to physical education for girls*. Sacramento, Calif.: State Department of Education, 1957.

Knapp, C., & Leonhard, P. H. *Teaching physical education in secondary schools*. New York: McGraw-Hill Book Co., 1968.

Kozman, H. C., & Rosalind, C. O. *Methods in physical education*. Dubuque, Iowa: William C. Brown Co., Publishers, 1967.

Lindeburg, F. *Teaching physical education in the secondary school*. New York: John Wiley & Sons, Inc., 1978.

Miller, A. G., & Massey, D. M. *Methods in physical education for the secondary schools*. Englewood Cliffs, N.J.: Prentice-Hall, Inc., 1961.

Miller, A. G., & Massey, D. M. *A dynamic concept of*

physical education for secondary schools. Englewood Cliffs, N.J.: Prentice-Hall, Inc., 1963.

Ridine, L., & Madden, J. *Physical education for inner city secondary schools*. New York: Harper & Row Publishers, Inc., 1975.

Vannier, M., & Fait, H. *Teaching physical education in secondary schools*. Philadelphia: W. B. Saunders Co., 1975.

PERCEPTUAL-MOTOR LEARNING

AAHPER. *Perceptual-motor foundations*. Washington, D.C.: The Alliance, 1969.

AAHPER. *Annotated bibliography on perceptual-motor development*. Washington, D.C.: The Alliance, 1978.

AAHPER. *Children learn physical skills*. Washington, D.C.: The Alliance, 1978.

AAHPER. *Foundations and practices in perceptual-motor learning: a quest for understanding*. Washington, D.C.: The Alliance, 1978.

Bell, V. L. *Sensorimotor learning from research to teaching*. Pacific Palisades, Calif.: Goodyear Publishing Co., 1970.

Carron, A. *Laboratory experiments in motor learning*. Englewood Cliffs, N.J.: Prentice-Hall, Inc., 1971.

Corbin, C. B. *A textbook of motor development*. Dubuque, Iowa: William C. Brown Co., Publishers, 1973.

Cratty, B. J. *Perceptual motor tasks*. Philadelphia: Lea & Febiger, 1968.

Cratty, B. J. *Movement behavior and motor learning*. Englewood Cliffs, N.J.: Prentice-Hall, Inc., 1974.

Cratty, B. J. *Perceptual and motor development in infants and children*. Englewood Cliffs, N.J.: Prentice-Hall, Inc., 1978.

Cratty, B. J., & Hutton, R. S. *Experiments in movement behavior and motor learning*. Philadelphia: Lea & Febiger, 1969.

Drowatzky, J. N. *Motor learning: principles and practices*. Minneapolis: Burgess Publishing Co., 1975.

Espenschade, A. S., & Eckert, H. *Motor development*. Columbus, Ohio: Charles E. Merrill Publishing Co., 1967.

Gallahue, D. *Motor development and movement experiences*. New York: John Wiley & Sons, Inc., 1976.

Gallahue, D., Werner, P., & Luedke, G. *A conceptual approach to moving and learning*. New York: John Wiley & Sons, Inc., 1975.

Godfrey, B., & Kephart, N. *Movement patterns and motor education*. New York: Appleton-Century-Crofts, 1969.

Harvat, R. W. *Physical education for children with perceptual-motor learning disabilities*. Columbus, Ohio: Charles E. Merrill Publishing Co., 1971.

Humphrey, J. H. *Improving learning ability through compensatory physical education*. Springfield, Ill.: Charles C Thomas, Publisher, 1976.

Kirchner, G., Cunningham, J., & Warrell, E. *Introduction to movement education*. Dubuque, Iowa: William C. Brown Co., Publishers, 1970.

Latchaw, M., & Egstrom, G. *Human movement*. Englewood Cliffs, N.J.: Prentice-Hall, Inc., 1969.

Lockhart, A., & Johnson, J. M. *Laboratory experiments in motor learning*. Dubuque, Iowa: William C. Brown Co., Publishers, 1970.

Mosston, M. *Developmental movement*. Columbus, Ohio: Charles E. Merrill Publishing Co., 1965.

Oxedine, J. B. *Psychology of motor learning*. New York: Appleton-Century-Crofts, 1968.

Robb, M. *Dynamics of motor-skill acquisition*. Englewood Cliffs, N.J.: Prentice-Hall, Inc., 1972.

Sage, G. H. *Introduction to motor behavior: a neuropsychological approach*. Reading, Mass.: Addison-Wesley Publishing Co., Inc., 1971.

Schmidt, R. *Motor skills*. New York: Harper & Row, Publishers, Inc., 1975.

Singer, R. *Motor learning and human performance*. New York: Macmillan Publishing Co., Inc., 1968.

Singer, R. *The psychomotor domain movement behaviors*. Philadelphia: Lea & Febiger, 1972.

Singer, R. *Readings in motor learning*. Philadelphia: Lea & Febiger, 1972.

Smith, H. *Introduction to human movement*. Reading, Mass.: Addison-Wesley Publishing Co., Inc., 1968.

Stallings, L. *Motor skills: development and learning*. Dubuque, Iowa: William C. Brown Co., Publishers, 1973.

Sweigard, L. *Human movement potential: it's ideokinetic facilitation*. New York: Harper & Row, Publishers, Inc., 1974.

Werner, P., & Rini, L. *Perceptual-motor development equipment*. New York: John Wiley & Sons, Inc., 1976.

Wickstrom, R. L. *Fundamental motor patterns*. Philadelphia: Lea & Febiger, 1977.

GAMES AND RHYTHMICAL ACTIVITIES

AAHPER. *How we do it game book*. Washington, D.C.: The Alliance, 1959.

AAHPER. *Games teaching*. Washington, D.C.: The Alliance, 1978.

Blake, W. O., & Volp, A. M. *Lead-up games to team sports*. Englewood Cliffs, N.J.: Prentice-Hall, Inc., 1964.

Cratty, B. *Active learning: games to enhance academic abilities*. Englewood Cliffs, N.J.: Prentice-Hall, Inc., 1971.

Cratty, B. *Learning about human behavior: through*

active games. Englewood Cliffs, N.J.: Prentice-Hall, Inc., 1975.

Edgren, H. D., & Gruber, J. *Teacher's handbook of indoor and outdoor games.* Englewood Cliffs, N.J.: Prentice-Hall, Inc., 1963.

Fleming, G. *Creative rhythmic movement: boys and girls dancing.* Englewood Cliffs, N.J.: Prentice-Hall, Inc., 1976.

Geri, F. H. *Illustrated games, rhythms and stunts for children.* Englewood Cliffs, N.J.: Prentice-Hall, Inc., 1957.

Hall, J., et al. *Until the whistle blows: a collection of games, dances, and activities for four to eight year olds.* Englewood Cliffs, N.J.: Prentice-Hall, Inc., 1977.

Harris, J. A. *File o' fun.* Minneapolis: Burgess Publishing Co., 1972.

Hindman, D. A. *Handbook of active games and rhythms.* Englewood Cliffs, N.J.: Prentice-Hall, Inc., 1951.

Jaruis, M. *Your book of swimming games and activities.* Levittown, N.Y.: Transatlantic Arts, Inc., 1978.

Latchaw, M. *A pocket guide of games and rhythms.* Englewood Cliffs, N.J.: Prentice-Hall, Inc., 1956.

Latchaw, M., & Pyatt, J. *A pocket guide of dance activities.* Englewood Cliffs, N.J.: Prentice-Hall, Inc., 1958.

Mason, B. S., & Mitchell, E. D. *Active games and contests,* New York: A. S. Barnes & Co., Inc., 1935.

Nagel, C. *Play activities for elementary grades* (2nd ed.). St. Louis: The C. V. Mosby Co., 1964.

Nagel, C., & Moore, F. *Skill development through games and rhythmic activities.* Palo Alto, Calif.: National Press, 1966.

Richardson, H. A. *Games for the elementary school grades.* Minneapolis: Burgess Publishing Co., 1962.

Staley, S. C. *Games, contests and relays.* New York: A. S. Barnes & Co., Inc., 1924.

Stuart, F. R., & Ludlam, J. S. *Rhythmic activities (three sets—Series I, II, III).* Minneapolis: Burgess Publishing Co., 1962.

Winters, S. *Creative rhythmic movement for children of elementary school age.* Dubuque, Iowa: William C. Brown Co., Publishers, 1975.

Wirth, M. *Teacher's handbook of children's games: a guide to developing perceptual-motor skills.* Englewood Cliffs, N.J.: Prentice-Hall, Inc., 1976.

SPECIAL EDUCATION

AAHPER. *A guide for programs in recreation and physical education for the mentally retarded.* Washington, D.C.: The Alliance, 1968.

AAHPER. *Adapted physical education guidelines: theory and practices for the 1970's and 1980's.* Washington, D.C.: The Alliance, 1978.

AAHPER. *Annotated listing of films: physical education and recreation for impaired, disabled and handicapped persons.* Washington, D.C.: The Alliance, 1978.

AAHPER. *Annotated research bibliography in physical education, recreation and psychomotor function of mentally retarded persons.* Washington, D.C.: The Alliance, 1978.

AAHPER. *Aquatic recreation for the blind.* Washington, D.C.: The Alliance, 1978.

AAHPER. *Dance for physically disabled persons: a manual for teaching ballroom, square and folk dances to users of wheelchairs and crutches.* Washington, D.C.: The Alliance, 1978.

AAHPER. *Early intervention for handicapped children through programs of physical education and recreation.* Washington, D.C.: The Alliance, 1978.

AAHPER. *Guide to information systems in physical education and recreation for impaired, disabled, and handicapped persons.* Washington, D.C.: The Alliance, 1978.

AAHPER. *Integrating persons with handicapping conditions into regular physical education and recreation programs.* Washington, D.C.: The Alliance, 1978.

AAHPER. *Involving impaired, disabled and handicapped persons in regular camp programs.* Washington, D.C.: The Alliance, 1978.

AAHPER. *Making workshops in physical education and recreation for special populations.* Washington, D.C.: The Alliance, 1978.

AAHPER. *Motor fitness testing manual for the moderately mentally retarded.* Washington, D.C.: The Alliance, 1978.

AAHPER. *Physical activities for impaired, disabled and handicapped individuals.* Washington, D.C.: The Alliance, 1978.

AAHPER. *Physical activities for the mentally retarded/ideas for instruction.* Washington, D.C.: The Alliance, 1978.

AAHPER. *Physical education for cerebral palsied individuals.* Washington, D.C.: The Alliance, 1978.

AAHPER. *Physical education for individuals with multiple handicapping conditions.* Washington, D.C.: The Alliance, 1978.

AAHPER. *Physical education for the visually handicapped.* Washington, D.C.: The Alliance, 1978.

AAHPER. *Physical education, recreation and related programs for autistic and emotionally disturbed children.* Washington, D.C.: The Alliance, 1978.

AAHPER. *Physical education, recreation and sports*

for individuals with hearing impairments. Washington, D.C.: The Alliance, 1978.

AAHPER. *Practical guide for teaching the mentally retarded to swim.* Washington, D.C.: The Alliance, 1978.

AAHPER. *Programming for the mentally retarded in physical education and recreation.* Washington, D.C.: The Alliance, 1978.

AAHPER. *Special fitness program for the mentally retarded.* Washington, D.C.: The Alliance, 1978.

AAHPER. *Special Olympics instructional manual— from beginners to champions.* Washington, D.C.: The Alliance, 1978.

AAHPER. *Testing for impaired, disabled, and handicapped individuals.* Washington, D.C.: The Alliance, 1978.

Adams, R. C., Daniel, A., & Rullman, L. *Games, sports and exercises for the physically handicapped.* Philadelphia: Lea & Febiger, 1975.

Amary, I. B. *Creative recreation for the mentally retarded.* Springfield, Ill.: Charles C Thomas, Publisher, 1975.

Arnheim, D. D., Auxter, D., & Crowe, W. C. *Principles and methods of adapted physical education and recreation* (3rd ed.). St. Louis: The C. V. Mosby Co., 1977.

Beter, T., & Cragin, W. E. *The mentally retarded child and his motor behavior.* Springfield, Ill.: Charles C Thomas, Publisher, 1972.

Clarke, H., & Clarke, D. *Developmental and adapted physical education.* Englewood Cliffs, N.J.: Prentice-Hall, Inc., 1978.

Cratty, B. *Developmental sequences of perceptual-motor tasks: movement activities for neurologically handicapped and retarded children and youth.* Freeport, N.Y.: Educational Activities, Inc., 1967.

Crowe, W. C., Auxter, D., & Arnheim, D. *Laboratory manual in adapted physical education and recreation: experiments, activities, and assignments.* St. Louis: The C. V. Mosby Co., 1977.

Daniels, A., & Davis, E. *Adapted physical education.* New York: Harper & Row, Publishers, Inc., 1975.

Drowatzky, J. N. *Physical education for the mentally retarded.* Philadelphia: Lea & Febiger, 1971.

Fait, H. *Special physical education.* Philadelphia: W. B. Saunders Co., 1978.

Geddes, D. *Physical activities for individuals with handicapping conditions.* St. Louis: The C. V. Mosby Co., 1978.

Hirst, C., & Michaelis, E. *Developmental activities for children in special education.* Springfield, Ill.: Charles C Thomas, Publisher, 1972.

Kelly, E. *Adapted and corrective physical education.* New York: John Wiley & Sons, Inc., 1965.

McClenaghan, B., & Gallahue, D. *Fundamental movement, a developmental and remedial approach.* Philadelphia: W. B. Saunders Co., 1978.

Moran, J. M., & Kalakian, L. H. *Movement experiences for the mentally retarded or emotionally disturbed child.* Minneapolis: Burgess Publishing Co., 1977.

Newman, J. *Swimming for children with physical and sensory impairments.* Springfield, Ill.: Charles C Thomas, Publisher, 1976.

Rarick, G., Dobbins, P., & Broadhead, G. *The motor domain and it's correlations in educationally handicapped children.* Englewood Cliffs, N.J.: Prentice-Hall, Inc., 1976.

Sherrill, C. *Adapted physical education and recreation: a multi-disciplinary approach.* Dubuque, Iowa: William C. Brown Co., Publishers, 1976.

Vannier, M. *Physical activities for the handicapped.* Englewood Cliffs, N.J.: Prentice-Hall, Inc., 1977.

Vodola, T. *Individualized physical education program for the handicapped child.* Englewood Cliffs, N.J.: Prentice-Hall, Inc., 1973.

Wehman, P. *Helping the mentally retarded acquire play skills.* Springfield, Ill.: Charles C Thomas, Publisher, 1977.

Wessel, J. A., et al. *Planning individualized education programs.* Northbrook, Ill.: Hubbard Scientific Co., 1977.

Winnick, J. P., & Jansma, P. (Eds.). *Physical education inservice resource manual for the implementation of the Education for All Handicapped Children Act.* Brockport, N.Y.: State University College, 1978.

MEASUREMENT AND EVALUATION

AAHPER. *Proficiency testing in physical education.* Washington, D.C.: The Alliance, 1978.

AAHPER. *Skill tests series: archery, basketball, football, softball, volleyball, tennis.* Washington, D.C.: The Alliance, 1978.

AAHPER. *What research tells the coach about: baseball, swimming, tennis, wrestling, sprinting, football.* Washington, D.C.: The Alliance, 1978.

AAHPER. *Youth fitness test manual.* Washington, D.C.: The Alliance, 1978.

American College of Sports Medicine. *Guidelines for graded exercise testing and exercise prescription.* Philadelphia: Lea & Febiger, 1975.

Barrow, H., & McGee, R. *A practical approach to measurement in physical education.* Philadelphia: Lea & Febiger, 1971.

Baumgartner, T. A., & Jackson, A. S. *Measurement for evaluation in physical education.* Boston: Houghton Mifflin Co., 1975.

Bloom, B. S., Hastings, J. T., & Madaus, G. F. *Hand-*

book on formative and summative evaluation of student learning. New York: McGraw-Hill Book Co., 1971.

Bovard, J. F., Cozens, F., & Hagman, P. E. Tests and measurements in physical education. Philadelphia: W. B. Saunders Co., 1949.

Clark, H. H. Application of measurement to health and physical education. Englewood Cliffs, N.J.: Prentice-Hall, Inc., 1976.

Clarke, H., & Clarke, D. Research processes in physical education, recreation and health. Englewood Cliffs, N.J.: Prentice-Hall, Inc., 1970.

Collins, D. R., & Hodges, P. A comprehensive guide to sports skills tests and measurement. Springfield, Ill.: Charles C Thomas, Publisher, 1978.

Cozens, F. W., Trieb, M. H., & Neilson, N. P. Physical education achievement scales for boys in secondary schools. New York: A. S. Barnes & Co., Inc., 1956.

Dotson, C., & Kirkendall, D. Statistics for physical education, health and recreation. New York: Harper & Row, Publishers, Inc., 1975.

Eckert, H. M. Practical measurement of physical performance. Philadelphia: Lea & Febiger, 1974.

Felishman, E. A. Examiner's manual for the basic fitness tests. Englewood Cliffs, N.J.: Prentice-Hall, Inc., 1964.

Felishman, E. A. The structure and measurement of physical fitness. Englewood Cliffs, N.J.: Prentice-Hall, Inc., 1964.

Franks, B. D., & Deutsch, H. Evaluating performance in physical education. New York: Academic Press, 1973.

Glassow, R. B., & Broer, M. R. Measurement achievement in physical education. Philadelphia: W. B. Saunders Co., 1939.

Haskins, M. J. Evaluation in physical education. Dubuque, Iowa: William C. Brown Co., Publishers, 1971.

Ismail, A. H., & Gruber, J. J. Integrated development: motor aptitude and intellectual performance. Columbus, Ohio: Charles E. Merrill Publishing Co., 1967.

Johnson, B., & Nelson, J. Practical measurements for evaluation in physical education. Minneapolis: Burgess Publishing Co., 1974.

Kibler, R., Cegala, D., Barker, L., & Miles, D. Objectives for instruction and evaluation. Boston: Allyn & Bacon, Inc., 1974.

Kryspin, W. J., & Feldhusen, J. F. Developing classroom tests. Minneapolis: Burgess Publishing Co., 1974.

Larson, L. A., & Yocum, R. D. Measurement and evaluation in physical education and recreation. Englewood Cliffs, N.J.: Prentice-Hall, Inc., 1951.

Latchaw, M., & Brown, C. The evaluation process in health education, physical education and recreation. Englewood Cliffs, N.J.: Prentice-Hall, Inc., 1962.

Mathews, D. Measurement in physical education. Philadelphia: W. B. Saunders Co., 1978.

McCloy, C. H. Tests and measurements in health and physical education. New York: Appleton-Century-Crofts, 1954.

Meyers, C. Measurement in physical education. New York: John Wiley & Sons, Inc., 1974.

Montoye, H. An introduction to measurement in physical education. Boston: Allyn & Bacon, Inc., 1978.

Morehouse, C. A., & Stull, G. A. Statistical principles and procedures with applications for physical education. Boston: Allyn & Bacon, Inc., 1978.

Neilson, N. P., & Jensen, C. R. Measurements and statistics in physical education. Belmont, Calif.: Wadsworth Publishing Co., Inc., 1973.

Penman, K. A. Using statistics in teaching physical education. New York: John Wiley & Sons, Inc., 1976.

Safrit, M. Evaluation in physical education: assessing motor behavior. Englewood Cliffs, N.J.: Prentice-Hall, Inc., 1973.

Scott, M. G., & French, E. Evaluation in physical education. St. Louis: The C. V. Mosby Co., 1950.

Sheehan, T. J. An introduction to the evaluation of measurement data in physical education. Reading, Mass.: Addison-Wesley Publishing Co., Inc., 1971.

Shephard, R. J., & Lavallee, H. Physical fitness assessment. Springfield, Ill.: Charles C Thomas, Publisher, 1978.

Stadulis, R. Research and practice in physical education. Champaign, Ill.: Human Kinetics Publishers, 1977.

VanDalen, D. Understanding educational research. New York: Harper & Row, Publishers, Inc., 1973.

Vincent, W. J. Elementary statistics in physical education. Springfield, Ill.: Charles C Thomas, Publisher, 1976.

Weber, J. C. Statistics and research in physical education. St. Louis: The C. V. Mosby Co., 1970.

Weiss, R. A., & Phillips. M. Administration of tests in physical education. St. Louis: The C. V. Mosby Co., 1954.

CONDITIONING

AAHPER. Fundamentals of athletic training for women. Washington, D.C.: The Alliance, 1978.

AAHPER. Nutrition for athletes. Washington, D.C.: The Alliance, 1978.

Allsen, P. Conditioning and physical fitness: current

answers to relevant questions. Dubuque, Iowa: William C. Brown Co., Publishers, 1978.

Allsen, P., Harrison, J., & Vance, B. *Fitness for life, an individualized approach.* Dubuque, Iowa: William C. Brown Co., Publishers, 1976.

Annarino, A. A. *Developmental conditioning for women and men* (2nd ed.). St. Louis: The C. V. Mosby Co., 1976.

Annarino, A. A., & Purvis, D. *Calisthenic programs for physical education.* Cincinnati, Ohio: Tri-State Co., 1961.

Arnheim, D. D., & Klafs, C. F. *Athletic training: a study and laboratory guide.* St. Louis: The C. V. Mosby Co., 1978.

Barney, V. A., Hirst, C., & Jensen, C. *Conditioning exercises.* St. Louis: The C. V. Mosby Co., 1965.

Behnke, A., & Wilmore, J. *Evaluation and regulation of body build.* Englewood Cliffs, N.J.: Prentice-Hall, Inc., 1974.

Bender, J., & Shea, E. J. *Physical fitness: tests and exercises.* New York: The Ronald Press Co., 1964.

Casady, D. R., Mapes, D. F., & Alley, L. *Handbook of physical fitness activities.* New York: Macmillan Publishing Co., Inc., 1965.

Daniels, J., Fitss, R., & Sheehan, G. *Conditioning for distance running, the scientific aspects.* New York: John Wiley & Sons, Inc., 1978.

Darden, E. *Especially for women.* West Point, N.Y.: Leisure Press, 1978.

Dayton, O. W. *Athletic training and conditioning.* New York: John Wiley & Sons, Inc., 1965.

DiGennau, J. *Individualized exercise and optimal physical fitness.* Philadelphia: Lea & Febiger, 1974.

Falls, H. B., Wallis, E. L., & Logan, G. A. *Foundations of conditioning.* New York: Academic Press, 1970.

Foss, M. L., & Garick, J. G. *Ski conditioning.* New York: John Wiley & Sons, Inc., 1978.

Fox, E., & Mathews, D., *Interval training conditioning for sports and physical fitness.* Philadelphia: W. B. Saunders Co., 1974.

Garrison, L. *Fitness and figure control: the creation of you.* Palo Alto, Calif.: Mayfield Co., 1974.

Getchell, B. *Physical fitness: a way of life.* New York: John Wiley & Sons, Inc., 1976.

Hillcourt, W. *Physical fitness for boys.* New York: Golden Press, 1967.

Hillcourt, W. *Physical fitness for girls.* New York: Golden Press, 1967.

Hockey, R. V. *Physical fitness: the pathway to healthful living.* St. Louis: The C. V. Mosby Co., 1977.

Hooks, G. *Weight training in athletics and physical education.* Englewood Cliffs, N.J.: Prentice-Hall, Inc., 1974.

Jensen, C. *Scientific basis of athletic conditioning.* Philadelphia: Lea & Febiger, 1978.

Johnson, W., & Buskirk, E. R. *Science and medicine of exercise and sport.* New York: Harper & Row, Publishers, Inc., 1974.

Jones, K., Shainburg, L., & Byer, C. *Total fitness.* New York: Harper & Row, Publishers, Inc., 1972.

Kasch, F., & Boyer, J. *Adult fitness: principles and practice.* Palo Alto, Calif.: Mayfield Co., 1968.

Klafs, C., & Arnheim, D. *Modern principles of athletic training: the science of sports injury prevention and management* (4th ed.). St. Louis: The C. V. Mosby Co., 1977.

Lindsey, R., Van Whitney, A., & Jones, B. J. *Body mechanics: posture, figure, fitness.* Dubuque, Iowa: William C. Brown Co., Publishers, 1978.

Morehouse, L., & Rasch, P. *Sports medicine for trainers.* Philadelphia: W. B. Saunders Co., 1963.

Mott, J. *Conditioning and basic movement concepts.* Dubuque, Iowa: William C. Brown Co., Publishers, 1977.

Muckle, D. S. *Sports injuries.* Boston: Routledge & Keagan Paul Ltd., 1978.

Murray, J., & Karpovich, P. *Weight training in athletics.* Englewood Cliffs, N.J.: Prentice-Hall, Inc., 1956.

Novich, M. M. *Training and conditioning of athletes.* Philadelphia: Lea & Febiger, 1970.

O'Donoghue, D. *Treatment of injuries to athletes.* Philadelphia: W. B. Saunders Co., 1976.

Olson, E. *Conditioning fundamentals.* Columbus, Ohio: Charles E. Merrill Publishing Co., 1968.

Percival, J., Percival, L., & Taylor, J. *Complete guide to total fitness.* Englewood Cliffs, N.J.: Prentice-Hall, Inc., 1977.

Peterson, J. A. *Conditioning for a purpose.* West Point, N.Y.: Leisure Press, 1978.

Pollack, M., Wilmore, J., & Fox, S. *Health and fitness through physical activity.* New York: John Wiley & Sons, Inc., 1978.

Rasch, P. *Weight training.* Dubuque, Iowa: William C. Brown Co., Publishers, 1977.

Reiter, M. J., & Cata, N. *Dynamic posture and conditioning for women.* Minneapolis: Burgess Publishing Co., 1970.

Ricci, B. *Physical and physiological conditioning for men.* Dubuque, Iowa: William C. Brown Co., Publishers, 1977.

Riley, D. P. *Strength training.* West Point, N.Y.: Leisure Press, 1978.

Roby, F., & Davis, R. P. *Jogging for fitness and weight control.* Philadelphia: W. B. Saunders Co., 1970.

Scholz, A. E., & Johnson, R. E. *Body conditioning for college men.* Philadelphia: W. B. Saunders Co., 1969.

Sorani, R. *Circuit training*. Dubuque, Iowa: William C. Brown Co., Publishers, 1977.

Stone, W. J., & Kroll, W. *Sports conditioning and weight training*. Boston: Allyn & Bacon, Inc., 1978.

Vermes, J. C. *The girls book of physical fitness*. New York: Association Press, 1972.

Vitale, F. *Individualized fitness programs*. Englewood Cliffs, N.J.: Prentice-Hall, Inc., 1973.

Williams, M. H. *Nutritional aspects of human physical and athletic performance*. Springfield, Ill.: Charles C Thomas, Publisher, 1976.

Wilmore, J. H. *Athletic training and physical fitness*. Boston: Allyn & Bacon, Inc., 1977.

Wilson, P. K., et al. *Policies and procedures of a cardiac rehabilitation program*. Philadelphia: Lea & Febiger, 1978.

Young, D. K. *Physical performance, fitness and diet*. Springfield, Ill.: Charles C Thomas, Publisher, 1977.

COACHING AND SPORTS

AAHPER. *Coaches' manual*. Washington, D.C.: The Alliance, 1978.

AAHPER. *Development of human values through sports*. Washington, D.C.: The Alliance, 1978.

AAHPER. *Drugs and the coach*. Washington, D.C.: The Alliance, 1978.

AAHPER. *Evaluating the high school athletic program*. Washington, D.C.: The Alliance, 1978.

AAHPER. *Motivation in coaching a team sport*. Washington, D.C.: The Alliance, 1978.

AAHPER. *Programs that work—Title IX*. Washington, D.C.: The Alliance, 1978.

AAHPER. *What research tells the coach about*. Washington, D.C.: The Alliance, 1978.

AAHPER. *The winning edge*. Washington, D.C.: The Alliance, 1978.

AAHPER. *Women's athletics: coping with controversy*. Washington, D.C.: The Alliance, 1978.

AAHPER. *Youth sports guide—for coaches and parents*. Washington, D.C.: The Alliance, 1978.

Alderman, R. *Psychological behavior in sport*. Philadelphia: W. B. Saunders Co., 1974.

Allen, D., & Fahey, B. W. *Being human in sport*. Philadelphia: Lea & Febiger, 1977.

Coakley, J. J. *Sport in society, issues and controversies*. St. Louis: The C. V. Mosby Co., 1978.

Corbin, C. *The athletic snowball*. Champaign, Ill.: Human Kinetics Publishers, 1978.

Cratty, B. *Psychology in contemporary sport: guidelines for coaches and athletes*. Englewood Cliffs, N.J.: Prentice-Hall, Inc., 1973.

Fisher, A. C. *Psychology of sport*. Palo Alto, Calif.: Mayfield Publishing Co., 1976.

Frost, R. *Psychological concepts applied to physical education and coaching*. Reading, Mass.: Addison-Wesley Publishing Co., Inc., 1971.

Gerber, E. W. *Sport and the body, a philosophical symposium*. Philadelphia: Lea & Febiger, 1972.

Harris, D. E. *Involvement in sport, a somatopsychic rationale for physical activity*. Philadelphia: Lea & Febiger, 1973.

Hart, M. *Sport in the sociocultural process*. Dubuque, Iowa: William C. Brown Co., Publishers, 1976.

Klafs, C. E., & Lyons, J. *The female athlete: a coach's guide to conditioning and training* (2nd ed.). St. Louis: The C. V. Mosby Co., 1978.

Loew, B. *The beauty of sport, a cross-disciplinary inquiry*. Englewood Cliffs, N.J.: Prentice-Hall, Inc., 1977.

Lucas, J. A., & Smith, R. A. *Saga of American sport*. Philadelphia: Lea & Febiger, 1978.

Magill, R., Ash, M., & Small, F. *Children in sport: a contemporary anthology*. Champaign, Ill.: Human Kinetics Publishers, 1978.

Martens, R. *Psychology of sport*. New York: Harper & Row, Publishers, Inc., 1975.

Martens, R. *Joy and sadness in children's sports*. Champaign, Ill.: Human Kinetics Publishers, 1978.

Methany, E. *Connotations of movement in sport and dance*. Dubuque, Iowa: William C. Brown Co., Publishers, 1965.

Miller, D. M. *Coaching the female athlete*. Philadelphia: Lea & Febiger, 1974.

Miller, D. M., & Russell, K. *Sport: a contemporary view*. Philadelphia: Lea & Febiger, 1971.

Neal, P. *Coaching girls and women*. Boston: Allyn & Bacon, Inc., 1975.

Neal, P., & Tutko, T. A. *Coaching girls and women: psychological perspectives*. Boston: Allyn & Bacon, Inc., 1975.

Oglesby, C. E. *Women and sport*. Philadelphia: Lea & Febiger, 1978.

Poindexter, H., & Mushier, C. L. *Coaching competitive team sports for girls and women*. Philadelphia: W. B. Saunders Co., 1973.

Rushall, B. S. *The development and control of behavior in sport and physical education*. Philadelphia: Lea & Febiger, 1972.

Sabock, R. *The coach*. Philadelphia: W. B. Saunders Co., 1973.

Singer, R. *Coaching athletics and psychology*. New York: McGraw-Hill Book Co., 1972.

Slusher, H. S. *Man, sport, and existence: a critical analysis*. Philadelphia: Lea & Febiger, 1967.

Thompson, W., & Clegg, R. *Modern sports officiating—a practical guide*. Dubuque, Iowa: William C. Brown Co., Publishers, 1974.

Tutko, T. A., & Richards, J. W. *Coach's practical guide to athletic motivation.* Boston: Allyn & Bacon Inc., 1972.

Vanek, M., & Cratty, B. J. *Psychology and the super athlete,* New York: Macmillan Publishing Co., Inc., 1970.

ANATOMY AND PHYSIOLOGY

Anthony, C. P. *Basic concepts in anatomy and physiology: a programmed presentation* (3rd ed.). St. Louis: The C. V. Mosby Co., 1974.

Anthony, C. P. *Anatomy and physiology laboratory manual* (10th ed.). St. Louis: The C. V. Mosby Co., 1978.

Anthony, C. P., & Alyn, I. *Structure and function of the body.* St. Louis: The C. V. Mosby Co., 1976.

Anthony, C. P., & Thibodeau, G. A. *Textbook of anatomy and physiology* (10th ed.). St. Louis: The C. V. Mosby Co., 1978.

Ashley, R. *Human anatomy.* New York: John Wiley & Sons, Inc., 1976.

Astrand, P., & Rodahl, K. *Textbook of work physiology.* New York: McGraw-Hill Book Co., 1977.

Brooks, S. M. *Basic science and the human body: anatomy and physiology.* St. Louis: The C. V. Mosby Co., 1975.

Brown, R. C., & Kenyon, G. S. *Classical studies on physical activity.* Englewood Cliffs, N.J.: Prentice-Hall, Inc., 1968.

Clarke, D. H. *Exercise physiology.* Englewood Cliffs, N.J.: Prentice-Hall, Inc., 1975.

Clarke, H. H. *Muscular strength and endurance in man.* Englewood Cliffs, N.J.: Prentice-Hall, Inc., 1966.

Crouch, J. E. *Functional human anatomy.* Philadelphia: Lea & Febiger, 1978.

Crouch, J. E., & McClintic, J. R. *Human anatomy and physiology.* New York: John Wiley & Sons, Inc., 1976.

Davies, J. *Human developmental anatomy.* New York: John Wiley & Sons, Inc., 1963.

Davis, E., Logan, G. A., & McKinney, W. C. *Biophysical value of muscular activity.* Dubuque, Iowa: William C. Brown Co., Publishers, 1965.

Dawson, H. L. *Basic human anatomy.* New York: Appleton-Century-Crofts, 1966.

DeVries, H. A. *Laboratory experiments in physiology of exercise.* Dubuque, Iowa: William C. Brown Co., Publishers, 1971.

DeVries, H. A. *Physiology of exercise for physical education and athletics.* Dubuque, Iowa: William C. Brown Co., Publishers, 1975.

Edington, D. W., & Edgerton, V. R. *The biology of physical activity.* Boston: Houghton Mifflin Co., 1976.

Elhardt, W. P., & Orth, O. S. *Physiological anatomy.* St. Louis: John S. Swift Co., 1936.

Falls, H. *Exercise physiology.* New York: Academic Press, 1968.

Francis, C. C., & Martin, A. H. *Introduction to human anatomy* (7th ed.). St. Louis: The C. V. Mosby Co., 1975.

Fulton, J. F. *A textbook of physiology.* Philadelphia: W. B. Saunders Co., 1950.

Gray, H., & Goss, C. M. *Gray's anatomy of the human body.* Philadelphia: Lea & Febiger, 1973.

Grinnell, A., & Barber, A. A. *Laboratory experiments in physiology* (9th ed.). St. Louis: The C. V. Mosby Co., 1976.

Grollman, S. *The human body: its structure and physiology.* New York: Macmillan Publishing Co., Inc., 1974.

Hamilton, W. J. (Ed.). *Textbook of human anatomy* (2nd ed.). St. Louis: The C. V. Mosby Co., 1976.

Hole, J. *Human anatomy and physiology.* Philadelphia: W. B. Saunders Co., 1978.

Jones, K., Shainberg, L., & Byer, C. *The human body.* New York: Harper & Row, Publishers, Inc., 1971.

Karpovich, P., & Sinning, W. *Physiology of muscular activity.* Philadelphia: W. B. Saunders Co., 1971.

Lamb, D. *Physiology of exercise responses and adaptations.* New York: Macmillan Publishing Co., Inc., 1978.

Leyshon, G. A. *Programmed functional anatomy.* St. Louis: The C. V. Mosby Co., 1974.

Matthews, D., & Fox, E. *The physiological basis of physical of physical education and athletics.* Philadelphia: W. B. Saunders Co., 1976.

Matthews, D., Stacey, R., & Hoover, G. *Physiology of muscular activity and exercise.* New York: John Wiley & Sons, Inc., 1964.

Morehouse, L. E., & Miller, A. T. *Physiology of exercise* (7th ed.). St. Louis: The C. V. Mosby Co., 1976.

Paterson, D., & Cunningham, D. *The physiological basis of physical education and athletics.* Philadelphia: W. B. Saunders Co., 1977.

Ricci, B. *Experiments in the physiology of human performance.* Philadelphia: Lea & Febiger, 1970.

Schade, J. P. *Introduction to functional human anatomy.* Philadelphia: W. B. Saunders Co., 1970.

Schottelius, B. A., & Schottelius, D. D. *Textbook of physiology* (18th ed.). St. Louis: The C. V. Mosby Co., 1978.

Sharkey, B. *Physiology and physical activity.* New York: Harper & Row, Publishers, Inc., 1975.

Sinning, W. *Experiments and demonstrations in exercise physiology.* Philadelphia: W. B. Saunders Co., 1975.

Sproul, E. E. *The science of the human body*. New York: Pocket Books, Inc., 1963.

KINESIOLOGY AND BIOMECHANICS

Barham, J. N. *Mechanical kinesiology*. St. Louis: The C. V. Mosby Co., 1978.

Barham, J. N., & Thomas, W. *Anatomical kinesiology—a programmed text*. New York: Macmillan Publishing Co., Inc., 1969.

Barham, J. N., & Wooten, E. P. *Structural kinesiology*. New York: Macmillan Publishing Co., Inc., 1973.

Bowen, W. P. *Applied anatomy and kinesiology*. Philadelphia: Lea & Febiger, 1953.

Broer, M. *Efficiency of human movement*. Philadelphia: W. B. Saunders Co., 1973.

Broer, M. *Laboratory experiences: exploring efficiency of human movement*. Philadelphia: W. B. Saunders Co., 1973.

Cooper, J. M. *Selected topics on biomechanics*. Chicago: Athletic Institute, 1971.

Cooper, J. M., & Glassow, R. B. *Kinesiology* (4th ed.). St. Louis: The C. V. Mosby Co., 1976.

Drury, B. J. *Muscles in action*. Palo Alto, Calif.: The National Press, 1962.

Dyson, G. *The mechanics of athletes*. New York: Holmes & Meier Publishers, Inc., 1978.

Groves, R., & Camaione, D. *Concepts in kinesiology*. Philadelphia: W. B. Saunders Co., 1975.

Harris, R. *Kinesiology, workbook and laboratory manual*. Boston: Houghton Mifflin Co., 1977.

Hay, J. *The biomechanics of sports techniques*. Englewood Cliffs, N.J.: Prentice-Hall, Inc., 1978.

Hinson, M. *Kinesiology*. Dubuque, Iowa: William C. Brown Co., Publishers, 1977.

Jensen, C., & Schultz, G. *Applied kinesiology*. New York: McGraw-Hill Book Co., 1977.

Kelley, C. *Kinesiology: fundamentals of motion description*. Englewood Cliffs, N.J.: Prentice-Hall, Inc., 1971.

Krause, J. V., & Barharn, J. N. *The mechanical foundations of human motion: a programmed text*. St. Louis: The C. V. Mosby Co., 1975.

Logan, G. A., & McKinney, W. C. *Kinesiology*. Dubuque, Iowa: William C. Brown Co., Publishers, 1970.

Logan, G. A., & McKinney, W. C. *Anatomic kinesiology*. Dubuque, Iowa: William C. Brown Co., Publishers, 1977.

Miller, D., & Nelson, A. C. *Biomechanics of sport*. Philadelphia: Lea & Febiger, 1973.

Northrup, J. W., & Logan, G. A., & McKinney, W. *Introduction to biomechanics analysis of sport*. Dubuque, Iowa: William C. Brown Co., Publishers, 1974.

Rasch, P., & Burks, R. *Kinesiology and applied anatomy*. Philadelphia: Lea & Febiger, 1974.

Scott, G. *Analysis of human motion*. New York: Appleton-Century-Crofts, 1963.

Spence, D. W. *Essentials of kinesiology—a laboratory manual*. Philadelphia: Lea & Febiger, 1975.

Steindler, A. *Kinesiology*. Springfield, Ill.: Charles C Thomas, Publisher, 1977.

Thompson, C. W. *Manual of structural kinesiology* (8th ed.). St. Louis: The C. V. Mosby Co., 1977.

Wells, K. F., & Luttgens, K. *Kinesiology—scientific basis of human motion*. Philadelphia: W. B. Saunders Co., 1976.

Williams, M., & Lissner, H. *Biomechanics of human motion*. Philadelphia: W. B. Saunders Co., 1977.

TEAM, INDIVIDUAL, AND DUAL ACTIVITIES
General

AAHPER. *DGWS sports guides*. Washington, D.C.: The Alliance.

AAHPER. *Encyclopedia of physical education, fitness and sport*. Washington, D.C.: The Alliance, 1978.

AAHPER. *Self-teaching sports techniques*. Washington, D.C.: The Alliance, 1978.

Andrews, E., et al. *Physical education for girls and women*. Englewood Cliffs, N.J.: Prentice-Hall, Inc., 1963.

Andrews, G., Saurborn, J., & Schneider, E. *Physical education for today's boys and girls*. Boston: Allyn & Bacon, Inc., 1960.

Annarino, A. A. *Fundamental movement and sport skill development*. Columbus, Ohio: Charles E. Merrill Publishing Co., 1973.

Armbruster, D. A., Irwin, L. W., & Musker, F. F. *Basic skills in sports*. St. Louis: The C. V. Mosby Co., 1963.

Broer, M. *Individual sports for women*. Philadelphia: W. B. Saunders Co., 1971.

Casady, D. R. *Physical education activities for men*. New York: Macmillan Publishing Co., Inc., 1973.

Cratty, B. J. *Teaching motor skills*. Englewood Cliffs, N.J.: Prentice-Hall, Inc., 1973.

Dewitt, R. T. *Teaching individual and team sports*. Englewood Cliffs, N.J.: Prentice-Hall, Inc., 1972.

Dintiman, G. B. *A comprehensive manual of physical education activities for men*. New York: Appleton-Century-Crofts, 1970.

Dratz, J. P., & Coker, H. L. *Men's physical education handbook*. Dubuque, Iowa: William C. Brown Co., Publishers, 1961.

Edgren, H., & Gruber, J. *Teacher's handbook of indoor and outdoor games*. Englewood Cliffs, N.J.: Prentice-Hall, Inc., 1963.

Fait, H., Shaw, J. H., & Fox, G. I. *A manual of physical*

education activities. Philadelphia: W. B. Saunders Co., 1956.

Fox, E., & Sysler, B. *Life-time sports for the college student*. Dubuque, Iowa: William C. Brown Co., Publishers, 1972.

Hale, P. *Individual sports—a textbook for teachers*. Dubuque, Iowa: William C. Brown Co., Publishers, 1974.

Hess, L. A. *Merrill Sports Series*. Columbus, Ohio: Charles E. Merrill Publishing Co.

Lawther, J. *Learning and performance of physical skills*. Englewood Cliffs, N.J.: Prentice-Hall, Inc., 1977.

McCue, B. F. *Physical education activities for women*. New York: Macmillan Publishing Co., Inc., 1969.

Means, L. E. *Physical education activities, sports and games*. Dubuque, Iowa: William C. Brown Co., Publishers, 1952.

Miller, K. *Physical education activities for men and women*. Dubuque, Iowa: William C. Brown Co., Publishers, 1963.

Mushier, C. *Team sports for girls and women*. Philadelphia: W. B. Saunders Co., 1973.

Paterson, A., & West, E. L. *Team sports for girls*. New York: The Ronald Press Co., 1971.

Physical education activities series. 31 vols., Dubuque, Iowa: William C. Brown Co., Publishers.

Purdue University Department of Physical Education for Women. *Physical education for women*. Minneapolis: Burgess Publishing Co., 1958.

Saunders physical education series. Philadelphia: W. B. Saunders Co.

Seaton, D. C., & Clayton, I. A., Leibee, H. C., & Messersmith, L. *Physical education handbook*. Englewood Cliffs, N.J.: Prentice-Hall, Inc., 1974.

Sports education series. Boston: Allyn & Bacon, Inc.

Stanley, D. K., & Waglow, J. F. *Physical education activities handbook for men and women*. Boston: Allyn & Bacon, Inc., 1966.

Thompson, D., & Carver, J. *Physical activities for women*. Englewood Cliffs, N.J.: Prentice-Hall, Inc., 1974.

Van Huss, V., Friedrich, J., Neimeyer, R., & Olson, H. *Physical activity in modern living*. Englewood Cliffs, N.J.: Prentice-Hall, Inc., 1969.

Vannier, M., & Poindexter, H. *Individual and team sports for girls and women*. Philadelphia: W. B. Saunders Co., 1976.

Wadsworth sports skill series, 26 vols. Belmont, Calif.: Wadsworth Publishing Co.

Specific
Archery

AAHPER. *Archery—a planning guide for group and individual instruction*. Washington, D.C.: The Alliance, 1978.

Annarino, A. A. *Archery: individualized instructional program*. Englewood Cliffs, N.J.: Prentice-Hall, Inc., 1973.

Campbell, D. *Archery*. Englewood Cliffs, N.J.: Prentice-Hall, Inc., 1970.

McKiney, W. C. *Archery*. Dubuque, Iowa; William C. Brown Co., Publishers, 1975.

Pszczola, L. *Archery*. Philadelphia; W. B. Saunders Co., 1976.

Badminton

Annarino, A. A. *Badminton: individualized instructional program*. Englewood Cliffs, N.J.: Prentice-Hall, Inc., 1973.

Bloss, M., & Brow, V. *Badminton*. Dubuque, Iowa; William C. Brown Co., Publishers, 1975.

Johnson, S. J. *Badminton*. Philadelphia: W. B. Saunders Co., 1974.

Pelton, B. C. *Badminton*. Englewood Cliffs, N.J.: Prentice-Hall, Inc., 1971.

Poole, J. *Badminton*. Pacific Palisades, Calif.: Goodyear Publishing Co., 1973.

Wright, L. *Your book of badminton*. Levittown, N.Y.: Transatlantic Arts Inc., 1978.

Wynn, R. *Badminton, advanced*. Philadelphia: W. B. Saunders Co., 1970.

Bait casting

Liotta, E. J. *The technique of bait casting*. Englewood Cliffs, N. J.: Prentice-Hall, Inc., 1949.

Baseball

Alston, W., & Weiskopf, D. *The complete handbook: strategies and techniques for winning*. Boston: Allyn & Bacon, Inc., 1972.

Siebert, D., & Vogil, O. *Baseball*. New York, Sterling Publishing Co., Inc., 1978.

Watts, L. *The fine art of baseball: a complete guide to strategy, skills and system*. Englewood Cliffs, N.J.: Prentice-Hall, Inc., 1973.

Basketball

Barnes, M., *Girl's basketball*. Boston: Allyn & Bacon, Inc., 1978.

Bell, M. *Women's basketball*. Dubuque, Iowa: William C. Brown Co., Publishers, 1973.

Cathcart, J. *Multiple-continuous offense for high school basketball*. Englewood Cliffs, N.J.: Prentice-Hall, Inc., 1968.

Cooper, J. N., & Siedentop, D. *The theory and science of basketball*. Philadelphia: Lea & Febiger, 1975.

Ebert, F., & Cheatum, B. A. *Basketball—five players*, Philadelphia: W. B. Saunders Co., 1977.

Hanson, D. *Basketball*. Englewood Cliffs, N.J.: Prentice-Hall, Inc., 1972.

Miller, K. D., & Horky, R. U. *Modern basketball for women*. Columbus, Ohio: Charles E. Merrill Publishing Co., 1970.

Mumford, K., & Wadsworth, M. *Beginner's guide to basketball*. Levittown, N.Y.: Transatlantic Arts Inc., 1978.

Schaafsma, F. *Basketball for women*. Philadelphia: W. B. Saunders Co., 1977.

Wilkes, G. *Basketball for men*. Philadelphia: W. B. Saunders Co., 1977.

Bicycling

Fithter, G. S., & Kingsbay, K. *Bicycling*. New York: Golden Press, 1972.

Wagenvoord, J. *Bikes and riders*. Levittown, N.Y.: Transatlantic Arts Inc., 1978.

Bowling

Annarino, A. A. *Bowling: individualized instructional program*. Englewood Cliffs, N.J.: Prentice-Hall, Inc., 1973.

Bellisimo, L. *Bowler's manual*. Englewood Cliffs, N.J.: Prentice-Hall Inc., 1975.

Casady, D., & Liba, M. *Beginning bowling*. Belmont, Calif.: Wadsworth Publishing Co., 1962.

Day, N., & Rayner, M. *Bowling*. Chicago: Athletic Institute, 1974.

Mackey, R. *Bowling*. Palo Alto, Calif.: Mayfield Publishing Co., 1974.

Martin, J., & Tandy, R. *Bowling*. Dubuque, Iowa: William C. Brown Co., Publishers, 1975.

Schunk, C. *Bowling*. Philadelphia: W. B. Saunders Co., 1976.

Dance

AAHPER. *Dance as education*. Washington, D.C.: The Alliance, 1978.

Ellfeldt, L. *Folk dance*. Dubuque, Iowa: William C. Brown Co., Publishers, 1969.

Ellfeldt, L. *Dance: from magic to art*. Dubuque, Iowa: William C. Brown Co., Publishers, 1976.

Fallon, D., & Kuchenmeister, S. A. *The art of ballroom dancing*. Minneapolis: Burgess Publishing Co., 1977.

Gilbert, C. *International folk dance at a glance*. Minneapolis: Burgess Publishing Co., 1974.

Gilbert, P., & Lockhart, E. *Music for the modern dance*. Dubuque, Iowa: William C. Brown Co., Publishers, 1977.

Harris, J. A., Pittman, A., & Walker, M. S. *Dance awhile: handbook of folk, square and social dance*. Minneapolis: Burgess Publishing Co., 1978.

Jensen, C., & Jensen, M. B. *Beginning square dance*. Belmont, Calif.: Wadsworth Publishing Co., Inc., 1966.

Kleinman, S. *Social dancing, fundamental*. Columbus, Ohio: Charles E. Merrill Publishing Co., 1968.

Lockhart, A., & Pease, E. *Modern dance*. Dubuque, Iowa: William C. Brown Co., Publishers, 1973.

Mynatt, C., & Kaiman, B. *Folk dancing for students and teachers*. Dubuque, Iowa: William C. Brown Co., Publishers, 1975.

Nash, B. *Tap dance*. Dubuque, Iowa: William C. Brown Co., Publishers, 1969.

Norris, D., & Shriner, R. *Keynotes to modern dance*. Minneapolis: Burgess Publishing Co., 1969.

Pease, E. *Modern dance*. Dubuque, Iowa: William C. Brown Co., Publishers, 1976.

Phillips, P. *Contemporary square dance*. Dubuque, Iowa: William C. Brown, 1968.

Pillich, W. *Social dance*. Dubuque, Iowa: William C. Brown Co., Publishers, 1967.

Schlaich, J., & DuPont, B. (Eds.) *Dance: the art of production*. St. Louis: The C. V. Mosby Co., 1977.

Spiesman, M. *Folk dancing*. Philadelphia: W. B. Saunders Co., 1970.

Wakefield, E. *Folk dancing in america*. Columbus, Ohio: Charles E. Merrill Publishing Co., 1966.

Fencing

Bower, M. *Fencing*. Dubuque, Iowa: William C. Brown Co., Publishers, 1976.

DeBeaumont, C. L. *Your book of fencing*. Levittown, N.Y.: Transatlantic Arts Inc., 1978.

Moody, D. L., & Hepner, B. J. *Modern foil fencing, fun and fundamentals*. California: B & D Publications, 1972.

Wyrick, W. *Foil fencing*. Philadelphia: W. B. Saunders Co., 1971.

Field hockey

Barnes, M. *Field hockey: the coach and player*. Boston: Allyn & Bacon, Inc., 1978.

Delano, A. *Field hockey*. Dubuque, Iowa: William C. Brown Co., Publishers, 1968.

Lees, J., & Shellenberger, B. *Field hockey*. New York: Ronald Press Co., 1971.

Reed, B., & Walker, F. *Advanced hockey for women*. Levittown, N.Y.: Transatlantic Arts Inc., 1978.

Wein, H. *The science of field hockey*. Levittown, N.Y.: Transatlantic Arts Inc., 1978.

Football

Fuoss, D. *Championship football.* Englewood Cliffs, N.J.: Prentice-Hall, Inc., 1974.

Kingsford, T. *Playing with a football.* New York: Sterling Publishing Co., Inc., 1978.

Golf

AAHPER. *Ideas for golf instruction.* Washington, D.C.: The Alliance, 1970.

Annarino, A. A. *Golf: individualized instructional program.* Englewood Cliffs, N.J.: Prentice-Hall, Inc., 1973.

Cheatum, B. *Golf.* Philadelphia: W. B. Saunders Co., 1975.

Diaz, C. *Golf: a beginner's guide.* Palo Alto, Calif.: Mayfield Publishing, 1974.

Dobereiner, P. *Golf explained.* New York: Sterling Publishing Co., Inc., 1978.

Ford, D. *Start golf young.* New York: Sterling Publishing Co., Inc., 1978.

Hudson, D. *Your book of golf.* Levittown, N.Y.: Transatlantic Arts Inc., 1978.

Myers, R., & Gordin, R. *Golf fundamentals.* Columbus: Ohio: Charles E. Merrill Publishing Co., 1973.

Nance, V., & Davis, E. C. *Golf.* Dubuque, Iowa: William C. Brown Co., Publishers, 1975.

National Golf Foundation, *Golf lessons.* Chicago: The Foundation, 1969.

National Gold Foundation, *Speedy golf.* Chicago: The Foundation, 1969.

Thompson, B. *How to play golf.* Englewood Cliffs, N.J.: Prentice-Hall Inc., 1939.

Wiren, G. *Golf.* Englewood Cliffs, N.J.: Prentice-Hall, Inc., 1971.

Gymnastics and tumbling

Annarino, A. A. *Teaching tumbling in physical education.* Cincinnati, Ohio: Tri-State, 1960.

Baley, J. *Gymnastics in the schools.* Boston: Allyn & Bacon, Inc., 1965.

Boone, W. *Illustrated handbook of gymnastics, tumbling and trampolining.* Englewood Cliffs, N.J.: Prentice-Hall Inc., 1976.

Bowers, C. *Judging and coaching women's gymnastics.* Palo Alto, Calif.: Mayfield Publishing Co., 1972.

Carter, E. *Gymnastics for girls and women.* Englewood Cliffs, N.J.: Prentice-Hall, Inc., 1968.

Cooper, P. *Feminine gymnastics.* Minneapolis: Burgess Publishing Co., 1973.

DeCarlo, T. *Handbook of progressive gymnastics.* Englewood Cliffs, N.J.: Prentice-Hall, Inc., 1963.

Drury, B., & Schmid, A. *Introduction to women's gymnastics.* Palo Alto, Calif.: Mayfield Publishing Co., 1973.

Frederick, B. A. *Gymnastics action cards.* Minneapolis: Burgess Publishing Co., 1965.

Frederick, B. A. *Gymnastics for men.* Dubuque, Iowa: William C. Brown Co., Publishers, 1966.

Frederick, B. A. *Gymnastics for women.* Dubuque, Iowa: William C. Brown Co., Publishers, 1966.

Gedney, J. *Tumbling and balancing: basic skills and variations.* Englewood Cliffs, N.J.: Prentice-Hall, Inc., 1977.

Hennessy, J. *Trampolining.* Dubuque, Iowa: William C. Brown Co., Publishers, 1968.

Hughes, E. *Gymnastics for girls.* New York: The Ronald Press Co., 1971.

Kaneko, A. *Olympic gymnastics.* New York: Sterling Publishing Co., Inc., 1978.

LaBue, F., & Norman, J. *This is trampolining.* Dubuque, Iowa: William C. Brown Co., Publishers, 1958.

Loken, N. *Gymnastics.* New York: Sterling Publishing Co., Inc., 1978.

Loken, N., & Willoughby, R. *The complete book of gymnastics.* Englewood Cliffs, N.J.: Prentice-Hall, Inc., 1977.

Ryser, O. *A manual for tumbling and apparatus and stunts.* Dubuque, Iowa: William C. Brown Co., Publishers, 1976.

Salmela, J. H. *The advanced study of gymnastics.* Springfield, Ill.: Charles C Thomas, Publisher, 1976.

Schmid, A., *Modern rhythmic gymnastics.* Palo Alto, Calif.: Mayfield Publishing Co., 1976.

Schmid, A., & Drury, B. *Gymnastics for women.* Palo Alto, Calif.: Mayfield Publishing Co., 1977.

Sweeney, J. *Olympic gymnastic fundamentals.* Columbus, Ohio: Charles E. Merrill Publishing Co., 1973.

Taylor, B., Bajin, B., & Zivic, T. *Olympic gymnastics for men and women.* Englewood Cliffs, N.J.: Prentice-Hall, Inc., 1972.

Vincent, W. *Gymnastic routines for men.* Philadelphia: W. B. Saunders Co., 1972.

Wachtel, E. *Girls gymnastics.* New York: Sterling Publishing Co., Inc., 1978.

Handball

Nelson, R., & Berger, H. *Handball.* Englewood Cliffs, N.J.: Prentice-Hall, Inc., 1971.

Reznik, J. W. *Championship handball.* West Point, N.Y.: Lesiure Press, 1978.

Rowland, B. J. *Handball—a complete guide.* Levittown, N.Y.: Transatlantic Arts Inc., 1978.

Yessis, M. *Handball.* Dubuque, Iowa: William C. Brown Co., Publishers, 1977.

Zafferano, G. *Handball basics.* New York: Sterling Publishing Co., Inc., 1978.

Ice hockey

Hayes, D. *Ice hockey.* Dubuque, Iowa: William C. Brown Co., Publishers, 1972.

Walford, G. *Ice hockey.* New York: The Ronald Press Co., 1971.

Lacrosse

Delano, A. *Lacrosse for girls and women.* Dubuque, Iowa: William C. Brown Co., Publishers, 1970.

Orienteering

Rand, J., & Walker, T. *This is orienteering.* Levittown, N.Y.: Transatlantic Arts Inc., 1978.

Racquetball/paddleball/squash

Allsen, P., & Witbeck, A. *Racquetball/paddleball.* Dubuque, Iowa: William C. Brown Co., Publishers, 1977.

Bloss, M. *Squash,* Dubuque, Iowa: William C. Brown Co., Publishers, 1977.

Hammer, H. *Paddleball: how to play the game,* New York: Grosset & Dunlap, Inc., 1972.

Hawkey, R. *Beginners guide to squash.* Levittown, N.Y.: Transatlantic Arts Inc., 1978.

Verner, B., & Skowrup, D. *Racquetball.* Palo Alto, Calif.: Mayfield Publishing Co., 1977.

Running

Campbell, G. *Marathon, the world of the long distance athlete.* New York: Sterling Publishing Co., Inc., 1978.

Roby, F., & Davis, R. *Jogging for fitness and weight control.* Philadelphia: W. B. Saunders Co., 1970.

Self-defense/judo/karate

Kim, D. *Judo.* Dubuque, Iowa: William C. Brown Co., Publishers, 1977.

Kim, D. *Karate and personal defense.* Dubuque, Iowa: William C. Brown Co., Publishers, 1978.

Wyness, J. *Practical personal defense.* Palo Alto, Calif.: Mayfield Publishing Co., 1975.

Skiing

Heller, M. *Skiing.* Levittown, N.Y.: Transatlantic Arts Inc., 1978.

Soccer

Annarino, A. A. *Teaching soccer in physical education.* Cincinnati, Ohio: Tri-State, 1956.

Bailey, C. I., & Keller, F. L. *Soccer.* Philadelphia: W. B. Saunders Co., 1970.

Goldman, H. *Soccer.* Boston: Allyn & Bacon, Inc., 1969.

Herbin, R., & Rethacker, J. *Soccer, the way the pros play.* New York: Sterling Publishing Co., Inc., 1978.

Hupprich, F. *Soccer and speedball for girls.* New York: The Ronald Press Co., 1971.

Lammich, G., & Kaddow, H. *Warm up for soccer: more than 100 ways to have fun practicing the fundamentals.* New York: Sterling Publishing Co., Inc., 1978.

Mott, J. *Soccer and speedball for women.* Dubuque, Iowa: William C. Brown Co., Publishers, 1972.

Nelson, R. *Soccer for men.* Dubuque, Iowa: William C. Brown Co., Publishers, 1976.

Schmid, I., McKeon, J., & Schmid, M. *Skills and strategies of successful soccer.* Englewood Cliffs, N.J.: Prentice-Hall, Inc., 1968.

Trimby, R. *Your book of soccer.* Levittown, N.Y.: Transatlantic Arts Inc., 1978.

Softball

Dobson, M., & Sisley, B. L. *Softball for girls.* New York: The Ronald Press Co., 1971.

Kneer, M., & McCord, C. *Softball: slow and fast pitch.* Dubuque, Iowa: William C. Brown Co., Publishers, 1976.

Noren, A. *Softball.* New York: A. S. Barnes & Co., Inc., 1940.

Swimming-aquatics

AAHPER. *Action in aquatics.* Washington, D.C., The Alliance, 1978.

AAHPER. *Aquatics for all.* Washington, D.C.: The Alliance, 1978.

AAHPER. *The new science of skin & scuba diving.* Washington, D.C.: The Alliance, 1978.

AAHPER. *Swimnastics is fun.* Washington, D.C.: The Alliance, 1978.

Armbruster, D. A., Allen, R. H., & Billingsley, H. S. *Swimming and diving* (6th ed.). St. Louis: The C. V. Mosby Co., 1973.

Balder, A. P. *Sport diving,* New York: Macmillan Publishing Co., Inc., 1978.

Barone, M. *Beginning diving.* Palo Alto, Calif.: Mayfield Publishing Co., 1973.

Bartels, R. *Swimming fundamentals.* Columbus, Ohio: Charles E. Merrill Publishing Co., 1969.

Councilman, J. *The science of swimming.* Englewood Cliffs, N.J.: Prentice-Hall, Inc., 1968.

Councilman, J., & Drinkwater, B. *Beginning skin and*

scuba diving. Belmont, Calif.: Wadsworth Publishing Co., Inc., 1964.

Gabrielsen, M. B. S., & Gabrielsen, B. *Aquatics handbook.* Englewood Cliffs, N.J.: Prentice-Hall, Inc., 1968.

Gaughram, J. *Swimming, advanced.* Dubuque, Iowa: William C. Brown Co., Publishers, 1977.

Gould, S. *Swimming the Shane Gould way.* New York: Sterling Publishing Co., Inc., 1972.

Hodgson, D. *Dive! dive! dive!* Levittown, N.Y.: Transatlantic Arts Inc., 1978.

Hogg, J. *Success in swimming.* Levittown, N.Y.: Transatlantic Arts Inc., 1978.

Jarvis, M. *Your book of swimming and lifesaving.* Levittown, N.Y.: Transatlantic Arts Inc., 1978.

Jones, F., & Lindeman, J. *The components of synchronized swimming.* Englewood Cliffs, N.J.: Prentice-Hall, Inc., 1975.

Lundholm, J., & Ruggieri, M. J. *Introduction to synchronized swimming.* Minneapolis: Burgess Publishing Co., 1976.

McKeown, J. *Learning and teaching swimming.* Levittown, N.Y.: Transatlantic Arts Inc., 1978.

Rackham, G. *Diving complete.* Levittown, N.Y.: Transatlantic Arts Inc., 1978.

Rackham, G. *Synchronized swimming.* Levittown, N.Y.: Transatlantic Arts Inc., 1978.

Ryan, J. *Learning to swim is fun.* New York: John Wiley & Sons, Inc., 1960.

Swimming, lifesaving, and diving. Washington, D.C.: American Red Cross, 1974.

Tillman, A. *Skin & scuba diving.* Dubuque, Iowa: William C. Brown Co., Publishers, 1962.

Torney, J., & Clayton, R. *Aquatic instruction, coaching and management.* Minneapolis: Burgess Publishing Co., 1970.

Table tennis

Bloss, M. V. *Table tennis.* Dubuque, Iowa: William C. Brown Co., Publishers, 1967.

Cartland, D. *Table tennis, illustrated.* New York: A. S. Barnes & Co., 1953.

Wasserman, S. *Table tennis.* New York: Sterling Publishing Co., Inc., 1978.

Tennis

AAHPER. *Ideas for tennis instruction.* Washington, D.C.: The Alliance, 1970.

AAHPER. *Tennis group instruction.* Washington, D.C.: The Alliance, 1978.

Annarino, A. A. *Tennis: individualized instructional program.* Englewood Cliffs, N.J.: Prentice-Hall, Inc., 1973.

Barnaby, J. *Advantage tennis.* Boston: Allyn & Bacon, Inc., 1975.

Brown, J. *Tennis: teaching, coaching, & directing programs.* Englewood Cliffs, N.J.: Prentice-Hall, Inc., 1976.

Brown, J. *Tennis without lessons.* Englewood Cliffs, N.J.: Prentice-Hall Inc., 1977.

Driver, H. *Tennis for teachers.* Philadelphia: W. B. Saunders Co., 1940.

Gensemer, R. T. *Tennis.* Philadelphia: W. B. Saunders Co., 1975.

Gould, D. *Tennis anyone?* Palo Alto, Calif.: Mayfield Publishing Co., 1975.

Jaeger, E., & Leighton, H. *Teaching tennis for school and recreation.* Minneapolis: Burgess Publishing Co., 1963.

Johnson, J., & Xanthos, P. *Tennis.* Dubuque, Iowa: William C. Brown Co., Publishers, 1976.

Jones, C. M. *Improving your tennis.* Levittown, N.Y.: Transatlantic Arts Inc., 1978.

Jones, C. M. *Your book of tennis.* Levittown, N.Y.: Transatlantic Arts Inc., 1978.

Jones, C. M., & Buxton, A. *Starting tennis.* Levittown, N.Y.: Transatlantic Arts Inc., 1978.

Kenfield, J. *Teaching and coaching tennis.* Dubuque, Iowa: William C. Brown Co., Publishers, 1976.

Leighton, H. *Junior tennis.* New York: Sterling Publishing Co., Inc., 1978.

Leighton, J. *Inside tennis; techniques of winning.* Englewood Cliffs, N.J.: Prentice-Hall, Inc., 1969.

Metzer, P. *Fine points of tennis.* New York: Sterling Publishing Co., Inc., 1978.

Murphy, C. *Tennis, advanced.* Dubuque, Iowa: William C. Brown Co., Publishers, 1976.

Murphy, C., & Murphy, B. *Tennis for the player, teacher and coach.* Philadelphia: W. B. Saunders Co., 1975.

Newcombe, J. *Advanced tennis.* New York: Sterling Publishing Co., Inc., 1978.

Newcombe, J. *Getting started in tennis.* New York: Sterling Publishing Co., Inc., 1978.

Pearce, W., & Pearce, J. *Tennis.* Englewood Cliffs, N.J.: Prentice-Hall, Inc., 1971.

Roy, H. *Tennis for schools.* Levittown, N.Y.: Transatlantic Arts Inc., 1978.

Tikmanis, G., & VanDerMeer, D. *Advanced tennis for coaches.* Philadelphia: Lea & Febiger, 1975.

Track and field

Bowers, R. *Track and field events.* Columbus, Ohio: Charles E. Merrill Publishing Co., 1974.

Bush, J., & Weiskopf, D. *Dynamic track and field.* Boston: Allyn & Bacon, Inc., 1978.

Clarke, R., & Boyle, R. *Successful track and field.* New York: Sterling Publishing Co., Inc., 1978.

Cretzmeyer, F. X., Alley L. E., & Tipton, C. M. *Track*

and field athletics. (8th ed.) St. Louis: The C. V. Mosby Co., 1974.

Doherty, K. J. *Modern track and field.* Englewood Cliffs, N.J.: Prentice-Hall, Inc., 1953.

Foreman, K., & Husted, V. *Track and field.* Dubuque, Iowa: William C. Brown Co., Publishers, 1977.

Jackson, N. *Track and field for girls and women,* Minneapolis: Burgess Publishing Co., 1968.

Jordan, P., & Spencer, B. *Champions in the making: quality training for track and field.* Englewood Cliffs, N.J.: Prentice-Hall, Co., 1968.

Robinson, C., et al. *Modern techniques of track and field.* Philadelphia: Lea & Febiger, 1974.

Thompson, D. *Modern track and field for girls and women.* Boston: Allyn & Bacon, Inc., 1973.

Wakefield, F., Harkins, D., & Cooper, J. M. *Track and field fundamentals for girls and women* (4th ed.). St. Louis: The C. V. Mosby Co., 1977.

Volleyball

Allen, G., & Weiskopf, D. *Handbook of winning volleyball.* Boston: Allyn & Bacon, Inc., 1976.

Annarino, A. A. *Teaching volleyball in physical education.* Cincinnati, Ohio: Tri-State, 1962.

Anthony, D. *Success in volleyball.* Levittown, N.Y.: Transatlantic Arts Inc., 1978.

Egstrom, G., & Schaafsma, F. *Volleyball.* Dubuque, Iowa: William C. Brown Co., Publishers, 1972.

James, D. *Volleyball for schools.* Levittown, N.Y.: Transatlantic Arts Inc., 1978.

Schaafsma, F., & Heck, A. *Volleyball for coaches and teachers.* Dubuque, Iowa: William C. Brown Co., Publishers, 1971.

Scrates, A., & Ward. J. *Volleyball.* Boston: Allyn & Bacon, Inc., 1976.

Shondell, D., & McManama, J. *Volleyball.* Englewood Cliffs, N.J.: Prentice-Hall, Inc., 1971.

Slaymaker, T., & Brown, V. *Power volleyball.* Philadelphia: W. B. Saunders Co., 1976.

Thigpen, J. *Power volleyball for girls and women.* Dubuque, Iowa: William C. Brown Co., Publishers, 1974.

Weight training

Fodor, R. V. *Competitive weightlifting.* New York: Sterling Publishing Co., Inc., 1978.

Massey, B. H., et al. *The kinesiology of weight lifting.* Dubuque, Iowa: William C. Brown Co., Publishers, 1959.

Wrestling

Carlton, R. F., & Patterson, B. *Principles of championship wrestling.* New York: A. S. Barnes & Co., Inc., 1972.

Perry, R. *Wrestling.* New York: Sterling Publishing Co., Inc., 1978.

Umbach, A., & Johnson, W. *Successful wrestling: its bases and problems.* Dubuque, Iowa: William C. Brown Co., Publishers, 1972.

Umbach, A., & Johnson, W. *Wrestling.* Dubuque, Iowa: William C. Brown Co., Publishers, 1977.

U.S. Naval Institute. *Wrestling.* New York: A. S. Barnes & Co., Inc., 1942.

APPENDIX B Selected reading articles

PART ONE

1. Annarino, A. A. The quest for physical education. *JOPER*, May 1971, p. 27.
2. Annarino, A. A. Physical education objectives: traditional vs. developmental. *JOPER*, Oct. 1977, p. 22.
3. Annarino, A. A. Operational taxonomy for physical education objectives. *JOPER*, Jan. 1978, p. 54.
4. Ariel, G. Physical education: 2001? *Quest*, Winter 1974, *21*, 49.
5. Bain, L. Description of the hidden curriculum in physical education. *Research Quarterly*, May 1976, 47(2), 154.
6. Bain, L. Status of curriculum theory in physical education. *JOPER*, March 1978, p. 25.
7. Bucher, C. National adult physical fitness survey: some implications. *JOPER*, Jan. 1974, p. 25.
8. Burton, D. Shaping the future. *JOPER*, March 1976, p. 20.
9. Caldwell, S. F. Toward a humanistic physical education. *JOPER*, May 1972, p. 31.
10. Cassidy, R. The cultural definition of physical education. *Quest*, Spring 1965, *6*, 11.
11. Cassidy, R. Societal determinants of human movement. *Quest*, June 1971, p. 16.
12. Cheffers, J. T. Bridging the theory into practice gap in curriculum. Paper presented at NASPE Curriculum Academy, AAHPER, Kansas City, Apr. 1978.
13. Clein, M. I., & Stone, W. J. Physical education and the classification of educational objectives: psychomotor domain. *The Physical Educator*, 1970, 27(1), 34.
14. Costner, C. E. Contributions to thought on physical education by selected contemporary philosophers. *Proceedings NCPEAM*, 1975, p. 51.
15. Davis, R. Writing behavioral objectives. *JOPER*, Apr. 1973, p. 47.
16. Davis, R. Writing behavioral objectives. *JOPER*, Jan. 1974, p. 47.
17. Hartman, B., & Clement, A. Adventure in key concepts: the Ohio guide for girls secondary physical education. *JOPER*, March 1973, p. 20.
18. Jewett, A. E. Who knows what tomorrow may bring? *Quest*, Winter 1974, *21*, 49.
19. Jewett, A. E., Jones, S., Lyneke, S., & Robinson, S. Educational changes through a taxonomy for writing physical education objectives. *Quest*, Winter 1971, *15*, 32.
20. Klesius, S. E. Physical education in the seventies: where do you stand? *JOPER*, Feb. 1971, p. 46.
21. Kneer, M. Exit competencies in physical education for the secondary school student. *JOPER*, Jan. 1978, p. 46.
22. Knight, R. Ohio-Michigan conference on curriculum improvement in secondary physical education. *JOPER*, Jan. 1970, p. 58.
23. Ley, K. Teaching understandings in physical education. *JOPER*, Jan. 1971, p. 21.

24. Lipton, E. D. Initiate reforms now. *JOPER*, Nov.-Dec. 1972, p. 24.

25. Locke, L. Implications for physical education. *Research Quarterly*, 1972, 43(3), 374.

26. Loughrey, T. Secondary school curriculum process. *JOPER*, March 1978, p. 20.

27. Marsh, R. L. Physically educated—what will it mean for tomorrow's high school student? *JOPER*, Jan. 1978, p. 50.

28. McIntyre, M. A model for the 70's. *JOPER*, Nov.-Dec. 1973, p. 29.

29. Melagrano, V. Status of curriculum practice. *JOPER*, March 1978, p. 27.

30. Mohr, D. Identifying the body of knowledge. *JOPER*, Jan. 1971, p. 23.

31. Murphy, B. L. The proper focus of our field is the study of sport. *JOPER*, June 1970, p. 27.

32. Newcombe, J. Urban involvement. *JOPER*, Nov-Dec. 1977, p. 24.

33. O'Donnell, C. Carry-over physical education in the elementary school. *JOPER,* Jan. 1973, p. 69.

34. Pease, D., & Crase, D. Commitment to change. *JOPER*, Apr. 1973, p. 35.

35. Rhea, H. A modern curriculum. *The Physical Educator*, March 1977, 34(1), 26.

36. Schmidt, C. Fantastically exciting and worthwhile educational experience. *JOPER*, June 1970, p. 29.

37. Schmidt, C. Education for a humane physically interacting society. *JOPER*, Jan. 1972, p. 33.

38. Sherman, W. D. Performance objectives. *JOPER,* Sept. 1971, p. 37.

39. Shockley, J. M. Needed: behavioral objectives in physical education. *JOPER*, Apr. 1973, p. 44.

40. Society of State Directors. A statement of basic beliefs about the school programs in HPER. *JOPER,* June 1973, p. 22.

41. Taylor, T., & Geisler, J. Improving elementary school programs. *JOPER*, March 1978, p. 31.

42. Terry, J. Changing habits by changing attitudes. *JOPER*, Sept. 1977, p. 13.

43. Triplett, E. Physical education's principal emphasis is upon building a fit America. *JOPER*, June 1970, p. 30.

44. Ulrich, C. The ultimate athlete: a review. *JOPER*, Jan. 1976, p. 12.

45. Varnes, P. Physical education should help the child enhance his physical me. *JOPER*, June 1970, p. 26.

46. Vogel, P. Battle Creek physical education curriculum project. *JOPER*, 1969, 40, 25.

47. Walker, D. A. A naturalistic model for curriculum planning. *School Review*, 1971, 80, 51.

48. Welsh, R. Futurism and physical education. *JOPER*, Oct. 1973, p. 28.

49. Young, S. Learning to cope with change and reality. *JOPER*, Jan. 1972, p. 28.

50. Zatz, D. H. How do you motivate students to learn? *JOPER*, March 1927, p. 26.

51. Zoloff, E. H. Physical education is a foundation for the development of democratic living in American life. *JOPER*, June 1970, p. 28.

PART TWO

1. AAHPER and NEA Conference Report. The young child: the significance of motor development. *JOPER*, May 1971, pp. 29-35.

2. Bird, J. Physical education and the middle school student. *JOPER*, March 1973, p. 25.

3. Blackmarr, S. Every child a winner. *JOPER*, Oct. 1974, p. 14.

4. Case, R. Piaget's theory of child development and its implications. *Phi Delta Kappan*, Sept. 1973, p. 20.

5. Collard, R. R. Exploration and play in human infants. *JOPER*, June 1972, p. 35.

6. Curry, N. Self concept and the educational experience in physical education. *The Physical Educator*, Oct. 1974, 31(3), 116.

7. Darst, P. W. Learning environments to create lifelong enjoyment of physical activity. *JOPER*, Jan. 1978, p. 44.

8. DeMaria, C. R. Movement education: an overview. *The Physical Educator*. May 1972, 2, 29.

9. Ellis, M. J. Play: practice and research in the 70's. *JOPER*, June 1972, p. 29.

10. Finchum, B., & Hanson, M. Who says the young child can't? *JOPER*, June 1972, p. 16.

11. Gilmore, J. B. Summary of play research. *JOPER*, June 1972, p. 42.

12. Granza, A. F. A measured approach to improvement of play environments. *JOPER*, June 1972, p. 43.

13. Herkowitz, J. Movement experiences for preschool children. *JOPER*, March 1977, p. 15.

14. Inbar, M. The socialization effect of game playing on pre-adolescents. *JOPER*, June 1972, p. 49.

15. Leaf, B. Happenings. *JOPER*, March 1973, p. 40.

16. Lewis, M. Sex differences in play behavior of the very young. *JOPER*, June 1972, p. 38.

17. Little, R. Project adventure. *JOPER*, June 1977, p. 13.

18. Mancini, V. H., Cheffers, J. T., & Zaichkowsky, L. D. Decision making in elementary children: effects on attitudes and interaction. *Research Quarterly*, March 1976, 47, 80.

19. Moffitt, M. Play as a medium for learning. *JOPER*, June 1972, p. 45.

20. Poll, T. Dance, self-esteem and motor acquisition. *JOPER*, Jan. 1979, p. 64.
21. Riley, M. Games and humanism. *JOPER*, Feb. 1975, p. 47.
22. Schafermeyer, H. Adventure programming—wilderness and urban. *JOPER*, Jan. 1978, p. 30.
23. Seefeldt, V. Middle schools: issues and future directions. *JOPER*, Feb. 1974, p. 32.
24. Shapiro, D. C. Knowledge of results and motor learning in preschool children. *Research Quarterly,* March 1977, *48,* 154.
25. Singer, R. N., & Lockhart, A. S. What do we mean by the expert in motor learning? *JOPER*, Feb. 1971, p. 34.
26. Slooten, P. V. Four theories of development and their implications for the physical education of adolescents. *The Physical Educator,* Dec. 1974, *31*(4), 181.
27. Snodgrass, J. Self-concept. *JOPER*, Nov.-Dec. 1977, p. 22.
28. Stafford, E. Middle schools: status of physical education programs. *JOPER*, Feb. 1974, p. 25.
29. Sterne, M. L. Way out games in the classroom. *JOPER*, June 1977, p. 38.
30. Stone, G. P. The play of little children. *Quest,* Spring 1965, *6,* 23.
31. Sutton-Smith, B. Play as a transformational set. *JOPER*, June 1972, p. 32.
32. Torbert, M., & Normandeau, C. New games. *JOPER*, Nov.-Dec. 1977, p. 16.
33. Webster, S. Project Adventure—a trip into the unknown. *JOPER*, Apr. 1978, p. 39.
34. Weinberg, H. Middle schools: selected annotated bibliography. *JOPER*, Feb. 1974, p. 35.

PART THREE

1. Anderson, E. New role expectations for contract teaching. *JOPER*, Oct. 1974, p. 37.
2. Annarino, A. A. I.I.P. *JOPER*, Oct. 1973, p. 20.
3. Annarino, A. A. Another way to teach. *JOPER*, Oct. 1974, p. 43.
4. Annarino, A. A. University basic instructional program—a new approach. *The Physical Educator,* Oct. 1974, *31*(3), 131.
5. Annarino, A. A. High school mini-activity physical education programs based on a multi-media individualized approach. *The Physical Educator,* Dec. 1975, *32*(4), 190.
6. Annarino, A. A., Taulman, R., & Otto, S. Tapes teach tumbling to Indiana youngsters. *JOPER*, Apr. 1977, p. 64.
7. Arnold, D. Compliance with Title IX in secondary school physical education. *JOPER*, Jan. 1977, p. 19.
8. Austin, D. A. A developmental physical education program. *JOPER*, Feb. 1978, p. 36.
9. Brynteson, P. Fitness for life: aerobics at Oral Roberts University. *JOPER*, Jan. 1978, p. 37.
10. Burlingame, M., & Pease, D. Educational change in the teaching of physical education. *Quest,* Jan. 1971, p. 15.
11. Cochrane, J. Student-centered physical education. *JOPER*, Sept. 1973, p. 25.
12. Cogan, M. Innovative ideas in college physical education programs. *JOPER*, Feb. 1973, p. 28.
13. Corbin, C. Changing consumers mean new concepts. *JOPER*, Jan. 1978, p. 43.
14. Cousens, C. Adapted sports and recreation for the handicapped child. *JOPER*, Nov.-Dec. 1972, p. 53.
15. Crisafulli, R. C. Equality in recreation for special needs children. *JOPER*, March 1978, p. 50.
16. Cutler, S. The nongraded concept and physical education. *JOPER*, Apr. 1974, p. 30.
17. DiRicco, P. Preparing for the mainstreamed environment: a necessary addition to preservice curriculums. *JOPER*, Jan. 1978, p. 24.
18. Driscoll, S., & Mathieson, D. A goal-centered individualized learning. *JOPER*, Sept. 1971, p. 27.
19. Ersing, W. The nature of physical education programming for the mentally retarded and physically handicapped. *JOPER*, Feb. 1974, p. 89.
20. Fast, B. Contingency contracting. *JOPER*, Sept. 1971, p. 31.
21. First National Conference on Secondary School Physical Education. The whole thing. *JOPER*, May 1973, p. 21.
22. Foster, L. E. A tool for flexibility. *JOPER*, Oct. 1974, p. 38.
23. Frederickson, V. I can. *JOPER*, May 1972, p. 33.
24. Fry, K. Simulation in curriculum planning. *Quest,* Summer 1975, *24,* 85.
25. Geddes, D. Physical activity: a necessity for severely and profoundly mentally retarded individuals. *JOPER*, March 1974, p. 73.
26. Greene, L. Learning centers: a humanistic approach to the educational process. *JOPER*, May 1978, p. 30.
27. Grieve, A. Try it—you'll like it. *JOPER*, May 1972, p. 34.
28. Hill, C. E. Computer-based resource units in health and PE. *JOPER*, June 1975, p. 26.
29. Hook, A., et al. Computer monitored physicist education. *JOPER*, Sept. 1973, p. 24.
30. Kelly, B. Implementing Title IX. *JOPER*, Feb. 1977, p. 27.
31. Kline, J. Inglemoor High School's outdoor educa-

tion recreation program. *JOPER*, Nov-Dec. 1974, p. 81.

32. Kraft, R. E. The students' view of contract teaching. *JOPER*, Oct. 1974. p. 47.

33. Lawson, H., & Lawson, B. An alternative program model for secondary school physical education. *JOPER*, Feb. 1977, p. 38.

34. Locke, L. Prepackaged sports skill instruction: a review of selected research. *JOPER*, Sept. 1971, p. 57.

35. Locke, L. Research on teaching physical education: new hope for a dismal science. *Quest*, Summer 1977, *28*, 2.

36. Locke, L., & Lambdin, D. Personalized learning in physical education. *JOPER*, June 1976, p. 32.

37. Lopiano, D. A. A fact-finding model for conducting a Title IX self-evaluation study in athletic programs. *JOPER*, May 1976, p. 23.

38. Mather, J. Contracts can motivate physical underachievers. *JOPER*, June 1978, p. 23.

39. Mayer, F. C., & Grant, J. L. Operation self-image. *JOPER*, May 1972, p. 64.

40. McDonald, L. J. An elective curriculum. *JOPER*, Sept. 1971, p. 28.

41. Meyers, E. G. Exercise physiology in secondary schools: a three dimensional approach. *JOPER*, Jan. 1975, p. 30.

42. Mundy, J. Performance based contract teaching. *JOPER*, Oct. 1974, p. 39.

43. Munson, C., & Stafford, E. Middle schools: a variety of approaches to physical education. *JOPER*, Feb. 1974, p. 29.

44. Nash, R. P. Giving seniors a chance. *JOPER*, Sept. 1973, p. 29.

45. Oliver, J. N. Physical education for the visually handicapped. *JOPER*, June 1970, p. 37.

46. Overskei, L. Coeducational lottery system. *JOPER*, Sept. 1973, p. 27.

47. Owen, B. H. Mainstreaming at Dae Valley Camp. *JOPER*, May 1978, p. 28.

48. Owens, L. E. Principles of scheduling. *The Physical Educator*, March 1970, *27*(1), 18.

49. Oxedine, J., & Roberts, J. E. The general instruction program in physical education at four-year colleges and universities: 1977. *JOPER*, Jan. 1978, p. 21.

50. Parchmann, L. L. Experiences with contract teaching. *JOPER*, Oct. 1974, p. 41.

51. Pastor, G. Student-designed elective course. *JOPER*, Sept. 1971, p. 30.

52. Perrigo, R. Individualizing PE for intermediate grades. *JOPER*, Feb. 1976, p. 51.

53. Poole, R. Using community resources. *JOPER*, Sept. 1973, p. 26.

54. Rhudy, E. An alternative to Outward Bound programs. *JOPER*, Jan. 1979, p. 26.

55. Riley, M. Title IX. *JOPER*, June 1975, p. 31.

56. Rothstein, H., & Adams, R. F. The quinmester extended school year plan. *JOPER*, Sept. 1971, p. 30.

57. Sadowski, G. M. Student choice of independent study units. *JOPER*, Sept. 1971, p. 25.

58. Short, F. X. Team teaching for developmentally disabled children. *JOPER*, Oct. 1975, p. 45.

59. Shrader, R. Individualized approach to learning. *JOPER*, Sept. 1971, p. 33.

60. Shulman, S. An experimental high school. *JOPER*, Sept. 1973, p. 23.

61. Singer, R. A systems approach to teaching physical education. *JOPER*, Sept. 1974, p. 33.

62. Stanhope, C. Independent study option. *JOPER*, Sept. 1971, p. 24.

63. Trevena, T. M. Integration of the sightless student into regular physical activities. *JOPER*, June 1970, p. 42.

64. Trump, J. L. Flexible scheduling. *Phi Delta Kappan*, May 1963, p. 361.

65. Wagman, E. Physical education for the disadvantaged. *JOPER*, March 1973, p. 29.

66. Winnick, J. Techniques for integration. *JOPER*, June 1978, p. 22.

PART FOUR

1. Adkins, R. Almost anything goes at ECU. *JOPER*, Feb. 1978, p. 44.

2. Basco, J. Winning at all costs, costs! *The Physical Educator*, March 1977, *34*(1), 35.

3. Bula, M. R. Competition for children: a real issue. *JOPER*, Sept. 1971, p. 40.

4. College and University Physical Education Council. Standards for the general college physical education program. *JOPER*, Sept. 1975, p. 24.

5. Gilliam, T. Fitness through youth sports: myth or reality. *JOPER*, March 1978, p. 41.

6. Heywood, L., & Warnick, R. B. Campus recreation: the intramural revolution. *JOPER*, Oct. 1976, p. 52.

7. Jackson, C. O. Just boys, not little adults. *The Physical Educator*, Dec. 1974, *31*(4), 171.

8. Jandris, T. P. Responding to today's diversity. *JOPER*, Feb. 1978, p. 48.

9. Johnson, L. Cold sports in high school. *JOPER*, Jan. 1977, p. 23.

10. Kroll, W. Psychological scaling of proposed Title IX guidelines. *Research Quarterly*, Oct. 1976, *47*(3), 548.

11. Lohmiller, V. Intramural mini-courses. *JOPER*, Feb. 1977, p. 35.

12. Maas, G. Promoting high school intramurals. *JOPER*, Feb. 1978, p. 40.
13. McCarthy, J. Athletics and the cult of the individual. *The Physical Educator*, Oct. 1974, 31(3), 157.
14. National Intramural Sports Council. Coeducational recreational activities. *JOPER*, May 1976, p. 16-22 (seven articles).
15. Pankau, M. A. New twists to old routines. *JOPER*, Feb. 1978, p. 45.
16. Razor, J., & Grebner, F. Elective PE programs: expansion vs. limitations. *JOPER*, June 1975, p. 23.
17. Seefeldt, V., & Haubenstricker, J. Competitive athletics for children. *JOPER*, March 1928, p. 38.
18. Slaughter, M. Should women athletes be allowed to play on men's teams? *The Physical Educator*, March 1975, p. 9.
19. Stumph, P. The expanded intramural concept. *JOPER*, March 1973, p. 55.
20. Summerline, S. L. Initiating public school intramurals. *JOPER*, Feb. 1979, p. 43.
21. Wittenhauer, J. Voluntary physical education: a sound practice. *JOPER*, May 1975, p. 23.

PART FIVE

1. Anderson, W. Descriptive analytic research on teaching. *Quest*, Jan. 1971, 15, 1.
2. Bain, L. An instrument for identifying implicit values in physical education programs. *Research Quarterly*, Oct. 1976, 47(3), 307.
3. Bayless, J. Conflicts and confusion over evaluation. *JOPER*, Sept. 1978, p. 54.
4. Bobo, M., & Bushong, J. Skill testing: a positive step toward interpreting secondary school physical education. *JOPER*, Jan. 1978, p. 45.
5. Bonanno, D., Dougherty, N., & Feigley, D. Competency by contract: an alternative to traditional competency testing techniques. *JOPER*, Nov.-Dec. 1978, p. 49.
6. Carmichael, L., & Vogel, P. Research into practice. *JOPER*, March 1978, p. 29.
7. Cheffers, J. Observing teaching systematically. *Quest*, Summer 1977, 28, 17.
8. Cooper, S. Hope for the future: a view of research in teacher effectiveness. *Quest*, Summer 1977, 28, 29.
9. Dougherty, N. J. A plan for the analysis of teacher pupil interaction in physical education classes. *Quest*, Jan. 1971, 15.
10. Field, D. Accountability for the physical educator. *JOPER*, Feb. 1973, p. 37.
11. Greenberg, J. S. How videotaping improves teaching behavior. *JOPER*, March 1973, p. 36.
12. Harrington, W., & Enberg, M. L. Developing competencies: questions and consequences. *JOPER*, Nov.-Dec. 1978, p. 52.
13. Heitmann, H. Curriculum evaluation. *JOPER*, March 1978, p. 36.
14. Hunsicker, P., & Reiff, G. Youth fitness report: 1958-1965-1975. *JOPER*, Jan. 1977, p. 31.
15. Lewis, G. T. A practical system for observing and analyzing student behavior in physical education. *The Physical Educator*, March 1977, 34(1), 12.
16. Marsh, D. B. Competency based curriculum: an answer for accountability in physical education. *JOPER*, Nov.-Dec. 1978, p. 45.
17. McGee, R. Measuring affective behavior in physical education. *JOPER*, Nov.-Dec. 1977, p. 29.
18. Melograno, V. Supervision by objectives. *JOPER*, March 1973, p. 27.
19. Nygaard, G. Interaction analysis of physical education classes. *Research Quarterly*, 1975, 46, 351.

Name index

415

Subject index